Total Operations Solutions

Total Operations Solutions

Ron Basu and J. Nevan Wright

ELSEVIER
BUTTERWORTH
HEINEMANN

AMSTERDAM • BOSTON • HEIDELBERG • LONDON • NEW YORK • OXFORD •
PARIS • SAN DIEGO • SAN FRANCISCO • SINGAPORE • SYDNEY • TOKYO

Elsevier Butterworth-Heinemann
Linacre House, Jordan Hill, Oxford OX2 8DP
30 Corporate Drive, Burlington, MA 01803

First published 2005

British Library Cataloguing in Publication Data
A catalogue record for this book is available from the British Library

Library of Congress Control Number: 2005924347
A catalogue record for this book is available from the Library of Congress

ISBN   0 7506 6465 7

For information on all Elsevier Butterworth-Heinemann
publications visit our website at http://books.elsevier.com

Typeset by Charon Tec Pvt. Ltd, Chennai, India
www.charontec.com
Printed and bound in Great Britain

Working together to grow
libraries in developing countries

www.elsevier.com | www.bookaid.org | www.sabre.org

ELSEVIER   BOOK AID
            International   Sabre Foundation

To Didi, my only sister, who moulded my formative years

R.B.

To my grandchildren, Daniel and Brad, Georgia and Austin,
and Sam

J.N.W.

Contents

Preface

Unless value is being added no organization will survive long. Value can be in the form of manufactured goods, value can be in the form of knowledge and intellectual capital, and value can be in the form of service. In the final analysis value will be judged by the customer. If value is not being added, failure will result.

Since the Industrial Revolution the traditional paradigm of wealth creation has been the adding of value to raw resources through the transformation process of manufacturing. During the past twenty years the focus has shifted to knowledge and intellectual capital which has resulted in more dependence on service industries and lately on alliances and partnering. It is estimated that over 75% of the GDP of advanced economies is dependent on the service sector. However, there is a considerable risk that if an economy does not have a strong manufacturing base it would not be able to support service industries. The driving engine of manufacturing cannot be ignored.

This book shows how to add value to the organization through the efficient use of resources to provide improved customer satisfaction. Resources are defined as all available resources, whether owned or borrowed along the complete supply chain, from the supplier's supplier, through to the customer's customer. Borrowed includes alliances and partnering.

This book builds on concepts that were introduced in *Total Manufacturing Solutions* (Basu and Wright, 1997). It demonstrates how this holistic approach of operational excellence, driven by a self-assessment methodology, can be applied equally to manufacturing, service or public sectors.

An implementation programme to put the methodology into practice is included. A differentiating feature of this book is impact analysis and comparison with new developments such as e-business, outsourcing, Six Sigma, EFQM and ISO 9000:2000.

This book will be of interest and value to:

- Functional managers, participants and practitioners in operational excellence; they will find this book provides them with a comprehensive insight into tools and techniques of continuous improvement in one package. A step-by-step guide is provided for the application of the appropriate tools to their improvement process. This book could be used as an essential handbook for all employees in a Six Sigma programme.
- Senior executives, in both the manufacturing and service industries, will find that this book will give them a better understanding of basic tools and techniques and help them to support a quality improvement initiative and sustain a strong competitive position.
- Professional management and training consultants will find the comprehensive approach of tools and techniques essential as a handbook for Six Sigma-related assignments and seminars.
- Management schools and academies and research associations will find this book valuable to fill the visible gap in basics of operational excellence.

Acknowledgements

The publication of this book, which draws heavily from *Total Manufacturing Solutions* (Basu and Wright, 1997), would not have been possible without the encouragement of Maggie Smith at Butterworth Heinemann, and the full support of Nevan Wright, my friend and co-author. I am indebted to them both. I am also grateful to Ross Milne for his contribution to Chapter 5, Supply Chain Management, and to Petra and Christopher Theunissen for their input to Chapter 9, Intellectual Capital.

Finally, the project could not have been completed without the tolerance and support of my family.

Ron Basu

I am indebted to Professor Ray Wild, past Principal of Henley Management College, for introducing me to Ron Basu some ten years ago. Ron and I have now co-authored three books, and I wish to acknowledge how much I enjoy working with Ron. As has Ron, I too wish to place on record grateful thanks for the support of Maggie Smith, and for the input from Petra and Chris Theunissen and Ross Milne. I also thank all my colleagues and friends at AUT (NZ) and Henley Management College (worldwide), and as always my wife Joy has been a tower of strength.

Nevan Wright

Chapter 1

The Concept of Value

The textbook mission, or reason for being, for an organization is to provide goods and services as efficiently as possible to the satisfaction of the customer. Without a customer the organization will cease to exist. This would seem so obvious that it does not need mentioning. But, in the real world of commerce the overriding demand on the chief executive is to provide up-to-date financial information and the public spotlight is on the share price. The obsession with the share price and its daily movement means in turn that managers' daily concerns are with stock turns, head counts, debtors' days, short-term paybacks on investments and consideration of outsourcing to enhance balance sheet ratios. Value in this sense is represented by profits, return on investment, or in the case of government departments, cost cutting and creative ways of measuring and reporting 'performance' (such as reduction of hospital waiting lists by referral of patients back to local practitioners). Consequently senior management are obliged to focus on short-term financial results ahead of customer satisfaction. In short, customer satisfaction, although colourfully featured in mission statements, has become a secondary objective for senior management.

Value-based management

In recent times software companies and consultants have jumped onto the value bandwagon, and the acronym of the moment is VBM, value-based management. VBM is claimed to be an integrated (integrated is a much overused word that has all but replaced holistic) framework of measurement and management tools. One blurb says 'VBM delivers dynamic, high performance organization results. It builds on the strengths of financially focused tools, such as economic value and its derivatives, by adding the perspectives of customers and other stakeholders.'

This hype would suggest that VBM is just another addition to a long line of three-letter acronyms (TQM, TPM, TCI, JIT, BPR, SCM, CRM). Experience shows that for each new initiative or fad, over time, the original promise does not materialize or if there are initial gains they are not maintained. Management, always in a hurry and driven by the need for quick results, moves onto the latest academic offering. In recent times Balanced Score Cards (BSC) and Six Sigma have had their champions, and their detractors. Even when an initiative such as Six Sigma realizes benefits, often, as found by Basu and Wright in *Quality Beyond Six Sigma* (2003), the benefits are not sustained.

In *Quality Beyond Six Sigma*, the concept of the value stream is discussed and the point is made that 'organizations that can produce the best products at competitive prices, and provide excellent service, will have an added advantage if resources are not wasted on activities that do not add value' (p. 73).

Value and non-value adding activities

In the introduction to this chapter we said that the reason for being for an organization is to provide goods and services as efficiently as possible to the satisfaction of the customer. From this, our concept of value is any activity that adds value in the process of creating a good or delivering a service. Non-value adding activities are any activity that adds a cost but does not directly add to the value of the good or service. Efficiency means the elimination of non-value adding activities unless a compelling reason can be demonstrated for keeping them. It is not possible to eliminate all non-value adding activities, indeed any organization will find that it has whole departments that do not directly add value to the good or service. For example, overhead departments and support departments, such as the finance department and the human resource department, do not directly add value to the good or service, but they most certainly add to the overall cost. Interestingly, when an organization goes into receivership the first department to be closed by the receiver or the liquidator is the human resource department. This suggests that statutory managers and receivers do not see the human resource department as adding value. Likewise, the compiling of and filing of accounting reports to the stock exchange or to the tax office does not add value, but these are a regulatory or legal necessity. At the other end of the scale pot plants and artwork in the staff cafeteria do not add value to the product or service, but they do create a pleasant atmosphere and might help staff relax and feel that this is a pleasant place to work (motivational value). Thus not all non-value adding activities or costs can or indeed should be eliminated. But, they should be identified (known) and recognized as non-value adding.

Efficiency

Our contention is that if an organization is internally efficient, i.e. resources are not being wasted, jobs are done 'right' first time and every time, people are not being employed on meaningless tasks, and non-value adding activities or expenditure are known and kept to a minimum, then the organization will be in better shape to add value for the benefit of the customer and in the long run for the stakeholders.

Internal efficiency means making the best use of resources and minimization of non-value adding activities.

World class and best practice

'World class' was a term used by Hayes and Wheelwright (1984) to describe successful Japanese and German export companies. Since then, 'world class' has grown to mean organizations that have adopted just-in-time lean production, are the leaders in reputation for product and service, are employers of choice by staff and jobseekers, and who are continuously improving and leading the market in their field.

World class organizations are totally efficient, and each department or function meshes with the rest of the organization to support the drive to achieve the common mission.

Best practice refers to the most efficient way of doing a specific activity or process benchmarked against competitors. Best practice has its origins in Frederick Taylor's best method. Taylor, a late nineteenth century efficiency guru, used scientific means of determining the best method for a job or task; once the best method was identified workers were trained in the best method. To keep the best method in place bonuses were paid and a high degree of supervision was used. This was a very top-down approach, with managers doing the thinking and workers doing what they were told! Today's best practice approach requires two-way communication with workers encouraged to feed back to management suggestions for improvements in methods etc. None the less, any move to best practice requires leadership and direction from the top.

It should be noted that what was best practice and what was considered to be world class last year will not necessarily be best or world class this year. It should also be noted that relying on incremental continuous improvement is not enough to keep pace with world class standards. Reliance on continuous improvement will leave an organization well behind if a competitor launches a much improved product, or, owing to changes in technology or new processes, is able to dramatically drop the price.

Value stream approach

The value stream approach transcends the traditional manner of departmentalizing stages of the business process. The value stream highlights the importance of the operations manager being involved in all aspects of the process, from supply right through to the customer and if possible to the customers customer. The 'old' approach was that one department or function would be responsible for purchasing goods and services, another for planning. Scheduling of activities was often a separate function as was warehousing and distribution, and operations were just one step in the whole process of providing services. With the value stream approach functional boundaries become irrelevant and in many organizations it is now accepted that the operations manager has to control the whole process from buying in goods and services to the final stage of satisfying the customer. Marketing, accounting, human resources and other support functions do not show up on the value stream as such

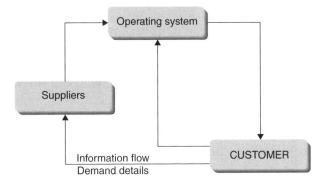

Figure 1.1   Flow of information for the value chain

but, as discussed below, operations managers must be vitally interested and involved in these internal functions of the organization. The value chain, derived from Porter (1990), is shown in Figure 1.1.

External efficiency

External efficiency is measured by customer satisfaction and by market share. To achieve customer satisfaction the organization requires, and is dependent on, the timely receipt of goods and services to specification by external suppliers. The efficiency of suppliers to the organization is of as much concern as the ultimate satisfaction of the customer. The key to the whole process is information flow and team work within the organization, and with suppliers at one end of the value stream and customers at the other.

Suppliers

In some organizations suppliers are treated with distrust and the business strategy adopted is to shop around and to get the best deal on each occasion. With this approach little loyalty is shown to any supplier and the supplier is almost treated as an adversary. The value stream approach is to treat key suppliers of goods and services as part of the team. Key suppliers are those that are important to the smooth operation of the system. In some cases the supplier can become involved in the day-to-day operations of the organization and might be expected to advise and to assist. Cost no longer becomes the key issue. Instead suppliers will be judged not on price but on their loyalty and ability to deliver goods and services to the required standard and on time. Suppliers can also become part of the information-gathering arm of the organization; often suppliers have a different perspective as to what competitors are up to (changes in buying patterns, timetables, new packaging, use of new materials and so on). Suppliers are also in a good position to offer technical advice regarding new technology and alternative materials. Chapter 5 takes a new approach to the supply chain from suppliers and partnership through the operational process out to the customer and the customer's customer.

The prudent organization will always have a fall-back position. No matter how well intentioned your supplier, it is foolish to be in a position where you are so reliant on one supplier that you are seriously embarrassed if the supplier is unable to perform for some reason (a fire or an unfriendly takeover).

Generally, organizations are divided into functional departments; and even if the organization has re-engineered, and no matter how flat the structure, some people's tasks will be primarily marketing, others will be primarily concerned with accounting; others will be purely administration and so on. In our value stream approach it is important that the operations department has the responsibility for purchasing goods and services, the process of manufacture, and the delivery of the goods or service to the customer. From supplier to customer the process has to be seamless, or as a Japanese saying has it, 'it flows like water'.

The customer and marketing

The total quality management approach of the 1980s propounded the philosophy of delivering a quality in excess of customer expectations. 'Surprise the customer' was the catch-phrase. But any organization can have satisfied customers and go out of business! What is provided has to be within an organization's capability, it has to be sustainable and affordable. Customers are hard to satisfy and show little loyalty. Today's customer is well informed, well travelled and has been conditioned to expect continuous improvements in quality of product and of service but at little extra or even at less cost. This is a major challenge for organizations: how to provide more for less!

The customer is the central focus for any organization. It has been said that marketing is too important to be left to the marketing department; everyone in an organization should be vitally interested in marketing the organization. None the less, it is the function of the marketing department to know what the customer wants and what the competition is doing or is likely to do. Marketing specify the product and its attributes. The importance of a close relationship between the key functions of marketing and operations is explored in Chapter 4.

Bunker mentalities

Communication, to be meaningful, has to be two-way and has to be aimed to help rather than to apportion blame or to criticize. With traditional hierarchical organizations a bunker mentality can develop whereby each function is walled off from the other and any suggestion, no matter how helpful, is taken as a threat or a challenge. World class organizations are noted by the manner in which the figurative walls that separated functions have been broken down, and by the team work that exists between all functions to achieve common goals as determined by the business policy. This requires that everyone in the organization knows what the goals and objectives are and that the culture is conducive to the enthusiastic pursuit of the goals for the common good of the whole. Information is open to all, and there are no secrets.

Finance and accounting issues

Many new businesses have a very short life span (over 70% of small businesses fail within five years of beginning operations), and every month there are reports of medium and large businesses in financial difficulties. Like it or not, the continued success of any organization relies on financial stability. Often operations managers see the accountants as soulless people devoid of imagination, interested only in short-term returns on assets. However, unless there is a positive cash flow and a strong balance sheet, long-term business plans for the future are meaningless. It is vital that any organization has a reliable accounting system in place to provide fast and accurate information. The minimum requirement is a budget and reliable feedback of actual results for comparison to the budget, in time for corrective action to be taken where required. Performance measurements are covered in Chapter 7 and the importance of financial management is discussed in Chapter 8.

Summary

In this chapter the concept of value is discussed, along with terms such as 'world class' and 'best practice'. The direct interrelationships of an operations manager with internal functions and with the external elements (suppliers and customers as part of the extended process) of the value chain are considered.

Chapter 2

Why Total Operations Solutions?

In the 1980s, service rather than manufacturing was seen by many in the developed nations as the way of the future. In the 1990s the inherent weaknesses in the reliance on service became increasingly exposed. It is now recognized that in the global market place a whole systems supply/value chain approach has to be taken embracing service and manufacturing as a whole. This chapter describes a total systems approach to the analysis of organizations so as to determine gaps in key areas of performance. The correction of gaps is addressed in later chapters.

Trend towards service

In the United Kingdom statistics show that 78% of the workforce are engaged in service industries (www.statistics.gov.uk), and in the USA 80% are employed in service industries (www.census/gov/). Although a shift back to manufacturing has been identified (Basu and Wright, 1997), it is obvious that the greater percentage of the workforce of developed nations will continue to be employed in service activities. There are two reasons for this:

1   Continual advances in technology mean that manufacturing is considerably less labour-intensive than previously. Automation, robotics, advanced

information technology, new materials and improved work methods all have led to the reduction of manual labour.

2 For larger organizations, manufacturing has become internationalized. For example, a company might outsource its manufacturing to overseas contractors or allied companies and itself concentrate on design, marketing and distribution.

Additionally, organizations can no longer regard themselves as being purely in manufacturing and hope to survive. The market first and foremost now takes for granted reliability of product and expects good service.

Market expectations of the level of quality are driven by perceptions of what technology is promising and by perceptions of what the competition is offering. Organizations now operate in a global market where national barriers, tariffs and customs duties no longer provide protection for a home market. Any manufacturer, even if the focus has been on supplying a local market, is in reality competing on the world stage. Competition is no longer limited to other local organizations, and the fiercest competition in the home market will be from goods and even services produced overseas or provided by overseas organizations. For example, a bus service in New Zealand is owned and operated by the Scottish company 'Stagecoach', based 20 000 km away. And McDonald's for over 30 years has competed, and indeed set the benchmark, for fast food providers all around the world.

This overseas involvement in a home market means that manufacturers (and service providers) can no longer make products just to suit their engineering strengths, but must now be aware of what the market wants and what global competition is offering. In manufacturing what the competition is offering, apart from well-engineered products, is service in the form of delivery on time, marketing advice, training, installation, project management, or whatever else is required to provide a total service as well as a reliable product.

Never before has the customer been better travelled, more informed and had higher expectations. Many of these expectations began with the quality movement of the 1980s, where it was trumpeted that the customer was king, and these expectations have been kept alive by continuously improved products and services, global advertising and, for the past decade, the Web.

If they are honest with themselves, most organizations realize that their products actually differ very little from those of their competitors, and any technological improvement is soon copied; thus the difference – the 'competitive edge' – comes from service.

Service separated from production operations

If no serious operation can ignore market demands for service and world class quality, why bother to try to separate manufacturing from service in the study of operations management? Indeed, for a manufacturing organization aspiring to world class status (as described in Chapter 1) we would most emphatically agree that the managements of such organizations must concern themselves with service and quality if they are to compete on the world stage.

But managers in service industries such as health, retail, distribution, education, travel, real estate, consultation, brokering, law, accounting, administration of central and local government, transportation of goods or people – where no direct manufacturing is involved, or where the manufacturing is light and simple (such as in a restaurant) – do not have to know much about manufacturing. Naturally all the above industries are reliant on manufacturers to varying degrees for the equipment they use, or in the case of a retailer for the goods they sell, but the physical heavy work of making the goods is not their concern. The analogy is that of a driver of a car: one can be a very good driver without knowing much about what happens under the bonnet. Some knowledge of when to change gear, and the danger of overheating due to lack of oil or water will be of advantage, but not much more is really necessary (for example, for the past five years some cars have even been able to 'tell' the driver when tyre pressures are low). Likewise a retail sales person of washing machines does not need a detailed knowledge of high-tech mass production line balancing. For the sales person some knowledge of lead times for deliveries, operating instructions and the capacity of the washing machine will be sufficient as a basis for good service to the customer.

Thus there can be a separation of operations management into two broad streams: the management of production including service, and the management of operations in service industries where only some rudimentary knowledge (if any) of manufacturing is required. But irrespective of whether a manager is involved primarily in production or service a total system approach is needed based on the supply or value chain philosophy.

For organizations involved directly in production and manufacturing, management needs to be well versed in strategies, tactics and methodologies of production operations management and also has to be very aware of what constitutes service and quality from the customer's point of view. A total operations approach to providing a quality product coupled with the service required is essential.

Managers of service industries will benefit from some basic knowledge of production systems and methodologies.

Total Manufacturing Solutions

The traditional operations management definition for manufacturing is the conversion of materials, energy and information into a product for customers. In *Total Manufacturing Solutions* (Basu and Wright, 1997), we defined total manufacturing to include all the interactions between the conversion process inside a 'factory' with all other business processes, including marketing, research and development, supply chain management, financial and information management, and human resource management – also with external factors such as environmental concerns, customer care and competition. The method of analysis, which in effect determined strengths, weaknesses and gaps in performance, was developed around 200 questions which were designed for self-benchmarking against world class standards. The structure of the benchmarking was to measure the performance of the business against 20 defined areas of the business, which were described as foundation stones. There were ten questions for each foundation stone, the aim being to get the right balance of foundation stones to support the pillars of the business. The pillars in Total Manufacturing Solutions were:

- Understanding the market place
- Supply chain management
- Environment and safety
- Manufacturing facilities
- Procedures
- People.

The new model: Total Operations Solution

In the new model we call Total Operations Solutions we continue to provide a process of self-assessment to systematically measure all aspects of an organization. This includes both internal functions and external relationships. We show how the concepts of Six Sigma as further developed in *Quality Beyond Six Sigma* (Basu and Wright, 2003) can be used without too much fuss to determine strengths and weaknesses. Quality Beyond Six Sigma is written around FIT SIGMA. FIT SIGMA was developed by Ron Basu to build on strengths and to understand where weaknesses are so that corrective action can be taken to gain a competitive advantage.

Over the past eight years we have refined the six pillars and their 20 foundation stones to give a greater emphasis on service and relationships with suppliers, and customers. Partnering and alliances are also included in our new model.

The six pillars now are:

- Marketing and innovation
- Supply chain management
- Safety and environment
- Infrastructure facilities
- Systems and procedures
- Intellectual capital.

The process comprises five steps:

1 Definition and understanding of the six pillars, and of the underpinning 20 foundation stones
2 Completion of a questionnaire for each foundation stone
3 Gathering of information and measurement of performance against an operational excellence factor
4 Establishment of strengths and weaknesses (gaps) against best practice and world class
5 Determination of actions to be taken to improve efficiency and competitiveness.

The self-assessment approach enables corrective action to be taken within the organization using FIT SIGMA techniques, or if this is not possible we show how to best brief external consultants to address self-recognized areas for improvement.

Table 2.1 Pillars and foundation stones of Total Operations Solutions

Pillars	*Foundation stones*
1 Marketing and Innovation	1 Understanding the market place
	2 Understanding the competition
	3 Product and process innovation
2 Supply Chain Management	4 Enterprise resource planning
	5 Supply chain and supplier partnership
	6 Distribution management and working with customers
3 Environment and Safety	7 Product safety
	8 Occupational safety and health
	9 Environment and resource management
4 Infrastructure Facilities	10 Sourcing strategies
	11 Appropriate technology and integrated systems
	12 Flexibility and lean process
	13 Reliability and maintenance
	14 Performance management and Balanced Scorecard
5 Systems and Procedures	15 Quality management
	16 Financial management
	17 Information and communication technology
6 Intellectual Capital	18 Leadership and organization capital
	19 Human resource policies and human capital
	20 Knowledge management and information capital

Success and future

The success and future of any organization rests on the six pillars and relies on specific and defined foundation stones. The foundation stones and pillars are shown in Table 2.1 and illustrated in Figure 2.1.

Self-assessment by 200 questions

There are ten questions for each of the 20 foundation stones (200 questions in total). The questions are easy to interpret and can be adapted to suit any organization. For the first pass a score is given for each question using a five-point scale.

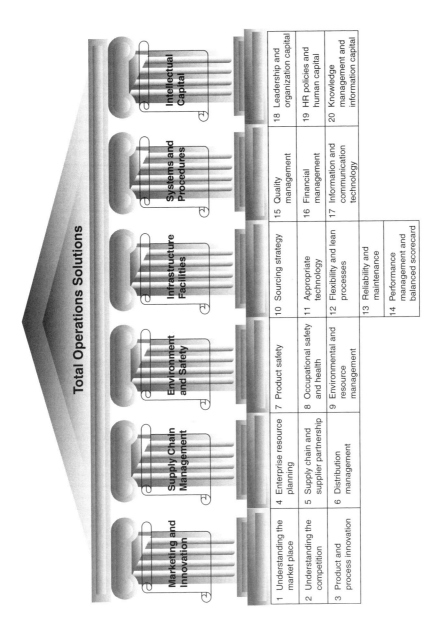

Figure 2.1 Pillars and foundation stones of Total Operations Solutions

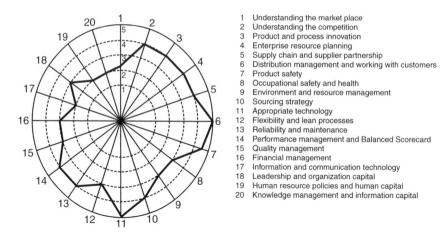

1   Understanding the market place
2   Understanding the competition
3   Product and process innovation
4   Enterprise resource planning
5   Supply chain and supplier partnership
6   Distribution management and working with customers
7   Product safety
8   Occupational safety and health
9   Environment and resource management
10 Sourcing strategy
11 Appropriate technology
12 Flexibility and lean processes
13 Reliability and maintenance
14 Performance management and Balanced Scorecard
15 Quality management
16 Financial management
17 Information and communication technology
18 Leadership and organization capital
19 Human resource policies and human capital
20 Knowledge management and information capital

Figure 2.2   Operations excellence profile ('spider diagram')

01 = Poor
02 = Fair
03 = Good
04 = Very good
05 = Excellent.

A spider diagram, as shown in Figure 2.2, can be used to profile the 'health' of the business. The aim will be to get totally 'fit' and once fit to sustain fitness.

True mission

Before any action is taken to get the business fit, the organization needs to take stock of what its objectives and true mission are. The mission, in the true sense of the word, is the reason for being. The mission should not to be confused with grandiose statements such as to be the world's best etc. For example, there is no point in a mission that says 'We value our customers and we value our people' if the policy is to reduce service and to reduce the numbers of staff. The true short-term mission for an organization could well be as simple as 'to survive'. Obviously such a mission will not appear on the letter head, but if survival is the case staff have to be aware of the true situation, and realize that this is the mission. If in survival mode the action has to be to turn the organization around. It is no secret that when William Ford took over Ford in 2003 that the mission was indeed survival.

The analysis begins with determining the baseline health of the organization and progresses to the important pillars of the business (that is, those pillars most important for making the mission happen). For example, if an organization saw that its mission was marketing and innovation then a low score for the pillar Marketing and Innovation, coupled with low scores for Intellectual Capital and World Class Performance would indicate that foundation stones 1, 2 and 3, and 18, 19 and 20 need attention. (Note; it could be that that all pillars are of equal importance.)

Improvement process

The improvement process will depend on the magnitude of change required. Where a major shortfall is identified the focus will be with finding a fix for that area. This is known as focused improvement and rapid, perhaps major, changes might be needed. Where less drastic action is required the process will be continuous incremental improvement. The improvement process is discussed in some detail in following chapters.

Summary

This chapter has established the need for a total approach, not only within the organization but encompassing various levels of suppliers through to the direct customer and out to the end user. It was shown that no manufacturing company can ignore service, and that no service organization can ignore its supply base. In short, a total systems approach is needed if organizations are to compete at world class levels.

The method for achieving this is introduced as Total Operations Solutions. Total Operations Solutions includes 200 questions designed for self-assessment by an organization of its strengths and weaknesses against world class standards. The analysis is at three levels:

- Establishing the baseline health of the organization
- Determining which pillars are essential for the achievement of the mission, and
- Answering searching questions for each of the foundation stones on which the pillars are set.

The analysis is concentrated on the pillars most relevant to achieving the true mission of the organization.

Chapter 3

Understanding Total Operations Solutions

O wad some Power the giftie gie us
To see oursels as others see us!
    Robert Burns, 'To a Louse'

In Chapter 2 we said organizations could no longer regard themselves as being purely in manufacturing and hope to survive. The market first and foremost now demands quality of product and service. Any technological improvement is soon copied; thus the difference – the 'competitive edge' – comes from service.

The aim of manufacturing is the creation of a product. Creation of a product occurs through the transformation of raw materials into a finished article. The transformation process uses resources of people, materials and capital (in the form of plant, machinery and buildings). The efficiency of the transformation process can be measured, in terms of units of output, quality of product, return on assets and so on. This measurement is dependent on the accurate and timely flow of information. So much is self-evident. For pure service industries, however, measurement is not always so obvious or easy. Much of the delivered service is measured in terms of customer perception.

Our concerns for any type of organization are two-fold: first, with the efficient use of resources and the elimination of activities that do not add value to the process, and second, with understanding and streamlining of external and internal flows of information.

Why 200 questions?

The six pillars and their foundation stones with the 200 questions (see Appendix) are designed to show the way to efficiency in the total supply/value chain, the elimination of unnecessary expense, and the simplification and improvement of information flow.

We pose the questions. The questions diagnose the problems and opportunities. The answers are dependent on individual circumstances. We believe that if the right questions are asked then the answers will often become self-evident. Knowing which questions to ask is part of the answer, but it is also important not to be fooled and to accept the first glib, easy answer that is offered.

The Japanese have an approach known as the five 'whys'. Davidow and Malone (1992) give an example of this. Suppose a machine stopped functioning:

1 Why did the machine stop?
   There was an overload and the fuse blew.
2 Why was there an overload?
   The bearing was not sufficiently lubricated.
3 Why was it not lubricated sufficiently?
   The lubrication pump was not pumping sufficiently.
4 Why was it not pumping sufficiently?
   There was no strainer attached and metal scrap got in.
5 Why was no strainer attached?
   There was no preventative maintenance schedule.

Repeating why five times in this manner will help determine the root problem so that corrective action can be taken. If in this example the five whys had not been asked the fuse and/or perhaps the pump shaft might have been replaced. If these were the only actions taken, then the problem would recur in a few months. The objective is to eliminate the root cause rather than to patch up the effects. Wright and Race (2004) use the same approach in an example of incorrect invoicing, also see Imai (1986). The five whys is a variation on the classic work-study problem-solving approach of why, what, where, when, who and how. For a discussion on this approach see Wild (2002).

Answering each of the 200 questions is not in itself final. Each question should suggest or indeed trigger further questions. We also appreciate that not every organization will find that the six pillars and all of the 200 questions will be totally relevant to their situation. Nor do we suggest that each organization should slavishly attempt to apply each of the foundation stones.

Which type of organization is most suited?

Our approach is relevant to any type or indeed size of organization.

In the past, textbooks have categorized manufacturing processes into job, batch or assembly line. However distinctions have become blurred. For example, with the just-in-time approach, supposing a traditional assembly line is still in use, but whereas previously the products were once made in batches of 100 (so as to give what was known as benefits of scale), now on the same assembly line work might be scheduled in batches of one. In one organization we visited, which makes white-ware products (refrigerators, cookers, washing machines, etc.), there are 3000 different line items and 900 units are made a day. Previously production was scheduled in batches of no less than 100 units; today batches are scheduled in units of one. Previously it took up to eight hours to change the line over and to set up for a batch; today the change-over and set-up time is down to less than three minutes. Another example is with Toyota where they are working towards the concept of a 72 hour car. The idea is that the purchaser will visit a showroom and be able to see a car indicative of the type of product that Toyota makes. There will not be a wide range of vehicles to inspect; instead the purchaser will be shown on a computer screen the various models available and a list of optional specifications. The purchaser will then select, by keying into the computer, the basic car model and required details such as size of engine, type of transmission, colour scheme, type of upholstery, sound system and so on, but all chosen from a given list. This information will now be electronically transmitted to the factory and to the suppliers of the factory. Within 72 hours the car will be delivered to the purchaser. The benefits include the customer getting what they want. But in fact the customer is now more than just a customer; the customer is now very much part of the manufacturing process. In effect, by keying in their requirements the customer initiates the whole process, raises the raw materials order for the factory, and updates the production schedule. From Toyota's point of view there is a further substantial benefit. Presumably the purchaser will pay on delivery, so there will be no cash flow problems (within a 72 hour period it is unlikely that Toyota will have paid for the materials or for the direct labour).

As Taiichi Ohno of Toyota said, we are 'Looking at the time line from the moment the customer gives us an order to the point where we receive the cash. And we are reducing the time line by removing the non-value wastes.'

Obviously, a system such as this does not, and cannot, make allowances for mistakes. It relies on good planning by management, quality designed into the product, well-trained workers who are empowered to work as a team, suppliers who are trusted to supply when required and who are also part of the team, an integrated computer system and the elimination of 'non-value wastes'.

Does it matter then how we would classify a manufacturing process? It could be said that in Toyota's case they are using a production line to make one-off jobs, and that the customer rather than drawing from the system is now an integral part of the production and service system.

The relative importance of each pillar is likely to be different depending upon the types of processes and products. However, regardless of whether the business is concerned with manufacturing commodity products or consumer products, or whether it is a continuous chemical process or a discrete metal-cutting operation, or at the other end of the spectrum a pure service operation providing consultancy advice, each business exists to satisfy customers and will rely on suppliers of goods, utilities and services. Thus the supply chain exists for all businesses. By applying the same rationale, each organization to some extent is involved in activities represented by our six pillars. For example, our first pillar, Marketing and Innovation, has the foundation stones of:

- Understanding the market place
- Understanding the competition
- Products and process innovation.

What organization can totally ignore any of these issues? Likewise with the other five pillars:

- Supply Chain Management
- Safety and Environment
- Infrastructure Facilities
- Systems and Procedures
- Intellectual Capital.

We have no doubt that our six pillars, and each of their foundation stones, are of enduring relevance to all organizations.

Although this book is applicable to any organization, the origin of the approach is with our book *Total Manufacturing Solutions*. There, we related to fast-moving consumer goods (FMCG), on the basis that the concepts and problems associated with this type of production are readily applied to all types of manufacture.

FMCGs are those goods that are consumed, that is generally they can only be used a few times, and in some instances only once. For example, we would consider a BIC ballpoint pen to be a consumable, but a £100 Parker pen could be said to be a durable. The overall approach to the manufacture of either might well be very similar. In other words the lessons learnt in the production of a fast-moving consumable BIC pen might be equally applicable to a Parker. However, if we compare a BIC throw-away razor with an electric razor, although they are designed to do the same job, one is definitely a consumable and the other is a durable.

Notwithstanding the differences in consumables and durables, or pure consultancy service we would argue that by considering your product or deliverable, prestigious though it might be, as a consumable, you will get a more direct focus on the complete supply chain, from supplier through to the end user.

Total business process

The pillars and foundation stones are designed to give us a framework for thinking about our organization and the total business processes. We have not written a textbook on each pillar and we would certainly not claim that a slavish following of the 200 questions is a blueprint for success. Each organization is different and each organization has different problems and different priorities.

Each pillar can be considered alone. It will be noted in Figure 2.1 that each pillar is shown as standing on its own because each pillar can be worked on independently. They are interrelated but are not rigidly interconnected. In this sense we have not devised a systems dynamic approach. If one pillar is disturbed it may not necessarily affect the others, although if one pillar is weak then the whole structure will be vulnerable. Our approach enables the identification of weak pillars. Action can then be taken to correct weaknesses and to reinforce.

None the less, it is important that a 'big picture approach' is applied and all the pillars of the business are examined. The synergy that results from the benefits contributed by all elements as a whole far exceeds the aggregate of benefits given by individual elements. The integrated approach is truly more than the sum of its elements. If one concentrates exclusively on isolated areas, a false impression may be inevitable and inappropriate action taken.

This maxim can be illustrated by the Indian folk tale of four blind men who were confronted with a new phenomenon, an elephant! The first man, by touching its ear, thought that the elephant was a fan. A second was hit by the elephant's tail and concluded that it was a whip. The third man bumped into a leg and thought it was a column, while the fourth, on holding the trunk, decided that it was an oversized hose. Each man, on the evidence he had, came to a logical conclusion, but all had made an erroneous judgement by failing to deduce that the total object was an elephant. As with all feedback devices where a basic message is given, inferences and decisions may be drawn from isolated data, which will be false and misleading.

A story in the business context will further underline the limitation of tackling only a part of a total problem. The technical director of a multinational company, having been to a conference, decided that line performance improvement must be the best thing in manufacturing. So he organized his technical team, called in experts from the corporate headquarters, and set up a line efficiency exercise. The team did an excellent job on two production lines by systematically eliminating all machine-related downtime problems (with the aid of high speed video techniques). As a result the production efficiency of the lines increased by 20%. However, it soon transpired that the product for one of the lines was going to be discontinued and the other line, despite its excellent standard of reliability and efficiency, encountered a severe long-term shortage of materials due to planning and procurement problems. Therefore, in isolation the line efficiency programmes did not improve the overall business performance.

Own benchmarking

There are many proponents of a 'single' method of problem-solving, usually designated with a buzzword or a three-letter acronym, whether it be called business process re-engineering, customer relationship management or whatever the flavour of the month may be. Consultants can get away with this kind of one-track package as long as their market (that is you and your management) is relatively ignorant of appropriate options. Over the past decade, however, business people have become increasingly aware of the need for company-wide methods and approaches. The art of management has grown much more widespread. One cannot therefore blame managers if they now make cynical remarks when they come across a 'packaged' approach from consultants.

Our recommendation is that managers need to do their own benchmarking. To do this self-assessment they need a comprehensive method of benchmarking. Our intention, with the 200 questions, is to provide a comprehensive approach. Once a weak point is diagnosed a specialist or consultant may be employed to effect a cure or act as a catalyst.

In Chapters 4 to 9 we examine each of the six pillars and their foundation stones to give the background for each question so that a total operations solution can be constructed, just and perfect in all its parts. What is required is for you to consider yourself a new breed of manager. Your first step will be to familiarize yourself with the six pillars and 20 foundation stones (Chapters 4–9) in the context of your organization. You should then be able to benchmark your business by using the 200 questions. The methodology of data collection and analysis is given in Chapter 12. Once this is done it is likely that changes will be necessary, which could well entail a change in culture. Chapter 13 deals with how to implement a change, including a change in organizational culture.

Mission statements of the 1990s were often poorly worded and lacked credibility. Properly worded, the mission statement should define exactly what is required. Words such as 'to be the best', 'to be world leaders', are mere rhetoric. Rather, we see the mission as being a statement of the purpose of the organization, i.e. the reason for being, in short why the organization exists. A well-worded mission gives a focus for strategy.

For example, supposing the vision was to set up an ambulance service in a small town. The mission could well read:

'To provide a speedy response, transport and first aid service for the sick and injured'.

Note the brevity of this statement: no mention of to be the best, or to be professional, etc. All these attributes might be highly desirable but for a succinct mission statement, getting back to basics will help crystallize exactly what we are trying to achieve.

From this statement we can then list what will be required to make the mission happen. In this example:

- *To provide a speedy response* ... This would mean we would need a 24-hour service, and we would thus need to have staff on call 24 hours a day. A communication system will be necessary. Ideally, to give a speedy response, a central location would be desirable.
- *transport and first aid service* ... This suggests reliable vehicles and equipment, and competent staff. If we are to perform then the vehicles and equipment will need to be well maintained, and the staff will need to be well trained. Maintenance and training will need to be ongoing.
- *for the sick and injured.* This reminds us why the service exists and defines who our customers are.

To make our mission happen we would need to consider the following list of 'things to do':

1 Select and acquire vehicles
2 Maintain vehicles
3 Select and acquire equipment
4 Maintain equipment
5 Recruit skilled staff
6 Ongoing training of staff
7 Select a location
8 24-hour service, staffing and communication
9 Network with hospitals and other emergency services.

The above is a simplified example. Likewise with our approach in this book. It is not for us to be experts on your organization. We provide a framework for you to apply. From our own practical experience we can testify to the effectiveness of our approach.

Your own benchmarking, using our 20 foundation stones and 200 questions, will position your business against a backdrop of criteria comprising both performance and practices. The exercise cannot have any practical value to your business unless the general profile can be matched with the specific mission and objective of your organization. In Chapter 12 we provide a methodology that allows the scoring of each foundation stone to be 'weighted' according to individual business priorities to determine an Operational Excellence

Factor. The Operational Excellence Factor will identify the gaps in your business and show where further improvements are needed.

Chapter 13 discusses improvement strategies and shows a plan of how to start the improvement process and how to make things happen. In Chapter 14 four case studies offer a set of proven practices. In Chapter 15 we reflect on the totality of our approach. We conclude that Total Operations Solutions is for the whole organization and cannot be limited to just the operations function.

Summary

To summarize, we take a practical, application-based approach. However, we are not simply propounding 'back to basics'. We are providing a conceptual framework to enable organizations to rethink what they are doing and why. The aims are two-fold: first, the elimination of non-value added activities, and second, the improvement of the flow of information throughout the total organization (internally), and externally with and between, suppliers and customers. Our overall approach is to examine each pillar and each foundation stone for weaknesses but not to ignore the whole by concentration on just one area. Our intention is to allow you to construct an organization which is just and perfect in all its parts.

Chapter 4

Marketing and Innovation

Two roads diverged in a wood, and I –
I took the one less travelled by,
And that has made all the difference.
  Robert Frost, 'The Road Not Taken'

It is said that today the priority for top management is to deliver a quality product to meet and even to exceed customers' expectations. This has to be achieved within the constraints of what the organization can afford to provide and is capable of providing. Shareholders and investors still measure management's performance in terms of the bottom line. On the other hand, customers, driven by intense international competition coupled with the promises of technological advances, are continually setting higher levels of quality and service, all at less cost. This chapter deals with maintaining a competitive advantage through innovation and marketing.

Generally businesses are organized around functions. Even in organizations that have re-engineered, and no matter how flat the structure, some people's prime function will be marketing and some people's prime function might be manufacturing. Others will be involved in accounting, administration, human resources and so on. Our main concern in this chapter is with the marketing and operational functions.

The essential job of the marketing function is to define a product or service that will sell. Definition of the product/service includes the features or attributes the customer wants. Attributes may range from the absolutely essential, through to the desirable, down to the lower level of nice to have but not really important. Attributes can include the finish and aesthetic appearance (to some customers appearance and status of a product can be every bit as important as the performance). Often some of the features required by the customer arise as the result of marketing pushing (selling) features that the customer had not previously considered important. As well as defining the product, marketing also has to establish the price the customer will be prepared to pay, plus the likely level of demand. The customer's expectations of attributes, quality and price will be driven by their perception of what they have previously experienced, what they believe the competition can now offer, and what they expect will be available (technological advances) in the near future. Often what the producer sees as being state of the art can well be seen by the customer (beguiled by technological promises and exaggerated promises of competitors), as simply old hat.

Once marketing believe that they know what is wanted and what will sell, then operations has the problem of determining feasibility. That is to say, can the product, with all the desired features, actually be made and or delivered? Does the business have the technology (the know-how and/or the specialized plant or equipment), and does it have the capacity (what else has to be delivered and what are the priorities)? If, after taking all the above into account, it is decided that it can be done (there is sufficient capability and spare capacity, and thus the demand can be met within the time frame advised by marketing), then the crucial question must be 'is it possible to deliver and make a profit within the price set by marketing'?

Thus arise the traditional conflicts of marketing and operations. Marketing see themselves as the opportunists; they are the innovators, the go-getters, they are the trigger for making things happen. For them the bottle is always half full whereas they believe that their colleagues in operations would describe the same bottle as half empty! Operations see themselves as the realists, they also see their job as making things happen, but it is their responsibility to balance conflicting demands with scarce resources. They know only too well who will get the blame when delivery is late and not to specification, or the customer has to queue for service!

Thus marketing often see the response of operations as being negative. They believe operations looks for reasons as to why things cannot happen rather than looking for ways in which to make things happen. On the other hand, operations see that marketing has little or no appreciation of the problems of capacity and scheduling, and the time and effort required to develop/prepare new products or services. Then again, marketing always seem keen to add to the range of product lines or stock-keeping units.

Table 4.1 Marketing *vs.* operations

Marketing	Operations
Why do we never seem to have enough capacity?	We need accurate long-range forecasts
Why are our lead times so long?	We need accurate medium-term forecasts
Why do we have stock outs?	
Or	
Why do customers have to queue?	Why is your short-term forecasting so erratic?
Why are our costs so high?	Extended product lines, rushed deliveries, fancy extras and high-quality finish all cost money

These conflicts are highlighted in a question/response type scenario, as shown in Table 4.1. The exchange can escalate to the extent that it can be likened to children throwing stones at each other across a garden wall (with each side determined to throw back a bigger stone or brick with each retaliation). We are sure that from the reader's experience other similar questions and replies will spring to mind. The pointlessness of such an exchange is obvious.

Part of the problem is communication and lack of understanding by both functions. Much of this is due to the traditional hierarchical structure of organizations whereby functions are walled off from each other. This can be described as the bunker mentality whereby each function sees the other as a possible threat or a challenge. In this atmosphere of mistrust responsibilities and demarcations are jealously guarded and suggestions, however helpfully meant, can be seen as examples of meddling or trying to usurp authority. The bunker phenomenon is more obvious between the factory and the marketing department, where often the two are separated by physical distance as well as by philosophy.

This problem of intra-functional communication is not much different in a service organization. In addition to the conventional demarcation between the service-generating marketing and sales team and the service-providing operations team there are other conflicts in a service firm. Levitt (1980) observed, 'customers do not buy goods or services, they buy what goods and services provide them'.

Gronroos (2000) has identified differences between the *service perspective* compared to *core product perspective* in customer relationship management. A service perspective relates to the role of the service component as a competitive advantage. A core product perspective is a traditional approach where the cost and quality of the core solution is considered to be the main source of competitive advantage. This is comparable to the conflict generated by the effectiveness and efficiency of the service.

If we want to do it right we need Total Operations Solutions. This requires not only bringing all people together by breaking down the walls, but also a good understanding of:

- The market place
- The product innovation process
- The competition (who they are and what they are doing).

As shown in Chapter 2, the pillar for Marketing and Innovation comprises three foundation stones:

1 Understanding the market place
2 Understanding the competition
3 Product and process innovation.

Foundation 1: Understanding the market place

Some managers will tell you that they thrive on chaos and that they enjoy the challenge of crisis management. There is a place for people like this: ideally, with the competition! Certainly it is important to be able to react quickly to threats and problems as they arise, but in reactive-type situations the best possible result is seldom achieved. Surely it is far more desirable to be in a position to anticipate what is going to happen and to plan accordingly? The ideal situation is to be the market leader, and for you to be making things happen, and to put your competitors in the position of playing to catch up.

The first stage of developing any business, strategy, or improvement plan is to analyse and understand the nature and trend of the market you are in, to be in a position of understanding what is happening and what is going to happen it is necessary to know:

- The size and trend of the market
- Customer perceptions
- Distribution channels
- Global opportunities.

Size and trend

In order to obtain a better knowledge of the size and trend of the market, the starting point can be trade, consumer and government statistical publications. It is also important to understand the local demography, the culture and habits. At a basic level if you want to open a fast food business you do not use pork in Israel or beef in India. At a more subtle level, if you want to market a brand image (e.g. Gucci) a large population alone (e.g. China) does not determine the market size. A growing market offers opportunities for future profits if a dominant position can be obtained.

The product/market matrix of Ansoff (1987) is a sound framework for identifying market growth opportunities. As shown in Figure 4.1, the *x*-axis shows the dimensions of the product, and the *y*-axis represents the current and the new market.

There are four generic growth strategies arising from Ansoff's grid. These are:

1 Current product/current market. The strategy for this combination is 'market penetration'. Growth will take place through the increase of market share for the current product/market mix.
2 Current product/new market. In this situation the strategy for growth is 'market development'. The pursuit will be for exploring new markets for current products.

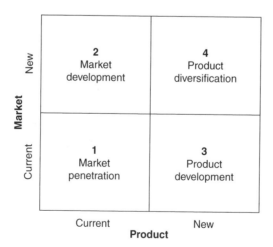

Figure 4.1 Ansoff's product/market matrix

3 New product/current market. The strategy of 'product development' is followed to replace or to complement the existing products.
4 New product/new market. The strategy of 'product diversification' is pursued when both the product and market are new in the business.

Ansoff has also identified a number of specific strategies for the diversification quadrant depending on the different market and product combinations:

• Vertical integration: when the organization decides to move into the suppliers' business
• Horizontal diversification: when entirely new products are introduced in the existing market.

Ansoff's model is traditionally in the domain of marketing managers for projecting the direction of business growth. In addition to establishing the scope of the product and market mix the model has been applied in other aspects of shaping the corporate strategy, including business growth, competitive advantage, defensive/aggressive technology, synergy and make or buy decisions.

When used in conjunction with the corporate objectives of an organization, the above five aspects of the model can be applied in the development of the business strategy. The model on its own is ineffective to evaluate the best strategy, but it provides an excellent framework for exploring strategic discussions on products and markets. This accounts for the fact that it is still popular with marketing strategists and business school students.

Every organization must develop its business plan and marketing strategy based on quantitative market research tempered by market intelligence. According to Kotler (2001), market research provides 'results data' while market intelligence supplies current 'happening data'. The marketing team collects market intelligence by reading books and publications, listening to media, visiting websites and meeting stakeholders. The data for market research can be obtained in a number of ways, including surveys by an in-house market research group or an external agency. Kotler suggests a five-stage process of market research as:

• Define the problem and research objectives
• Develop the research plan
• Collect the information

- Analyse the information
- Present the findings.

Customer perception

For a given cost of a product, a customer's requirements will fall into three categories: time, quality and service. Time includes the lead time for new products, i.e. the time between the start of the product definition and the time when the first shipment is made. For existing products time means the lapsed time from the date of making the order to the date of delivery. Quality includes the defect level of products as perceived by the customers and quality also includes delivery on time. Service is as judged by the customer.

It has been said that if it can't be measured it can't be managed. Some measurements are internal and some external. Internally, on the shop floor it should be a straightforward task to record and measure the cost of scrap, reworks, downtime of machines and idle time of workers. Likewise delivery dates should be known and it should be standard practice to record the percentage of deliveries made on time. Measurement of a service is not so easily achieved from within, but the percentage of deliveries made in time to customer specification is one measurement that can be made.

There are some other measures and ways of determining how your customer perceives your service levels. First, establish who your top 20% of customers were last year. (Statistically about 80% of your total sales will be from 20% of your customers.) If marketing doesn't have this information, the accounts department will easily be able to extract it. Now compare this year's sales against last year's. Have sales dropped for any of the major customers? If so, go and talk to them. If approached in the right manner (a genuine desire to improve quality and service, and an avoidance of excuses) then customers usually will only be too pleased to tell you what you are doing wrong. If there is some doubt that you can perform, be careful of making promises to get it right the next time. Failure to get it right next time will totally destroy the credibility of your organization!

Distribution channels

It is also important to recognize who your real customers are. Are they the agents, the wholesalers, the retailers or the end consumers?

Analysis of the distribution channel will help to determine exactly who the customer is and who is driving demand. Once this is known, then by talking to the real customer, it can be found what attributes are really required of the product. How important is the finish, the price and so on? By following the distribution channel back to the end user, one manufacturer found that a costly feature was never used by the end consumer and thus could be removed from future models. (It had been added to meet a whim, albeit advised in an authoritative manner, of the wholesaler.)

Once the distribution channels of products or services have been developed it is important to determine what factors are likely to influence the flow of goods and services throughout the supply chain. As described in more detail in Chapter 5, there are two key factors affecting this flow. One is the 'collaborative supply chain' as growth in outsourcing and dependence on supplier partnership. The other factor is the so called e-supply chain contributing to the speed and sharing of information through e-commerce.

Global opportunities

It is also important to be aware of potential customers. For example, the emerging markets of what were the communist blocs and the gradual removal of tariff barriers have all resulted in a huge growth in world trade and for most companies this has opened up opportunities in the global market place. Conversely, an opportunity can just as easily be a threat. As Creech (1994) writes, 'Go to the Annual Consumers Electronics Association Convention in the United States ... Japanese, Koreans and others from Oriental countries so overwhelmingly dominate the sales personnel and display booths as if some exotic malady has wiped out the American suppliers'.

Foundation 2: Understanding the competition

Having established a good understanding of the nature and trend of the market place, the next stage is understanding your market position and the position and strength of the competition in the market. Activities include:

- Establishing your 'core' business
- Analysing your product portfolios
- Identifying the competitors, the setting of performance criteria based on the competition, and the measuring of your current performance against these criteria
- 'SWOT' analysis (strengths, weaknesses, opportunities and threats) to compare your business, internally and externally, against the competition (current and possible competition).

Core business

The first step in establishing the 'core' business is to examine the product range and roughly establish the margin or profitability of each product or group of products, and then look for products within this group that have 'differentiation', i.e. the products that are perceived to be superior to those your competitors are marketing. Differentiation can take many forms, such as:

- Brand image, e.g. Coca-Cola
- Technology, e.g. Sony Camcorder
- Service, e.g. Singapore Airlines.

The 'core' business may also evolve as a subset of categories as a 'focused' strategy to a restricted area of the market. An example of this strategy is Porsche, with a niche market in prestige sports cars.

Product portfolios

The analysis of establishing the 'core' business into categories is, however, extremely general. The next stage is to convert these generalities into specifics by further analysis of product portfolios. (A product portfolio is a grouping of products which compete in the market place in identical ways, e.g. a London–New York air ticket).

There are several measures for analysing the relative importance of a product portfolio, including contribution, market share, growth of market share and market growth. But seldom can one measure be taken in isolation (a product with an excellent margin is not core business if only a few items are sold each year). The importance of contribution, market share, growth of market share and market growth is discussed below.

- Contribution: Contribution or profit margin of a product is an indication of how potentially profitable a particular product portfolio is.
- Market share: If your product has a good profit margin and a high market share, especially if the product is a price leader in the market, then you are in a very strong position.
- Growth of market share: If the product's market share is increasing, particularly in a growing market, and it is the price leader, then the product has a very real competitive advantage.
- Market growth: This is an indication of future opportunities for the product portfolio.

The analysis of product portfolios is more complex than the simplified description of the above measures.

One popular and established approach is the BCG (Boston Consulting Group) matrix of 'stars', 'wild cats', 'cash cows' and 'dogs' against the two axes of market share and growth, as illustrated in Figure 4.2:

- A *cash cow* is a product with high sales but which is static in market growth. With a cash cow, because good sales are still being made, the

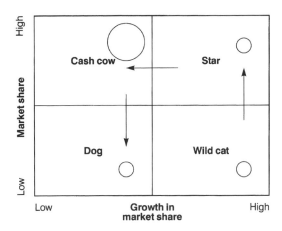

Figure 4.2 The Boston Consulting Group (BCG) matrix

danger is that unless market share is known and is being monitored it will not be realized what is happening. With a cash cow unless action is taken, for example the addition of new features or a new model, then the product is likely to become a dog.

- A *dog* is a product with a low share of the market and with no growth in the market share.
- A *wild cat* can become a star. A wild cat has a low share of the market but its share is growing.
- A *star* has a high share of the market and its share is growing.

Although the BCG matrix is a useful way to obtain a quick picture of the position of the product portfolios, it is often difficult to collect reliable data of the market share. Another approach is to carry out a similar analysis of products into A, B, C or D against two axes, one of contribution and one of growth, as illustrated in Figure 4.3.

Products have a high contribution and their sales are growing. At the other end of the scale D products have a low contribution and their sales are not growing. For B products, although contribution is low, growth is high, and with C products although they have a high contribution their market growth is low. For C products the question is: can the margin be sustained in a falling share of the market? Without a change in product features the only way to increase market share will be to reduce the price, but if this doesn't work then not only has contribution been reduced but the product is likely to slide down into the D category.

Information for the above analysis is easier to obtain and is more accurate than the BCG analysis because all the information required

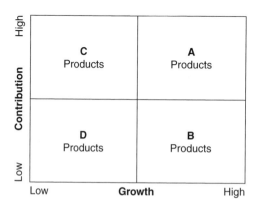

Figure 4.3   The contribution/growth matrix

is available within the company. However this does not provide a direct measure of competition.

Another useful approach is to plot trends in percentage contribution, percentage market share and market size (£, tonnage or units) over a number of years, as illustrated by Figure 4.4(a), Figure 4.4(b) and Figure 4.4(c), respectively. Once this information is plotted and analysed, then the core business of important products should be readily identifiable.

Having identified the important product portfolios, the next stage is to identify competitors in each portfolio and the competitive performance criteria.

Competitors

Identification of existing competitors should not be difficult. It is a poor sort of marketing department that cannot identify the existing competitors!

Performance criteria will depend on what product and what market you are in. For example, for a manufacturer of fast-moving consumer goods (FMCGs) the chosen criteria could include measurements of:

- Innovation and success ratio
- Cost, quality and service of products
- Capacity and performance of manufacturing units
- Efficiency of distribution.

The method of assessing your own performance against your competitors is popularly known as 'external benchmarking'. Establishing a benchmarking partnership with direct competitors may not be easy as it is an unaccustomed situation to 'dance with the enemy'. However, the problems of access may not be so acute when the partners to benchmarking are operating in a different market. In some respects businesses in competition have a clear interest in benchmarking each other in common peripheral areas – such as purchasing of commodity type raw materials – and thus are willing to cooperate. Where the competitor is not interested in cooperating your own market intelligence and the use of external consultation give sufficient information to establish key benchmark measurements.

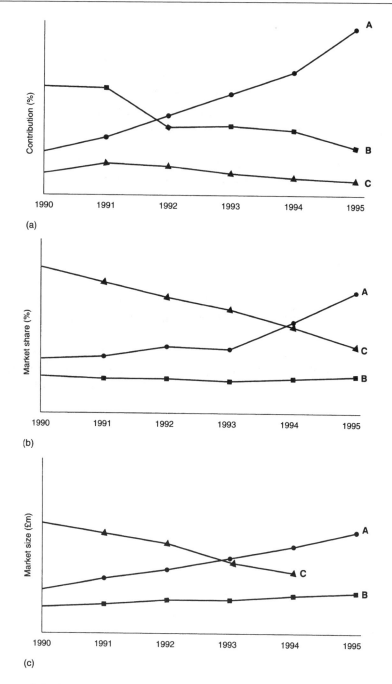

Figure 4.4 Product trend graphs: (a) percentage contribution; (b) percentage market share; (c) market size

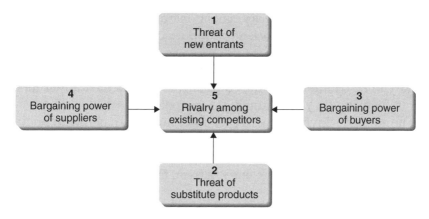

Figure 4.5 Porter's Five Forces model

Much comparison work can be done without the cooperation of competitors or without resorting to consultants to get the information. Manufacturers of cars have for many years obtained competitors' models and stripped them down to see what the differences are and to determine what advances have been made. In other cases the vehicle may not be stripped down but checked against in-house standards as to how the competition for the same class of vehicle measures up in terms of paint quality, fitting of panels, and so on – the aim being to determine how good 'we' are compared to 'them'. Annual reports, brochures and advertising also provide useful information on the standards that the competitors are publicly setting for themselves. Even if the competitors are not achieving these standards, these are, none the less, the standards that are being advised to the market and consequently shape and form the perceptions by which your customers and potential customers will judge the performance of your business and your products.

Porter's (1985) 'Five Forces' model has been most widely used in the strategic analysis of competition. This model for competitive analysis relates to five different forces (see Figure 4.5).

1 New entrants: threat of entry from other organizations. (Example: online banks challenging high street banks.)
2 Substitutes: availability and competition from substitute products. (Example: e-mail as a threat to fax machines.)
3 Buyers: bargaining power of buyers. (Example: supermarkets' increasing power related to suppliers.)
4 Suppliers: bargaining power of suppliers. (Example: Trained specialist required by an industry.)

5 Existing competitors: rivalry among existing competitors. (Example: Vodafone and T-Mobile jockeying for position in the 3G market.)

The model emphasizes the external forces of competition and how these can be countered by the company. It implies the danger inherent in focusing on your immediate competitors.

The elements involved with each force are shown below to prepare for competition.

- New entrants: Examine the entry barriers for new entrants including
  - economies of scale
  - brand identity
  - capital requirements
  - switching cost
  - access to distribution
- Substitute: Analyse the determinants of substitution threats including
  - relative price performance
  - switching cost
  - buyer's inclination to substitute
- Buyer: Examine to what extent buyers can bargain by considering
  - buyer volume
  - buyer information
  - decision-maker's incentives
  - switching costs
  - differentiated products
  - impact on quality/performance
- Supplier: Competitive forces from suppliers mirror those of buyers. Examine the determinants of supplier power, including
  - differentiation of inputs
  - supplier volume
  - substitute inputs
  - switching cost
  - forward integration to your customers
- Existing competitors: Analyse the rivalry determinants related to existing competitors. These factors could include:
  - industry growth
  - diversity of competitors
  - fixed cost and asset bases
  - switching cost
  - brand identity
  - exit barriers.

Porter's model of the Five Forces has been most widely used in strategic analysis and business schools. However, the model is more useful for developing a reactive strategy. It is weak in developing a proactive strategy building upon the core strengths of a company.

SWOT analysis

Armed with the best market information available the next self-analysis that can be carried out is SWOT analysis.

Traditionally SWOT analysis is done from two perspectives: internal and external. Internally, we identify our strengths and weaknesses and externally we look for the opportunities in the market place, and conversely what are the likely external threats. When we look at our strengths we consider what we are doing well with what we have and what else we could be doing; in other words, what advantages do we have. Advantages could include our specialized equipment, our committed workforce, and a strong financial backing. Likewise, the same approach is taken to identify internal weaknesses. Weaknesses could include a lack of cooperation between marketing and manufacturing. Opportunities are external and as discussed earlier could be the lowering of tariff barriers and the opening up of new markets (of course lowering of tariff barriers could also be a threat). Threats, once again from without, will not only be the competition or likely new competitors but will also include possible legislation, technological advances (which could also be an opportunity) and other issues such as the environment and the green movement.

Foundation 3: Product and process innovation

Having identified the competition, the core business and the market position for the 'core' business it is now time to assess the 'gap' in the existing product portfolio and to move to improve existing products and processes, and/or to innovate new products with expanded capabilities to fill the gap.

Innovation is essential to keep pace with what the competition is doing. Innovation includes the search for new products as well as the improvement of existing products. Since the number of entirely new products will normally be few, development will largely be the introduction of adaptations, improvements and the addition of features. In this regard the technique of 'value analysis' has proved important. Value analysis looks at existing products, in an organized way, element by element, with the aim of reducing cost without reducing the performance or reliability. For example, the replacement of a brass casing with an alloy or even a plastic material might reduce the cost and actually improve the product (now lighter to carry around yet performance has not been reduced and it is much cheaper and easier to produce).

For new innovations Ray Wild (2002), has identified six stages of development. These are:

1 Exploration, including research, i.e. the continual search for new ideas
2 Systematic, rapid screening to eliminate less promising ideas
3 Business analysis, including market research and cost analysis
4 Development of the remaining possibilities
5 Testing the offerings developed
6 Launching on a commercial scale.

There are several strategies available to a business with the development of new products. Some, a few, will position themselves as the market leaders and will, through high investment in research and development, bring forth new products. Others will seek quickly to copy the innovations of others and will attempt to join in the initial growth phase of a new product. Others will join in with adaptations before market saturation sets in and will endeavour to perhaps find a niche market. Others will add nothing new to the innovation but will rely on mass production to enter the market at lower prices.

For any organization, whichever of the strategies are adopted for innovation, certain conditions have to be met:

• First, close links between marketing, research and development, and manufacturing are essential.
• Second, innovation lead time has to be minimized.
• Third, there has to be a continuous analysis of the 'product life cycle'.

'Product policy – what to make and how to make it – is the most pressing issue that manufacturing companies face today.'

Shapiro, 1988

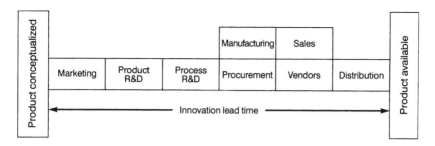

Figure 4.6 Traditional innovation project (adapted from Tompkins, 1989)

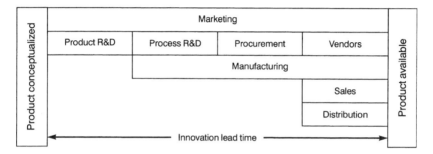

Figure 4.7 Integrated innovation project (adapted from Tompkins, 1989)

Business process re-engineering includes the concept of 'integrated product line management', wherein all the major functions – marketing, R&D, engineering, manufacturing, logistics and sales – are involved and the innovation lead time is reduced by interactive and concurrent activities. Figures 4.6 and 4.7 illustrate the innovation processes by two methods.

In a conventional innovation strategy companies invested in internal R&D which led to many breakthrough discoveries. These discoveries have been closely guarded as intellectual property (IP). Figure 4.8 shows an innovation cycle of a pharmaceutical company. Ideas flow into the organization on the left and flow out to the market to the right. These are screened and filtered through defined 'gates' during the research process and surviving ideas are selected for development and then commercialized for the market. Chesbrough (2003) describes this strategy as a 'closed innovation paradigm'. However, with the growing mobility of highly experienced technologists and the need to market a product faster the innovation strategy is moving towards an 'open innovation paradigm'. In the open paradigm an idea originates from the company's research laboratory, but some of those ideas may

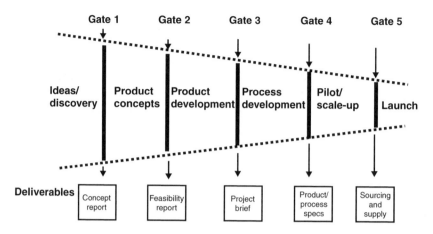

Figure 4.8   An innovation cycle

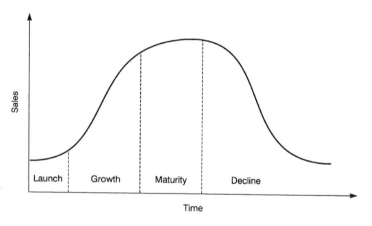

Figure 4.9   The product life cycle

seep out of the company to be commercialized by another partner. Similarly, the company may acquire a viable entity from another research organization and develop it for its own market.

It is generally accepted that products have a life which goes through a cycle of launch (incubation), rapid initial growth, followed by a period of maturity and then an eventual and often rapid decline. A new product with new technology has a switch point when the new takes over from the old technology. An example can be seen with technology-associated recorded music when the cassette tape (which had taken over from the 33- and 45-rpm record discs) was in turn superseded by the compact disc (CD). This pattern is shown in Figure 4.9.

Different actions or decisions will be required for each stage of the life cycle, and each decision will have an impact on manufacturing requirements. For example, in the launch and the growth stages it will be essential for manufacturing to have the capability to keep pace with the demand. In the maturity stage production requirements will be more predictable and work can be scheduled with some degree of certainty. The decline stage will bring different problems, because to arrest the decline, price changes or additional features might be attempted. Manufacturing will be expected to react quickly and be able to reduce costs or add new features at no extra cost.

Product life cycles for fast-moving consumer goods can be as little as six months, whilst for capital-intensive products such as aircraft the cycle can be several years. Often with fast-moving consumer goods even before the launch the next product is in research and development, thus rendering the new product outmoded in a matter of months or even weeks.

Summary

In this chapter we have discussed how customer's expectations are fuelled by what the competition offers or is perceived to offer, and by the promises, as widely publicized in the media, of what technological advances will soon offer.

We say that competitive advantage is hard to maintain, and can only be maintained through innovation and marketing. We agree that the marketing function's role is to know the market place and to be abreast of what the competition is doing. However, marketing is too important to be left to just one section of a company. It is important that all functions, especially manufacturing and service operations, be aware of what the competition is doing, and what the key (i.e. the top 20%) of customers want and expect. Marketing and operations are in it together and must work together, and not throw bricks at each other. (Bouquets are okay!)

We are firm believers in measurement. Much interesting and important marketing data should already exist in a company, and in this chapter key measures and indicators are considered.

With the subject of product innovation, in this chapter we introduce the concepts of 'integrated product line management', 'open innovation' and the reduction in lead time by interactive and concurrent activities.

Above all in this chapter, we stress the need for functions to work together and to try to understand and support rather than to criticize or damn with faint praise.

CASE EXAMPLE 1: Product innovation at Elida Fabergé, UK

Background

Elida Fabergé, UK is a subsidiary of Unilever Group and manufactures and supplies personal care products like shampoo, deodorants and toothpastes. The company examined the way in which innovation takes place in the business and how it is managed and controlled. The purpose of this review was to develop a clearly mapped transparent process for new products delivery ahead of competition with the optimum use of resources. The relaunch of a major shampoo brand (Timotei) in March 1992 was the pilot project using this process.

The relaunch involved four variants of shampoo in four sizes and two variants of conditioner in three sizes and incorporated the main technical changes of a new dispensing cap and changes in formulations.

Approach

A multidisciplinary task force was set up to develop the new process in readiness for a company-wide launch in April 1993. The innovation process used by Elida Fabergé was based on the principles of 'phases and gates' (see Figure 4.10) and consisted of:

- A logical sequences of phases and exit gates
- The use of empowered multidisciplinary core teams
- Using gates as key points where 'gate keepers' review progress and decide whether a project may proceed or be terminated
- Monitoring progress at each gate and for the overall project using key performance measures.

The project team had a membership representing the key processes, such as brand development, supply chain, quality management and customer development. The members received additional training in project management and the use of SPC tools. A project leader coordinated the team's efforts and reported the progress to the 'gate keepers'.

Implementation

Using the multi-process team approach as described, the Timotei project was launched and managed to the implementation stage (Phase 4) by a team led by

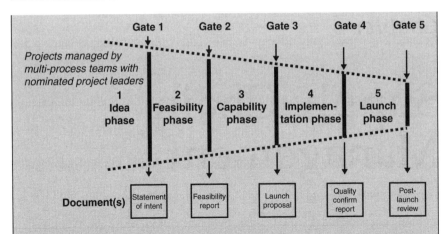

Figure 4.10 Elida Fabergé: innovation process

a brand manager. A second team was set up under the technical leadership of a development manager to see the project through to launch, in particular to set up supply lines, production trials and production start-ups.

Two other teams were also involved: a separate packaging supply chain team, and a TQ team on the Timotei start-up production line. Technical audits were also set up at three packaging supply sites and corrective actions were issued. The sites were revisited to ensure that all corrective actions have been satisfactorily achieved.

Results and learning points

The Timotei project was a success both in terms of sales and as a managed innovation process. There were no notable problems with materials supply. However, the considerable sales success of the product overstretched the bottle supplier, so that a second supplier was brought on stream. The quality and performance ratings of the production line achieved targets.

The key learning points of the project included:

- The use of a multi-process team allowed actions to be taken swiftly with shared ownership and resources at the team's disposal.
- The additional training of team members in project management and SPC tools ensured that the project was managed in a systematic, organized and disciplined manner.
- The effective use of phases (with multiple project leadership) and gates contributed to the development of the 'innovation funnel' of Unilever which was introduced to all product groups.

Chapter 5

Supply Chain Management

The real voyage of discovery
Is not seeking new lands
But seeing with new eyes.
　　　Marcel Proust

To gain a competitive edge, to satisfy customers and to keep costs down many operations have used the incremental improvement approach of total quality management (TQM) and the often drastic restructuring approach of business process re-engineering (BPR). Each of these approaches has their proponents and each approach, or elements of each approach, can result in great advances. Equally each approach has been criticized and there have been many reported examples where an attempt to impose TQM or BPR has resulted in disappointment and even disaster. Some of these disasters can be explained away by saying 'they didn't do it right'. Likewise, often when a business is in real difficulties it is too late to hope for a miracle cure. Turning a business around is like turning the *QE2* around – it doesn't happen all at once.

In addition, each organization – manufacturing or service – is in some way unique, and although there is a tendency to exaggerate this, it is still a fact that what will work for one business will not necessarily work as effectively for another. There can be a variety of reasons why one technique, seemingly successful for one organization, will not work quite as well for another. Reasons can include the type of business, the management style of the chief executive and the overall culture of the organization. Often a change to TQM or to BPR will require a major change in management styles and in the culture of the organization.

There is however one approach that is becoming increasingly recognized as a certain way of meeting customer specifications and reducing effort and wastage of resources but which does not require a major change in direction and culture. This approach constitutes our second pillar: Supply Chain Management.

What is a supply chain?

If you asked people involved in business to define the term supply chain you would get many different answers. Each definition would reflect the nature of the business and the inputs and outputs that it produced. For some, supply chain is related to purchasing and procurement, to others it is warehousing, distribution and transportation. Yet for others it would be sources of capital and labour.

In a typical supply chain, raw materials are procured and items are produced at one or more factories, shipped to warehouses for intermediate storage and then shipped to retailers or customers. Melnyk and Swink (2002) give the following holistic definition of the supply chain as:

> *The entire network of organizations involved in:*
>
> 1 *converting raw materials and information into products and services*
> 2 *consuming the products and services, and*
> 3 *disposing of the products and services.*

They further state that 'this definition treats the supply chain as a product cradle-to-grave concept, including all value added activities required to plan, source, make and deliver products and services that meet customer needs'.

The supply chain in manufacturing

Supply chain management in a manufacturing and supply organization considers demand, supply and inventory needs for each item of production and in particular looks at how inventory flows through the system to achieve output to the customer's specification on time and at least cost. With supply chain management, customer service is increased through the reduction of lead times and the product is always exactly as specified and it is always delivered on time. Costs are reduced through the elimination of any activity that doesn't add value and through the elimination of any non-essential increment of material.

Activities and measures based on customer requirements, as explained in Chapter 4, are very important in improving business performance. But externally driven customer-based measures have to be matched by measures of what the company can do (feasibility, capacity, know-how and resources) to meet its customers' expectations. A high standard of customer performance derives from planning decisions, processes and actions which take place across the whole organization.

Supply chain management focuses on the critical measures of all elements of the supply chain. Externally the measures include the suppliers at one end and the customer at the other end of the supply process, and match these externals with the internal requirements of the manufacturing process. The focus is two-fold: to satisfy customer needs and to keep costs to a minimum.

In reality the elements of supply chain management are not new – we have all been managing parts of the supply chain for years (e.g. buying, planning, scheduling, stock control, warehousing, logistics, distribution, etc.) without realizing the significance of the whole chain concept. Likewise the cost of the various elements of supply has been long recognized.

In 50 years between 1870 and 1920 the cost of distributing necessities and luxuries has nearly trebled, while production costs have gone down by one fifth – what we are saving in production we are losing in distribution

Barsodi, 1929

It is, however, new to view the supply chain as a single integrated flow across all the functions of the business. Traditional, specialist functions like purchasing, planning, manufacturing and distribution are substituted by the flows of materials and information across the traditional functional boundaries, as shown in the simplified model depicted in Figure 5.1.

Traditionally the information flow was the domain of the commercial division while the conversion process of materials flow was a manufacturing or technical division responsibility. With an integrated supply chain approach the responsibility for all elements of supply

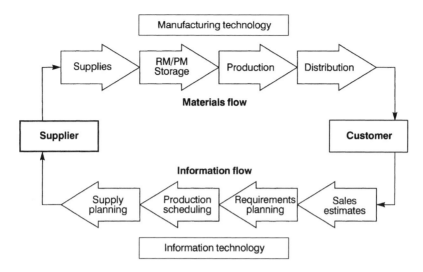

Figure 5.1 Supply chain management

is now with operations management or supply chain management. In many businesses, the integrated approach is being extended to include all suppliers through the manufacturing processes to each level of customer (including wholesalers and retailers where appropriate through to the end user or consumer). This is known as the extended supply chain.

The supply chain in services

As a result of the heightened expectations of customers, operations managers in service sectors also have been forced to focus their attention on managing the value adding system underpinned by the principles of supply chain management. Thus we have seen the emergence and growth of supply chain management as a dominant force for operational success.

But what exactly is supply chain management in a service context? Simchi-Levi *et al.* (2003) define it as follows:

> *Supply chain management is a set of approaches utilized to efficiently integrate suppliers, manufacturers, warehouses and stores, so that merchandise is produced and distributed at the right quantities, to the right locations, and at the right time, in order to minimize system-wide costs while satisfying service level requirements.*

What does this definition suggest? It suggests that supply chain management must consider every organization and facility involved in making the product and the costs involved in doing so. It also implies that the objective is to be cost-effective across the whole supply chain, which requires a system-wide approach to optimization. The supply chain of a service organization also contains suppliers, products or services, customers and their demand for products and service level agreements. The service inventory can be in the form of information databases and stationery items.

Swank (2003) described a successful application of supply chain management and lean production principles in Jefferson Pilot Financial (JPF), a typical insurance service company in the USA. JPF believed that the processing of their almost tangible 'service product' was comparable to a car assembly process. Swank quotes: 'Like an automobile on the assembly line, an insurance policy goes through a series of processes, from initial application to underwriting or risk assessment to policy issuance. With each step value is added to the work in progress – just as a car gets doors or a coat of paint.'

What about logistics management? Is there a difference between 'logistics' and 'supply chain' management? The Council of Logistics Management defines logistics management as:

> *The process of planning, implementing and controlling the efficient, cost-effective flow and storage of raw materials, in-process inventory, finished goods, and related information from point of origin to point of consumption for the purpose of conforming to customer requirements.*

If we consider this definition we see it is very similar to the first and we can conclude that for our purposes, at least in a manufacturing and supply organization, we can consider logistics and supply chain management to be synonymous. If one is inclined to separate the physical movement of logistics in a service organization, we can see that there is but a fine border between logistics and supply chain management in the service sector.

The pillar of supply chain management stands on our pillars number 4, 5 and 6:

4 Enterprise resource planning
5 Supply chain and supplier partnership
6 Distribution management and working with customers.

We now look at the philosophy for each in turn.

Foundation 4: Enterprise resource planning

Supply chain management is distinguished by its role to provide a strategic and integrating function at all levels of logistics including the suppliers. Ideally the supplier becomes part of the team and is involved in the planning process, not only for scheduling of deliveries when required but in the design stage for new products. The business objective to convert customer demand by optimizing the utilization of resources to deliver effective customer service applies to all organizations regardless of whether they are in manufacturing or service sectors.

MRP II to ERP

In most manufacturing companies the main objective is to set up a materials requirements plan for inbound logistics so as to achieve an appropriate balance of stock and provide a desired service level to customers.

Materials requirement planning (MRP) is the set of techniques that uses bills of material, inventory on hand and on-order data, and the production schedule or plan to calculate quantities and timing of materials. Such a plan is incomplete if it does not take into account whether manufacturing resources (e.g. plant, people, energy, space) will be available at the desired time. *Manufacturing resource planning* (MRP II) arose from an appreciation of the need to time and phase materials with resource availability so as to achieve a given output date. Manufacturing resource planning is an integrated computer-based system. A computer-based approach is essential due to the amount of data required. Various software systems are available, each based on the same principles. MRP II is depicted in Figure 5.2.

With manufacturing resource planning the planning process arises from the innovation of new products and the strategic marketing plan. Starting with this information a business plan is constructed to determine and communicate estimates of the sales volume of each product range. The business plan should be developed at least once a year and during the year periodic updates will be required.

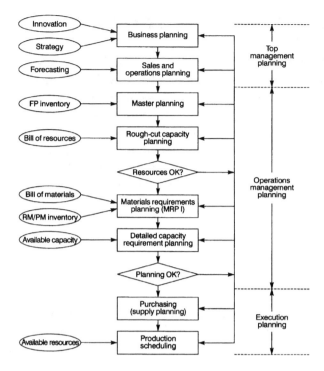

Figure 5.2 Manufacturing resource planning (MRP II)

From the business plan, an operations plan is formulated which covers the materials and other resources needed to translate the business plan into reality. It follows that to keep the operations plan in line with updates to the business plan, regular communication is required between the various functions involved. This updating process is best achieved by face-to-face meetings, which we recommend should take place at least once a month and always with all parties present at the one time. There is a very real danger of misunderstandings and ambiguities if meetings are not face-to-face and if all concerned are not present at the same time. Meetings need not be long-drawn-out affairs. From experience we believe that any planning meeting that takes longer than an hour is wasting time. The key managers at these meetings will be from sales, operations and planning. The issues that will be agreed will include time and availability of resources, and conflicting requirements and priorities will be resolved. Above all demand is the crucial issue, and as future demand can never be certain there should be a formal mechanism of

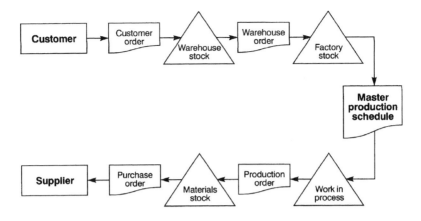

Figure 5.3 Order flow in materials requirements planning

forecasting using the best combination of historical models, past results from promotions, data from customers and market intelligence. Likewise the inventory data system has to be up to date and accurate with details of raw materials on hand, goods on order, lead times and finished goods on hand.

Only with up-to-date information, and with the continuous review and management of information, can an organization hope to achieve a balance of resources and stocks of inventory to meet planned service levels. The master planning and production scheduling process therefore has to be continuously monitored and updated to ensure that this occurs.

The master production plan or master schedule is at the heart of materials requirements planning (MRP), where both the timing and quantity of orders are determined from offsetting from the current stock the demand during the lead time to meet the master production plan.

As shown in Figure 5.3, the concepts of MRP underpinned by the master plan can be extended also to the distribution channel to allow integrated scheduling throughout the supply chain. The approach of distribution requirements planning (DRP) is compatible with MRP as used in the factory.

The next stage is to follow a rough-cut capacity planning process to assess to what extent the capacity of manufacturing facilities could meet the master schedule. The feedback loop at this level tests the master plan against problem areas such as known bottlenecks and other critical resource areas. Often, as this is a short- to medium-term approach, action has to be taken to make the best use of existing resources rather than to add extra long-term resources. The company should decide which alternative to follow if the existing resources are not adequate, e.g. review the schedule, increase resources, work extra shifts, delay maintenance, outsource to third parties and so on. With computer systems it is relatively straightforward to simulate using 'what if' scenarios to evaluate alternative courses of action.

Having established that the resources are sufficient, or having adjusted the plan to fit the resources, then the next step is the detailed materials requirements planning and the detailed capacity requirements planning for day-to-day operations. This stage includes the production of detailed bills of materials for each product or batch of products. With the revised master schedule for each product and for each stock-keeping unit (SKU) and bills of material for each SKU, the materials required for each item of raw materials (RM) and packaging materials (PM) are then matched with the current inventory levels to derive the additional procurement requirements. The requirements are modified, if required, after comparing with the detailed capacity planning process. The execution of the planning process then commences with the final production scheduling and purchasing (supply planning) processes.

We have outlined a generic description of the manufacturing resource planning process. There are of course variations – more significantly between batch production processes and continuous production processes and between so-called 'push' or 'pull' demand systems. With the 'push' system stocks of materials and of finished goods are used to ensure maximum plant capacity utilization by having level production. The 'pull' system is driven by customer orders and just-in-time principles which can result in some underutilization of capacity. It is said that just-in-time requires greater flexibility and reliability of plant plus a multi-skilled workforce. In its simplistic form just-in-time is reactive (demand pull), whereas MRP II can be described as proactive. MRP II looks forward and determines what will be needed to achieve a desired output date. Internally MRP II is a push system; inventory is driven through the process by the schedule. Thus customer requirements are linked to the resources and materials necessary so as to precisely meet a just-in-time delivery date. From a customer's point of view it could be argued that as long as the goods arrive on time and meet the specifications, the system used by the manufacturer is irrelevant!

To be effective, MRP II has to be an integrated computerized system and should be on-line and accessible to all interested parties. It follows therefore that data has to be kept up to date on the system. For example, if engineering changes are made to the design of a product the MRP II database has to be updated otherwise the bill of materials for procurement purposes will not be in line with the new design. It is clear that MRP II cannot be effective unless a 'single set of numbers' is used by all functions (i.e. marketing/sales, finance, manufacturing, human resources and information technology) of the organization or enterprise. This has led to the migration of MRP II to ERP or *enterprise resource planning*. ERP takes over the old stand-alone computer systems in finance, manufacturing, HR and distribution and replaces them with a single unified software system divided into software modules that approximately represent the old stand-alone systems. The growing market of ERP systems is dominated by SAP R/3 and followed by Oracle, PeopleSoft, Baan, JD Edwards and MfgPro. It is fundamental to note that if you simply install the software without rationalizing the processes or changing the way people do their jobs you may not see any value at all.

ERP in service enterprises

There are five major factors why companies undertake ERP systems:

1 Integrate financial information
2 Integrate customer order information and demand plan
3 Standardize and speed up supply processes
4 Reduce inventory
5 Standardize HR information.

It is true that ERP is basically a second-generation MRP II system which is predominantly in manufacturing organizations. However, if we consider the above five reasons from the standpoint of a service organization we see that all factors, arguably with the exception of 'reduce inventory', are applicable to justify an ERP system. More importantly, if you consider the ERP process rather than the software it is evident that the interaction between all functions with a 'single set of numbers' is equally important for an effective service enterprise.

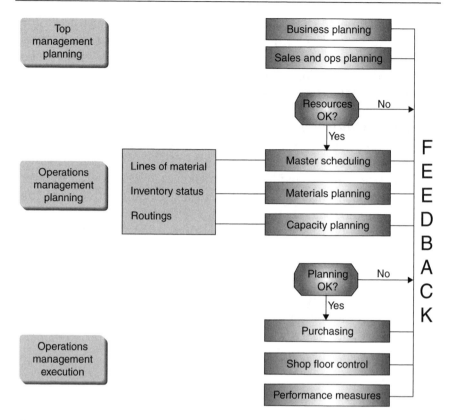

Figure 5.4   Operations resource planning

The second and third factor of applying ERP relate to resource planning. Every service company has customers, demands, in-house resources and suppliers and therefore requires resource planning to deliver an effective customer service. We call this *operations resource planning* (ORP), as illustrated in Figure 5.4.

It is evident from Figure 5.4 that although ORP is not so detailed as MPR II the key steps of the process are similar. From the business plan, a sales and operations plan is developed which covers key products and resources needed to deliver the business plan. The monthly sales and operations planning meeting by senior managers approves the master operations plan. The operations team will review the product portfolio, supplier status and the capacity of own resources and ensure that purchase orders are raised to procure appropriate resources or services from suppliers. If the capacity of own resources is adequate then an internal control document for the customer order is processed.

But a partnership with customers and with suppliers can and will achieve very obvious benefits to all. A partnership with suppliers and a partnership with customers are the beginnings of a radical change in supply chain management. As a result, the service provider, the supplier and the customer achieve benefits in:

- Lower operating cost
- Improved service level
- A greater certainty of a continued relationship.

> *The boundaries between companies will blur as they view themselves as part of an ecosystem, supply chain, or value chain.*
> Hasso Platner, co-founder and vice chairman, SAP

Foundation 5: Supply chain and supplier partnership

Peter Drucker once said, 'Alliances are where the real growth is' (cited by Heller, n.d.). In the market-driven competitive world, businesses are continuously seeking new strategies and business models to excel. They strive to update the process and metrics used to measure and improve performance. The Internet is providing companies both with new challenges and potential solutions. Arguably the biggest external factor that is revolutionizing business culture is the power of the Internet. One such area of impact is the collaborative supply chain.

The idea of a collaborative economy is not entirely new. Over the past decades strategic collaborations and global sourcing have become a familiar business strategy. Even during the 1970s and 1980s multinational companies were setting up manufacturing sites to meet local demand and regulatory requirements. In terms of industrial relations it was considered a high risk strategy to focus sourcing from a small number of sites. However, with gradual deregulation and the improved manufacturing capabilities of the developing markets, the strategy of global sourcing and third party supply began to advance. Perhaps the biggest transformation in collaborative economy has been enabled by the Internet and information systems. The visibility of real-time information, round the clock on-line trading and the gradual shift in power from suppliers to customers have accelerated this transformation.

Supply chain to supply web

The traditional supply chain has been concerned with a linear flow of information and products/services from customers to suppliers through various stages of processes (see Figure 5.1). Traditionally the information flow was the domain of the commercial division while the conversion process of materials flow was a manufacturing or technical division responsibility. During the 1990s the concept of total supply chain management shifted the responsibility for all elements of supply to operations management or supply chain management.

According to Basu (2002), the Internet-enabled integrated supply chain or e-supply chain has extended the linear flow of the supply chain to an eco system or a supply web (see Figure 5.5). It now includes all suppliers and customers to the end user or consumer's suppliers' customers and customers' suppliers and so on. The front runners of the new collaborative business model, such as Dell, are sourcing materials and products in response to customer demand and minimizing both inventory and dealers. The collaborative culture has enabled these companies to become adept at managing relationships between customers, suppliers and multidisciplinary company functions with a sharing of transparent information and knowledge exchange.

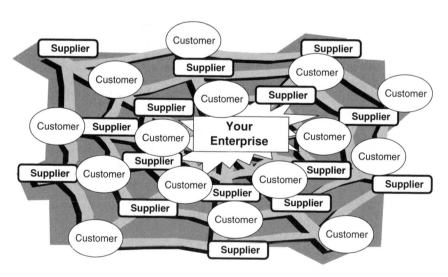

Figure 5.5   An e-supply chain web

Shift from enterprise to network

A little more than a decade ago the companies were urged to attain so-called 'world class' performance within the enterprise. The departments within a company were striving for islands of excellence and then with a succession of operational excellence initiatives (e.g. TQM, BPR, MRP II and Six Sigma) the fences between departmental turfs were gradually demolished. The organizations started to become customer-focused and with established performance metrics in all areas of the business (e.g. 'Balanced Scorecard') began to emerge. However, it is fair to say that both the business model and the performance metrics were site-centric or at most were confined within the company or enterprise. However, with Web-based technologies now accelerating the collaborative supply chain it is becoming imperative to rethink the selection and implementation of the external metrics. This shift is not only in the measurement criteria but also in the mind-set of business practices. Collaboration requires a capacity to 'work in association, sometimes, with an enemy' and does not achieve its business success at the competitor's expense. To maximize the advantages of collaboration the buy-in and commitment of employees to the new mind-set is essential. The following are a few reasons for this fundamental shift from a site-centric linear supply chain to a collaborative network of supply web:

- Demands for the flexibility of partnership. In today's market place consumers have degree of choice and greater ability to make comparisons. As a result their expectations are rising and needs constantly changing. Value in this environment is a moving target. Organization must be flexible to be able to adapt to these changes. It is very difficult for a single organization to possess all the capabilities required to keep up. Organizations now look for suppliers who can provide the skills and capabilities needed as they require them. A firm can easily form partnerships with appropriate skilled suppliers that last as long as the need exists. As demand changes so too can the partnership arrangements.
- Advances in technology. The merging of information and communications technologies has supported the growth in supply chain partnerships. These technologies have enabled extensive connectivity. Today's computer networks, open systems standards and the Internet enable people working in different areas of the supply chain to maintain constant contact. Since information transactions have become so easy, there is

less of a need to restrict operations to within traditional organizational boundaries.

These new capabilities offer the ability for supply chain partners to share information in real time. This enables the partnering firms to hold lower inventories and incur fewer transactions costs. These lower costs can in turn be passed on to the customer in the form of lower prices and better value. Or alternatively, retained as increased profits!

• Collaborative networks. Companies have now recognized that great improvements in value can be attained by coordinating the efforts of partners along the supply chain. When firms focus only on their internal operations they are making decisions in isolation and as a result this can lead to the overall performance of the supply chain deteriorating. As we will see later, firms who work together and share their plans and other information are actually able to improve the overall supply chain performance to their mutual benefit.
• Recognition of core competencies. Recently there has been a shift away from focusing on markets and products towards considering what the organization's capabilities are. A focus on core competencies allows a firm to concentrate on those few skills and areas of knowledge that make the organization distinct and competitive. These competencies are what provide the firm with its competitive advantage. Recognizing what processes they are best at allows the firm to concentrate on these processes. This had led to firms rationalizing what they do. This has the effect of producing supply chains where each of the partnering organizations focuses on what they do best.

Supplier partnership

Reviewing the impact of new technologies on supply chain provides an interesting development of partnering with suppliers. In the past many manufacturers regarded their suppliers with some suspicion, almost as adversaries. Little loyalty was shown to the suppliers and consequently the supplier was never certain as to their future relationship with an organization. Often the purchasing or procurement department would see their role as screwing the best deal possible from a supplier. The huge growth in outsourcing and more importantly the on-line access to information by the Internet have changed that. Companies have realized that achieving world class excellence in their own sites is not enough. It is like being in a high performance car in a traffic jam. It is important to raise the standards of suppliers as well as learn from them by working in partnership with them. The tightly controlled service level agreements are being replaced by joint service agreements with free exchange of data and knowledge. However, the success of the benefits will depend on mutual trust, a highly developed commercial relationship and an efficient system of data exchange. In order to improve the effectiveness of data exchange, companies are sharing with their suppliers (and customers) common systems such as EAN standards (European Article Numbering), EDI (Electronic Data Interchange) and Web-based Extranets. For example EDI enables companies to communicate with each other. Purchase orders to suppliers can be eliminated by using customers' order schedules. And by EDI and Extranets, the supplier could be authorized to link directly into the manufacturer's MRP II or ERP system. The emergence of the Internet protocol has helped the interaction between powerful supply chain systems such as i2, Manugistics, Ariba, Oracle and SAP/R3 to name a few.

Foundation 6: Distribution management and working with customers

There is no doubt that supply chain order fulfilment is the Achilles' heel of the e-business economy. At the end of every e-commerce, on-line trading and virtual supply chain there is a factory, a warehouse and a transport system. The Internet has elevated the performance of information accessibility, currency transactions and data accuracy, but the real effectiveness of supply chain from the source to customer cannot be achieved without the physical efficiency of the supply chain. Web-based software and e-market places are increasing the alternatives available to e-supply chain managers in all operations, including the service industry. More opportunities may also mean more options and complexity. Therefore it is vital that a process is in place to ensure the performance of the e-supply chain for both virtual and physical activities. This foundation stone, distribution and working with customer, addresses this challenge under two headings: physical distribution and strategic alliances.

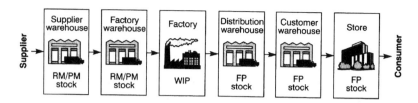

Figure 5.6   Outbound logistics

Physical distribution

In the same way that enterprise resource planning is concerned with information flow, suppliers and inbound logistics, distribution management is likewise concerned with materials flow, customers and outbound logistics. Inbound logistics is characterized by demand variability, and outbound logistics is characterized by variable service levels. A simple model of distribution management in a manufacturing process is illustrated in Figure 5.6.

With the management of distribution, that is the physical transportation of goods from the factory to the customer, invariably some stock is held to buffer the variability of demand and supply lead times. The focus on outbound logistics is to balance customer service level against cost. Cost of distribution is not just transportation costs but also includes warehousing, including special requirements such as refrigeration, insurance and financing of stock, and stock slippage (deterioration, damage, pilfering and obsolescence). The more stock that is held, the greater the cost of storage and the greater the chances of losses.

The main components of distribution management are:

• Distribution strategy
• Warehouse operations
• Stock management
• Transport planning.

Distribution strategy

It is important that a company in a consumer-focused business has a defined distribution strategy. The first criterion of the strategy is to

Table 5.1 Distribution strategy mixes

	Warehousing		Transport	
	Building	Operation	Trunking	Delivery
Strategy A	Own	Own	Own	Own
Strategy B	Rented	Own	Leased	Own
Strategy C	Rented	Own	Third party	Third party
Strategy D	Own	Own	Third party	Third party
Strategy E	Rented	Third party	Third party	Third party
Strategy F	Rented	Own	Own	Own
Strategy G	Own	Own	Third party	Own

decide whether the management of activities should be by the company or by a third party. With assets (buildings, equipment and transport vehicles) the strategy can go three ways: own the assets or some of the assets, lease or rent assets, or use contractors. Some of the various strategy mixes are shown in Table 5.1. Note there are 64 possible combinations, e.g. own premises, leased premises, own management of premises, third party management of premises, own transport, leased transport, or third party supplied and managed transport, and so on.

There are some obvious advantages of distribution management by a third party, e.g. the distribution expertise of third party companies, and the avoidance of capital outlay and underutilized equipment. However, as the delivery of the finished products is closest to the customer on the supply chain, there could be some degree of risk if the management of outbound logistics is totally left to third parties.

It is important that, for a manufacturer of fast-moving consumer goods (FMCGs), the distribution strategy should consider the opportunities for both present and future business through an appropriate mix of the channels of distribution, e.g. supermarkets, wholesalers and direct to retailers. The distribution strategy should also include the company policy of exclusive agents or stockists and of direct mail order to consumers. Figure 5.7 illustrates an example of the channels of distribution in a typical FMCG business. The selection of a strategy may be influenced by the cost of distribution and it should be tempered by the business judgement of customer service and future opportunities.

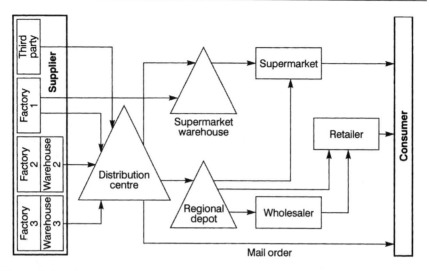

Figure 5.7 Channels of distribution

The location, design and operations of distribution warehouses are all vital ingredients of a supply chain – not only for cost optimization but also for the quality and safety standards of products and for improving customer service by a faster turnaround at the warehouse. There are computer simulation models available for determining the size and location of a distribution centre, but local body planning regulations, the proximity of a highway and a big demand centre very often will be the prime determinants of the location.

Warehouse operation

The operations of a distribution warehouse in general can be represented by Figure 5.8. There are good opportunities of 're-engineering' the warehouse functions when the total process from reception to despatch is critically examined.

The design issues of a warehouse include:

- Storage systems:
  - block stock
  - back-to-back racking

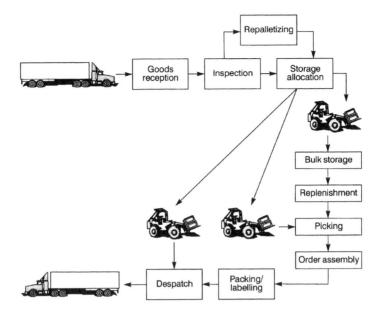

Figure 5.8   Warehouse operations

- double deep racking
- narrow aisle racking
- drive-through racking
- mobile racking
- Handling systems
  - counterbalanced trucks
  - reach trucks
  - turret trucks
  - stacker cranes
  - automated guided vehicles
  - overhead cranes
- Product quality
  - ambient
  - chilled store (e.g. margarine)
  - cold store (e.g. ice cream)
- Safety and control systems
  - detection systems
  - sprinkler and fire hydrants
  - warehouse management system software.

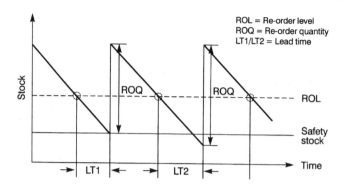

Figure 5.9   A basic ROL/ROQ model for a 'pull' system

Stock management

As indicated earlier, stocks are kept as a buffer along the supply chain in various warehouses, factories (work in process) and retail store shelves. These inventories can cost from a minimum of 15% up to 40% of their value per year (storage space, handling costs, energy costs including heating and refrigeration, stock slippage and insurance). Therefore careful management of stock levels makes good business sense.

In traditional stock management there are two basic approaches: the pull approach and the push approach. In a pull system (Figure 5.9) a warehouse is viewed as independent of the supply chain and inventory is replenished with order sizes based on a predetermined stock level for each warehouse. The stock management model for the pull system is normally geared to establish ROL (re-order level) and ROQ (re-order quantity). That is, when the stock drops to a certain level, a re-order is triggered of a predetermined amount. The re-order quantity takes into account past demands and the lead times for a re-order to be satisfied. The aim is to have as small amount of inventory as possible on hand at any one time, and the re-order quantity should likewise be as small as possible. However, in some processes, such as a batch system, there will be a minimum amount that can be produced and in other cases there can be economies of scale which will determine the optimal size of an order. The push method is used when economies of scale in procurement outweigh the benefits of minimum inventory levels as achieved in the pull method (Figure 5.10). That is, the warehouse does not decide the quantity of the order but

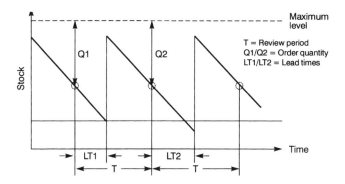

Figure 5.10　A basic fixed interval model for a 'push' system

will receive a delivery as determined by the production schedule. Normally a fixed interval review model with a forecast demand for manufacturing planning is used in a push system.

With the support of information technology, businesses are moving towards a virtual inventory system with a single stock concept which can be held anywhere in the system, be it on order with the supplier, in production or at the point of sale. This is the concept of virtual inventory management (VIM) or electronic inventory. Thus instead of considering stocks of raw materials, work in progress at the various stages of production and finished goods in warehouses each as separate stocks of inventory, purely because of their physical location, inventory is now considered as being part of one single stock.

Transport planning

Transport planning is a key decision area of distribution management. Transportation is a non-value added item to the cost of the product and absorbs, in general, the biggest share of the logistics cost. Students often argue that unless a product is in the right place it is of little value and thus transportation does add value. Not so! The concept of adding value relates to the transformation process, that is the conversion of inputs of raw materials, labour and machinery into a finished product. Storage, inspection and transportation all add cost but do not add value. Some of these costs will be unavoidable; materials have to be moved, goods have to be distributed, but storage,

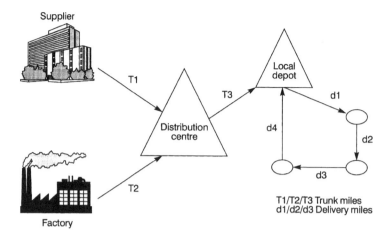

Figure 5.11 Distribution routes

handling and movement only add to the cost, and not to the value of the product.

The main factors in transport decisions are (see Figure 5.11):

- Transport mode selection
- Trucking routing
- Delivery planning.

There are various means of transportation, such as railway, river, canal, coastal shipping and pipelines for products such as oil. In some countries, for some products, air transport might prove to be the most viable option. Generally, however, because of dependability, flexibility, speed and door-to-door service, road transport has proved to be the best option. For Great Britain the Channel Tunnel has added to the convenience of road transport.

There are significant opportunities in optimizing the selection of hauliers or type of trucks. In order to take advantage of the competitiveness and the up-to-date development of vehicles, companies are building partnerships with hauliers.

After the selection of the mode, the planning of trunking or primary transport for single-drop repetitive journeys between known or well-known locations (e.g. factory to warehouse) is relatively straightforward. However, the routing and scheduling of delivery vehicles to customers is extremely variable and therefore requires more systematic planning. There are computer-based procedures to optimize delivery to customers. The objective is not to minimize the total mileage but to maximize the utilization of vehicle time (delivery window) and space (by volume or weight) and ensuring customer service.

Strategic alliances

In order to achieve an integrated supply chain the various players need to work together. The four most important types of distribution management strategic alliances are third party logistics (3PL), retailer–supplier partnerships (RSP), distributor integration (DI), and customer relationship management (CRM).

Third party logistics (3PL)

The use of a third party to take over some or all of a company's logistics responsibilities is becoming more prevalent. 3PL is simply the use of an outside company to perform all or part of the firm's materials management and product distribution function. 3PL relationships are typically more complex than traditional logistics supplier relationships. Modern 3PL arrangements involve long-term commitments and often multiple functions or process management. As organizations focus on their core competencies they are looking for other specialist organizations to partner with.

Retailer–supplier partnerships

As customer satisfaction becomes more imperative and margins get tighter it makes sense to create cooperative efforts between suppliers and retailers in order to leverage the knowledge of both parties. The types of retailer–supplier partnerships can be viewed on a continuum. At one end is information sharing. At the other is a consignment scheme of vendor-managed inventory (VMI), where the vendor completely manages and owns the inventory until the retailer sells it.

In a simple quick response strategy, suppliers receive POS data from retailers and use this information to synchronize their production and inventory activities with actual sales at the retailers. In this strategy the retailer still prepares individual orders, but the POS data is used by the supplier to improve delivery performance and hence reduce supply variability.

In a continuous replenishment strategy, sometimes called rapid replenishment, vendors receive POS data and use this data to prepare shipments at previously agreed upon intervals to maintain specific levels of inventory.

In a vendor-managed inventory system, the supplier decides on the appropriate inventory levels of each product and the appropriate policies to maintain these levels. The goal of many VMI programmes is to eliminate the need for the retailer to oversee specific orders for replenishment. The ultimate is for the supplier to manage the inventory and only receive payment for it once it has been sold by the retailer; in essence the retailer is providing an outlet for the supplier!

Distributor integration (DI)

Modern information technology has enabled this strategy in which distributors are integrated so that expertise and inventory located at one distributor is available to the others. DI can be used to address both inventory-related and service-related issues. In terms of inventory, DI can be used to create a large pool of inventory across the entire distributor network thus lowering total inventory costs while raising customer service levels. Similarly, DI can be used to meet the customer's specific needs by directing those requests to the distributor best suited to address them.

The influence of the Internet on the economy in general and business practice in particular has been tremendous. The direct business model employed by industry giants such as Dell Computer and amazon.com enables customers to order products over the Internet and thus allows these companies to sell their products without relying on third party distributors apart from those providing the physical delivery service.

Similarly, the Internet and the emerging e-business models have produce expectations that many supply chain problems will be resolved merely by using these new technology and business models. Whilst it has promised so much in reality the expectations have not been achieved. In many cases the downfall of some of the highest profile Internet businesses has been attributed to their logistics strategies.

Whilst the success of the business to customer concept has not yet eventuated, the use of the Internet for business to business integration has more likelihood of success. Integration of the supply chain players is made possible with the use of the Internet and the associated technologies.

Reviewing the impact of the new technologies on the supply chain provides an interesting development. The Internet and the evolving supply chain strategies has seen a shift in transportation and order fulfilment strategies away from case and bulk shipments to single item and smaller-size shipment and from shipping to a small number of stores to serving highly geographically dispersed customers. This shift has seen the importance of partnerships with parcel and LTL industries. It has also increased the importance and complexity of reverse logistics, that of handling the significant numbers of product returns. Thus one of the big winners in the new developments is the parcel industry. Indeed one of the important advantages of the parcel industry is the existence of an excellent information infrastructure that enables real-time tracking. Those players in this industry who work to modify their own systems in order to integrate it with their customers' supply chains are likely to be successful.

As businesses come to understand the role of the Internet we will see new models of business evolving. As yet what those models will be is unsure, but one thing is for certain, the Internet will have an impact on how supply chains of the future will be managed.

Customer relationship management (CRM)

The recent growth in availability of customer relationship management (CRM) systems has led to access to data that can be used to improve overall supply chain performance. The objective of CRM is to develop a customer-centred organization that ensures every opportunity is used to delight customers, foster customer loyalty and build long-term relationships that are mutually beneficial. The ultimate goal is to ensure that each individual customer's current and future wants and needs can be satisfied. What this involves is the capture of individual customer transaction details and from this historical data developing a picture of what that customer needs and what that customer's purchasing habits are.

CRM's relevance to overall supply chain management lies in the need to integrate such systems with the management of the supply side. The information gathered by the CRM systems can be used to improve the overall performance of the complete supply chain. As the need for supply chain transparency increases, businesses are looking for ways to improve the efficiency of supply. This has led to the development of the concept of total demand chain management.

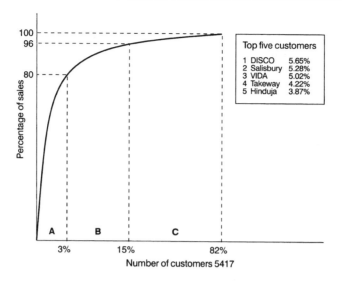

Figure 5.12   ABC analysis – customers

The partnership with customers is the mirror of working with suppliers, but with the role reversed. Ideally the relationship will be that the customer involves the manufacturer in the market research phase so that together the best product can be designed to meet the end consumers' needs. Likewise the customer through electronic data information (EDI) or Extranet can input directly into the ERP system. Improved internal relationships within the business between manufacturing and logistics staff interfacing directly with the customers should achieve a more precise specification of customer needs and sharing data (e.g. EDI or B2C web).

Thus it is useful to carry out an ABC analysis (Pareto chart) to identify the top customers, as shown in Figure 5.12. The Pareto theory is that 20% of the customers will account for roughly 80% of the business. ABC analysis takes this a step further by dividing customers into three groupings, as shown in Figure 5.12. Normally the division will be the top 5%, the next 15% and the balance of customers – 80%. In this example the analysis has been further broken down so that it can be seen that the top five customers account for 24% of the sales, and overall just 3% of the customers account for 80% of the sales.

Another challenge of working with customers is to identify the true profitability of all customers and then to improve the profitability of key customers. Figure 5.13 illustrates a point made by Christopher

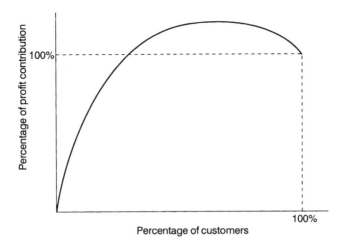

Figure 5.13   Customer profitability (adapted from Christopher, 1992)

(1992), that a 'tail' of unprofitable customers actually reduces the total profit contributions.

In one organization we encountered, the top 5% of the customers accounted for 40% of the sales, and because of their importance to the company they had been able to negotiate volume discounts and special delivery arrangements. When these benefits were examined and costed out it was found that whereas the balance of the customers were providing the company with a true 40% gross profit margin on sales, these top 5% were only providing the company with a margin of 10%. Thus overall the gross margin on all sales for the company was reduced to 28% whereas the budget had allowed for 40%. This had not been apparent as the discounts had been shown in the accounts as an overhead expense and the extra transport costs had also been included as an overhead cost. There were also other reasons as to why the drop in true margin was not obvious.

In order to assess the true profitability of customers it is necessary to move away from the average allocation of cost (e.g. cost per tonne) and conventional cost accounting. Logistics managers are now working towards what is known as 'activity-based costing' (ABC) where cost is allocated according to the level of activity that consumes the resources. For example, the picking cost of an order will vary according to its work content depending on whether the order is in full pallet or small units, number of lines or SKUs or whether it requires additional packaging.

Supply chain performance

In this chapter we have identified supply chain performance as a key driver of Total Operations Solutions because:

- We need to have a grip over the various parameters of the supply chain in their true perspective, and
- The performance measures can be used not only to drive continuous improvement of the business process but also to set directions for future strategy.

Therefore the criteria for performance measures should cover a balanced approach to all key parameters of the supply chain and should provide operational measures rather than financial measures. Measures should be simple, easy to define and easy to monitor.

In determining what should be measured it is useful to get away from standard accounting measures. Operations' requirements are different from those of the accountants. In determining our own measurements we should ask:

- What should be measured and why?
- What is the benefit of this measure, how does it help us to achieve our goal?

Once we decide what should be measured, then we can determine how it should be measured.

Measurements are only of any use if they are fed down to the workers and if the workers understand what the measurements mean. Ideally if a worker receives a measurement then that worker should be encouraged to become involved in finding ways to improve the system so as to achieve improved results.

Measurements should never be used as a means of levelling blame to one department or to criticize any one individual. Measurements should be aimed at finding where problems occur so that action can be taken so as to prevent future mistakes. After all, no one section or department works alone; we are all in this together. If the company goes down we all go down!

The methods given in Figure 5.14 are fairly standard and should fit into most systems without upsetting the accountants. None the less, no measurement is sacrosanct and each measurement should be

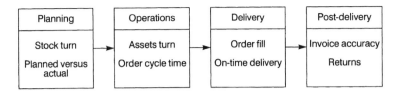

Figure 5.14 Supply chain performance

challenged. A measurement that does not help to improve the system is an unnecessary cost.

Planning performance

'Stock turn' is the ratio of the total sales (or throughput of a product) and the actual stock at any time, both being expressed in either money or volume. The objective is to maximize the stock turn (i.e. minimize average stock level) but also to maintain stock availability. Stock availability (the percentage of demand that can be met from available stock) is another measure of performance; availability can also be measured by the number or percentage of orders satisfied within a given target time frame.

The unit of stock turn is a number or ratio. It is also a common practice to express stock profile in terms of equivalent weeks or days of stock. For example if the cost of goods sold (raw materials plus direct labour and other manufacturing costs but not overheads) is £25 000 and the amount of stock of finished goods on hand totals £5000 then the number of days of finished goods equals 73 days ($5000/25 000 \times 365 = 73$). That is, on past performance it is going to take just on two and half months to sell all the finished goods we have on hand. Assuming that we have already paid the suppliers and have paid our workers' wages and paid the other costs of production, this obviously means that our inventory of finished goods is putting pressure on our cash flow. The same types of calculations can be made for stocks of raw materials and work in progress.

One company we visited was proud of the fact that in their high street stores they only ever had seven days of retail stock (own product) on hand. Their re-order system to their central warehouse was on-line and re-orders were delivered within 24 hours. The

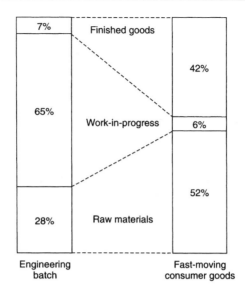

Figure 5.15   Stock profile: percentage of total stock

warehouse of finished goods held six months' stock, and the stock-pile of raw materials for production amounted to seven months' supply. Assuming suppliers were paid within one month of supply this meant that this company was waiting 12 months and seven days to recover the cost out-laid for stock! Not really anything to be proud of when looked at in this fashion.

The share of stock by primary materials (i.e. raw materials and packaging materials), work in progress and finished products varies according to the products and method of manufacturing, as illustrated in Figure 5.15.

'Planned versus actual' (also known as planning efficiency) is a simple measure of whether the plan is being achieved. This measure can be for any period, i.e. this month we planned to produce 80 000 units, but our actual production was 70 000 units. Therefore we were 87.5% efficient. This measure is of little use if we cannot trace back to why production was short of the plan, not with a view to criticize but with a view of correcting the system so that we will be more efficient in future. It is more meaningful when planning efficiency is expressed for each product or SKU rather than for total volume. Sometimes this measurement will be more hard-hitting if it is expressed in lost sales.

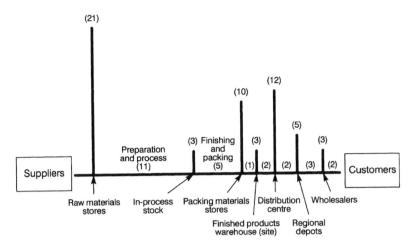

Figure 5.16   Pipeline map of an FMCG product

It is a common practice to express both the planned and actual production of each week in graphs and calculate planning efficiency figures for the week and cumulative year to date. But all this effort is only of any use if the information, however expressed, leads to corrective action being taken. Too many measures too often will only serve to confuse the real issues.

Scott and Westbrook (1991) introduced an apparently simple tool, called a pipeline map, to present a snapshot of the total stock in a supply chain. As shown in Figure 5.16, the supply chain of an FMCG product is mapped by a series of horizontal lines representing the average time spent in major processes between stock-holding points, and a series of vertical lines showing in the same scale (e.g. days) the average stock cover at each point. Pipeline volume is the sum of both the horizontal and vertical lines and represents the time needed to 'flush' the inventory in the supply chain at an average rate of throughput. Pipeline mapping is a useful tool to understand the planning performance of a supply chain, but additional analytical techniques should be used to identify the key areas of improvement.

Operations performance

'Asset turn' is the ratio of total sales and fixed assets. It is important that the value of fixed assets is updated by taking into account the

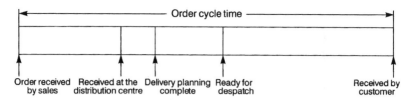

Figure 5.17   Order cycle time

depreciation rate for the type of asset according to a defined accounting policy of the company. Assets utilization (time-based) is more relevant to all manufacturing performance. However, the measure of assets turn (value-based) provides an indication of investment in the supply chain. In the short to medium term this measurement is of little use as the investment in the assets has already been made and the measurement is against a past decision. In biblical terms the sins of the fathers are being visited on the next generation.

'Order cycle time' (also known as lead time) is the elapsed time from the placement of an order by the customer to the receiving of delivery (see Figure 5.17). It is important to state standards to suit customer requirements and analyse the total cycle time into relevant components.

Lynch and Cross (1991) claim that only 5% of cycle time is devoted to adding value. In many cases the product is waiting to be worked on 95% of the time. (This excludes raw materials in stock and finished goods in the warehouse.)

Delivery performance

'Order fill' is the percentage of first time satisfied orders. From the customer's point of view this is probably the most important measurement. The order is the correct quantity and quality. The next most important measure as far as the customer is concerned is if the delivery is on time!

'On time delivery' can be expressed as a percentage of full orders delivered on time. 'On time' may be determined by the standards of order cycle time set for a customer or the agreed date of delivery as set by the customer.

Past delivery performance

The times a customer normally comes into contact with the company will be when they are placing an order, that is when the sale is made, when they receive the goods, and when they pay for them. These are the three crucial times for the customer. These are the times that your customer will judge you. Whatever happens in between in the manufacturing process, the supply management or whatever, is not of any great interest to the customer.

Payment will generally be against your invoice. It follows that if the invoice is incorrect (wrong quantities shown, incorrect prices and discounts not allowed) that the customer will be irritated. An incorrect invoice also gives a customer an excuse to delay payment. From our experience, few customers need any excuse to delay payment.

With invoicing, time is of the essence. Most organizations have a cut-off date for passing invoices for payment. If the cut-off date is the twelfth of the month and your invoice is not received until the fifteenth, then for the sake of three days you are going to wait 30 extra days for payment.

If your company is having problems with a large number of incorrect invoices, then measurement of the number of invoices wrong as a percentage of total invoices could well prove worthwhile. It will not be difficult to determine if there is a problem. Five minutes with the accounts receivables' clerks over a cup of coffee should be sufficient.

Likewise a target date should be set for despatch of invoices. There is no reason why invoices cannot be mailed out within 24 hours of delivery of the goods. With an integrated system the release of goods for delivery should automatically trigger an invoice.

Return of goods is another key measure. Goods will be returned because they are not what were ordered, or because they are defective or delivery is late. Our motto should be 'never give the customer a reason to leave'. Delivering faulty goods, or the wrong goods, or delivering late is giving the customer the perfect reason to leave.

Measurement of returns can be expressed as the number returned, or the value of returned goods or as a percentage of deliveries. The value of goods returned is not the true cost. The cost includes the cost of putting right and the loss of confidence experienced by the customer.

Any error can be measured in monetary terms or as a percentage, and don't forget the cost of making the corrections. What cannot be measured is equally important. What cannot be readily measured is loss of confidence by the customer, loss of future orders, loss of reputation with possible new customers, loss of morale amongst workers, an acceptance that being right 90 per cent of the time is good enough. Imagine what would happen at Heathrow if the air traffic controllers were only right 98 per cent of the time, or if 5 per cent of babies were dropped by the doctor at delivery? Anything but a target of 100 per cent correctness is telling workers that we expect there will always be some mistakes and so therefore mistakes are acceptable.

Customer service

As Christopher (1992) says, 'Customer service is one of the most powerful elements available to the organization in its search for competitive advantage and yet is often least well managed.'

The output and performance of all supply chain management activity are relevant to customer service. However, the indices of both delivery performance and past delivery performance are directly related to customer service. It is useful to monitor the indices separately. It is also possible to calculate a 'composite index' by attaching a weight to each service index. The weighting should reflect the relative importance that the customers attach to these elements.

Table 5.2, as shown by Christopher (1992), illustrates an example of composite customer service index.

No matter how good our internal measurements are, the best way of finding out how good we are at customer service is to ask the customer what is important to them, and then to take action to achieve what the customer wants. It could be, for example, that the customer can never get through on the telephone. We could therefore set a target that no telephone should ever ring more than three times before it is answered and that no matter who is passing they should pick up the telephone and at least take a message. To stress the point that we should always be seen as easy to communicate with, we could also set a target that all faxes are to be answered within 24 hours, and so on. These targets do not have to be measured. It will be a matter of changing the culture of the company so that such actions become

Table 5.2 Composite customer service index

Service index	Weighting (%) (a)	Performance (%) (b)	Weighted score a × b
Order fill	45	70	0.315
On time	35	80	0.28
Invoice accuracy	10	90	0.09
(100 − returns)	10	95	0.095
			0.78

Composite customer service is 78%

Source: Christopher, 1992

standard practice: 'this is the way we do things around here'. No manner of measures will ever make up for a strong culture driven by pride in achievement and getting things right first time and every time.

Summary

We began this chapter with a quote from Proust, and the importance of 'seeing with new eyes'. We continue from where we left off in Chapter 4, with the need for measurement and for a customer focus. We extend this approach to include a supplier focus.

In the past the attitude in business was secrecy and restricting information to a 'need to know' basis. This especially applied to suppliers, where the aim was to achieve the best deal possible.

Supply chain management asks us to see with new eyes: to see customers and suppliers as part, and indeed partners, in our overall production process. As partners both suppliers and customers can be, and should be, involved in the planning process.

A major tool in achieving this is the computer-driven MRP II system which is discussed in detail in this chapter. Other key areas discussed here are distribution strategies, materials handling, warehouse management and stock management. Our main lesson in this chapter is to open our eyes, to appreciate how much we can benefit through honesty and loyalty to suppliers and to customers.

CASE EXAMPLE 2: Supply chain logistics at National Starch, USA

Background

National Starch and Chemical Company, based in Chicago, began measuring shipping performance on a corporate basis in the early 1990s. The initial results indicated that, at best, the Adhesives Division was achieving 80–85% on time delivery performance. This is a business where there is a need to ship a multitude of products in a variety of containers with varying lead times from customers. The logistics department set an objective to reduce shipping delays from 15% to 5% and at the same time reduce overall inventories.

Approach

The approach the division took was to classify their products in specific containers by ABC categories. The categories represented volume of product and the customer base purchasing the product. The lead time for shipping the product and the inventory held were related to the A, B and C designations, with A being shorter lead time with available inventory.

Implementation

A number of local cross-functional teams were formed comprising Sales, Manufacturing, Technical Service, Materials Management and Customer Service. The task of the teams was to work on ABC product classification and delivery service standards. Essentially every product in each container was evaluated based on the volume and number of customers purchasing it. The Chicago plant reviewed over 200 products in approximately 15 different containers for more than 700 orders per month.

The next task was to develop a tracking system to report on delays against standard lead times and compare them with the date agreed with the customer.

After agreement was reached on the ABC products and their safety stocks the order patterns of these products were reviewed and minimum, maximum and re-order levels were established. The employees were thoroughly trained and the system was also presented at each regional sales meeting. It was important to gain support of sales stuff since they needed to 'sell' it to the customers.

To ensure that the ABC and safety stocks reflect changing market demands, a cross functional team reviews the product ABC designations and inventory lists every month.

Results and learning points

The improvement in shipping performance was dramatic following the implementation of the ABC system, as shown by the figures of shipping delays as follows:

Year 0 overall: 14.7%
Year 1 overall: 3.8%
Year 2 overall: 1.2%

There were other benefits in the supply chain operations and performance, including:

- Sales team increased the amount of time to work proactively with customers
- A reduction in finished goods and raw materials inventory
- Decreased 'last minute' expedited freight charges
- Improved communication between departments especially between sales and logistics.

Chapter 6

Environment and Safety

The River Rhine, it is well known,
Doth wash your city of Cologne;
But tell me, Nymphs, what power divine
Shall henceforth wash the river Rhine?
   Samuel Taylor Coleridge, 'Cologne'

Environment and safety are not popular issues with most manufacturers or service organizations. Costs of compliance, audits and inspections are non-value adding. This chapter shows why environment and safety issues should be considered critical success factors. For example, poor health and safety leads to illnesses and accidents – and significant costs for the organization. Wasted energy consumption damages the environment and damages profits. Good health and safety and environmental practice can also be used in marketing the organization – internally and externally – as a caring organization, to staff, the local community and to customers. Add to these considerations moves by institutional investors, such as the State Treasurer of California (the United States' third largest pension fund, with assets of US$250 billion), who demand environmental accountability and disclosure before investing in company stocks.

Since Wickham Skinner of the Harvard Business School published his famous article, 'Manufacturing – the missing link' in 1969, hundreds of books and articles have been written on manufacturing strategy, mission or policy for industries. Few of these publications describe the importance of environment and safety issues as an integral part of manufacturing policy or process. What references there are seem to emphasize either a 'structuralist' philosophy where it is believed that success in a manufacturing business comes from vision, planning, measuring and monitoring the performance – or a 'behaviourist' approach where it is believed that success is achieved through leadership, motivation, involvement, learning and empowerment. Other than meeting legal and regulatory requirements, environment and safety issues are seldom seen as critical success factors.

Not surprisingly, there are instances in recent history where the profit of manufacturing businesses was drastically affected due to negligence in environment and safety standards. A failure in product safety caused children to be born with deformities and is still haunting the manufacturers of thalidomide. The gas escape of 1984 in Bhopal, India, killed over 1000 people and permanently damaged the business of the manufacturer. Environmental pollution by Pacific Gas and Electric in California (as recounted in the Julia Roberts film *Erin Brokovich*) resulted in numerous legal battles. Readers will probably remember other such stories.

On a global scale, industrial pollution is said to be the main contributor to the 'greenhouse' effect, to global warming and to acid rain. (For details of the causes of the greenhouse effect see www.bbc.co.uk/science.) It is generally accepted that increased emission of gases, particularly carbon dioxide (vehicle exhausts) increase the global temperature. Another major problem are chlorofluorocarbons (CFCs), which in the past have been widely used in aerosols (hair spray etc.), refrigerator coolants and air-conditioners, which are believed to be destroying the ozone layer. These issues gained such prominence that in 1997 the Kyoto treaty was drawn up to implement the United Nations framework to combat climate change. The Kyoto treaty largely binds industrial nations to reduce the emission of greenhouse gases by an average of 5.2% below their 1992 levels over the next decade (1997–2007). As a result of some governments making grandiose promises and overexaggerated claims by the green movement some credibility has been lost. None the less, increasingly individual nations are passing legislation that will require commercial organizations to clean up their act. Some legislation or threatened legislation has been rather misguided; for example the government of New Zealand considered taxing farmers for flatulence by cattle so as to reduce methane emissions (the tax gathered was intended to research how to reduce emissions by cattle through changes of diet etc.). Eventually, the government, reacting to a strong farming lobby, did not proceed with taxing the flatulent bovines.

Manufacturing industries are major players in environment issues. Companies that take the lead, such as Toyota with their hybrid petrol and battery driven car (the Prius), will only continue to do so if there is a market. The consumer has the final vote. If consumers do not buy environmentally friendly products manufacturers will continue to make what sells. Other examples are solar energy, collection of water from house roofs, recycling of 'grey' water (dish water, washing machine water for gardens), toilets with inbuilt systems (non-chemical) that do not require sewerage disposal. All this technology is readily available, generally simple to install, but not at all widely adopted by house owners in the developed nations. The saving in money terms is simply not there. The initial cost of installing solar water heating takes over five years to recover from savings in energy costs. When building a new home the owner (usually already overstretched financially) simply cannot see the cost benefit.

But for larger organizations cost benefits from being eco friendly are being realized. British Petroleum announced in 2000 that it would reduce greenhouse gas emissions 10% by 2010. This was achieved by 2003 and they claim they have saved $US650 million a year. Much of this was achieved by good house keeping. The Japanese company Canon in 1998 adopted the principle 'plants that fail to protect the environment should not be in operation'. They have five headings under which environment issues are addressed, namely:

1 Green procurement
2 Energy conservation
3 Resource conservation
4 Elimination of hazardous waste
5 Risk management.

The Canon environment report, detailing substantial savings made through recycling as well as from the five initiatives listed above, can be found at www.canon.com/about/environment.

Environment International Limited found that Interface, the world's largest carpet manufacturer, has eliminated more than $US165 million in waste over 10 years; Baxter Healthcare saved $US75 million in raw materials, energy costs, disposal and packaging costs in 2000; and others who increased profits through implementing environmental management include DuPont, Georgia Pacific, Lucent Microelectronics, Anheuser-Busch, Sunoco, and aspen/Snowmass. Other savings quoted by Environment International are half a billion tons of pollutants eliminated by 3M Corporation as well as an 84% reduction in manufacturing releases to water with an overall saving of

$US750 million over 20 years. Texas Instruments now saves $US23 million per year through recycling and $64 million per year by optimizing resources; an investment of $US1 million on CFC reduction by Nortel Communications resulted in a saving of $US4 million in the first year.

In service industries there is not so much obvious scope for environmental savings. But substantial savings can be made in large offices by measures such as becoming energy conscious (turning off lights at night, replacing incandescent lamps with compact fluorescent lamps, using time controls, double glazing etc.), not using polyurethane cups for coffee, siting recycling bins for paper, metal, plastic, glass etc., saving paper through double-sided photocopying, recycling printing cartridges and toner bottles and not having stocks of stationery but printing from templates on demand. If a team is set up to find ways of reducing environment costs it is surprising how much can be achieved. Did you know that it takes 70 trees to produce one tonne of paper!

If your organization owns buildings, the biggest single cost will be in energy (electricity and gas), and lighting accounts for 50% of energy costs. If a manager of a large building wants to get waste costs down the first step is to get the various cleaning contractors on side, and show them that waste management will actually make their jobs easier. For example, the waste compactor should be located so that the cleaners have to pass recycling bins for paper, cans and bottles, and each floor should have strategically placed wheelie bins for recycling paper and so on. The Vero Tower manager (40 floors in down town Auckland, New Zealand) reported that they had 16 tonnes of compact waste per month; within three months, with the support of the three largest tenants and the cleaners, 16 tonnes was reduced to 9 tonnes. Twelve months later the compacted waste had climbed back up to 12 tonnes, showing that continual monitoring is necessary! However, if they had not measured the waste in the first place they would not have had a benchmark to compare to.

In manufacturing industries, there is much scope for environment and safety accidents to occur and likewise there are many opportunities to prevent accidents. Where operations are repetitive in nature, common environment and safety factors can readily be identified and controlled. Fuji Xerox, in their non-manufacturing operations in 1997, instituted a zero injury programme and reduced injuries by 50%. They also introduced annual medical check-ups for staff and reduced absences from illness by 47%.

From these examples it can be seen that environment and safety are not just social or political issues, they are vital ingredients contributing to the performance of any organization.

We have categorized the pillar of Environment and Safety into three foundation stones:

7 Product safety
8 Occupational safety and health
9 Environment and resource management.

Foundation 7: Product safety

Too often do we see advertisements requesting drivers of a particular model to return their car for some safety modification. What sort of message does this give the market place? Have you ever wondered how much the cost of the recall really is, not only the cost of advertising, but the cost of putting the product right, and of course the lost opportunity costs. The waste of time, effort and money can usually not be fully quantified and when an organization does go through the trauma of a product recall or even a withdrawal, direct money costs may well be the least of the problems.

An extreme example is the much-publicized Ford/Firestone debacle which saw 13 million tyres being recalled in 2001 after more than 200 deaths – with an initial cost of US$3 billion. Eventually this recall, and the ensuing bad feeling and bad publicity between the two companies, led to the early retirement of chief executives at Bridgestone (Firestone's parent company) and at Ford. In 2003, after several further recalls of hundreds of vehicles for various reasons such as faulty brakes, jamming safety belts, and after Ford had posted huge losses with a resulting collapse in the share price, the new chief executive, William Clayton Ford, reacting to stock market and institutional pressure, announced the closure of five North American plants and layoffs of 35 000 workers. It would appear that Ford has now turned the corner and reputation is being restored, but as the Duke of Wellington said after the battle of Waterloo, it was a close run thing.

A major incident in product safety, especially if related to consumable and brand products, can seriously damage the brand and also work against the goodwill and business of the whole company, as in the Ford example above. This is particularly obvious in food products. If all the faulty products are not quickly identified and recalled the result could be extremely costly both in terms of health and money. If the faulty products contain toxic materials, they could be absorbed either through the respiratory system, or through the skin or gastro-intestinal tract. If micro-organisms are present in a product their fast propagation rate will spoil the quality of the product. Some micro-organisms may produce toxic substances and others may be harmless to health but they can have adverse effect on the quality of consumable products. A concentration of ten million bacteria per gram of a food product generally means that the product is spoiled. Only one micro-organism in water can generate seven hundred million micro-organisms in just 12 hours. The physical damage of a product down the supply chain may be costly but will be less harmful than chemical damage.

Organizations, particularly in food and pharmaceutical industries, are closely monitored by regulatory bodies. The Food and Drug Administration (FDA) of the USA is a powerful body for ensuring the safety of new and existing food and pharmaceutical products. In the UK a similar organization, the Medicines and Healthcare products Regulatory Agency (MHRA), replaced in April 2003 both MDA (the Medical Devices Agency) and MCA (the Medicines Control Agency). This Agency is committed to safeguarding public health by ensuring the medicines, healthcare products and medical equipment meet appropriate standards of safety, quality and performance and are used safely (MHRA, 2004).

Cost of product safety

In addition to its effect on goodwill and health, the financial cost related to a product safety incident is generally compounded by costs at various levels, such as:

- Cost of investigation
- Cost of sterilization of the plant and storage areas
- Cost of production downtime as the plant is shut down until a certified clearance is obtained
- Cost of recall from the customers and consumers
- Cost of salvage if the returns are worth salvaging through reprocessing or repackaging

- Cost of dumping if the returns could cause health and environment problems
- Legal costs and damages.

And of course it is not only your immediate customers who will be dissatisfied; withdrawals and recalls of products, no matter how well handled, will be well publicized by the media to the whole market place – potential customers and competitors alike, as shown above in the Ford example.

Control of product safety hazards

The safety hazards of consumable manufactured products are manifested in various forms including:

- Toxicological: the presence of poisonous or toxic substances in a product or process
- Micro-biological: the presence of micro-organisms or bacteria in a product, plant or process
- Chemical: corrosive actions or chemical reaction with other agents and decomposition under heat
- Physical: damage to the product and by the product or its packaging at any stage during manufacture, storage or distribution
- Environmental: pollution of the environment by the product and its packaging materials, especially if they are not biodegradable.

In a manufacturing and supply chain process, where activities are repetitive, the above hazards can be prevented by measures as illustrated in Figure 6.1.

Development and design engineers must avoid features in product design that enhance the probability of errors or safety hazards at the subsequent stages of the supply chain. A formal safety clearance of all new products regarding toxicological hazards must be mandatory.

Plant and equipment for the processing and packaging of consumer products, especially edible products, must follow the hygiene design aspects with regard to ease of cleaning and micro-biological impermeability. 'Hygiene, design and operation of food plants', by Jowitt and Horwood (1989), is recommended to those engaged in the operation of a food plant.

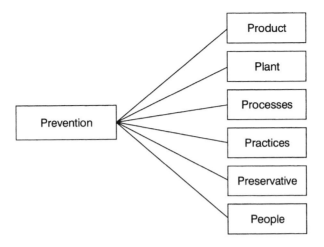

Figure 6.1 Product safety measures

A clear understanding of the sources of contamination is vital to ensure product safety in a manufacturing process. Raw materials can be controlled by micro-biological tests before the start of the process. Water is the main source of micro-organisms, and a water decontamination system (such as chlorination, pasteurization) is an essential part of a process containing water. A process with a cleaning-in-place (CIP) system is also recommended.

The code of practice at each stage of the supply chain, including raw material approval, sanitation, housekeeping, storage and handling and fault precautions, and the strict adherence to them, is the preferred practice of product safety. Many companies have formalized the quality assurance procedures through ISO accreditation.

Preservatives are an essential ingredient of a consumable product to prevent accidental contamination and to protect against normal processes of degradation. However, the reliance on preservatives offers only a low level of protection and product safety.

People are the key to the success to any programme, including one for product safety. The company's organizational structure should include a quality assurance manager qualified in microbiology to ensure the quality standards of the product. This manager's team should be supported by a multi-functional team from the factory and a continuous training programme to ensure the safety and quality standards of products.

The hazards and preventive measures of product safety at different stages of the supply chain are summarized in Figure 6.2.

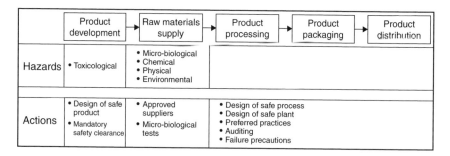

Figure 6.2 Hazards and measures of product safety

Foundation 8: Occupational safety and health

Accidents in the work place mean lost production time plus time-wasting inspections by government officials and legal costs. There will also be the cost of correcting the situation so that the accident will not occur again. It is said that if an accident can happen then it will, and usually at the worst possible time! Apart from humanitarian concerns, prevention and training in safe practice will be always cheaper than putting things right after an adverse event.

Since the days of the Industrial Revolution safety standards at the work place have steadily and significantly improved. However, processes and equipment have attained a high degree of complexity. We are now dealing with over a million chemicals and compounds with a massive reserve of energy in process. Unfortunately, many managers assume that accidents are part of doing business and that costs are borne by insurance companies. It is important to understand that the same factors which are creating accidents are also creating losses in production, quality, sales and profit. It is not surprising that the most respected organization specializing in industrial safety is called the International Loss Control Institute (ILCI).

The major industrial accidents in recent times, including Three Mile Island, the Mexico LPG fire, Bhopal and Chernobyl, were all well publicized because of their high fatality and serious injury rates. However, there are many more minor accidents that are taking place in manufacturing industries – as demonstrated by a study of 1.75 million industrial accidents in 1969 by the ILCI (Bird and Germain, 1990). This is known as the 1–10–30–600 ratio, as illustrated in Figure 6.3.

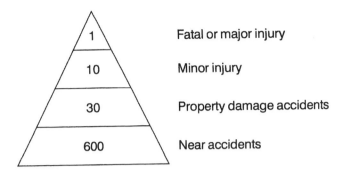

1	Fatal or major injury
10	Minor injury
30	Property damage accidents
600	Near accidents

Figure 6.3 Accident ratio triangle

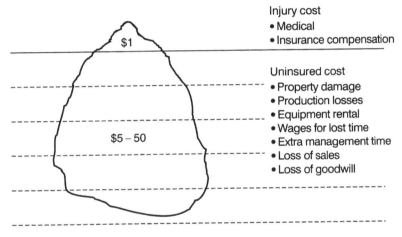

Injury cost
- Medical
- Insurance compensation

Uninsured cost
- Property damage
- Production losses
- Equipment rental
- Wages for lost time
- Extra management time
- Loss of sales
- Loss of goodwill

Figure 6.4 Accident cost iceberg (adapted from Bird and Germain, 1990)

The injury or illness costs, which are usually claimed from an insurance company, are a relatively small part of the total cost, as shown in the 'accident cost iceberg' illustrated in Figure 6.4.

Causes of accidents

According to the ILCI, an accident is usually the result of contact with a substance or a source of energy above the threshold limit of the body or structure. Dominoes have been used by ILCI to illustrate the causes and prevention of accidents (Figure 6.5).

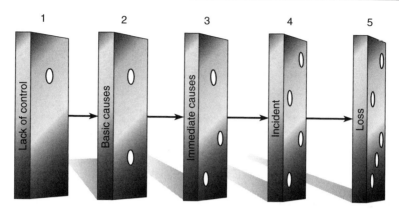

Figure 6.5   Causes of accidents

The result of an accident includes losses to people, property or process. An incident is the event that precedes the loss; it is the contact with energy or substance. The immediate causes of accidents are the circumstances that immediately precede the contact. They are usually substandard acts and unsafe conditions. Basic causes are the real reasons why substandard acts or conditions occurred. There are two categories of basic causes, either personal factors (e.g. lack of skill, stress, laziness, taking short cuts, and stupidity) and job factors or work environment (e.g. poor engineering, no safety guards, poor training, lack of maintenance of equipment, etc.).

There are three common causes for lack of management control:

- An inadequate programme
- Inadequate programme standards
- Inadequate compliance with standards.

In a more practical sense, major factors contributing to accidents in a factory (i.e. basic causes relating to job factors) are:

- Material hazards
- Process hazards
- Mechanical/electrical equipment
- Working practices.

The hazards for frequently used chemicals such as ammonia (toxic), hydrogen (explosive) and hexane (highly inflammable), must be taken into account in the handling, storage and processing of these materials.

The hazards of mechanical and electrical equipment include unguarded moving equipment, pressure vessels and electric shock.

Lack of protective wear, inadequate training, improper tools and procedures are examples of working practices conducive to accidents.

Prevention and control

The three stages of accident prevention and control are:

• Pre-contact control
• Contact control
• Poor contact control.

Pre-contact control is aimed at the prevention of accidents. The leading manufacturing companies of the UK are increasingly commissioning HAZOP (HAZards and OPerability) studies to identify potential hazards both before and after the installation of a manufacturing plant or process.

Contact control measures are applied to minimize the amount of energy exchange or harmful contact. The ILCI guidelines for contact control include:

• Substitution of alternate energy forms (e.g. electric motors to replace shafts and butts)
• Reducing the amount of energy used (e.g. low voltage equipment, or use of transformers)
• Placing barriers between the source of energy and people (e.g. firewalls, guards, fire-fighting equipment)
• Modifying contact surfaces (e.g. padding points of contact).

Poor contact control applies to actions after the accident such as the implementation of emergency action plans. This does not prevent the accident but minimizes the damage.

Fire-fighting equipment, systems and procedures should embrace all three stages of accident prevention. Depending on the size and type of operation, the key fire-fighting features should cover:

• Equipment
• Hydrant system
• Water storage

- Extinguishers
- Systems
- Sprinklers
- Smoke detectors
- Fire alarms
- Procedures
- Fire-fighting organization
- Fire escape markings
- Fire-fighting drill.

Implementation and monitoring

Each factory should deploy a properly trained safety manager to implement and monitor safety programmes. A continuous safety training programme for everyone in the factory should be in place. The management should promote safety awareness by encouraging safety posters, safety weeks and safety awards.

It is important to measure and monitor the accident rate of the factory. The most widely used index is measured thus:

$$\text{Accident rate} = \frac{\text{Number of accidents} \times 200\,000}{\text{Employee's hours of exposure}}$$

It is encouraging to note that there has been a gradual reduction of accident rates in most of the industrialized countries.

For an individual organization a formal audit by accredited safety auditors is a sensible way to assess that safety standards are being met and to learn of improvements that can be made. Many leading companies follow ISRS (International Safety Rating Systems). Another recognized standard is the HSG (Health and Safety Guidelines).

Foundation 9: Environmental protection

Environment protection is an important international issue and industrialized countries are spending between 0.5 and 1.5% of their gross national product (GNP) on the control of pollution. It is a big subject and any attempt to make a comprehensive analysis of all the issues is beyond the scope of this book. Our emphasis is focused on the impact of environment in manufacturing companies. The Advanced Studies Centre of the Massachusetts Institute of Technology, back in 1976, studied the cause and effect of environmental factors on the performance of a wide range of companies from different industrial sectors. It found in all cases that those companies that were most advanced in environment protection were also the most profitable. On reflection it is not surprising that an efficient (and profitable) company will be safety-conscious and environmentally aware and will be following best practices. It is, however, surprising that investment in environment protection by manufacturing companies swings with the political pendulum rather than business objectives. Environment protection is going in cycles without showing a continuous improvement. In the 1970s the environment was a political hot potato but as we became accustomed to the issues, and without doubt some issues were overstated, interest tended to wane. But now, during the 2000s, influenced by the Kyoto treaty, pressure groups like Friends of the Earth and well-publicized activities of Greenpeace, environment issues are again at the forefront.

Environment protection relates to pollution control in two stages. Conventional controls or 'first generation pollution' controls are applied to pollution in air and water and to noise created in the manufacturing process. Such controls are usually regulated by legislation. There is also a 'second generation pollution', which relates to the problems caused by the usage of certain products and chemicals over a long period. The most widespread example of such 'second generation pollution' is the contamination of land by pollutants that subsequently permeate through to ground water.

Causes of pollution

Pollution control engineering has essentially evolved from sanitary engineering and thus the solutions are primarily concerned with effects rather than causes, and with control rather than prevention. The overall ongoing economic impact of pollution has been largely neglected and most of the attention of manufacturing companies has been directed to the cost impact of pollution control.

The contamination of land is mostly caused by the disposal of solid wastes by manufacturing industries. With the introduction in the UK of the 'land fill tax' the disposal of solid wastes by incineration will be more cost-effective and environmentally friendly in the future.

The three main gases causing air pollution are carbon dioxide, sulphur dioxide and nitrogen oxides. For many years the consumption of combustion fossil fuels has been releasing carbon dioxide to the atmosphere faster than it can naturally be absorbed by photosynthesis (provided by trees and plants). As the proportion of CO_2 in the air increases, it absorbs heat and as a result the atmosphere warms up. Sulphur dioxide resulting from the combustion of coal and oil or any sulphur-burning process is another pollutant of air and one of the substances causing 'acid rain'. The damage by acid rain to plants and trees is very evident in parts of Europe. Other acidic gases are the oxides of nitrogen resulting from high temperature combustion processes in power plants.

Lead is a serious pollutant (neurotoxin) affecting nerves and brain. The sources of lead include emission from motor vehicles, lead pipes carrying drinking water, paint and other industrial processes. The Royal Commission on Environmental Pollution recommended in 1983 the benefits of banning the use of lead in petrol. A second pollution-bearing metal is cadmium which is used industrially in batteries, metal plating and micro-electronics. The discharge of cadmium from local industries in the Severn Estuary in the UK severely damaged the local shellfish industry. A third heavy metal is mercury, causing hazards to life even today. In the 1950s the discharge of industrial effluents with high levels of mercury in a Japanese bay led to 700 people being crippled and 200 deaths among villagers who ate fish from the bay.

Another harmful mineral is asbestos, causing painful and fatal diseases such as asbestosis and mesothelioma. Many domestic items such as textured ceilings, ovens, electrical heating equipment in the past contained asbestos. After campaigning by environmental pressure groups, asbestos lagging in power stations and electric sub-stations has been gradually eliminated in the UK.

The noise levels in many 'metal bashing' and packaging industries caused low performance and, more seriously, hearing impairment. Today there are established preventive and protective measures of noise control.

Cost of pollution

In addition to the long-term immeasurable damage done to vegetation, birds, animals and human beings by air and water pollution, there are many instances of huge sums being paid to victims by polluting industries, as exampled above in our reference to Erin Brokovich, who famously fought for such compensation in the USA.

Benefits of environmental protection

A sound environment protection policy can earn a company an extremely marketable environment-friendly image, leading to higher sales and profitability.

There are also several published examples of 'non-waste technology' where a project of environment control has turned out to be a profit-earner. One such example is the Dow Chemical Company's $7.2 million project for the reuse of cooling water, which produced over 10% return on investment and considerably reduced the pollution of a neighbouring river. The famous 3P programme (Pollution Prevention Pays) of the 3M company brought about major savings including $2 million from the elimination of hydrocarbon wastes from a reactive costing process. When 3M instigated this programme in 1974 the approach was to capture and control pollutions and emissions before they could damage the environment. This approach although effective has been changed to a philosophy of prevention rather than containment. The 3P programme now aims to prevent pollution at source by using different materials, changing the process, re-designing the plant and equipment, and through recycling waste.

Another example is provided by a distillery in Scotland, where an effluent treatment project for the control of suspended solids and BOD (biological oxygen demand) produced, with the addition of a drying plant, high-quality cattle feed.

Environmental strategies

In *Total Manufacturing Solutions* (1997) we suggested an eight-point strategy of environment protection for a manufacturing company:

1 Cut down waste by improving efficiency.
2 Sell wastes to someone else.
3 'Build on' extra plant to convert wastes into raw materials or products which are valuable to the company or to someone else.

4 Work with self-cleansing and dispersing power of the environment so as to permit maximum discharge or effluent.
5 Negotiate emission standards and subsidies with the authorities and the community.
6 Build the treatment facility needed for residual wastes jointly with another enterprise or the local authority.
7 Build the plant using company staff and know-how.
8 Sell the acquired know-how to others with the same problem.

The triple bottom line

In 1998 Elkington coined the phrase 'triple bottom line'. Since then the accounting fraternity has developed a triple bottom line framework to help organizations think about how they build and maintain relationships with communities in a way that better reflects the needs of the wider community. The concept of the integrated bottom line of corporate sustainability represents to date the most comprehensive approach to understanding and bringing together a business, namely the

• environmental
• social, and
• economic bottom lines.

It aims to show in annual reports and elsewhere a balanced view of overall corporate performance for all three activities. As the Centre for Innovation in Corporate Responsibility (2004) says:

> *A fundamental concern of many organizational managers is how to bring these fundamental, yet seemingly disparate pillars of sustainability together to form the integrated 'triple bottom line; of economic, social and environmental performance. Is measuring and assessing corporate performance in one or two, but not three sufficient? For open-minded managers, the answer is obvious: each of these spheres is connected with the others' ... and ... forward looking companies will realize that such good management will help to entrench and maximize the values inherent in each of the individual social, environmental and economic bottom lines.*

Fine words, but the issue is what to measure and what criteria to employ? For more information on the Centre for Corporate Responsibility see www.triplebottomline.com.

In practical terms, triple bottom line accounting means expanding the traditional reporting framework to take into account not just financial outcomes but also environmental and social performance. It will only be a matter of time before Standard Accounting Practices will include standards for triple bottom line reporting.

Summary

Every business has legal responsibilities to ensure health and safety of employees, safety of products and to protect the environment. But the right approach is not about doing just enough to meet legal requirements. As we have shown in this chapter, there are definite commercial advantages for organizations to be proactive in product safety, occupational safety and health and environmental management.

Good safety and health and environmental practices more than pay for themselves. They also improve the organization's reputation with customers, the community and employees. Failure to consider these issues will eventually mean a company will not be able to survive in the increasingly demanding political and economic environment.

CASE EXAMPLE 3: San Diego Refuse Disposal Division

San Diego is the sixth largest city in the United States. The Refuse Disposal Division (RDD) employed Environment International Limited as consultants and on 31 July 2002 gained ISO 14001 accreditation. By using Environment International's management system (EMS) RDD improved employees' participation in environmental issues as well as the city's overall environmental performance. This provided RDD with a competitive edge on issues such as privatization and was also seen by the city as a valuable public relations tool. The most notable gains, however, were financial savings. The city of San Diego's initial one-off investment was $220 000 and the annual savings are $2 162 000. This was achieved by shutting off heavy motive equipment during morning and lunch breaks, reuse of containers etc. and using reclaimed water rather than potable water.

Other parallel environmental gains were reduced emission of carbon dioxide exhaust by 1 400 000 tons, reduced emissions of nitrogen compounds by 39 000 tons, 31 million gallons of potable water saved, surplus storm water used for dust control resulting in benefits for neighbours etc. and less dust pollution for a local stream. (For more details see www.eiltd.net.)

Chapter 7

Infrastructure Facilities

Men, my brothers, men the workers, ever reaping something new:
That which they have done but earnest of the things that they shall do.
   Alfred, Lord Tennyson, 'Locksley Hall'

Global warming perhaps not only refers to changing weather patterns; it could equally apply to the changing global market. Globalization – the reduction of tariffs and virtual elimination of national barriers – has exposed management inadequacies that previously were hidden. Previously a company competed in its own country against local competition using like systems and with similar cultures. Inefficiencies and inadequacies were to a large extent hidden. Comparative economic isolation and protection and the advantages of technical expertise no longer exist. Technological advances are constant and are available to all. The only real opportunity for competitive advantage is to do things better and to achieve world class status.

Ever since God sent Moses down from the top of Mount Sinai to deliver the Ten Commandments we have been delegating work to third parties. The dynamic growth of technology, especially the digital technology, has opened up new opportunities and competition. Any business, whether in a manufacturing or service sector, cannot gain competitive advantage without the best use of both own and third party resources.

The pillars we have discussed in the last three chapters are 'external' pillars. We now turn to the 'core' pillars of an organization. The pillar that forms the subject of the present chapter is Infrastructure Facilities.

What are infrastructure facilities? They include factories, offices, equipment and hardware, conversion technology and third party resources. Infrastructure facilities does not include people, procedures and systems. This chapter considers the challenge for selecting the most appropriate infrastructure facilities, and whether this challenge differs for manufacturing and service industries?

The challenges of infrastructure facilities are far more complex than cash flow management, and the parameters are not of the short-term nature of labour and software. The outcome of an investment decision for a manufacturing facility is likely to last for 10–100 years. Likewise, it normally takes several years of disciplined effort to transform an existing weak service unit into a strong unit.

Manufacturing sector

Skinner (1969) described manufacturing facilities as either a corporate millstone or a competitive weapon depending on the strategy applied and pursued. Wheelwright and Hayes (1985) defined the four stages of manufacturing's strategic role, as illustrated in Table 7.1.

In a manufacturing business, a number of interrelated functions (such as marketing, innovation, engineering, purchasing, manufacturing and distribution) work towards a common objective of satisfying the customers and at the same time ensuring an attractive return on investment for the shareholders. This is illustrated in Figure 7.1. Of these, the manufacturing function has the majority share of the

Table 7.1 Stages in manufacturing's strategic role

Stage	Strategy	Role
Stage 1	Minimize manufacturing's negative potential: 'internally neutral'	Manufacturing is kept flexible and reactive
Stage 2	Achieve parity with competitors: 'externally neutral'	Capital investment is the primary means for catching up with competition
Stage 3	Provide credible support to the business strategy: 'internally supportive'	Longer-term manufacturing developments and trends addressed systematically
Stage 4	Pursue a manufacturing-based competitive advantage: 'externally supportive'	Long-range programmes pursued in order to acquire capabilities in advance of needs

Source: Wheelwright and Hayes, 1985

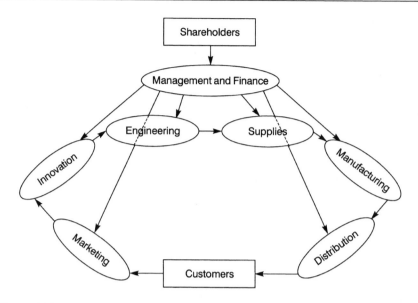

Figure 7.1 Total business process

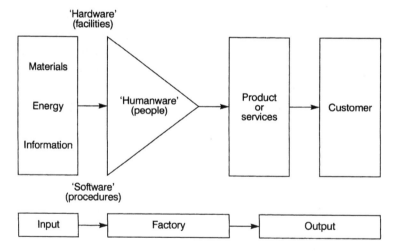

Figure 7.2 Manufacturing

company's assets and people. In a typical fast-moving consumer goods (FMCG) manufacturing business:

- 98% of the products sold are either own manufactured or co-produced
- 90% of the assets of the company are for manufacturing
- 75% of the people work in manufacturing.

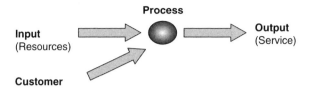

Figure 7.3 Service operations

A simple and popular model is shown in Figure 7.2. This illustrates the manufacturing process where the core conversion activities in a factory are performed by the three key elements of:

- Facilities or 'hardware'
- Procedures or 'software'
- People or 'human ware'.

It is not enough just to formulate and pursue an 'up front' manufacturing strategy, no matter how good the strategy is. To maintain a competitive advantage it is essential to support the strategic planning of facilities with the ongoing monitoring of performance and with continuous improvement programmes. The management of manufacturing facilities should be dynamic with the relentless pursuit of the elimination of unnecessary non-value adding expense, and always with the objective of adding value for customers. Competitive advantage once achieved through a strategy such as investment in new facilities will require hard work if the advantage is to be retained.

Service sector

For a service business the perceived value of the offering to the customer is determined by the service rendered rather than the product offered. The customer is close to the supplier and provides input to the process as shown in Figure 7.3. As Wright and Race (2004) say, 'A service organization exists to interact with customers and to satisfy customers' service requirements. For any service to be provided, there has to be a customer.' Without customer input the service cannot be provided. For example, from high-level personal interaction between the provider and the customer, such as a medical consultant, down to no direct interaction with staff of the provider, such as automatic

Table 7.2   Categories of services

	Direct service	*Isolated service*
Small-scale	Professional service (e.g. doctor, hairdresser)	Service shop (e.g. garage, tailor)
Large-scale	Mass service (e.g. university, supermarket)	Service factory (e.g. banks, post office)

Source: adapted from: Schmenner, 1993

barrier entry to a car park, some input from the customer is essential as an input into the service system.

This intimacy of a customer in a service function has led to the perception that service cannot be stored and has to be produced and consumed simultaneously. Of course, there are some services that have to be produced at the delivery point, such as emergency medical treatment. However, in a higher proportion of services the activities that can be isolated from the interaction of the customer are uncoupled from the organization. The isolated operations can be managed using the similar methods used in manufacturing operations. The examples of these types of services include tailors, banks and hotels. Whether it is a small-scale or a large-scale operation, all services can be grouped as direct services or isolated services, as shown in Table 7.2.

The strategic and operational considerations related to infrastructure facilities for isolated services are likely to be similar to those for manufacturing operations. For direct service also, it can be argued that manufacturing principles can be selectively applied such as the application in fast foods services. Mass service, such as the delivery of university courses, can be compared to pre-setting work outside the machine running cycle in a production line.

Foundation stones

To achieve and retain competitive advantage it is necessary to consider the five 'foundation stones' of the Infrastructure Facilities pillar namely:

10 Sourcing strategy: To ensure an operation advantage in a global market.
11 Appropriate technology: To define the optimum choice of processes and an appropriate level of technology.

12 Flexibility and lean process: To highlight the ability and agility of facilities to adapt the operation to the changing need of customers, process or materials.

13 Reliability and maintenance: To underline the operational measures for facilities for quality advantage, speed, dependability and efficiency (cost).

14 Performance management and Balanced Scorecard: To define the key indices with which the competitive parameters of infrastructure facilities can be measured, monitored and improved in the context of the total business.

Foundation 10: Sourcing strategy

The fundamental objective of a sourcing strategy is to determine where to make or buy a product or service and why. The sourcing strategies for both manufacturing and service organizations are discussed separately although there are many obvious common features between them. The sourcing strategy goes hand in hand with supply chain management as described in Chapter 5.

Manufacturing

There has been considerable hyperbole regarding world class manufacturing (WCM) and many articles and books have been written on the subject. There have been a number of interpretations of WCM. Some people associate WCM with working practices influenced by Japan's 'quality movement'. Others understand WCM to be manufacturing at the highest level of performance.

We define WCM as the term applied to organizations who achieve dominance in their segment of the global market and who sustain this dominance against world class competition.

Up until about 1990 manufacturing strategy tended to focus on the local area, e.g. for manufacturers in the United Kingdom the concern was the domestic market and the near neighbours of Europe. The emphasis has now moved to the determination of either a global strategy or regional strategy, not only for marketing, but for sourcing. Sourcing includes materials and labour, and also includes the basic decision of whether to make or buy.

The globalization of manufacturing began with sourcing and a search for low labour costs. Manufacturing was transferred from the

Western nations and Japan through the establishment of manufacturing facilities in Asia, the Indian Sub-Continent and Latin America. However, it soon transpired that once overseas investment is made in a country the cost of labour creeps up. Additionally as other overseas companies with similar products follow the lead (and move to a country where labour is cheaper) the initial competitive edge of cheap labour gained by the 'pioneer' company becomes a diminished advantage. There have been significant changes in the global market place, demanding a sound sourcing strategy for the manufacturing company as the changes accelerate. These changes include:

- Newly industrialized countries (the 'little dragons' such as Korea, Taiwan and Malaysia) and the People's Republic of China are acquiring world class manufacturing capabilities. Investors wishing to set up manufacturing in these countries will find labour is not as cheap in real terms as it was even 10 years ago. But more importantly these countries are now, without doubt, competitors of world class standing. Other Asian countries which show longer-term potential to achieve WCM in some areas of endeavour include India, Pakistan and Indonesia. Other regions which are emerging as WCM contenders include South America and South Africa.
- The gradual elimination of tariff barriers and the regional pacts for 'common markets' (e.g. Mercosur, NAFTA, Andina, EU, CER etc.) are encouraging competition from regionally based groupings of countries.
- The 'new' markets of what was the East European Communist bloc has provided new opportunities in the global market. Additionally manufacturers in this region are close to achieving the status of WCM.
- Improved logistics and electronic communication systems are assisting the implementation of sourcing strategies.
- The growing similarity of what people want to buy across the world is encouraging global product/process development and marketing.
- Investment costs for innovation and new technology are becoming too expensive to concentrate in one local market.

A sound sourcing strategy for a manufacturing company may well be a requirement for future survival. Catching up with the manufacturing performance of the competitors is not enough. The sourcing strategy of the company must move in step with the corporate strategy and reflect, as described in Chapter 4, the marketing strategy and innovation programmes of the company. The sourcing strategy should be dynamic in a relentless pursuit of value to customers in a changing market place. As Hamel and Prahalad (1994) accurately forecast some ten years ago, 'the market a company dominates today is likely to change substantially over the next ten years. There is no such thing as "sustaining" leadership, it must be regenerated again and again.'

In order to develop a sourcing strategy for manufacturing it is necessary to have a formal strategic planning process. The process should be flexible and simple to follow and it should be incorporated with other corporate planning processes. Our strategic planning process for sourcing for manufacturing consists of the eight steps described below.

1 Project brief

The process is best carried through by setting up a project team of about ten people and defining the brief of the project. The project team should consist of a project director (e.g. head of manufacturing), manufacturing staff (e.g. industrial engineer, plant engineer, manufacturing manager, quality manager), logistics staff (e.g. planning manager, distribution manager), marketing staff (e.g. brand managers), commercial staff (e.g. accountant, buyer and human resources staff).

When preparing the project brief it is useful to have those documents that cover current company activities such as capital investment, annual operating plans and long-term plans. In addition, any other relevant reports (such as information on competition, market place, economy and government regulations) of the countries covering the scope of the strategy will help with this activity. The project brief should clearly state the scope, time scale, deliverables and resources required for the project.

2 Operational mission and objectives

The manufacturing mission defines the aim of manufacturing in the corporate strategy or the business plan. The mission statement must fit the capabilities of the manufacturing function. Unless the mission is feasible it will be no more than mere words or rhetoric. Usually the mission statement is described in broad terms as illustrated by the following example:

> The manufacturing mission is to achieve the lowest unit manufacturing cost relative to competition without sacrificing high standards of quality, service and flexibility to the customer.

This mission statement has a priority on low cost. Alternative priorities could include one or more of: quality, customer service, rapid introduction of product, visible presence in emerging markets, combating a dominant competitor, etc. The point to note is that the mission has to be sufficiently specific for a clear objective or objectives to be readily distinguished.

Manufacturing objectives consist of performance measures that the company's manufacturing must achieve as part of the annual operating plan. Achievement of the objectives will result in the achievement of the mission.

3   Strategic factors

The understanding and analysis of strategic factors can determine the success of a sourcing strategy. Strategic factors relate to the longer-term implication of both the external and internal factors to project manufacturing into the future. These factors are competition, customer preferences, technology, environment, economic conditions and statutory regulations.

To develop a sourcing strategy for manufacturing, so as to gain a competitive advantage, a detailed competitive position analysis will be necessary. This analysis determines how the strengths and weaknesses of the company's manufacturing position relate to major competitors (both current and potential competitors). The dimensions for this analysis can be cost, quality, dependability, flexibility and innovation. Following this analysis the company should be able to identify any gaps in manufacturing competence and establish priorities for a future strategy so as to gain a competitive advantage.

The strategy of appropriate technology will be discussed later. However, it is critical to determine what should be made and whether to make or buy. Such decisions depend on the long-term volumes of the product and of the level of technology required. To identify the preliminary grouping of the sourcing of products, we propose an approach as illustrated in Figure 7.4. This grouping would be finalized after the quantitative evaluation in stage 6.

Systematic analyses of both external factors (such as environment, economic, cultural, social and political factors of the countries involved) and internal factors (such as research and development and marketing) should be made to determine how these factors will influence manufacturing.

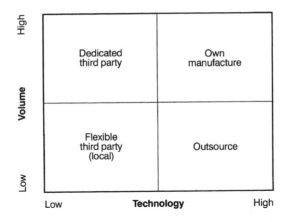

Figure 7.4 Sourcing strategy

The project brief may be reviewed and restated after the analysis of all strategic factors.

4 Data collection and data analysis

Once the revised project brief has been finalized, the next stage is the collection of data and the analysis of data. Although the need for data will vary, the following areas will need to be considered:

- General information
  - internal information of the company regarding annual plans, long-term plans, R&D and marketing
  - external information regarding competition, economic and political factors of countries involved, social and cultural aspects and environmental (green) issues
- Product information
  - future, 10-year sales forecast by products, and
  - past, 5-year sales history
- Plant information
  - present capacity of own plants
  - investment plan to increase capacity
  - present levels of efficiency
  - other manufacturing alliances, e.g. subcontractor capabilities
- Stock information
  - stock policy of materials and finished products
  - warehousing area (space and capacity) and method of storage
  - method of distribution to customers

- Personnel information
  - projection of people availability and skills
  - industrial relations of manufacturing sites
  - amenities required
- Cost information
  - manufacturing costs of products by site
  - distribution cost elements
  - cost of warehouse building per square metre
  - cost of office building per square metre
  - cost of an employee per year (total cost, i.e. wages, benefits and training).

The purpose of this stage is to calculate the capacity of plant and services for the projected volume and estimate the space required for each activity for each manufacturing site. It is normally sufficient to carry out these analyses for the current year, and at the mid stage and at the completion of the plan or when a significant event (e.g. the manufacture of a new product) occurs. The utilization of assets as determined at this stage should help to establish what to manufacture and where, and the profitability of each site.

5   Strategic options

Strategic options determine how sourcing or own manufacture is going to meet the objectives of the mission. It is useful to reiterate that the objectives refer to performance measures (such as cost, flexibility, quality, etc.) and strategy refers to how these objectives will be achieved.

Strategic options are normally expressed in a number of sourcing scenarios. These are derived from the understanding of the competitive strengths and weakness from the foregoing stages.

As a general rule there should not be more than eight scenarios. Eight scenarios are manageable and enable adequate attention to be given to each scenario. A critical analysis of each scenario is then carried out against the criteria of manufacturing objectives and strategic factors. Two or three scenarios are then shortlisted for quantitative evaluation.

6   Options evaluation

The aim of this stage is to evaluate two or three main options in order to select the best strategy for the future. The analysis should take

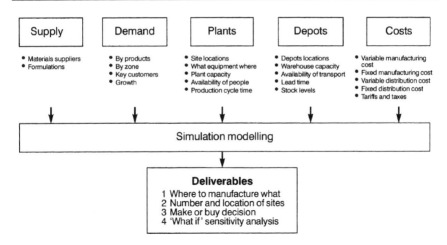

Figure 7.5   Sourcing strategy model

advantage of simulation modelling tools to select a strategy by optimizing the total operating cost (see Figure 7.5). Costs only need be broad estimates for the evaluation of options.

The strategy should then be further tested by comparing the investment costs of alternative development plans with quantitative tools such as discounted cash flow (DCF) analysis.

7   Implementation plan

The success of a sourcing strategy for manufacturing will depend on how effectively the changes have been implemented. There should be a structured implementation plan describing the phasing, responsibility, costs and obstacles that have to be overcome.

The strategy itself should not have major changes every year or there will be little chance of maintaining the strategic goal. However, tactics should be continually adjusted to meet changing circumstances.

8   Review

As stated above, there is a need for regular evaluation and review of progress to implement the strategy. In addition to the regular review the entire strategy should be formally reviewed on an annual basis.

Service sector

In the service sector the sourcing strategy buzzwords such as 'outsourcing', 'off-shoring' and 'in-sourcing' have gained currency. Outsourcing is the collaboration with a partner to manage a part of your business. An example is IBM supplying and managing on-site the information and technology function for Toyota.

There are distinct categories of outsourcing in the service sector:

- Information technology outsourcing (e.g. programming)
- Business process outsourcing (e.g. handling all administration)
- Managed services (e.g. call centres).

Background of outsourcing

A well documented example of business process outsourcing, albeit in manufacturing, is provided by the Coca-Cola Corporation. For over 100 years Coca-Cola has been producing syrup and marketing bottled products. The actual production and bottling of the product (to Coca-Cola's strict standards) is done locally by its global network of business partners.

A huge explosion of outsourcing can be attributed to the concept of 'core competence' popularized by Hamel and Prahalad (1994). The principle is fundamentally simple. For example, by analysing and understanding Porter's 'value chain' (1985) an organization can focus on the elements that are core to its business and outsource others while maintaining strategic control.

The examples of successful outsourcing companies include Dell and CISCO. Dell Computers Company has focused on its key activity as sales and outsourced non-core functions such as logistics and maintenance. CISCO has identified design and network solutions as its core activity and outsourced the manufacturing of infrastructure components.

Rationale of outsourcing

A particular advantage of outsourcing is cash flow, flexibility and releasing key management resources, but other benefits include external expertise and cost savings. There are several external factors driving the growth of outsourcing:

- The rapid change in the technology landscape, especially in information and communication technology (ICT); external vendors are often in a position to provide more effective solutions support in the new technology.
- Globalization is a strong catalyst in outsourcing by enhancing the transparency in financial reporting, wider choice of suppliers and more competition. Outsourcers offering service level guarantees have a powerful proposition.

Off-shoring

Off-shoring is a form of outsourced managed services where skilled labour is cheaper. Cost savings are primary benefits. Other benefits include time zone differences enabling 24 hour services and access to more willing well-qualified workers to tackle boring jobs. An example is call centres located in India serving callers (customers) in England.

There are some risks of off-shoring. These include:

- Services going down because of telecommunication problem and inadequate training
- Data and physical security are in potential danger
- Excessive foreign travel.

The ways to minimize these risks include minimizing foreign travel, keeping your software code and using a third party broker.

In-sourcing

In-sourcing means centralizing multiple, distributed operations into a semi-autonomous unit. This is managed separately and accountable to the business, like an outsourcer, but remains under the organization's control.

The advantages of in-sourcing include:

- The business maintains strategic control
- It avoids third party margins
- It is reversible.

Service level agreements and joint service partnerships

In a service level agreement (SLA) all three words carry equal importance. The document should define what services are to be delivered and the levels of performance expected. It is also an agreement between the customer and the supplier and not a unilateral declaration.

For simple functions like catering fixed price contracts by SLAs are easy to implement. However, they are highly limiting and inappropriate for strategic partnerships. The agreements (also known as joint service partnerships) should include:

• Shared gains or structured incentives based on added value beyond core services
• Shared risks
• Best practices, training and cost-effectiveness initiatives are freely shared
• Forecast data and planning processes are shared.

Foundation 11: Appropriate technology

Many people in both the manufacturing and service sectors may equate business competitiveness with the state of the art technology such as on-line e-commerce or robotics. On the other hand, 'Putt's law' says in jest, 'Technology is dominated by two types of people: those who understand what they do not manage and those who manage what they do not understand.' This may be a quip, but a study by Gartner (2002) concluded that when applying a new technology to a business, 70% of benefits are derived from improved business practices and only 30% from the actual implementation of technology. So do we need these technologies? Yes, appropriate but not necessarily advanced technology is essential to becoming and remaining a world class organization. In this section we discuss the key considerations for adopting technology in both manufacturing and service applications.

Manufacturing

Manufacturing technology is popularly seen as the main factor contributing to the manufacturing advantage more than any other elements or foundation stones. However a 'high tech' strategy is not necessarily the best strategy. Selecting or failing to select the correct technology can have long-term and serious repercussions for a business. Technology can give a competitive advantage if managed well. If not managed well, or if the wrong technology is selected then the results can be catastrophic. If an organization is inefficient and not capable of managing standard technology, the introduction of advanced technology will only create further problems.

An international benchmarking survey between the USA, Japan and Europe (Miller *et al.*, 1992) clearly established that 'robotics' ranked as the lowest pay-off of improvement programmes both in the USA and Europe. Technology is responsible for the added value conversion process. It is a vital foundation stone of Total Manufacturing Solutions, but it is the choice and application of technology appropriate to the product, volume and specifications that create and sustain the advantage. The key issues of appropriate technology are:

- Product and process technology
- Choice of technology
- Evaluation of technology.

Product and process technology

Product technology focuses on advanced product innovation to provide the basis for superiority in product performance.

Process technology relates to improvements in the processes of manufacturing a product that is already in existence. The process applies to any added value conversion operation whether chemical, metal cutting or packaging.

The benchmarking survey by Miller *et al.* indicates that different visions of the factory of the future are emerging in the USA, Japan and Europe. Both Americans and Europeans are emphasizing advanced product technologies while the Japanese companies focus more on process technology and the ability to make rapid design changes in highly customized products. United States manufacturers are moving toward the value factory of the future. European companies are moving toward the borderless factory of the future. In Japan manufacturers are working steadily to build the design factory of the future.

The strategy of product technology must be addressed at the innovation stage (see Chapter 4), but as process technology depends on the product, both process and product development should be carried out as closely as possible. The relationship could be overlapping, parallel or interactive, upstream for the product and downstream for the process. The early commitment of process technology in the design of a product is described as simultaneous or concurrent engineering. The philosophy is to involve participants from marketing, engineering, production, purchasing and quality to work together as a design team to design the process in parallel with the development of the new product.

A 'technological model' (see Figure 7.6) by Brown and Blevins (1989) depicts product technology at a higher plane relative to process technology and the authors argue that the USA has progressively moved from the process technology plane (with emphasis on productivity) to the product technology plane (with emphasis on innovation). This model predicts that Japan is also moving from the strategy of 'wait for a competitor to try a new product' towards the higher plane of product technology. During the 1970s and 1980s Japan's manufacturing productivity increased at an annual percentage rate in double figures and a key factor contributing to this is the extensive application of robotics. R&D expenditure of Japan is constantly rising but it is reported to be 1.8% of sales as compared to 3.4% of sales in the USA. In addition, ROI was the first consideration for US companies while market share was paramount in Japan. It is concluded that management philosophies in various companies are related to the local environments of those countries and not necessarily transportable.

Wheelwright and Hayes (1985), however, concluded that a number of sophisticated high-technology companies that regard product

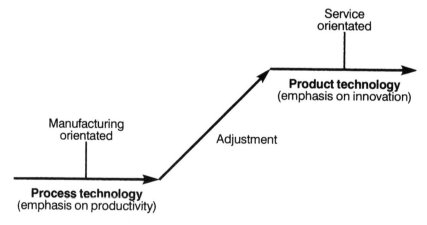

Figure 7.6 A technological model

technology as the key to competitive success and process technology are, at best, in Stage 1 of manufacturing (see Table 7.1). They should strive for a longer-term competitive advantage to progress towards Stage 4 by pursuing an 'externally supportive' manufacturing strategy including the management of process technology.

Although keeping up to date with the use of technology is vital, it must be remembered that the design or revision of a production system is more than just a way to use technology, it encompasses the development of a socio-technical system that reflects the nature of people and the way they work together (see also Dilworth, 1992; Boyer, 1999).

Numerous publications comparing the Japanese management techniques with Western techniques suggest that management techniques are not transportable and that the success of techniques depends on the technological and cultural environments of each country. Other writers such as Schroeder (1993), Creech (1994) and Reid and Sanders (2004) cite several examples of where Japanese techniques have been successfully used in the United States. Our view is that with some adjustments any technique can be applied in any country. After all the Japanese move to quality stemmed from work done by an American, Dr Deming.

Notwithstanding, common themes on technology are:

- Product technology development should be simultaneous (or concurrent) with process technology development during the innovation stage.
- There is significant scope for managing process technology. This should be appropriate to individual requirements against the technological, social and cultural background.

The contents of the following section relate primarily to process technology.

Choice of technology

The choice of process technology is not governed by exact science but by a combination of a number of logical criteria. We can group these criteria into two categories such as:

- General criteria
  - volume growth
  - variety growth
  - degree of sophistication

- Local criteria
  - user's experience and skill
  - supplier partnership.

The general criteria of choice are applicable to all companies and all countries. A chemical process such as a refinery or a spray-drying tower benefits from economy of scale whereas discrete processes such as metal cutting or packaging can benefit from small capacity increments. A large machine like a high speed packing line has the benefit of a lower capital cost per unit of capacity, but the choice of a high speed line must be balanced against the volume growth over the life cycle of the product, otherwise the machine will only be partly utilized during a single shift operation. Another general criterion of choice is the variety and the growth of a product. Smaller units of machines offer higher flexibility and lower unit manufacturing cost when the growth in product variation is high. Schonberger (1986) uses as an example the 'super machine cycle' and he clearly demonstrates the inflexibility and progressive inefficiency of increasing capacity in large increments.

The degree of sophistication of technology relates to one or more of the levels such as mechanization, automation and integration. With mechanization manual tasks are reduced but machine operators are required. Automation eliminates the operator for a small number of repetitive tasks (for example robotics). Integration is the higher level of automation with the combination of previously separated functions. A typical example of integration is a group of machines with reprogrammable controllers linked together by an automated materials-handling system and integrated through a central computer to enable the production of a variety of items. This is also known as flexible manufacturing systems or (FMS). A yet higher level of automated manufacture is computer-integrated manufacturing (CIM). This concept integrates information from product ideas to the output of high-quality products. Information from the core manufacturing activities plus input where relevant from marketing, customer orders, suppliers, inward transportation, is used. CIM includes master scheduling, capacity planning, materials requirements, inventory control, purchasing, quality reporting and logistics. The higher the level of the sophistication of technology, the higher is the intensity of capital. High capital investment in technology (including high software cost) is justifiable for high volume, high life cycle and high added value products (e.g. motor cars).

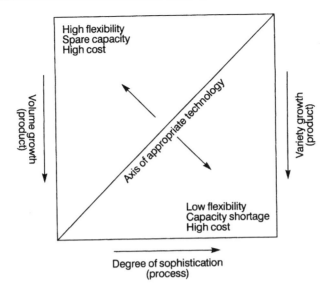

Figure 7.7 Choice of technology

Figure 7.7 illustrates the appropriate technology axis, along the diagonal of the product process matrix. The effectiveness of the choice of technology reduces with a gradual shift from the axis or diagonal.

The local criteria of choice depend on the cultural and technological environments of a country. The higher the technology the higher level of sophistication required of the workforce and the more efficient the infrastructure has to be (reliable energy sources and communications). The experience curve of the company on a known and proven technology should be a favourable criterion for choice. Where there is the necessary skill for managing technology then improved technology, as it becomes available, should be given serious consideration.

Partnership, with preferred vendors, offer longer-term benefits and should influence the choice and confidence in technology. These benefits include:

- Experience in proven technology
- Standardization of equipment (especially attractive to multinational companies)
- Involvement in the modification and design of equipment
- More rapid response from local representatives.

The 'turnkey' approach practised in Japan, where one supplier is responsible for all the plant in a complete production line, also has its merits. This avoids one supplier blaming the other. However the supplier must have the expertise in all processes in the production line.

Evaluation of technology

The primary tool used by Western companies in the evaluation of technology is the return on investment (ROI). ROI has received much criticism in recent years. Schonberger (1986) analysed the 'overstated role of capital' and argued that ROI should be revised to measure 'benefits of reduced variability'. Japan's investment in capital equipment in the past two decades has been twice that of its Western competitors. Japanese investment in the training of workers (necessary to cope with higher level technology) is also a lot higher per worker than in any other country. However it is their type of training that is important. Creech (1994) claimed that in the United States for every graduate engineer there are eight lawyers, whereas in Japan for every lawyer there are 10 graduate engineers. It is axiomatic that lawyers do not add value to a process.

The newer technology (e.g. flexible manufacturing systems) could not show high returns and became difficult to handle financially in the Western world. Another criticism is that investment decisions based on cost savings alone could lead to the continuation of historical constraints with 'out of date' equipment.

Hamel and Prahalad (1994) conclude that the corporate objective of ROI improvement (comprising two components: a numerator – net income – and a denominator – investment) has produced, in the USA and the UK, 'an entire generation of managers obsessed with denominators'. Denominator management is an accountant's short cut to asset productivity. They also warn that:

> in a world in which competitors are capable of achieving 5 per cent, 10 per cent or 15 per cent of real growth in revenues, aggressive denominator reduction under a flat revenue stream is simply a way to sell market share and the future of the company.

The rhetoric of the authors may be strong to make the point, but the message is clear. The primary goal of a company is the opportunity to compete in the future by creating new products and businesses rather than the need to meet short-term payback periods to make annual reports look good.

On the other hand, during the 1990s and continuing into this century, it has to be admitted that manufacturing companies in the Western world have faced a 'capacity glut' due to a combination of a number of factors:

- A recession which reduced consumer demand
- Aggressive restructuring and cost cutting initiatives which have identified redundant or poorly utilized plant
- Systematic re-engineering and continuous improvement programmes have increased the plant efficiency, thus releasing extra capacity
- A relatively free movement of goods across countries has encouraged outsourcing and resulted in an imbalance of capacity.

Thus many companies are carrying high asset values amounting to between 25 and 40% of the value of goods they produce with a significant amount of cash locked into underutilized assets. The need to provide high level attention to improve the productivity of capital assets continues.

From the above analysis it is evident that evaluation of technology should be based upon not just ROI alone, but also a number of strategic criteria. Slack *et al.* (2004) suggest a balanced approach by taking into account:

- The feasibility of investment – how difficult it is to install the technology?
- The acceptability of the investment – how much does it give competitiveness and a return on investment?
- The vulnerability of the investment – how much risk is involved in terms of what could go wrong?

Figure 7.8 shows a simplified diagram of the logical process for the selection and evaluation of appropriate technology. It is necessary to follow conventional capital investment appraisal procedures such as discounted cash flow (DCF) and net present value (NPV). The costs must include 'hidden' elements such as commissioning, training, software development and support. Non-financial benefits should also be examined, such as improved quality, saving of space, customer service, flexibility, avoidance of repetitive stress injury, lower stock holding and so on. If the ROI is less than the acceptable level of a conventional investment, then strategic considerations of the future (such as competitors' investment strategy) may be the decider when considering proposals for appropriate technology.

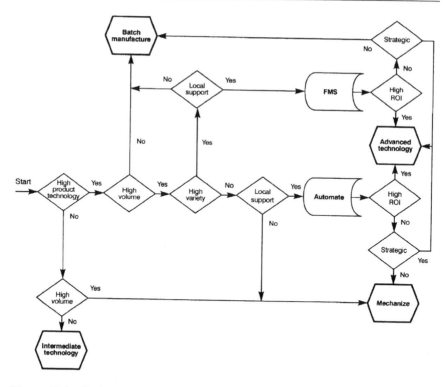

Figure 7.8   Technology selection and evaluation

Service sector

A myth still prevails that services are extremely difficult to standardize because services are often tailored for each unique customer. And
yet most of the early applications of information technology were in
offices and service functions, such as payroll and accounting reports.
A study by Quinn (1993) demonstrated that in the USA 85% of information technology is sold to the service sector and about 75% of all
capital investment goes to the service sector. The trend is for further
growth in the service sector and the scenario is comparable to Europe.
The impact of information and communication technology (ICT)
and the revolution of e-business will be discussed in Chapter 8.

It can be argued that the considerations of appropriate technology
for the manufacturing industry should be extended also to capital
investment in the service sector. In Figure 7.9 we propose a generic
technology strategy for the service sector based on Koyak (1993). It
is important to note the similarity of technology strategies for the

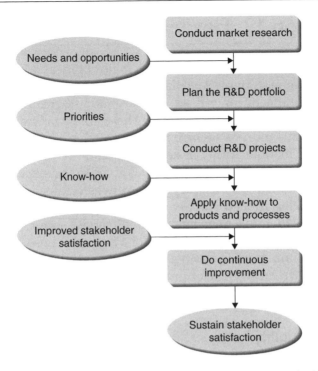

Figure 7.9 Technology strategy for services (adapted from Royak, 1993)

manufacturing industry and the service sector shown respectively in Figure 7.8 and Figure 7.9.

A proven way of establishing the technology strategy of a service organization is by understanding the products and services that an organization brings to the market and the interactions of those outputs with their underlying technology. This approach follows the principle of 'house of quality' or QFD (quality function deployment) (see Basu, 2004). Customer needs feed into the first planning 'house' and produce a number of strategy options to satisfy the market. These strategies in turn influence R&D programmes and these in turn feed into new products and services.

As indicated earlier and will be discussed further in Chapter 8, the growth in advanced economies is more likely to come from knowledge-based services. Intellectual services such as software will continue to be at the heart of service innovation and technology in the foreseeable future. Examples include enterprise resource planning (ERP) systems. Companies worldwide are investing more than $10 billion every year in ERP systems alone.

Foundation 12: Flexibility and lean processes

Encouraged by the Japanese investment in flexibility and their success in the just-in-time strategy, flexibility has become one of the most fashionable of manufacturing virtues. However, it also created confusion and ambiguity in the Western world. There are instances of failures during the 1980s and 1990s where companies invested in sophisticated FMS (flexible manufacturing systems) in pursuit of flexibility. At the other end of the scale all the attention was given to organizational flexibility (e.g. cultural and skills integration between craftsmen and operators), producing limited success. Recognizing a closer link between lean processes there is a huge interest in the service sector; also how to optimize the benefits of lean processes for a faster response to customer demand. It is important to clarify what we mean by flexibility in operations, what we mean by lean processes and how they are linked to flexibility, why we need flexibility and how we can improve flexibility.

What is flexibility?

Flexibility in manufacturing is the ability to respond quickly to the variations of manufacturing requirements in product volume, of product variety and of the supply chain.

The variability in volume is demonstrated by product launching, seasonal demand, substitution and promotional activities. The changes in variety relate to increased number of SKUs (stock keeping units) in new products, distributors' own brands (DOB), etc. The variations in the supply chain result from variability of lead times of both suppliers and customers, increased service level, change in order size, etc.

Slack *et al.* (2004) distinguishes between range flexibility (how far the operation can be changed) and response flexibility (how fast the operation can be changed).

What is a lean process?

Lean is a process philosophy with three main purposes:

- To eliminate wasted time, effort and material
- To provide customers with 'make to order' products
- To reduce cost while improving quality.

The philosophy of lean process has been described in detail in many articles and books, including *Quality Beyond Six SIGMA* (Basu and Wright, 2003). The origin of lean process is in manufacturing. The concept of Lean Enterprise – and make no mistake, 'lean' is more than a system it is a philosophy – began with Japanese automobile manufacturing in the 1960s, and was popularized by Womack, Jones and Roos in *The Machine that Changed the World* (1990), which is essentially the story of the Toyota way of manufacturing automobiles.

A visitor to a lean manufacturer will be struck by the lack of materials: there is no warehouse, no stocks of materials between workstations, and no stocks of finished goods. At first glance this suggests that lean is an inventory system, but it is more than this. Lean also means the elimination of 'muda'. *Muda* is a Japanese word that means waste, with waste being defined as any human activity that absorbs resource but creates no value. Thus the philosophy of lean is the elimination of non-value adding activities. The rough rule is the elimination of any activity that does not add value to the final product, and the taking of action so that the non-value activity never again occurs.

Before anything can be eliminated it first has to be identified. The Toyota approach to identifying areas of waste is to classify waste into seven mudas:

- Excess production
- Waiting
- Movement or transportation
- Motion
- The process
- Inventory
- Defects.

The approach is to identify waste, find the cause, eliminate the cause, make improvements and standardize (until further improvements are found). The usual approach is akin to flow process charting (as used by industrial engineers) to show operations, transports, delays and storage.

For non-manufacturing operations lean means the elimination of any wasteful activity (muda) that does not add value to the service provided to the customer. Typical examples of muda in a service operation such as secretarial administration are:

- Excess production: preparing reports, not acted upon
- Waiting: processing monthly or in batches, not continuously

- Transportation: fax machines and printers are at a distance from the workstation
- Motion: steps/data entry
- The process: signoffs
- Inventory: transactions not processed
- Defects: incorrect data entry/typing mistakes.

Staff are encouraged to take responsibility for their activities, to be proactive, and are encouraged to make suggestions for improvement of process (more efficient use of time and resources) and to make suggestions that will enhance the level of service provided to the customer. Team work, open communication and flexibility are accepted as part of the culture.

What is the link between flexibility and lean process?

With lean process the aim is to achieve a 'just-in-time' system. 'Just-in-time' means that materials are received directly into production from suppliers just when required. This means that suppliers have to be geared up to deliver to the right specification and on time. With just-in-time supply there is no room for errors in specification, or late delivery.

In order to achieve the agility of supply as demanded by 'just-in-time' the infrastructure will have to be flexible in product design, workstation design and capacity and scheduling management. Initial observations may suggest that characteristics of flexibility and lean appear to be in conflict, e.g. flexibility aims for a buffer and lean aims to eliminate waste. However, the aims of optimizing designs and responsive agile customer service are the same for both flexibility and lean.

Why be flexible?

Our strategy should be to improve our flexibility instead of depending on forecasting algorithms. The best way to improve performance and customer service is to create a highly responsive manufacturing and supply operation. Flexibility is usually achieved by adequate capacity, inventory and agile scheduling (e.g. kanban, see below). The cost of becoming flexible is often relatively small investment with greater returns. It is also a great insurance policy in case supply chain forecasting falls short of promises.

Flexibility is the ability to be responsive. In the past the manufacturers depended on a limited product range often supported by a protective market. Henry Ford and the days of the Model T car – 'You can choose any colour as long as it is black' – are long gone. Traditionally companies managed the variations in volume, variety and customer service by building stocks and/or excessive production capacity. This approach generated poor productivity and required heavy investment in stock piles of raw materials, work in progress and output stocks.

With the increased choices available to customers, often induced by competitors' marketing, the fragmentation of the market for increased product varieties will continue. Flexible manufacturing can offer a competitive advantage by giving customers greater choice of selection, and with less waiting time (for example, see Toyota's 72 hour car in Chapter 3).

Within the factory flexibility offers the following benefits:

- Reduced departmentalization of equipment leads to reduced movement and handling of materials which should result in less direct labour.
- Reduced capital investment as fewer and less specialized machines are needed. Multi-functional machines should lead to greater machine utilization.
- Set-up or change-over time should be reduced. One installation visited by us had reduced set-up time from 8 hours to 3 minutes.
- Factory workers are required to be multi-skilled and job enrichment is experienced. When workers have job satisfaction, productivity inevitably increases.

But there is little intrinsic merit in flexibility just for its own sake. Unlike cost, quality and service, companies do not sell flexibility. Flexibility within the plant is not of any concern to the customer. The customer does not care how a product is made as long as it is received on time and to specification.

Flexibility is the shock absorber of manufacturing to provide continuous customer service under conditions of uncertainty and variety (Figure 7.10).

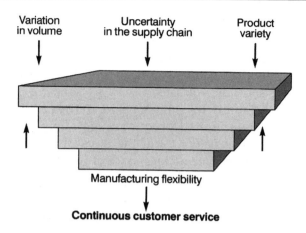

Figure 7.10   Flexibility as a shock absorber

How to improve flexibility in manufacturing?

A change to a flexible system will require careful planning, capital investment and a change in attitude by workers. Intensive training of workers will be required. During the change-over productivity is likely to drop. Additionally, flexibility does imply some slack in the system. The first consideration then must be to be certain that there are benefits to be gained from changing from long runs to a flexible system. Additionally, flexibility does suggest the acceptance of some slack in the system. Even if flexibility is achieved without cost, it should not be wasted in areas where it could be avoided.

A flexibility strategy, if adopted, should be applied at different stages of the business process across all functions. It is not the responsibility of manufacturing alone and should span product design, process design, operations management, human resources, suppliers, systems flexibility and modular design.

Product design

One important factor affecting the decision to adopt flexibility or not is product design philosophy aimed at reducing complexity. The harmonization of products and materials can reduce the number of SKUs and production change-over times without reducing the 'variety' for customers. For example, it is easy to standardize the shape and size of ice-cream cones and maintain different flavour and packaging so as to 'split' markets.

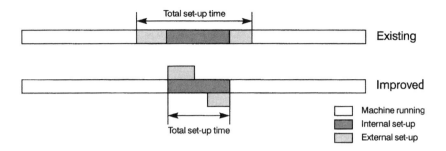

Figure 7.11 Set-up time reduction

Process design

We discussed the rationale of FMS in the previous section. Although advanced 'flexible' plants with programmable controls (e.g. FMS, robotics, CAD/CAM) offer efficient product change-over, the high initial capital cost and inadequate local support may impede their implementation. However, simple modifications (such as quick change-over parts) can be easily built into the conventional production plant to improve flexibility.

Operations management

One much-publicized approach to improving flexibility in current operations is SMED (single minute exchange of dies) developed for the Japanese automobile industry by Shigeo Shingo (1985). The SMED method involves the reduction of production change-over by extensive work study of the change-over process and identifying the 'in process' and 'out of process' activities and then systematically improving the planning, tooling and operations of the change-over process (see Figure 7.11). Shingo believes in looking for simple solutions rather than relying on technology. With due respect to the success of the SMED method, it is fair to point out that the basic principles are fundamentally the application of classical industrial engineering or work study.

Systems flexibility

The accuracy of planning data (e.g. stock records, production standards, capacity information), the reliability of products, plants and the planning tools (e.g. forecasting, materials requirements, production scheduling), worker training and attitudes, are all essential for improved systems flexibility for the total supply chain.

Layout flexibility

The flexible design of facilities enables incremental changes in equipment or a layout to handle growth in production. Layout flexibility achieves two objectives – lower additional cost of facilities and minimum disruption of current operations. Figure 7.12 (from Tompkins, 1989) illustrates a flexible design of facility expansion. By locating all utility services (e.g. steam, air, water, power) and the main passage for material handling along the 'spine', the disruption to processing is minimized.

Kanban

The Toyota Motor Company of Japan pioneered the kanban technique in the 1980s. As part of lean manufacturing concepts, kanban was promoted as one of the primary tools of just-in-time concepts by both Ohno (1988) and Shingo (1985). Inspired by this technique, American supermarkets in particular replenished shelves as they were emptied and thus reduced the number of storage spaces and inventory levels. With a varied degree of success outside Japan, kanban has been applied to maintain an orderly flow of goods, materials and information throughout the entire operation.

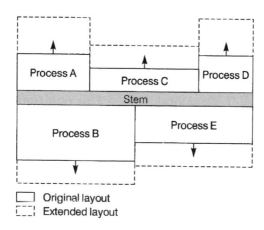

Figure 7.12   Layout flexibility

The Japanese word *kanban* literally means 'card'. It refers here to a (usually printed) card in a transparent plastic cover that contains specific information regarding part number and quantity. It is a means of pulling parts and products through the manufacturing or logistics sequence as needed. It is therefore sometimes referred to as the 'pull system'. The variants of the kanban system utilize other markers such as light, electronic signals, voice command or even hand signals.

Following the Japanese examples, kanban is accepted as a way of maximizing efficiency by reducing both cost and inventory.

The key components of a kanban system are:

- Kanban cards
- Standard containers or bins
- Workstations, usually a machine or a worktable
- Input and output areas.

The input and output areas exist side by side for each workstation on the shop floor. The kanban cards are attached to standard containers. These cards are used to withdraw additional parts from the preceding workstation to replace the ones that are used. When a full container reaches the last downstream workstation, the card is switched to an empty container. This empty container and the card are then sent to the first workstation, signalling that more parts are needed for its operation.

A kanban system may use either a single card or two cards (move and production) system. The dual card system works well in a high up-time process for simpler products with well-trained operators. A single card system is more appropriate in a batch process with a higher change-over time and has the advantage of being simpler to operate. The single card system is also known as 'withdrawal kanban' and the dual card system is sometimes called 'production kanban'.

The system has been modified in many applications, and in some facilities although it is known as a kanban system the card itself does not exist. In some cases the empty position on the input or output areas are sufficient to indicate that the next container is needed.

How to improve flexibility in services?

Many of the above approaches of improving manufacturing flexibility are also applicable to service operations, such as product design, process design, systems flexibility and layout flexibility.

A key area of improving flexibility in services, as also to a great extent in manufacturing, is by balancing of objectives. The two basic objectives for an operations manager are customer satisfaction and resource utilization. The key requirements of the customer, once understood, must then be matched with the resources available. If the objectives are driven primarily by the need for efficient use of resources then customer satisfaction will be more difficult to achieve. Given infinite resources any system, no matter how badly managed, might provide adequate service. The truth will be that there will not be infinite resources, and existing resources will often not completely mesh with the achievement of total customer satisfaction. Thus the service will be altered to meet the competencies of the organization, rather than extra resources being added to meet a higher level service. A matrix approach for customer satisfaction and resource utilization can be used, as shown in Table 7.3 for a travel agency service.

In this example of a travel agency it has been established that customers rate advice and accurate ticketing as most important (specification) and that they are prepared to wait for information and for tickets, but they do not expect to wait more than five minutes before a consultant is available. Cost, although important, is of a lesser consideration to accuracy and to receiving speedy service. Having established this rating the next step is to determine the most vital resources needed to give the customer satisfaction. In this example a reliable integrated computerized information and ticketing system is essential. When the system is 'down' little can be achieved, information on prices, schedules, and availability of seats cannot be provided, nor can bookings be made and tickets and vouchers issued. A back-up 'manual' system consisting of the telephone, bound books of pamphlets and hand-written tickets has proved in the past to be not only unwieldy and slow but expensive due to mistakes being made through information not being up-to-date and bookings being incorrectly recorded. Trained staff are important but of lesser importance

Table 7.3 Balance of objectives

Customer satisfaction			*Resource utilization*		
Specification	*Time*	*Cost*	*People*	*IT system*	*Space*
1	2	3	2	1	3

1 = Essential, 2 = Important, 3 = Less important

than the system, for without the system the staff can do little. Space is an issue, but in this example has not generally proved too much of a problem. With a good system and well-trained staff customers can be turned around quickly, when the system is slow or staff are inexperienced then the time taken to serve a customer is extended and space can become a problem. This example is derived from Wright and Race (2004).

An important approach to improving flexibility in service is lean process. As indicated in Chapter 5, Jefferson Pilot Financial has proved that service companies can use the philosophy of lean process to improve flexibility and push their performance to a new height. Swank (2003) suggests that a supermarket, which is traditionally based on an old concept in a retail service industry, is in its lean production sense a storage area where line managers and customers can shop for their required materials and components.

Another approach of enhancing flexibility in operations, particularly in services, is the theory of constraints (TOC). The theory of constraints is a management philosophy developed by Goldratt (1992). The theory is that the output of a system is limited (constrained) by internal resources, market factors and by policy. Resource constraint means not enough resources to meet demand, market constraints mean capacity is more than the market demands, and a policy constraint (i.e. a policy of no overtime) can limit output. TOC tries to improve system performance by focusing and eliminating constraints. In service operations where it is often difficult to quantify the capacity constraint TOC can be very useful. For companies that employ skilled workers and for many service organizations the constraint is often the time of one or a few key employees. The key steps in this process are:

1 *Identify*. The first step in applying TOC is to identify the constraining factor (bottleneck department or section).
2 *Exploit*. Determine the throughput per unit of the constraining factor (by department or section of a department).
3 *Subordinate*. Prevent the resources needed from waiting in a queue elsewhere (i.e. backing up at a non-constrained resource).
4 *Elevate*. If the constraint still exists find ways to increase the capacity of the constraining section.
5 Go back to step 1.

Implementation of TOC, although simple in principle, is often difficult because it may require a complete change in the way a company operates. For example, TOC requires a shift from cost-based decision-making to decision-making based on continuous improvement.

Foundation 13: Reliability and maintenance

Having established the selection and procurement of the appropriate infrastructure facilities for both the present requirements and longer-term competitive advantage, it is equally important to ensure dependability and reliability. If the plant is not reliable, in either availability or performance, companies must build up stocks or install excess capacity, thereby leading to poor capital utilization. Although the function of ensuring reliable manufacturing has been given different names to induce a higher profile (e.g. assets care, reliability engineering, etc.) it is best known as maintenance.

A maintenance strategy, for manufacturing and service industries, should cover three levels of action such as maintenance avoidance (longer term), maintenance reduction (medium term) and maintenance improvement (current or short term). Maintenance avoidance relates to longer-term 'right first time' measures at the selection and procurement stage of a capital project so that appropriate specifications and project management can ensure capital plant which is intrinsically reliable with associated low maintenance costs. Maintenance reduction relates to medium-term measures of existing equipment by continuous modifications of plant to eliminate weak points. Maintenance improvement relates to the policy, planning and control of the current maintenance activities.

Trends in maintenance

One traditional role of the maintenance function within a company up to the 1980s was as a simple cost centre whose main contribution was to keep the factory plant and office buildings running at a minimum cost. The trends away from labour-intensive to computer-controlled intensive production and from manufacturing for stock to just-in-time manufacturing have made efficient maintenance a key function. Maintenance is no longer a cost centre; it is a competitive weapon for manufacturing.

The cost of maintenance should be perceived at two levels. The visible cost incurred by own labour, materials and third party maintenance is only the tip of an iceberg. The less tangible maintenance-related costs (downtime, scrap, reworks, holding stocks of spare parts and even reserve machines, lost sales, poor workmanship, poor product quality and safety hazards) are many times more than the direct maintenance cost. Some of these costs can be measured, but some, such as lost sales due to poor quality or lack of reliable delivery, are unknown and unknowable.

Influenced by the change in technology, competition and work culture, the maintenance function has experienced a gradual transformation:

- **1960s:** Breakdown maintenance
- **1970s:** Time-based preventative maintenance
- **1980s:** Predictive maintenance
- **1990s:** Total productive maintenance and empowerment of workforce
- **2000s:** Reliability-centred maintenance and outsourcing.

Breakdown (or unscheduled or reactive or unplanned corrective) maintenance is the repair of a piece of equipment or asset as the fault occurs. This is not always the cheapest option. Preventative maintenance, including lubrication and correcting settings, can prevent expensive repairs. Likewise minimum direct maintenance will result in reduced availability and reliability. It is not unknown for equipment to break down at the least convenient time!

Time-based preventative maintenance is carried out at regular fixed intervals or after a fixed cumulative output or cycles of operation and follows documented procedures. Lubrication is in this category and is essential for all mechanical machinery. Figure 7.13 shows a model that is often used to illustrate the optimum level of preventative maintenance.

Condition-based predictive maintenance requires the measurement and monitoring of key parameters to look for changes in characteristics which indicate whether the equipment is approaching failure. Preventative action is then dependent on the analysis of the condition data. This approach is appropriate and effective for rotating equipment and critical plant. For example, vibration measurement (e.g. velocity in mm/second on rotating equipment which indicates faults in alignment, foundation or imbalance) (see Figure 7.14).

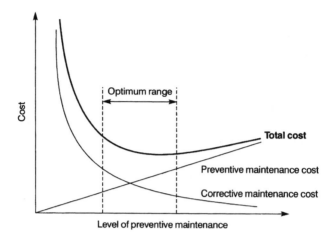

Figure 7.13   Optimum maintenance

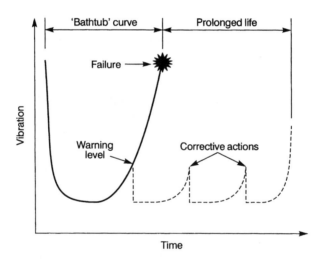

Figure 7.14   Condition monitoring

Inspection-based maintenance is aimed to establish the condition of the equipment by simple 'look, listen and feel' inspection. This simple approach can be effective when administered by experienced engineers and craftsmen.

Total productive maintenance (TPM) is a proven Japanese approach to maximizing overall equipment effectiveness and utilization, and relies on attention to detail in all aspects of manufacturing. TPM includes the operators looking after their own maintenance and thus encourages empowerment. TPM is described in more detail later.

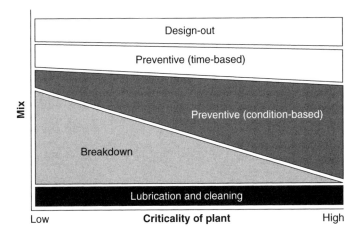

Figure 7.15 The maintenance mix

Reliability-centred maintenance (RCM) is a zero-based approach of determining the maintenance requirement of a plant based on its criticality and a risk or FMEA (failure mode and effect analysis). The origin of RCM dates back to maintenance practices in aircraft industries in 1970s. The modern approach of RCM (also known as RCM 2) follows a structured approach to develop a maintenance mix for the infrastructure (see Figure 7.15). Many organizations, particularly in the service sector and public sector, are contracting out either all or major maintenance activities to third parties specializing in facilities and infrastructure maintenance.

Maintenance policy in manufacturing

The present experience both in Japan and the rest of the world has demonstrated the virtues of TPM. However, it is also vital to establish the appropriate maintenance policy and infrastructure, both before and during the application of TPM principles, to sustain the reliability and safety of plant.

Although we have discussed the trend in maintenance policy over the past four decades, manufacturing companies are following (and quite rightly so) a mix of maintenance policies depending on the type and criticality of the equipment. There are elaborate tools and concepts such as RCM (reliability-centred maintenance) available to develop the optimum maintenance mix, see Figure 7.15.

The criticality of a piece of equipment can be determined by the role of the equipment in the total process, repair expenditure incurred and the production and quality consequences. The experience of the factory engineer and manufacturing manager should be sufficient to categorize each item of equipment and assess the criticality of that item. The following examples of maintenance mix could be used as a guide:

- All equipment: Lubrication and cleaning to be carried out to a formalized plan.
- Critical equipment: Assets with high production and quality consequences or repair expenditure to be put on condition-based predictive maintenance, e.g. rotary equipment should be on vibration monitoring.
- Packing lines: To be on periodic inspection-based maintenance with proper checklists. Overhaul (part or full should be taken only on the basis of inspection observations).
- Less critical equipment: Assets with lower production consequences to be on formalized look, listen and feel inspection coupled with corrective action.
- Services: Same approach as production equipment but third-party contracts will play a more important role here. Statutory regulations (e.g. for pressure vessels) could determine time-based preventative maintenance.
- Buildings: A long-term (e.g. 10 years) time-based preventative plan for setting up a specified repair budget plan. Building maintenance should be contracted out.
- Internal transport: A time-based preventative maintenance plan for this type of equipment (e.g. fork lift trucks), which should be carried out by specialist third parties.

In order to implement the maintenance mix, the company must provide maintenance infrastructure in the form of organization, workshops, engineering stores, planning procedures and information systems.

There are two aspects of maintenance organization: organization of skills and organization structure. Organization issues are discussed in Chapter 9. However, it is important to note that factories in the future will require fewer people but people with higher technical knowledge. It is therefore necessary to define basic educational standards, with the future in mind, for the recruitment of operators, team leaders and technicians to ensure that they will be capable of running and maintaining sophisticated machinery.

The maintenance workshop should contain machinery for emergency repairs, including welding equipment and instrumentation and monitoring equipment. Building maintenance, non-emergency repairs and specialist maintenance should be undertaken by third parties wherever possible. Each site should have one engineering store with appropriate coding and layout for both general parts and machine spares.

The planning procedures should be designed to obtain permits (where required), checklists for inspection and lubrication, and scheduling of large repair work. Excessive planning, on the other hand, risks the danger of a slow response. Finally, records should be kept of when each item was purchased and from whom, warranty details, and of what and when maintenance is carried out. Manufacturers' manuals should be filed and updated as required.

TPM (total productive maintenance) in manufacturing

The use of the word 'maintenance' here is misleading. Total productive maintenance includes more than maintenance; it addresses all aspects of manufacturing. The two primary goals of TPM are to develop optimum conditions for the factory through a self-help people/machine system culture and to improve the overall quality of the work place. It involves every employee in the factory. Implementation requires several years, and success relies on sustained management commitment. TPM is promoted throughout the world by the Japan Institute of Plant Maintenance (JIPM).

TPM is the manufacturing arm of total quality management (TQM) and is based upon five key principles:

- The improvement of manufacturing efficiency by the elimination of six big losses.
- The establishment of a system of autonomous maintenance by operators working in small groups.
- An effective planned maintenance system by expert engineers.
- A training system for increasing the skill and knowledge level of all permanent employees.
- A system of maintenance prevention where engineers work closely with suppliers to specify and design equipment that requires less maintenance.

TPM requires the manufacturing team to improve asset utilization and manufacturing costs by the systematic study and the elimination of the major obstacles to efficiency. In TPM these are called the 'six big losses' and are attributed to (i) breakdown, (ii) set-up and adjustment, (iii) minor stoppages, (iv) reduced speed, (v) quality defects and (vi) start-up and shut-down.

The process of autonomous maintenance is to encourage operators to care for their equipment by performing daily checks, cleaning, lubrication, adjustments, size changes, simple repairs and the early detection of abnormalities. It is a step-by-step approach to bring the equipment at least to its original condition.

Some managers may hold the belief that in TPM 'you do not need experienced craftsmen or engineers and all maintenance is done by operators'. This is not true. The implementation of a maintenance policy with appropriate infrastructure is fundamental to planned maintenance. Planned maintenance is the foundation stone of TPM. However, if the skill and education levels of operators are high then a good proportion of planned maintenance activities should be executed by operators after proper training. Cleaning, lubrication and minor adjustments together with an ability to recognize when a machine is not functioning correctly should be the minimum required of operators.

For TPM to succeed a structural training programme must be undertaken in parallel with the stages of TPM implementation. In addition 'one point lessons' can be used to fill in a specific knowledge gap. This uses a chart which is displayed at the work place and describes a single piece of equipment and its setting or repair method.

Whilst great progress can be made in reducing breakdowns with autonomous maintenance and planned maintenance, 'zero breakdowns' can only be achieved by the specification of parts and equipment which are designed to give full functionality and not to fail. All engineers and designers of the user company should work concurrently with the suppliers of equipment to achieve a system of maintenance prevention.

Although there is a special emphasis on input by different employees to different aspects of TPM (e.g. 'six big losses' for middle management, 'autonomous maintenance' for operators, 'planned maintenance' for middle management, 'maintenance prevention' for senior management), TPM involves all employees and the total involvement is ensured by establishing TPM work groups or committees. Figure 7.16 illustrates an example of a TPM organization.

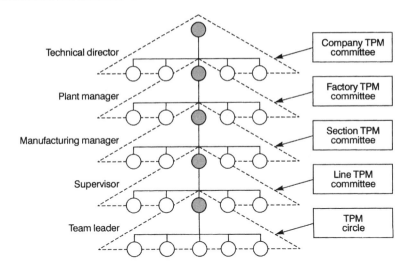

Figure 7.16 TPM organization

To summarize, TPM is a factory-wide continuous improvement programme with particular emphasis on changing the culture of the shop floor through improved attitudes and skills. TPM progress is measured by the stages of autonomous maintenance completed, and visible progress is also seen in the higher reliability of equipment, reduction of waste and improvements in safety statistics.

Maintenance strategy in services

As indicated earlier, three levels of maintenance strategy, i.e., maintenance avoidance, maintenance reduction and maintenance improvement, also apply to service industries. It is important to recognize that effectiveness of a core service process (e.g. hotel reception) depend on the reliability of the supporting infrastructure (e.g. computers, credit card transactions, fax machines etc.). Larger service organizations like insurance companies require big office buildings fitted with lifts, heating, lighting and ventilation systems. The delivery of services based in office buildings depends on the effectiveness and reliability of these supporting systems.

The maintenance activities in a service organization can be divided into four broad categories:

- Equipment maintenance: Maintenance of pumps, motors, generators, compressors and boilers installed in the office building

- IT infrastructure maintenance: Maintenance of computers, network and systems
- Facilities maintenance: Maintenance of buildings, furniture, painting, decorations, plumbing, electrical installations, gardens, and cleaning
- Office maintenance: Maintenance and layout of the office environment.

Equipment maintenance can easily follow the maintenance strategy (e.g. inspection-based maintenance) of manufacturing organizations. Large office buildings often carry an engineering team to ensure equipment maintenance. It is more common for smaller service organizations to deploy contract maintenance with either the supplier of equipment or a third party maintenance company.

IT infrastructure maintenance is also supported by own resources or outsourced to a third party depending on the size of the company.

It is a common current practice to outsource facilities management for all service organizations. It is a rare exception if an organization supports in-house resources for facilities management. There are many successful companies specializing in facilities maintenance and management for other organizations.

Following its success in Japan many organizations have applied TPM concepts, especially Five Ss, in office maintenance (Kesh, 2004). Five Ss represent a set of Japanese words for excellent house keeping:

- *Sein* – Sort
- *Seiton* – Set in place
- *Seiso* – Shine
- *Seiketso* – Standardize
- *Sitsuke* – Sustain.

Foundation 14: Performance management and Balanced Scorecard

When you can measure what you are speaking of, and express it in numbers, you know that on which you are discoursing. But if you cannot measure it and express it in numbers, your knowledge is of a meagre and unsatisfactory kind.

Lord Kelvin, c. 1900

The above quotation may be one hundred years old but it applies equally to today's businesses, whether they are in manufacturing or services. From our discussions in previous chapters we have established that some results can be quantified and expressed in numbers while some other situations are difficult to quantify. However, these intangible activities can be graded in a numeric scale by applying well-defined criteria. It is also important to recognize that the measurement requirements of a business initiative would vary according to the primary objectives of the business, but the fundamental philosophy of performance management equally applies to all initiatives and organizations.

Manufacturing performance

There may be a minority group of behaviourists who consider the measurement of performance is an impediment to the creativity and empowerment of employees. However, in the real business world, including Japan, successful companies are pursuing competitive parameters of manufacturing by continuous measurement, monitoring and improvement programmes. Adler (1993) demonstrated that by defining performance standards, quality and productivity at the Fremont plant (a GM–Toyota joint venture) went from worst in the General Motors' quality league (before Toyota got involved) to best shortly after Toyota became involved. The Toyota approach was centred on teams, with each team responsible for setting measurable objectives in the areas of quality, cost, production and safety. Wright and Race (2004) give examples of what should be measured and stress the importance of team work and common goals. It is now well documented that a faster rate of progress has been successfully sustained in companies where work groups have been involved in setting, monitoring and improving their own work standards.

Having established the strategies of sourcing, appropriate technology, flexibility and reliability it is imperative to measure the performance of manufacturing facilities in order to monitor how the strategies are delivering the expected competitive advantage. If it cannot be measured there is no method of determining whether an improvement has taken place. Or, as F.W. Taylor once said, 'if it can't be measured it can't be managed'. There are several benefits arising from manufacturing performance efforts.

First, by defining and measuring the key parameters, the company can identify areas for improvement and take early corrective action. Second, by comparing performance across units, organizations and industries, management can make decisions on both operational improvement and research needs. Any benchmarking exercise (whether 'internal' or 'external') cannot be effective without measured performance. Third, a planning and scheduling scheme is only as reliable as the data used and thus only measured performance data can ensure dependability in customer service. Fourth, performance measurement when carried out by teams made up of all levels of employees unites labour and management in seeking real productivity gains. Fifth, measuring performance also gives an organization the evidence it needs to quantify and celebrate gain, whether it is for employee incentive schemes or to demonstrate gains to interested stakeholders.

Our model of manufacturing performance has two elements – manufacturing efficiency and manufacturing effectiveness. Manufacturing efficiency is internal, factory focused and relates to the utilization of resources (namely assets, materials, energy and people). Manufacturing effectiveness is external, customer-focused and relates to quality, delivery and environment. Slack *et al.* (2004) gives parameters of manufacturing advantage as:

- Doing it right – the quality advantage
- Doing things fast – the speed advantage
- Doing things on time – the dependability advantage
- Changing what you do – the flexibility advantage
- Doing things cheap (without sacrificing quality) – the cost advantage.

Although they are not strictly identical, manufacturing efficiency is responsible for the 'cost advantage' and manufacturing effectiveness is responsible for the other 'advantages'.

Manufacturing efficiency

The measurement, monitoring and improvement of manufacturing efficiency are strongly established functions within the field of traditional industrial engineering. However, many companies – perhaps influenced by the tide of fashionable TLAs (three-letter acronyms) – abandoned the professionalism of 'efficiency experts'. Arguably, some companies misinterpreted W.E. Deming's statement, 'Eliminate numerical quotas for the workforce: as they disregard quality and put a ceiling on production.' (Deming also said, 'Use statistical methods to find the trouble spots.') There is some history of the abuse of labour standards to determine incentive payments (time studies and Taylorism). The leverage of efficiency has certainly moved away from labour with increased mechanization and automation of repetitive work, but it has shifted to the efficiency of assets, materials and energy. Measurement is still important, the issue now is to measure what matters.

Labour productivity

Labour productivity can be measured and expressed in one of three ways.

- Standard hours, where standard actual hours and output for a task or product are compared to actual time taken
- Input of resource, such as employees per unit or employee hours per tonne
- Output such as units of output per employee or tonnes per employee hour.

The need for and choice of work measurement tools (such as time study, pre-determined motion time systems, activity sampling, etc.) will depend on the nature of operations and the importance of labour in the total performance. Labour standards are valuable data for resource planning, standard costing and activity-based costing. Labour is also the most controllable of all manufacturing resources.

Materials productivity

In terms of cost the most important resource is materials. In an FMCG business raw and packaging materials account for 70–80% of the ex-works cost of a product. Because of the large number of line items or SKUs (stock-keeping units) involved in the bill of materials of a product, a popular method of expressing materials productivity has been financial indices such as the ratio of standard material cost to actual material cost. Cost performance provides an indicator of the trend of materials cost for the product by using a common unit for all materials (e.g. the cost), but it fails to give the yield or productivity of a specific material.

Other measures of material productivity are materials yield and loss rate by each material where:

$$\text{Material yield} = \frac{\text{Theoretical consumption}}{\text{Actual consumption}} \times 100$$

$$\text{Loss ratio} = \frac{\text{Reject or losses}}{\text{Actual consumption}} \times 100$$

The data collection and measurement of materials productivity can be complex and this can lead to inaccuracies. Hence companies achieve effective results by restricting the monitoring of materials productivity to key items selected by Pareto analysis (the 80/20 rule which says that 80% of the problems can be attributed to 20% of the causes). The reliable information on materials costs and productivity not only assists continuous improvement programmes but also leads to longer-term decisions on purchasing of materials and design/ formulations of products.

Energy efficiency

Energy management benefits in two areas – cost reduction (energy accounts for 15–30% of the conversion cost of a product) and environmental protection. There are a number of factors that would influence a longer-term improvement (e.g. choice of fuel, type of equipment, generation process, etc.). However, by eliminating losses and monitoring some simple indices, companies can implement a continuous energy efficiency programme. The main indices for an FMCG plant are:

- Steam: Tonnes of steam per tonne of product
- Electricity: kWh (kilowatt hour) per tonne of product
- Fuel: kg of fuel per tonne of product
- Overall: GJ (giga joule) per tonne of product.

It is important that the above indices are used for monitoring the trend of the factory. If inter-factory benchmarking is considered then appropriate metering of utilities would be necessary.

Plant efficiency

As the manufacturing operations have progressively become more process- and equipment-dependent, the utilization and efficiency of plant have become the most important driving element of manufacturing performance. A properly designed and administered plant efficiency scheme offers broad-ranging benefits and a comprehensive manufacturing performance system:

- It provides information for improving asset utilization and thus reduces capital and depreciation costs in the longer term.

- It highlights equipment faults and thus improves plant reliability and contributes to the designing out of weak points.
- Higher plant efficiency improves labour productivity by producing higher output without increasing the number of employees required.
- Plant efficiency information focuses on downtimes caused by services (steam, air, water, power) and a higher plant efficiency results in a higher energy efficiency.
- It identifies the direct losses caused by poor quality of materials and thus improves material productivity and product quality.
- It provides essential and reliable information for capacity planning.
- It provides information on downtime due to shortage of materials and thus improves materials planning.
- It provides information for effective scheduling of plant to shorten lead times, e.g. by changing the operation from two to three shifts.

A proven TPM approach of plant efficiency is overall equipment effectiveness (OEE). The critical success factor of OEE is that parameters must be well defined and measurements should not rely heavily on recorded downtime data. The OEE is an index of delivered performance of plant or equipment based on output.

The method of monitoring OEE is devised in such a way that it would highlight the losses and deficiencies incurred during the operation of the plant and identify the opportunities for improvement.

There are many ways to calculate OEE (see Hartmann, 1991; Shirose, 1992). In this section we describe the methodology of OEE that was developed and applied by Ron Basu at both Unilever and GlaxoWellcome.[1]

Overall equipment effectiveness (OEE) is defined by the following formula:

$$\text{OEE \%} = \frac{\text{Actual goods output}}{\text{Specified output}} \times 100$$

where Specified output = Specified speed $\times$ Operation time

---

[1] In Unilever plc, the methodology was known as PAMCO (plant and machine control); in GlaxoWellcome it was called CAPRO (capacity analysis of production).

Application

The application of OEE has been extensive, especially when driven by the TPM (total productive maintenance) programmes, to critical plant and equipment. It can be applied to single equipment, a packing line, a production plant or processes. In order to appreciate the usefulness of OEE it is important to understand equipment time analysis as shown in Figure 7.17 and described below.

- Total time defines the maximum time within a reporting period, such as 52 weeks a year, 24 hours a day, 8760 hours in a year.
- Available time is the time during which the machine or equipment could be operated within the limits of national or local statutes, regulation or convention.
- Operation time is the time during which the machine or equipment is planned to run for production purposes. The operational time is normally the shift hours.
- Production time is the maximum time during which the machine or equipment could be expected to be operated productively after adjusting the operation time for routine stoppages such as change-over and meal breaks.

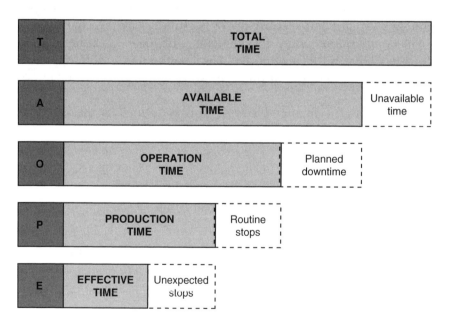

Figure 7.17   Equipment time analysis

- Effective time is the time needed to produce a 'good output delivered' if the machine or equipment is working at its specified speed for a defined period. It includes no allowances for interruptions or any other time losses.

It is important to note that effective time is not recorded; it is calculated from the specified speed as:

$$\text{Effective time} = \frac{\text{Good output}}{\text{Specified speed}}$$

where specified speed is the optimum speed of a machine or equipment for a particular product without any allowances for loss of efficiency. It is expressed as quantity per unit, such as tons per hour, bottles per minute, cases per hour or litres per minute.

In addition to OEE, two other indices are commonly used, as shown below:

$$\text{Production efficiency (\%)} = \frac{\text{Effective time (E)}}{\text{Production time (P)}} \times 100$$

$$\text{Operational utilization (\%)} = \frac{\text{Operation time (D)}}{\text{Total time (T)}} \times 100$$

As indicated earlier, a properly designed and administered plant efficiency scheme such as OEE offers a broad range of benefits and a comprehensive manufacturing performance system.

Manufacturing effectiveness

Manufacturing effectiveness is primarily external and customer-focused. However, there are some useful parameters (see Table 7.4) and indices of manufacturing effectiveness which are internal and factory-focused. Table 7.5 shows the key external parameters and indices for manufacturing performance that customers are looking for. We have covered some of these in previous chapters.

Table 7.4 Manufacturing effectiveness: internal

Parameter	Indices
Planning	Actual output versus planned output (by product)
Inventory/stock	Stock cover or stock turn
	Stock value as percentage of total sales
Safety	Loss time accident rate percentage
	First aid attendance
Environment	Percentage compliance of emission rate
Product quality	Defined waste as percentage of total sales
Training	Training days per employee
	Training cost as percentage of total sales

Table 7.5 Manufacturing effectiveness: external

Parameter	Indices
Customer service	Order fill percentage
	Lead time (days)
	On-time delivery percentage
Quality	Goods returned as percentage of total sales
	Complaints as percentage of number of invoices
Innovation	New product sales as percentage of total sales

Service performance

Our model for service performance is similar to the manufacturing model and it has two elements: service efficiency and service effectiveness.

Service efficiency is often termed as service productivity. The productivity equation is simple: it is output divided by input. A common way of measuring productivity is to measure directly the number of products or services provided per person. As the service organizations deal with more variations in their products it is often difficult to express productivity by a meaningful number.

Gronroos (2000) defines service productivity as a function of three parameters: internal efficiency, external effectiveness and capacity utilization:

Service productivity = Internal efficiency, external effectiveness,
               capacity utilization
          = Cost efficiency, revenue efficiency,
               capacity efficiency

$$\text{Cost efficiency} = \frac{\text{Customers served}}{\text{Cost of employees}}$$

$$\text{Revenue efficiency} = \frac{\text{Revenue}}{\text{Cost of resource}}$$

$$\text{Capacity efficiency} = \frac{\text{Required capacity}}{\text{Employee hours}}$$

Farrell (2003) presented the basic concept of productivity in the context of IT industries and proposed simple rules of improving productivity as follows:

Increase output	Increase number of units produced
	Increase labour efficiency
	Increase asset utilization
	Increase value of portfolio
	Sell new value added goods and services
	Shift to higher value added goods in current portfolio
	Realize more value from goods in current portfolio
Decrease inputs	Reduce labour costs
	Substitute capital for labour
	Deploy labour more effectively
	Reduce non-labour costs
	Reduce inventory holding costs, real estate costs, and so on

Service effectiveness is externally oriented and measured by customer service. The metrics of customer service have been described in Chapter 5: these include order fill, line fill, on time in full, and composite customer service (see Table 5.2).

It is important to recognize that many performance metrics of both manufacturing and service organizations can be identical, similar or at least interrelated.

The Balanced Scorecard

The concept of the Balanced Scorecard was first introduced by Kaplan and Norton in an article in the *Harvard Business Review* in 1992, 'The

Balanced Scorecard – Measures that Drive Performance'. This generated considerable interest for senior business managers and led to the next round of development of the scorecard. The focus was shifted from short-term measurement towards generating growth, learning and value added services to customers. This methodology was then published by Kaplan and Norton in a number of articles in the *Harvard Business Review* and culminated in their 1996 book *The Balanced Scorecard*.

Many companies are now using the Balanced Scorecard as the central organizing framework for important decision processes. The evolution of this technique has gradually transformed the performance measurement process into a strategic management system.

The Balanced Scorecard (BSC) is a conceptual framework for translating an organization's strategic objectives into a set of performance indicators distributed among four perspectives: financial, customer, internal business processes and learning and growth (see Figure 7.18).

The indicators are aimed to measure an organization's progress towards achieving its vision as well as the long-term drivers of success. Through the Balanced Scorecard an organization monitors both its current performance (e.g. internal processes, finance, customer satisfaction) and its effort to improve and sustain performance (e.g. innovation and employee development). It is also balanced in terms of internal efficiency and external effectiveness. Later David Norton (1999) extended the elements of the overall scorecard to six, these being:

- Return on investment
- Budget
- Shareholder value
- Customer
- People
- Quality.

Targets (scores) are formulated for each element, communicated and consensus achieved, executed and results are evaluated with corrective action taken so that the targets (scores) are achieved. Norton says that it is important that all elements are linked and not considered in isolation.

The Balanced Scorecard has been applied successfully in several organizations around the world. It is evident that the key performance

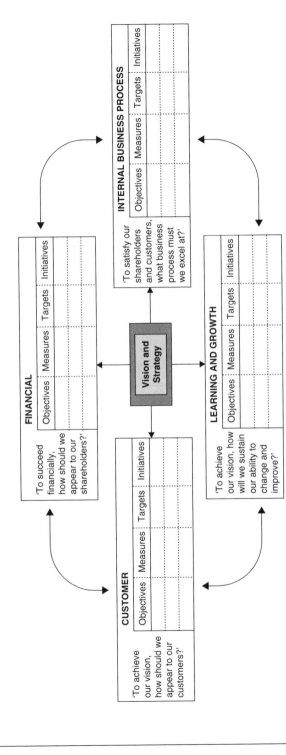

Figure 7.18 The Balanced Scorecard (adapted from Kaplan and Norton, *California Management Review*, 1996)

indicators of both manufacturing and service organizations, as we have described earlier, can be incorporated in to a properly designed Balanced Scorecard. The scorecard, with some customized changes, provides a management tool for senior executives primarily to focus on strategies and longer-term objectives. The organizations could vary from a large multinational business to a non-profit-making public service unit. The scorecard is sometimes named the 'Executive Dashboard'. The key performance indicators (KPI) are reported as:

- Current actual
- Target
- Year-to-date average.

When the actual performance value is on or above target then the value is shown as green. If the actual is below the target but within a given tolerance then the colour becomes amber. It is depicted in red when the value is below the tolerance limit of the target.

Another area of application is to assess the performance at the tactical operation level. Usually the top level indicators (also known as 'vital flow') are designed in such a way that they can be cascaded to 'component' measures and the root causes can be analysed.

The published case studies by Kaplan (1996) provide examples of the application of the Balanced Scorecard in three areas: Chemical Bank, Mobil Corporation's US Marketing and Refining Division and United Way, a non-profit-making community service based in Rhode Island, USA.

Basu (2002) emphasized the impact of new measures on the collaborative supply chain. The Internet-enabled supply chain or e-supply chain has extended the linear flow of supply chain to collaborative management supported by supplier partnerships. This has triggered the emergence of new measures especially in five areas:

- External focus
- Power to the consumer
- Value-based competition and customer relationship management
- Network performance and supplier partnership
- Intellectual capacity.

The design features and application requirements of the Balanced Scorecard can be adapted to the collaborative culture of the integrated supply chain.

Performance improvement

There is a risk of neglecting the opportunities for incremental improvement of the performance of the existing systems by downgrading the approach as 'tinkering'. While the vision must be to look for step changes in competitive advantages by strategic initiatives, the opportunities for continuous improvement cannot be ignored.

The whole theme and emphasis of this book is to identify the right balance of opportunities by a self-analysis in order to see the wood for the trees.

A continuous improvement programme can be in three stages.

1 *Monitoring.* The continuous monitoring of appropriate performance indices, ideally by professional industrial engineers, and regular discussions and corrective actions by all functions.
2 *Special studies.* When the trend of performance indicators shows chronic problems, special studies (such as video-based machine motion analysis, and failure mode effect analysis) are carried out by a team or task force.
3 *Change programmes.* In order to sustain the improvements in manufacturing performance, a company-wide change programme (such as total quality management or total productive maintenance) is implemented.

Summary

As Aristotle said, 'Give me a lever long enough and I will move the world.' This chapter covers the five foundation stones of the 'core' pillars of an organization, whether it is in the manufacturing or the service sector.

Management manufacturing facilities is the forgotten link in corporate competitive strategy, yet in manufacturing companies it is the factories that employ the major share of the companies' assets and the majority of the people.

To gain, and to maintain, a competitive advantage in a service organization it is essential to know and to understand each of the foundation stones of infrastructure facilities.

Foundation 10: Sourcing strategy deals with where we get our materials and people, and whether we make or buy. Sourcing requires a formal strategic plan. This plan must be in tune with the overall corporate strategy. We recommend a project team approach to develop a formal strategic sourcing plan.

Foundation 11: In this section we discussed the pros and cons of technology. Without proper planning – including product, process, choice of technology and evaluation of options – technology can well become a costly millstone. There are many well-publicized 'green-field' hi-tech factories which have proved to be white elephants. In this section we show how to plan so as to avoid costly mistakes that are hard to undo.

Foundation 12: Here we examine the fashionable subject of flexibility. We warn that there is little merit in flexibility for its own sake. After all, the customer does not care how the plant is organized providing the product is to specification and received on time. We point out that the crucial issues with flexibility are the training and attitude of workers. The workers have to be trained, and receptive, or flexibility will result in confusion and a drop in productivity.

Foundation 13: For this foundation stone we examine the various levels and ways in which maintenance can be planned so that the manufacturing process becomes more reliable. The highest level of maintenance is total productive maintenance (TPM). We describe TPM in some detail as we firmly believe that maintenance is a major issue in giving a company a competitive edge. The success of TPM is dependent on the quality and attitude of the workers.

Foundation 14: In this section on performance we revisit F.W. Taylor's statement, 'If it can't be measured, it can't be managed.' If the system does not have standards that are quantifiable how do we know if there has been an improvement, and how do we know if we are not actually losing ground? This section gives some key measures. Unless measurements are used, there is no point in taking them.

In all our activities we must be conscious of the aim. The aim is to add value and to reduce costs.

CASE EXAMPLE 4: Total productive maintenance (TPM) in Nippon Lever, Japan

Background

The Utsunomia plant in Japan was commissioned in 1991 on a greenfield site by Nippon Lever to manufacture household detergents products and plastic bottles for liquid detergents. The factory was experiencing 'teething' problems primarily due to the poor reliability and lack of local support of the imported equipment. Many of the employees were new to factory work.

To improve this situation the company used the help of the Japanese Institute of Plant Maintenance (JIPM), an organization which is working on TPM (total productive maintenance) with over 800 companies in Japan. TPM has been widely used in Japan, having been developed to support Lean/JIT and TQM. It was considered to be appropriate for the Utsunomiya plant. TPM focuses on machine performance and concentrates on operator training and team work.

Approach

A TPM programme was launched at the Utsunomiya plant in July 1992 with the objective of zero losses:

* Zero stoppages
* Zero quality defects
* Zero waste in materials and manpower.

Strong organizational support was provided by the Nippon Lever management in terms of:

* A top management steering team to facilitate implementation by removing obstacles.
* A manager to work full time supporting the programme.
* One shift per week set aside for TPM work.
* Training for managers, leaders and operators involving JIPM video training material.

The programme launch was initiated at a 'kick-off' ceremony in presence of the whole Nippon Lever Board and managers from other companies' and suppliers' sites.

Implementation

The initial thrust of the programme was the implementation of 'autonomous maintenance' following the JIPMs seven steps:

1 Initial clean-up
2 Elimination of contamination
3 Standard setting for operators
4 Skill development for inspection
5 Autonomous inspection
6 Orderliness and tidiness
7 All-out autonomous working.

To implement the Seven Steps, 'model machines' (those giving the biggest problems) were chosen. This approach helps to develop operators' knowledge of a machine and ensures that work on the model can be used as the standard for work on other machines. It also helps motivation, in that if the worst machine moves to the highest efficiency, this sets the tone for the rest of the process.

The improvements to the machines were made using 'kaizen' methodology (small incremental improvements), and were carried out by groups of operators under their own guidance. Two means of support were given to operators: a kaizen budget per line so that small repairs and capital expenses could be agreed without delay and the external JIPM facilitator provided encouragement and experience to workgroups.

Results and learning points

Substantial benefits were achieved within a year at the Utsunomiya plant, including:

- £2.8 million reduction in operating costs
- Reduced need for expensive third party bottles
- Production efficiency increased from 54% to 64% for high speed soap lines and from 63% to 80% for liquid filling lines
- A team of trained, motivated and empowered operators capable of carrying out running maintenance.

The success of the programme at the Utsunomiya plant led to the introduction of TPM to two other factories of Nippon Lever (Shimizu and Sagamihara). Over the next few years the Corporate Groups of Unilever encouraged all sites outside Japan to implement TPM, with remarkable successes achieved particularly in factories in Indonesia, Brazil, Chile, UK and Germany.

Chapter 8

Systems and Procedures

The golden rule is that there are no golden rules.
George Bernard Shaw, 'Maxims for Revolutionists'

Chapter 7 discussed infrastructure facilities, the 'hardware' of operations. We now turn to the 'software', that is systems and procedures, and the three foundation stones of:

15 Quality management
16 Financial management
17 Information and communication technology.

Earlier we considered the implications of issues such as shorter innovation cycles, more stringent product specifications, asset performance, standard on-time delivery to customers, closer relations with both suppliers and customers, and so on. Attention to these issues accentuates the need for new integrated and flexible management control systems.

Another important issue is improving the financial performance of the company. Under pressure to participate in fashionable improvement activities, or to become involved with the newest business wisdom, management may lose sight of the real issue – improving profitability. The aim of this book is to improve profitability of an organization by concentrating on adding value through operations management endeavours.

Foundation 15: Quality management

What is quality?

Quality has two levels, a basic level and a higher level. At the basic level common definitions, 'fitness for purpose', 'getting it right first time' and 'right thing, right place, right time' apply. (These definitions have all been so overused that they are almost clichés.) An understanding of what we mean by basic level and higher levels of quality can best be explained by illustration.

Consider a bus service. As passengers what are our basic requirements? First, unless the bus is going more or less where we want to go, we won't catch it. The second is timing. If we start work at 9 a.m. unless the bus gets us to the office before 9 we won't catch it. Another consideration will be cost. Therefore the basic requirements in this example are the route, the time and the cost, and depending on alternatives we would probably rank them in that order.

A bus service could meet all these requirements (right thing, right place, right time and right cost), but still not be a quality service. If the service was unreliable (sometimes late, sometimes early, sometimes did not keep to the route) then we would not consider it a reliable service. But supposing the bus met all our basic requirements, got us to work on time every time and at a reasonable cost, but it was dirty, the driver was surly, the seats were hard and the bus leaked exhaust fumes. Although it met our basic requirements we would not describe it as a quality service.

To meet our perception of quality there are certain basic requirements that have to be met, and there are certain higher order requirements that have to be met. In this case we would expect polite service, a clean bus, reasonably comfortable seating and certainly no exhaust fumes. A truly high-quality service would mean that the bus was spotlessly clean, had carpet on the floor, and perhaps piped music as well as all the other attributes. But no matter how comfortable the ride, how cheap the fare, unless the bus is going our way we shan't be interested in catching it. To have your product described as a quality product, the customer will expect higher level benefits. These higher level benefits are what gives an organization a competitive edge, and often the difference costs very little to achieve.

There are many different definitions and dimensions of quality to be found in books and academic literature.

- Performance
- Features
- Reliability
- Conformance
- Durability
- Serviceability
- Aesthetics
- Perceived quality

Figure 8.1   Garvin's (1984) product quality dimensions

One of the most respected definitions of quality is the eight quality dimensions developed by Garvin (1984) (Figure 8.1).

- *Performance* refers to the efficiency (e.g. return on investment) with which the product achieves its intended purpose.
- *Features* are attributes that supplement the product's basic performance, e.g. tinted glass windows in a car.
- *Reliability* refers to the capability of the product to perform consistently over its life cycle.
- *Conformance* refers to meeting the specifications of the product, usually defined by numeric values.
- *Durability* is the degree to which a product withstands stress without failure.
- *Serviceability* is used to denote the ease of repair.
- *Aesthetics* are sensory characteristics such as a look, sound, taste and smell.
- *Perceived quality* is based upon customer opinion.

The above dimensions of quality are not mutually exclusive, although they relate primarily to the quality of the product. Neither are they exhaustive. Service quality is perhaps even more difficult to define than product quality. A set of service quality dimensions (see Figure 8.2) that is widely cited has been compiled by Parasuraman, Zeithamel and Berry (1985).

- *Tangibles* are the physical appearance of the service facility and people.
- *Service reliability* deals with the ability of the service provider to perform dependably.
- *Responsiveness* is the willingness of the service provider to be prompt in delivering the service.

- Tangibles
- Service reliability
- Responsiveness
- Assurance
- Empathy
- Availability
- Timeliness
- Professionalism
- Completeness
- Pleasantness

Figure 8.2   Parasuraman *et al.*'s (1985) service quality dimensions

The quality of a product or service is the degree to which it satisfies customer requirements
It is influenced by:

- *Design quality:* the degree to which the *specification* of the product or service satisfies customers' requirements
- *Process quality:* the degree to which the product or service, which is made available to the customer, *conforms* to specification.

Figure 8.3   Wild's (2002) definition of quality

- *Assurance* relates to the ability of the service provider to inspire trust and confidence.
- *Empathy* refers to the ability of the service provider to demonstrate care and individual attention to the customer.
- *Availability* is the ability to provide service at the right time and place.
- *Timeliness* refers to the delivery of service within the agreed lead time.
- *Professionalism* encompasses the impartial and ethical characteristics of the service provider.
- *Completeness* addresses the delivery of the order in full.
- *Pleasantness* simply means the good manners and politeness of the service provider.

Our third definition of quality is from Ray Wild (2002: 644), as shown in Figure 8.3.

The list of quality dimensions by both Garvin and Parasuraman *et al.* are widely cited and respected. However, one problem with multiple dimensions is that of communication, and if allowed time,

Figure 8.4   Three dimensions of quality

the reader could probably identify additional dimensions. It is not easy to devise a strategic plan on quality based on specific dimensions which could be interpreted differently by different departments. Wild's definition of design/process quality however provides a broad framework to develop a company specific quality strategy.

None the less, one important dimension of quality is not clearly visible in the above models: the quality of the organization. This is a fundamental cornerstone of the quality of a holistic process and an essential requirement of an approved quality assessment scheme such as EFQM (European Foundation of Quality Management). Therefore, a three-dimensional model of quality has been developed (Basu, 2004). This is shown in Figure 8.4.

When an organization develops and defines its quality strategy, it is important to share a common definition of quality and each department within a company can work towards a common objective. The product quality should contain defined attributes of both numeric specifications and perceived dimensions. The process quality, whether it relates to manufacturing or service operations, should also contain some defined criteria of acceptable service level so that the conformity of the output can be validated against these criteria. Perhaps the most important determinant of how we perceive sustainable quality is the functional and holistic role we fulfil within the organization. It is only when an organization begins to change its approach to a holistic culture emphasizing a single set of numbers based on transparent measurement with senior management commitment that the

- Top management commitment
- Sales and operations planning
- Single set of numbers
- Using tools and techniques
- Performance management
- Knowledge management
- Team work culture
- Self-assessment

Figure 8.5   Organization quality dimensions

'organization quality' germinates. Figure 8.5 provides a set of key organization quality dimensions.

- *Top management commitment* means that organizational quality cannot exist without the total commitment of the top executive team.
- *Sales and operations planning* is a monthly senior management review process to align strategic objectives with operation tasks.
- *Single set of numbers* provides the common business data for all functions in the company.
- *Using tools and techniques* relates to the fact that without the effective application of tools and techniques, the speed of improvement will not be assured.
- *Performance management* includes the selection, measurement, monitoring and application of key performance indicators (KPI).
- *Knowledge management* includes education, training and development of employees, sharing of best practice and communication media.
- *Team work culture* requires that team work should be practised in cross-functional teams to encourage a borderless organization.
- *Self-assessment* enables a regular health check of all aspects of the organization against a checklist or accepted assessment process such as EFQM.

Hierarchy of quality

In this section we discuss the various ways in which quality can be managed. We also discuss the strengths and weaknesses of each method. Our 'hierarchy' of quality approximates the evolution of quality management from simple testing to a full total quality management system.

Quality by inspection

Traditionally in manufacturing, the concept of quality related to conformance to certain dimensions and specifications, the cliché being 'fitness for purpose'. Quality control was achieved by inspection and supervision. This, the most basic approach to quality, can be labelled as quality by inspection.

Quality by inspection, if every deviation from standard is detected by the inspector before despatch, will at least provide the customer with an acceptable product. Although an acceptable product might satisfy the customer it is not likely to encourage customer loyalty. It is our contention that a competitive edge can only be gained by providing the customer with more than they expect.

Quality inspection is an expensive method of achieving a basic level of quality. It requires the employment of people to check on the operators. Inspection and supervision do not add value to a product, they merely add to the cost!

The stage of the process where the inspection takes place is important. If the only inspection is at the end of the process then, if deviations from the standard are discovered, the cost of reworking could well double the cost of the item. If a deviation from standard is not detected, the customer becomes the 'quality inspector', by which time it is too late. If the product is found to be below standard by the customer, the provider has the problem of putting it right. Putting right could include the cost of scrapping the unit and giving the client a new one, or in extreme cases a total product recall with all the costs and loss of consumer confidence that this entails.

Quality inspection at a more advanced level includes checking and testing at various stages of production so that errors can be detected early and remedial action taken before the next stage of the process takes place. At a still higher level of inspection materials are inspected on receipt and then probably tested again before being drawn from the store. Of course all these tests and checks take time and cost money. The cost is easy to quantify when the checks are carried out by people whose prime job is to test and check the work of others.

When people know that everything they do is subject to testing and checking, then the onus is no longer on them to get the job right first time and they complacently rely on inspection 'down the line'. We believe that the inspector or supervisor will be conditioned to find a percentage of errors (that being the main reason for employing inspectors!). This attitude will be reinforced further by an error percentage being built into the standard costs. Thus, a level of error becomes accepted and is built into the cost of the product.

The costs of relying on inspection by people other than the operator are therefore two-fold:

1 A level of error becomes accepted as standard and is included in the price.
2 Inspectors do not add value to the product. Inspectors are an added cost.

Next in the hierarchy is quality control.

Quality control

With quality control, the aim is not only to monitor the quality at various stages of the process but to identify and eliminate causes of unsatisfactory quality so that they do not happen again. Whereas inspection is an 'after the fact' approach, quality control is aimed at preventing mistakes. With quality control, you would expect to find in place drawings, raw material testing, intermediate process testing, some self-inspection by workers, keeping of records of failure, and some feedback to supervisors and operators of errors and percentage of errors. The objectives are to reduce waste by eliminating errors and to make sure that the production reaches a specified level of quality before shipment to the customer.

Quality assurance

Quality assurance includes all the steps taken under quality control and quality inspection. It includes, where appropriate, the setting of standards with documentation for dimensions, tolerances, machine settings, raw material grades, operating temperatures and any other safety quality or standard that might be desirable. Quality assurance would also include the documentation of the method of checking against the specified standards. Quality assurance generally includes a third party approval from a recognized authority such as the ISO. However ISO accreditation in itself does not suggest that a high level of quality has been reached. The only assurance which ISO accreditation gives is that the organization does have a defined level of quality and a defined procedure which is consistently being met.

With quality assurance one would expect to move from detection of errors to correction of process so as to prevent errors. One would also expect a comprehensive quality manual, recording of failures to achieve quality standards and costs, use of statistical process control (SPC) and the audit of quality systems.

Total quality management (TQM)

The fourth and highest level in our hierarchy of quality is total quality management. The lower levels – quality inspection, quality control and quality assurance – are aimed at achieving an agreed consistent level of quality, first by testing and inspection, then by rigid conformance to standards and procedures, and finally by efforts to eliminate causes of errors so that the defined accepted level of quality will be achieved. This is a cold and sterile approach to quality. It implies that once a sufficient level of quality has been achieved, then apart from maintaining that level which in itself might be hard work, little more need to be done. This approach to quality has its roots in Taylorism. Taylor (1947) believed in finding the 'best method' by scientific means and then establishing this method as the standard. This approach is top-down, the bosses determine the level of quality to be achieved, and then the bosses decide on the best method to achieve the desired level of quality. Control methods of inspection and supervision are then set in place to ensure that the required level of quality is maintained. This does not mean that management is not taking into account what the customer wants or is ignoring what the competition is doing. It just means that they, as managers, believe they know what is best and how this can be achieved. To this end, supervision and inspection become an important method of achieving the aim with little input expected from the workers.

Total quality management is on a different plane. Total quality management does, of course, include all the previous levels of setting standards and the means of measuring conformance to standards. In doing this, SPC will be used, systems will be documented and accurate and timely feedback of results will be given. With TQM, ISO accreditation might be sought, but an organization that truly has embraced TQM will not need the ISO stamp of approval.

TQM requires a culture whereby every member of the organization believes that not one day should go by without the organization in some way improving the quality of its goods and services. The vision of TQM must begin with the chief executive. If the chief executive has a passion for quality and continuous improvement, and if this passion can be transmitted down through the organization, then, paradoxically, the ongoing driving force will be from the bottom up.

Generally, it is the lower-paid members of the organization who will physically make the product or deliver the service, and it is the sum of the efforts that each individual puts into their part of the finished product which will determine the overall quality of the finished article. Likewise, generally it is the lower-paid staff members, such as shop assistants, telephone operators and van drivers who are the contact point with the customer, and the wider public. They, too, have a huge part to play in how the customer perceives an organization. It is on the lower level that an organization must rely for the continuing daily level of quality. Quality, once the culture of quality has become ingrained, will be driven from the bottom up, rather than achieved by direction or control from the top. Management will naturally have to continue to be responsible for planning and for providing the resources to enable the workers to do the job. But, unless the factory operators, the telephone operators, the cleaning staff, the sales assistants, the junior accounts clerk and the van driver are fully committed to quality, TQM will never happen.

TQM, however, goes beyond the staff of the organization – it goes outside the organization and involves suppliers, customers and the general public.

Once a relationship has been built with a supplier, that supplier is no longer treated with suspicion, or in some cases almost as an adversary. Instead of trying to get the best deal possible out of the supplier, the supplier becomes a member of the team. The supplier becomes involved in the day-to-day problems and concerns of the organization and is expected to assist, help and advise. The supplier becomes part of the planning team. Price and discounts will no longer be the crucial issues, delivery of the correct materials at the right time will be the real issues, and suppliers will be judged accordingly. Once a supplier proves reliable, the checking and testing of inwards goods will become less crucial. Ideally, the level of trust will be such that the raw materials can be delivered direct to the operator's work place rather than to a central store.

Consider the difference to your organization if the raw materials were always there on time, were of the right quantity and quality, and were delivered to the operator's work place and not to a store; each operator knew the standards and got the job right first time every time; and so on right down the line. Then the organization would not need anyone involved in checking anyone else's work. Supervisors and middle management would no longer be policing each step of a job.

At the end of the process is the customer. TQM organizations are very customer-conscious. As the supplier is regarded as part of the team, so too is the customer. This is more than just casual slogans such as 'the customer is always right'; this means really getting alongside the customer and finding out exactly what they want. The ultimate is that the customer, like the supplier, becomes part of the process, as with the Toyota 72 hour car example described in Chapter 3.

We are now then looking at a totally new type of organization: the old bureaucratic style of management, with the associated rules relating to span of control, appraisal systems and incentive schemes is simply no longer appropriate. Instead, organizations have to be designed around the process. For example, instead of having a centralized purchasing department, why could not the operator, or a group of operators on the shop floor, phone, e-mail or fax through the daily order to the supplier (and for the materials to be delivered directly to production rather than to the store). If each group of operators around a process were working as a team, why would a large central human resources department be needed? Certainly, the operating team itself would not need a supervisor. Maybe a team leader would be necessary to hurry management along and to ensure that management planning was sensible. The aim here is not for the front-line operators to be working harder but for them to take control and accept responsibility for their operation. It does not mean fewer people turning out more, but it does mean the elimination of several levels of management and it does get rid of the matrix of responsibility for human resource and other 'service' or staff departments as shown on the old-fashioned organization charts. With fewer levels of management, communication becomes less confused, and responsibilities (and areas of mistakes) become much more obvious.

For TQM to work, a company has to go through a total revolution. Many people, especially middle managers, have to be won over. Workers, too, have to want to accept responsibility. TQM will mean a change of culture.

The cost of TQM can be measured in money terms. The emphasis will be on prevention rather than detection, thus the cost of supervision and inspection will go down. Prevention cost will go up because of the training and action-orientated efforts. But the real benefits will be gained by a significant reduction in failures – both internal

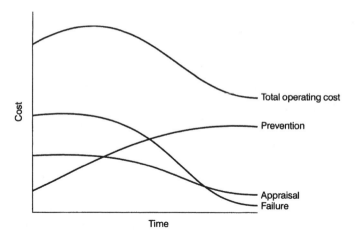

Figure 8.6   Cost of quality

(e.g. scrap, rework, downtime) and external (handling of complaints, servicing costs, loss of goodwill). The total operating cost will reduce over time (say three to five years), as shown in Figure 8.6.

ISO and TQM

In a discussion on the subject of quality it would be wrong to ignore the effect that the International Organization for Standardization (ISO) has had on quality. The ISO 9000 series (accrediting criteria revised 2000/2001) and the 14 000 environmental series have been developed over a long period of time. The origins can be traced back to military requirements, for example NATO in the late 1940s developed specifications and methods of production to ensure compatibility between NATO forces in weapons and weapons systems.

ISO certification means that an organization constantly meets rigorous standards, which are well documented, of management of quality of product and services. To retain certification the organization is audited annually by an outside accredited body. ISO on the letter-head of an organization demonstrates to the organization, to its customers and to other interested bodies that it has an effective quality assurance system in place.

Total quality management means more than just the basics as outlined in BS 5750 or ISO 9000, indeed BS 5750/ISO 9000 could be seen as running contrary to the philosophy of TQM. As Sayle (1991) pointed out:

> *It is important to recognize the limitations of the ISO 9000 series. They are not and do not profess to be a panacea for the business's ills. Many companies have misguidedly expected that by adopting an ISO 9000 standard that they will achieve success comparable to that of the overpublicized Japanese. One must not forget that the ISO 9000 standards did not exist when the Japanese quality performance improved so spectacularly: many Japanese firms did not need such written standards, and probably still don't.*

Primarily, ISO certification gives the customer confidence that the product or service being provided will meet certain specified standards of performance and that the product or service will always be consistent with those standards. Indeed, some customers will insist that suppliers are ISO accredited.

There are also internal benefits for organizations that seek ISO 9000 accreditation. First, by adopting ISO the methodology of the system will show an organization how to go about establishing and documenting a quality improvement system. To achieve accreditation, an organization has to prove that every step of the process is documented and that the specifications and check procedures shown in the documentation are always complied with. The recording and documenting of each step is a long and tedious job. Perhaps the most difficult stage is agreeing on what exactly the standard procedure is.

If an organization does not have a standard way of doing things, trying to document will prove difficult and many interesting facts will emerge. The act of recording exactly what is happening and then determining what the one set method should be is in itself a useful exercise. Non-value adding activities should be unearthed and, hopefully, overall a more efficient method will emerge and be adopted as standard procedure. Determining a standard does not imply that the most efficient method is being used. The standard adopted only means that there is now a standard method (not necessarily the most efficient), that the method is recorded and that the recorded method will be used every time. The standard method not only includes the steps taken in the process but will list the checks and tests that will be carried out as part of the process. This will often require the design of new and increased check procedures and a method of recording that each check or test has been done.

From this it can be seen that the adoption of ISO rather than stream-lining an organization might actually serve to increase the need for audits and supervision. ISO to this extent can therefore be seen to be contrary to the philosophy of TQM. With TQM staff members are encouraged to do their own checking and to be responsible for getting it right first time and supervision then becomes almost superfluous. With ISO the standard method will likely be set by management edict and, once set in place, the bureaucracy of agreeing and recording improvements may stultify creative improvements.

ISO tends to be driven from the top down and relies on documentation, checks and tests to achieve a standard, somewhat bland, level of quality assurance. TQM on the other hand, once established, relies on bottom-up initiatives to keep the impetus of continual improvement. However, as the Deming method of TQM does advocate a stable system from which to advance improvements, the adoption of the ISO approach will mean that there will be a standard and stable system. To this extent, ISO will prove a useful base for any organization from which to launch TQM.

As shown in Figure 8.7, ISO can be depicted as the wedge that prevents quality slipping backwards, but the danger is that it can also be the wedge that impedes progress.

Notwithstanding the benefits of obtaining a standard stable system through ISO procedures, it must be queried why a true quality company would need ISO certification. If the customer or potential customer is *not* insisting in ISO accreditation, then the time and effort (and the effort expended will be a non-recoverable cost) makes the value of ISO to an organization highly questionable.

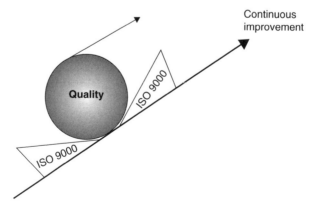

Figure 8.7   The wedge

TQM to **FIT SIGMA**

Today, depending on whom you listen to, Six Sigma is either a revolution slashing trillions of dollars from corporate inefficiency, or its the most maddening management fad yet devised to keep front-line workers too busy collecting data to do their jobs.

USA Today, *21 July 1998*

During the period since the above statement was made, the 'Six Sigma revolution' has created a huge impact in the field of operational excellence, yet conflicting views are still prevalent.

On a positive note, the success of Six Sigma in General Electric under the leadership of Jack Welch is undisputed. In the GE company report of 2000 their CEO was unstinting in his praise: 'Six Sigma has galvanized our company with an intensity the likes of which I have never seen in my 40 years of GE.' Even financial analysts and investment bankers compliment the success of Six Sigma in GE. An analyst at Morgan Stanley, Dean Witter, has estimated that GE's gross annual benefit from Six Sigma could reach 5% of sales and that share value might increase by between 10 and 15%.

However, the situation is more complex than such predictions would suggest. In spite of the demonstrated benefits of many improvement techniques such as total quality management, business process re-engineering and Six Sigma, most attempts by companies to use them have ended in failure (Easton and Jarrell, 1998). Sterman *et al.* (1999) conclude that companies have found it extremely difficult to sustain even initially successful process improvement initiatives. Yet more puzzling is the fact that successful improvement programmes have sometimes led to declining business performance, causing lay-offs and low employee morale.

To counter heavyweight enthusiasts like Jack Welch (GE) and Larry Bossidy (Allied Signal), there are sharp critics of Six Sigma. Six Sigma may sound new, but critics say that it is really statistical process control (SPC) in new clothing. Others dismiss it as another transitory management fad that will soon pass.

It is evident that, like any good product, Six Sigma should also have a finite life cycle. In addition, business managers can be forgiven if they are often confused by the grey areas of distinction between quality initiatives such as TQM, Six Sigma and Lean Sigma.

Against this background we examine the evolution of total quality improvement processes (or in a broader sense, operational excellence) from ad hoc improvement to TQM to Six Sigma to Lean Sigma.

Building on the success factors of these processes the key question is: how do we sustain the results? We call this sustainable process FIT SIGMA® (Basu and Wright, 2003; FIT SIGMA is a registered trademark of Performance Excellence Ltd).

What is FIT SIGMA? First, take the key ingredient of quality, then add accuracy of the order of 3.4 defects in 1 000 000 and implement this across your business with an intensive education and training programme. This is Six Sigma.

In a 'lean enterprise' the focus is on delivered value from a customer's perspective and strives to eliminate all non-value added activities ('waste') for each product or service along a value chain. The integration of these two, complementary, approaches – Six Sigma and Lean Enterprise – is known as Lean Sigma. FIT SIGMA is the next wave. If Lean Sigma provides agility and efficiency, then FIT SIGMA allows a sustainable fitness. In addition the control of variation from the mean (small sigma, σ) in the Six Sigma process is transformed to company-wide integration (capital sigma, Σ) in the FIT SIGMA process. Furthermore, the philosophy of FIT SIGMA should ensure that it is 'fit' for the organization.

The road map to FIT SIGMA (see Figure 8.8) contains three waves and the entry point of each organization will vary.

First wave: As Is to TQM   The organized division of labour to improve operations may have started with Adam Smith in 1776. However, it is the industrial engineering approach, which has roots in F.W. Taylor's 'Scientific Management', that is credited with the formal initiation of the first wave of operational excellence. The industrial engineering approach was sharpened by operational research and complemented by operational tools such as management accounting.

During the years following the Second World War, the 'first wave' saw through the rapid growth of industrialization, but in the short term the focus seemed to be upon both increasing volume and reducing the cost. In general, improvement processes were 'ad-hoc', factory-centric and conducive to 'pockets of excellence'. In the 1970s the holistic approach of total quality management (TQM) initiated the second wave of operational excellence. The traditional factors of quality control and quality assurance were aimed at achieving an agreed and consistent level of quality. TQM goes far beyond mere conformity to standard. TQM is a company-wide programme and requires a culture in which every member of the organization believes that not a single day should go by within the organization without in some way improving the quality of its goods and services.

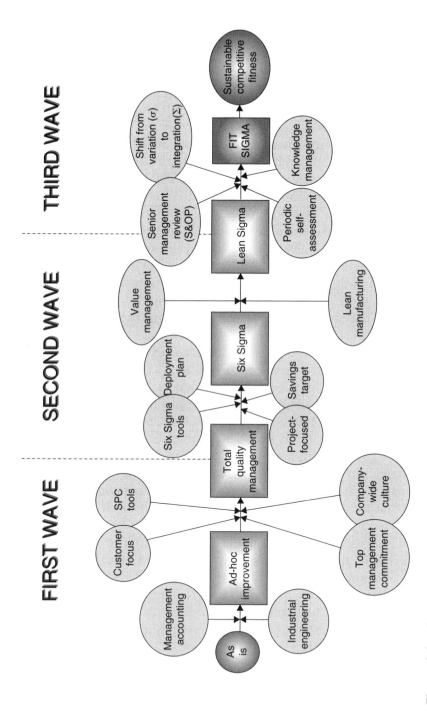

Figure 8.8 Operational excellence road map

Second wave: TQM to Lean Sigma Learning the basics from W.E. Demming and J.M. Juran, Japanese companies extended and customized the integrated approach and culture of TQM (Basu and Wright, 1997). The economic growth and manufacturing dominance of Japanese industries in the 1980s can be attributed to the successful application of TQM in Japan. The three fundamental tenets of Juran's TQM process are, first, upper management leadership of quality, secondly, continuous education on quality for all, finally, an annual plan for quality improvement and cost reduction. These foundations are still valid today and embedded within the Six Sigma/Lean Sigma philosophies. Phil Crosby and other leading TQM consultants incorporated customer focus and Demming's SPC tools and propagated the TQM philosophy to the USA and the industrialized world in the 1980s. The Malcolm Baldridge Quality Award in the USA, Deming Award in Japan and in Europe the EFQM (European Foundation of Quality Management) award and ISO kept TQM awareness high. Some of its definitions, such as 'fitness for the purpose', 'customer is king', 'getting it right first time', 'work smarter not harder' became so overused that they are almost clichés and thus the impact of TQM began to diminish.

To overcome perceived gaps in operation excellence high profile consultants marketed a series of three-letter acronyms (TLAs) such as JIT, TPM, BPR, SCM, CRM, MRP and SAP. Some are still alive and kicking. None the less, TQM the buzzword of the 1980s was viewed by many in the late 1990s, especially in the US quality field, as an embarrassing failure – a concept that promised more than it could deliver. Philip Crossby pinpointed the cause of TQM 'failures' as 'TQM never did anything to define quality, which is conformance to standards'. Perhaps the pendulum swung too far towards the concept of quality as 'goodness' and employee culture. It was against this background that Six Sigma emerged.

Six Sigma began in 1985 when Bill Smith, an engineer at Motorola, came up with the idea of inserting hard-nosed statistics into the blurred philosophy of quality. In statistical terms, sigma (σ) is a measure of variation from the mean and the greater the value of sigma the fewer the defects. Most companies produce results at around four sigma, which is more than 6000 defects per million opportunities. By contrast, at the six sigma level, there are only 3.4 defects per million.

Although 'invented' at Motorola, Six Sigma was experimented with by Allied Signal and perfected at General Electric. Following the recent merger of these two companies, GE is truly the home of

Six Sigma. During the past five years, Six Sigma has taken the quantum leap into operational excellence in many blue chip companies, including DuPont, Ratheon, Ivensys, Marconi, Bombardier Shorts, Seagate Technology and GlaxoSmithKline.

The key success factors differentiating Six Sigma from TQM are:

- The emphasis on statistical science and measurement
- A rigorous and structured training deployment plan (Champion, Master Black Belt, Black Belt and Green Belt)
- A project-focused approach with a single set of problem-solving techniques such as DMAIC (Define, Measure, Analyse, Improve, Control)
- Reinforcement of Juran tenets (top management leadership, continuous education and annual savings plan).

Following their recent application in companies like GlaxoSmithKline, Ratheon, Ivensys and Seagate, the Six Sigma programmes have moved to the Lean Sigma philosophy, which integrates Six Sigma with the complementary approach of Lean Enterprise. Lean focuses the company's resources and its suppliers on the delivered value from the customer's perspective. Lean Enterprise begins with lean production, the concept of waste reduction developed from industrial engineering principles and refined by Toyota. It expands upon these principles to engage all support partners and customers along the value stream. Common goals to both Six Sigma and Lean Sigma are the elimination waste and improvement of process capability. The industrial engineering tools of Lean Enterprise complement the science of the statistical processes of Six Sigma. It is the integration on these tools in Lean Sigma that provides an operational excellence methodology that addresses the entire value delivery system.

Third wave: Lean Sigma to FIT SIGMA   Lean Sigma is the beginning of the 'third wave'. The predictable Six Sigma precisions combined with the speed and agility of lean processes produces definitive solutions for better, faster and cheaper business processes. Through the systematic identification and eradication of non-value added activities, optimum value flow is achieved, cycle times are reduced and defects eliminated.

The dramatic bottom-line results and extensive training deployment of Six Sigma and Lean Sigma must be sustained, with additional features for securing the longer-term competitive advantage of a company. The process to do just that is FIT SIGMA. The best practices of

Six Sigma, Lean Sigma and other proven operational excellence best practices underpin the basic building blocks of FIT SIGMA.

Four additional features are embedded in the Lean Sigma philosophy to create FIT SIGMA. These are:

- A formal senior management review process at regular intervals, similar to the sales and operational planning process
- Periodic self-assessment with a structured checklist which is formalized by a certification or award, similar to EFQM award but with more emphasis on self-assessment
- A continuous learning and knowledge management programme
- The extension of the programme across the whole business with the shifting of the theme of variation control (σ) of Six Sigma to the integration of a seamless organization (Σ).

Foundation 16: Financial management

Historically the relationship between financial management and operations management has been like oil and water, 'them and us'. The 'quality movement' of the 1980s appeared to have encouraged some operations managers to move away from involvement in costs and measurements. Some operations managers, both in the manufacturing and service sectors, took the stance that cost and measurement were 'internally focused', the concern of the 'bean counters', whereas the quality movement was externally customer-focused. But in fact this was not what the quality gurus such as Deming, Juran, Crosby, Feigenbaum and Peters were saying. Their message was that measurement is important in achieving quality. For a start, without a scorecard of some type it is not possible to determine whether improvements are being made.

Traditionally accountants have seen themselves as the major channel through which quantitative information flows to management. Accountants work on historical data of what has happened, and their reports cover arbitrarily set periods of time, with little allowance that business activities do not stop on 30 June or 31 December (or whatever other date has been designated as the time to take a snap-shot of the financial position of the business). From a conventional point of view, and from the point of view of stakeholders, such as shareholders and bank managers, there has to be a way of measuring the performance of an organization and currently there is no better method than accounting reports. It follows therefore, that for accountants to do their job of reporting to meet the conventional requirements, information will be required from the operational arm of the business. This cannot be disputed. Therefore if information is being provided, then it is useful to try to use that information to improve the productivity of the organization.

In response to pressures from stakeholders there is a risk of overemphasis on short-term financial performance. Consequently this myopic approach results in overinvestment in short-term fixes and underinvestment in longer-term development plans. Furthermore, the emphasis for short-term results can cause organizations to reduce costs with across-the-board targets (say, costs have to be reduced by 10%) without any effective analysis of how, or alternative value-creating activities.

It makes sense that financial factors are integrated with operations and that operations managers be allowed to focus on the efficiency of the operating system. Improved quality, delivery and flexibility should eventually improve the profit margin, but additional operations costs go straight to the accountants' 'bottom line' and as such invite attention. There are indications that there has been a gradual shift in operations towards financial management, probably influenced by the following factors:

- The growth of the 'share owning' population has generated a new breed of consumers who are interested in the financial performance of a company.
- This has required financial management to become conscious of external requirements.
- With the increase in external sourcing and third party operations, the cost base and its control in manufacturing and services have been sharpened.
- The economic recession in the late 1990s forced many manufacturing and service industries to adopt restructuring and cost-reduction initiatives.
- Finally, in the well-publicized Balanced Scorecard the role of financial perspective, as one of the four perspectives, has been accepted by operations managers since 'financial measures are valuable in summarizing the readily measurable economic consequences of actions already taken' (Kaplan and Norton, 1996a).

It is therefore important for any company to focus on the key issues of financial management in order to enhance competitiveness through operations cost advantages. These issues include achieving financial objectives for the business, understanding strategic cost factors and cost-effectiveness.

Achieving financial objectives

We do not intend to delve into the sophisticated world of financial management involving the method of financing, tax implications, currency movements, etc. However, as indicated earlier, it is important that key financial parameters and objectives of the business should be understood and incorporated in manufacturing objectives. Key financial concepts are:

- Sales value: The total turnover of the business in money terms
- Net profit: The money made by the business after charging out all costs. This can be expressed before tax or after tax
- Capital employed: Total investment tied up in the business comprising shareholders' funds. With the double entry system of accounting, shareholders' funds, or capital, will always equal the total of all the assets less all the liabilities
- Working capital: Working capital refers to the funds available, and is the difference between current assets (debtors, inventory, bank balances and cash) less current liabilities (creditors, short-term loans and the current portion of long-term loans)
- Cash flow: Cash flow statements show where and how the working capital has increased or decreased.

There are only four basic sources for an increase in working capital and likewise only four basic uses to explain a decrease in working capital, namely:

- Increase in working capital
  - Profits from operations
  - Sale of fixed assets
  - Long-term borrowing
  - Increase of shareholders' funds through the issue of shares.
- Decrease in working capital
  - Losses from operations
  - Purchase of fixed assets

- Repayment of long-term loans
- Distribution of profits to shareholders (dividends).

The key financial indices influencing the financial objectives of a business are:

$$\text{Trading margin} = \frac{\text{Net profit}}{\text{Sales value}} = 100$$

$$\text{Asset turn} = \frac{\text{Sales value}}{\text{Capital employed}}$$

$$\text{Return on investment (ROI)} = \frac{\text{Net profit}}{\text{Capital employed}} \times 100$$

Balance sheet ratios

Balance sheet ratios are the cornerstones of financial accounting and are concerned with the longer-term and external requirements of creditors, shareholders, prospective investors, inspectors of taxes and persons outside the management as well as with the internal requirements of the management.

Operating ratios

The operating ratios are in the domain of management accounting for tactical management and these ratios can be classed as follows:

1 *Sales to capital.* This ratio measures the efficiency of the use of capital. The higher sales per pound of capital the more effectively is capital being employed.
2 *Cost of sales to stock and sales to debtors.* These ratios help to assess whether stock is too high or debtors are taking too long to pay.
3 *Return on investment and return on sales.* These ratios are widely used as measures of efficiency and performance evaluation. In addition, wide use is made of return on investment to assess the validity of new projects. Most companies set a minimum return on investment rate that must be exceeded before a new project can be proceeded with.

In spite of some recent criticisms, ROI has continued to be the most important single index of the financial objective of a manufacturing business. Value-based management methodology is favoured by many companies today. One such performance measure is EVA (economic value added), which is a trademark of Stern Stewart & Co. EVA accounts for the cost of doing business by deriving a capital charge. A positive EVA rating indicates that the company has created value. Often firms become so focused on earnings that they lose sight of the cost of generating those earnings in the first place. EVA has become a popular tool to which executives' bonuses may be linked.

$$EVA = (ROI - WACC) \times TCE$$

where WACC is the weighted average cost of capital and TCE is the total capital employed.

Hamel and Prahalad (1994) attacked managers obsessed with denominators (capital employed). The right approach of manufacturing is, as shown in Figure 8.5, to identify high leverage points of both increasing profits and reducing capital employed. Low-cost manufacturing is a desirable manufacturing objective as long as the investment decisions are geared to longer-term requirements and the measures do not affect the specified standards of quality, delivery and safety. The measures indicated in the ROI improvement tree (Figure 8.9) have been covered in other sections of the book, but it is useful

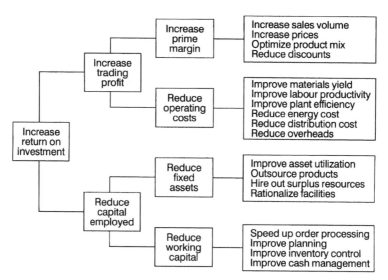

Figure 8.9 Company profitability: tree of improvement

to focus on a total picture of cost advantages so that the interrelationship between different elements and their relative weight can be visualized. In special cases, simulation of cost modelling is justifiable.

The financial objectives of a business, especially in the manufacturing sector, include increasing asset turn, improving profit margin and improving ROI, but these three indices may appear to be conflicting, as shown in Figure 8.10. For a given ROI, profit margin goes down with increased asset turn and vice versa. However, when analysed more closely by managing the improvement of both numerator and denominator (i.e. operations improvement and asset management), the company performance can move to a higher ROI curve and retain improvements in both profit margin and asset turn.

Understanding strategic cost factors

There are a number of strategic factors affecting the financial management that drive the business strategy of an organization in both manufacturing and service sectors. We shall review three areas:

- Revenue growth by volume and product mix
- Asset utilization and investment
- Cost-effectiveness.

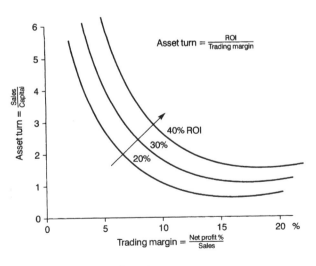

Figure 8.10 Capital assets productivity

Volume and mix

Costs are determined by volume (including variety and variations) and investment policy. These are strategic in a sense that they relate to the way the company may decide to react to the competition and to developments in the market place.

Volume, in general, is good for business as the higher volume reduces the overhead or fixed cost per unit of production. However, the advantage of 'economies of scale' should not be pushed beyond the natural capacity of a site as the unit cost could go up due to constraints in site capacity and services. As variety increases, unit cost of manufacturing may also increase due to technology cost, lower utilization of plant and increased overhead/infrastructure. As discussed in Chapter 7, with flexible manufacturing variety can be essential to be competitive in segmented markets. Manufacturing should in these cases accommodate variety by incorporating higher flexibility of plant and operations. Variation is another determinant of product cost. If there are unstable variations in sales demand, supplier lead time and plant performance, then the planning effectiveness will go down and buffers in stock, capacity and resources will be necessary.

Asset utilization

The criteria of investment decision have been covered in Chapter 7. It is important that formal investment appraisal procedures and investment policies are in place. However, the rate of discounted cash flow (DCF) yield should vary according to the type of investment, as indicated in Table 8.1.

Table 8.1 Discounted cash flow yields

Cost reduction projects	7.25%
Capacity expansion	
Replacement	20–25%
Strategic	15–20%
New technology	10–15%
Environment and safety	0–15%

Evaluation should include all tangible benefits and intangible benefits. The above table is indicative only to demonstrate the relative importance of investments. The actual limit of DCF yield is set by each company depending on financing charges, depreciation rate for a capital asset and the life cycle of the product.

Cost-effectiveness

Cost cutting or cost reduction exercises, if they are panic-driven, or 'chairman's 5 per cent reduction target' will only give short-term results and will cause imbalances and disruptions in operations. Other legitimate concerns will be the negative effect on quality, innovation and customer service. And although direct factory labour might account for only 5–15% of the total ex-works cost (see Figure 8.11), the overwhelming emphasis usually is given to the reduction of labour cost. New and Mayer (1986) claimed that, whole departments are maintained to control the direct labour content of unit cost. Yet there are many plants that spend twice as much on purchased materials as on direct labour that do not even attempt to measure purchasing performance realistically.

The real business focus should be to survive and to be capable of competing in the future. Although strategy and innovation are important, the hard fact is that unless there is a positive operational cash flow the business cannot plan for the future. Therefore it is vital to have cost improvement even in a profitable company, but the approach must be one of cost-effectiveness, not cost cutting.

The key principles of a cost-effectiveness programme are:

- Understand the strategic drivers of cost, i.e. volume/capacity, variety and variation and their impact in the market place and competition.
- Evaluate the effect of any company-saving measures on quality, safety and customer service.
- Identify the leverage of cost structure and set priorities of effort and 'go for gold'. But as a rough guide, the amount of effort allocated to operations cost reduction should be proportional to the rest of the costs of the company.

The programme should be company-wide.

The principles of value engineering should be applied in identifying and emphasizing operations where no value is added.

Cost-effectiveness is a continuous process for all businesses, but some businesses may require a quick and significant change in their cost structure. Study teams should then be formed to carry out

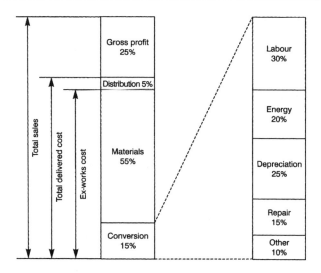

Figure 8.11   An example of a cost structure

ad hoc exercises, such as big scale value analysis, restructuring or site rationalization (including plant closure).

Value analysis is a technique used to examine each element of a process so as to find a cheaper material or better method with the aim of maintaining or enhancing the value of the product in performance terms and at the same time reducing the cost. Big scale value analysis (BSVA) uses value analysis technique but in addition examines the total delivered cost (see Figure 8.11) of the business and has a short time scale (usually less than one year), with emphasis on company-wide implementation. The cost model in Figure 8.11 is a typical example of an FMCG business and obviously the proportion of cost elements would vary depending on the product or service.

Accounting systems

It is vital that the company has a reliable accounting system in place to provide fast and accurate cost information. The minimum requirements should be standard costing and budgetary control.

As discussed in Chapter 5, some companies are moving towards activity-based costing (ABC), particularly for supply chain management. The accurate cost information provided by ABC can give a company a competitive advantage. However, the experience of Western companies, according to De Meyer and Ferdows (1990), suggests that the implementation of activity-based costing has not been successful, perhaps due to the historical inertia of standard costing. Any half-baked implementation could be more harmful than useful.

Foundation 17: Information and communication technology

Thirty-six years ago computer scientists at UCLA linked two bulky computers together using a 15 foot grey cable, testing a new way of exchanging data over a network, ultimately this experiment resulted in the Internet.

The focus of information technology within organizations has shifted dramatically over the past four decades; from improving the efficiency of business processes within organizations to improving the effectiveness of the value chain reaching suppliers, customers and consumers. During the 1960s and 1970s, businesses focused on the use of mainframes to process large quantities of data. In the 1980s and early 1990s organizations focused on using personal desktop computers to improve personal efficiencies. The past decade, with the rapid expansion of the Internet, has seen the use of technologies to create electronic communication networks within and between organizations and individuals. The implementation of Enterprise resource planning (ERP), websites, e-commerce and e-mail systems during the past ten years allowed individuals within organizations to communicate together and share data. Information technology (IT) has now grown into information and communication technology (ICT). In this ICT foundation stone we consider two broad areas:

- Information technology and systems
- e-Business.

Information technology and systems

Information technology (IT) is rapidly changing and becoming more powerful. It will be a continuing source of competitive advantage for manufacturers if used correctly. In 2005 the personal computer (PC) on the desk of an average operations manager has more computing power than was available to the average £100 million a year company 10 years ago. This IT revolution is available to everyone and how a company puts it to work will determine to a great extent its competitiveness in the global market. The advent of wireless networks enables communication to anywhere in the world. To take advantage of this mobility in communication requires an understanding that information technology has become a key part of business processes and organization structures are no longer dependent on the nineteenth-century military chain of command for communication. The chief executive is only a fingertip away from staff anywhere in the world.

Information technology has moved from being an important enabler of communication to becoming an integral part of the strategic planning process. On the other hand, Novelli (2004), writing in *Modern Healthcare*, warns that technology is a means not an end in itself.

Using health care in the United States as an example, he says that information technology is not adequately or routinely applied to the practice of medicine: 'more than 90% of the 30 billion annual medical transactions are conducted by phone, fax or stamped mail … Only one third of hospitals have computerized order-entry systems and fewer than 55 require their use. Only 5% of clinicians and 195 of provider organizations use electronic medical records … fewer than 5% of physicians write electronic prescriptions.'

Novelli believes that:

e-prescribing alone could mean:

- *A reduction of administrative costs for an estimated total savings of $13 billion annually*
- *A reduction (of $10 per prescription) for mail order drugs, worth about $11 billion annually*
- *Savings on formulary or generic drugs, estimated to be as much as $36 billion annually*
- *Savings because of reduction in prescription errors, a possible $36 billion*
- *And untold billions of dollars saved in the decline of prescription fraud and abuse.*

He also points out that doctors and nurses could make better use of IT to access information such as lab tests, X-rays and to generally improve communication between themselves and with patients.

Novelli adds that technology such as the telephone, fax or e-mail can hardly be thought of as 'technologies' any longer; 'they are home appliances. Yet many physicians are reluctant to communicate this way.'

Many of the technologies we need already exist. The challenge is to apply them. Despite all the promises the rapid growth of information technology has also created problems and challenges. Many senior managers of companies lack any detailed understanding of the complexity of technology. They either follow the fashion (e.g. 'no one was fired for choosing IBM') or they are discouraged by the cost of technology, or from a lack of evidence of savings in a new field. When executives read about all the clever things seemingly low cost computer technology can do they feel frustrated when the systems experts say, 'It will take three years to develop the software.' Most senior managers also feel lost in a blizzard of buzzwords.

Another issue is software application strategy and networking. Successful companies are using information technology and compatible software on the factory floor (CAD/CAM and process computing), in administration, planning and in the office (word processing, spreadsheets and PC workstations). Sophisticated global information networks (e-mail, the Internet, high speed data and video links) have simplified international operations. Electronic data interchange (EDI) technology has made possible extended supply chains between companies; for example, cash register transactions can trigger automatic reordering. On the down side there are also many failures when a company's software does not meet its requirements or wasted effort when IT managers try to re-invent the wheel by attempting to build software in-house when simple tested 'off-the-shelf' software would suffice.

When an organization looks for an IT solution to a problem without re-engineering the process, refining the existing database or training the end users, the application is doomed to fail. Real disasters can be very expensive. John Kost of Gartner believes that current procurement practices will doom every major government jurisdiction to at least one IT disaster in the next two years; that widespread outsourcing of public sector IT is only a few years away, unless human resources (HR) practices undergo change; and, that funding projects by 'silo' will effectively disrupt attempts to seamlessly integrate data and communications systems.

He gives the example where in Michigan during 2003 a new state welfare system collapsed under the weight of an expanding mandate. Under federal regulations, the new IT system had to be previously implemented in another state. The system transferred was from

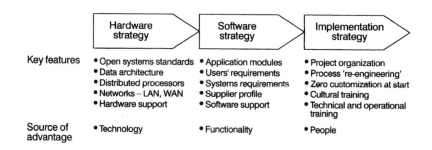

Figure 8.12   Information technology strategy

Connecticut and had close on 280 screens. 'That was a lot, even for a welfare system,' Kost said, 'But because everyone wanted this thing to be so feature rich and do so much more, by the time they finished the requirements design phase it was at 1300 screens. It was patently absurd, completely unmanageable and undoable. Nobody was empowered to say no, and the project ultimately was cancelled after 10 years and US$160 million' (Bray, 2003).

Figure 8.12 shows a framework of IT strategy comprising three levels: hardware strategy, software strategy and implementation strategy.

It is a common belief that many IT projects are not successful. However, as Zeichick, Scannell, Moore and Krill (2004) say, failure is relative. They quote Shepherd of MAMR Research who says that there are a myriad of ways that projects can experience problems, but that actual implementation usually succeeds. 'If a project is three months late or 5% over budget, that may be a disappointment, but it's not a failure. That's the case with most IT projects'; and 'Failure would be a situation where orders stopped being taken, or the books couldn't be closed off, or the project itself was simply abandoned'. As Zeichick *et al.* say, 'That's rare.'

Zeichick *et al.* cite the Standish Group, who surveyed 13 522 projects in 2003 which showed that only 34% of projects are unqualified successes, and that 15% of projects are 'out and out failures' (projects abandoned before completion). The balance (51%) had cost overruns, time overruns and 'projects not delivered with the right functionality'. Zeichick *et al.* quote Gaucherin of Sapient who claims that, in order of importance, the level of success can be tied to the degree of user involvement, executive management support, and the experience of the project manager. Gaucherin says, 'the larger the project, the greater chance of failure, and therefore the more effort you want to put behind managing risk.' Gaucherin recommends that projects be 'put on a value chart with plot points becoming project milestones plotted over a time line'. Obviously, when variances appear they would be investigated and action would be taken.

Open systems

Dramatic developments towards 'open systems' standards started in 1987 when AT&T in partnership with Sun Microsystems introduced the Unix Open Look operating system. This system was used by Wang, Oracle, Olivetti and Lucky Gold Star. Seven big computer companies led by IBM, Hewlett-Packard and DEC formed the Open Software Foundation (OSF) and introduced in 1990 their own competing standard operating system using IBM operating systems as core technology.

With the rapid development of application tools a proven hardware policy has been what is known as client-server computing. All 'servers' are open system large or mini computers (e.g. IBM-AIX) and 'client' computers are largely PCs.

The benefits of standards include the creation of local area networks (LANs) and wide area networks (WANs). A LAN can cover a large industrial complex while a WAN can offer inter-site communications on a national or international basis. In the early 1990s the companies were gradually migrating from previously popular network standards (such as PC LAN, Novell, Internet) to open systems network such as NFS-based systems. However by the mid-1990s Novell started to regain the market dominance.

The hardware strategy should also include the capability of local hardware support both by suppliers and the company's own staff. The support capability may influence the selection of hardware, whether IBM, HP, DEC or SUN or other. A sensible strategy is to go with the market leaders who are setting the de facto standards. Some smaller companies use only one brand of provider (i.e. homogenous), but larger companies inevitably become heterogeneous because of mergers and acquisitions.

Companies' desires to be global, to operate 24 hours a day seven days a week, and on the Internet, has resulted in heterogeneity. Zeichick *et al.* (2004) quote Goethal of IBM as saying that most companies today usually have a mix of server types:

If you look at what's typically on a desktop, for instance, that's going to be Intel. Depending on the departmental environments, they could have Intel-based servers or Unix servers, and when you get into the datacenter, you're going to find mainframes as well as Intel and Unix systems.

Both heterogeneity and homogeneity have their pros and cons. Open solutions give users a variety of technology choices, theoretically driving down costs. IT managers, however, will have the task of trying to integrate with a myriad of standards and procedures.

In 27 years of experience, Joe Poole, an IT official at Boscov's Department Stores and manager of technical support, has watched his organization grow and diversify from a mainframe-only environment to a mix of a mainframe running VM and Linux plus RISC Unix boxes and Intel systems. He found that some applications such as the company's merchandise conveyor system and its graphical applications simply ran much better on the newer platforms. Poole believes that, these days, no one can continue to be a single-platform operation.

Zeichick et al., 2004

IT software strategy

At the early stage of information technology, applications software was limited to financial and commercial areas. Now a company is faced with a bewildering array of software ranging from design/ process engineering, to manufacturing, to supply chain, to administration. Versions of specific software and systems technology will continue to change. Therefore it is vital that any organization formulates a software strategy by careful planning.

The first step is to identify the areas of application depending on the activities, size and priorities of the company. Figure 8.13 shows a framework of application software in five key areas, namely financial administration, supply chain management, administration, and 'client' workstation. The traditional computing modules of accounts and payroll are in financial management. The biggest area of application is in supply chain management and customer relationship management, starting from sales forecasting to customer service and electronic data interchange (EDI). At the factory shop floor there are two application areas, namely factory administration – comprising management information systems – and factory automation – comprising design, process engineering and automation of equipment. The software for client workstations is PC-based, covering word processing, desk top publishing, spreadsheets, computer graphics (e.g. Powerpoint), multi-tasking e-mail and conferencing. During

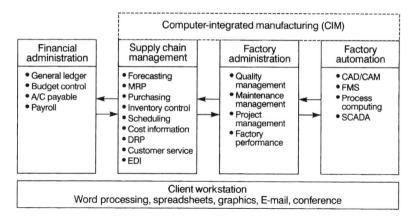

Figure 8.13 Application software modules

the late 1980s many manufacturing companies searched for one turnkey package and computer-integrated manufacturing (CIM) after initial limited success came of age. If a company follows an 'open systems' policy for hardware and relational database then different proprietary software packages stand a better chance of being interfaced and database information can be shared in a client–server environment. Probably their most significant advantage is in the enterprise-wide view of a business that ERP (enterprise resource planning) systems allow. ERP systems (such as SAP) are no longer costly or difficult to implement and allow integration with the systems of other organizations within a value chain.

The software policy should include standard packages for the company in specific areas of application. The selection of software should conform to the key criteria of user requirements, systems requirements, supplier profile and software support. The earlier examples of applications software were relatively inflexible and the approach was 'systematize the customer' rather than 'customize the system'. Many disillusioned customers attempted to build their own software and burnt their fingers in the process. In the present climate the software tools have become flexible, the IT technology continues to advance rapidly and competitive expert support is provided by specialist software houses. It is prudent to buy appropriate software rather than to develop one's own (see Figure 8.14). The software should conform to open systems requirements and the supplier should be both reputable and locally available for support. The company should also build up its own IT support staff, especially a 'user support' (help desk) service.

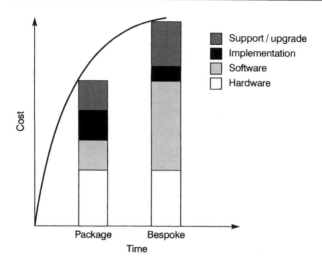

Figure 8.14   Software development strategy

Implementation strategy

The success of an IT strategy depends as much on the selection of appropriate hardware and software as on their implementation.

Similar to a company-wide programme such as TQM, the implementation must have top management commitment. This should be reflected in setting up a project team comprising members from users (marketing, logistics, manufacturing, accounts) and business systems. The project manager is usually chosen from the main user group. For example, if the application software is for supply chain management then the project manager should ideally have a logistics background.

The project team should receive both technical training and operational training (functionality of the software). The project manager then prepares a clearly stated action plan with target dates and resources for key activities. The plan must include review points and steering by the members of the board.

It is essential that the existing procedures and processes are thoroughly and systematically reviewed. There are various tools for analysing the flow and requirements of the existing systems. Statistical process control (SPC) techniques are widely used. Nowadays some companies are using computer-aided software engineering (CASE) tools to analyse the structure, database and flows of the existing process and compare them with the proposed software for implementation. With the success of the business process re-engineering (BPR) approach of Hammer and Champy (1993), some companies are using an IT application as a catalyst and applying the principles of BPR to re-engineer the total business processes of the company. The approach should depend on the depth and breadth of the application systems, but there is no doubt that the existing systems must be reviewed and refined when implementing a new system.

One important rule is that the user should not try to customize the system at the outset. Often after acquiring experience on the new system the user may find that the need and nature of customization could be different. However, it is necessary that a 'prototype' is tested for a new system using the company's own data.

After the training of the project team the training programmes should be extended to all potential users of the system. The training features should contain both cultural education to establish acceptance by everyone concerned and operational training to understand the functionality and operations of the new system. Training documents are designed specifically for the users' needs. The next stage is the data input and 'dry run' of the new system in parallel with the existing system before the system goes live. There are benefits from forming users' group for exchanging experience with users drawn from within and from outside the company.

e-Business

It would appear, from today's press, that all business problems can be solved by e-business whilst, at the same time, all business failures and any economic downturn can be blamed on e-business as well! Given the volume of news items, it may appear that defining 'e-business' is to state the obvious. Or is it?

It is apparent that very often all e-business is perceived as a collection of pure-play dot.com organizations. Such an 'umbrella view' means the distinctions between e-commerce, e-marketplace and e-business are poorly interpreted. For example, the most popular perception of e-business is personal online shopping – convenient for 'workaholics' with no time to get to the shops. Let us clarify some items:

- e-Commerce is transactional electronic exchange for the buying and selling of goods and services.

- The 'e-marketplace' is the online intermediary for electronic transactions between buyers, sellers and brokers. This is also referred to as the digital market place, portals, or hubs.

e-Business is the exchange of information across electronic networks at any stage in the value chain, whether paid or unpaid. It can take place:

- *within an organization*
- *between businesses*
- *between businesses and consumers*
- *between public and private sectors.*

UK Government PIU Report@its.best.uk (1999)

In 2001, in the face of a decline in US productivity, the main contributing factor was said to be the 'collapse' of the 'new economy' (*The Economist*, 12 May 2001). This doom and gloom report was premature. The key players have regrouped and a significant realignment has taken place in various business sectors.

Early opportunities were observed in the enabling infrastructures and Internet-based networks (Internet, intranet and extranet), replacing existing telephone, fax, and EDI networks. The early success of e-procurement vendors (e.g., Commerce One, Ariba, Info Bank) was well received. The old suppliers suffered many problems, including that of authorization, with no conformity of systems between business partners. It was like having different telephone systems for each of the people to whom you speak. This has been transformed by trading portals that interconnect different suppliers making them usable by all buyers.

Basu (2002) has simplified the complex web and infrastructure of e-business applications, as shown in Figure 8.15, to illustrate the 'building blocks'.

There are five key types of e-business application systems that enable businesses to trade and conduct electronic transactions or communications. These are:

- e-Commerce solutions for both sell-side and buy-side applications
- Market-making applications that enable multiple buyers and sellers to collaborate and trade
- CRM solutions to facilitate improved business partnerships with customers
- ERP solutions for site-based planning and execution of operations
- SCM solutions for optimizing the demand and supply in the total supply network, including the suppliers.

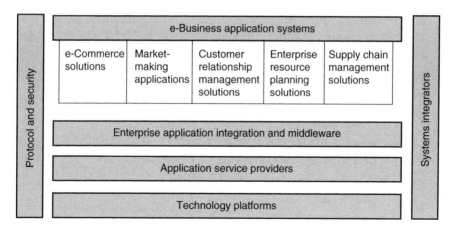

Figure 8.15 e-Business building blocks

In order to support the interfacing and integration of application systems, there are technology building blocks. These include enterprise application integration (EAI) and middleware applications, ASPs and technology platforms.

e-Commerce solutions

The buy-side applications of e-commerce, initially targeted at larger buyers, enable companies to levy across new or existing vendors. Solutions are increasingly aiming at integrating ERP systems with the organization's own suppliers and customers. The new application developers are utilizing the opportunities created by the lack of integration of ERP systems with other Internet systems and outside companies.

Initially the buy-side application vendors (including Commerce One and Ariba) were driven by pure-play solutions for the purchase of MRO (maintenance, repairs and operations) or indirect goods. The huge potential of e-procurement offered up by 'pure companies' has been recognized and seized by established ERP vendors such as SAP and Oracle, and software vendors like Netscape and Datastream.

The buy-side vendors, whether pure-play or not, are focusing on packaged buy-side application suites and looking to move into the direct procurement area. This requires a greater degree of understanding of business processes in specific industries and rigorous validation of the data processing.

The sell-side application vendors are looking to provide services content management and transaction processing. Hence, there are some sub-categories of software within this group. These include cataloguing, profiling, configurations and payment technologies. As a result, this sector is highly fragmented. There is a close interface with CRM solutions.

There are three broad categories of vendors in the sell-side market. They are (a) dominant software houses (e.g., IBM, Microsoft, AOL); (b) ERP vendors (e.g., Oracle, SAP); and (c) EDI vendors and B2C vendors (e.g., Harbinger, Broadvision).

Market-making applications

There are broadly two types of market-making applications. The first allows businesses to buy or sell by online auctions or bidding. Buyers place an open order to purchase an item and the sellers have the opportunity to bid. The second mechanism is the exchange or two-way auction platform containing a high speed bid/ask bartering process.

Enterprise resource planning (ERP) applications

Internet technology has certainly enhanced the collaborative business culture by enabling online transparent information and transactions. The company-centric enterprise application vendors (including SAP, Oracle, J D Edwards and PeopleSoft) are now building partnerships or alliances with supply chain vendors (e.g., Manugistics, i2) and looking to extend their customer relationship applications and e-commerce solutions out into the Web.

Customer relationships management (CRM) solutions

It is fair to state that most businesses regard the retention of customers as an important goal and therefore the criteria of CRM are not new for most enterprises. However, the collaborative Internet-based network has enhanced the need for customer intimacy and personalization. A number of software solutions have been developed (e.g., Siebel, Vantive) to provide some powerful holistic functionalities, including:

- Customer database for knowing and understanding customer characteristics
- Managing the relationship with key business partners (e.g., customers)
- Providing value added services to retain customer loyalty
- Transparency and real-time acceptability of information for both customers and suppliers
- Optimizing cross-selling opportunities.

Supply chain management (SCM) solutions

The emerging dot.com companies may be 'fireflies before the storm' (Lou Gerstner, ex CEO of IBM), but most companies now recognize that the Internet has a profound effect on supply chain performance. Applications that fall into this category are essentially decision support software packages for optimizing multiple levels of demand and supply in the global supply chain. These solutions take into account the constraints of transportation, supply capacity and inventory requirements. The ultimate objective is order fulfilment within the time and cost parameters acceptable to customers.

The leading vendors' niche in the market, (e.g., i2 and Manugistics), is being challenged by ERP vendors such as SAP, Oracle and J D Edwards.

EAI and middleware

The benefits of using an e-business solution increase in direct proportion to the degree of integration between the customer and the market place. It is impractical to make any attempt to change the software and platform of the acquired customer to those of the acquirer. Therefore, the effectiveness of handling real-time transactions in an e-business environment will depend on the technology 'building blocks' enabling the integration and interfaces of all parameters.

As outlined in Figure 8.15, the key set of 'building blocks' are EAI (enterprise application integration) and middleware applications that bring together the information the exchange needs from disparate internal systems. This is often referred to as 'back-end integration' and can account for up to 75% of the costs of going online.

Application service providers (ASPs)

ASPs assemble the functionality needed by organizations and package it with outsourced maintenance.

The growth of ASP solutions started with packaged services provided by e-commerce application software vendors (e.g., Ariba, Commerce One, Broadvision). The penetration of the market came from the ASPs' ability to take responsibility for system development and maintenance while avoiding the overhead of expensive IT staff. This means that smaller firms are being offered fully managed, and large organizations are receiving part-managed, ASP services.

Technology platforms

Technology platforms are supported by two groups of vendors. Hardware technology is provided by established computer companies (such as IBM, HP, Compaq and SUN). The other group supporting network technology comprises the telecommunication operators (e.g. BT, MCI, France Telecon, Deutsche Telecom, AT&T) and infrastructure companies (e.g., CISCO, EXODUS).

Technology companies are forming strong partnerships or alliances to provide end-to-end technology solutions, especially to SMEs. Examples include the partnership deals between Compaq and Cable and Wireless as well as SUN's alliance with Oracle.

Protocol and security

Protocol and security are the key building blocks of data transmissions and data security.

The Internet uses a special language or protocol to ensure safe arrival of data at its intended destination. This language has two parts:

- TCP (Transmission Control Protocol)
- IP (Internet Protocol).

TCP divides the data into small 'packets' adding information that allows the receiving computer to assure undamaged transmission. IP puts end 'address labels' on each packet. HTML (HyperText Markup Language) is the TCP and XML (eXtensible Markup Language) allows the dynamic logging of text in documents. This enables internal systems at the customer and the market place to send machine-readable messages to each other. XML is hailed as the 'lingua franca' for data transfer in the cyber realm. The flexible formats of XML offer a transition from EDI fixed formats to self-identifying data.

System integrators

The final piece of the 'building block' is the art and science of pulling together all elements of an e-business project and making it work. The lower end of the market for SMEs and start-up companies has been addressed by ASPs working together with hardware vendors (IBM, HP, Compaq) and software vendors (Microsoft).

However in a multi-functional, multi-site large application business it is necessary to redesign the way the business works in terms of both processes and culture in order to gain sustainable benefits from e-business. This requires not only the integration of IT systems between businesses but also process improvement and continuous education. There is a large gap between software functionality and the existing business process. Furthermore, the number of users in an e-business project is many times more than those expert users of an ERP application. Thus the shift of culture presents a much greater challenge.

Summary

This chapter has covered quality management, financial management and information technology. We are far from suggesting that we have written a complete accounting textbook or the definitive work on information technology. With quality management we have, however, gone into greater depth. Quality management is not a discipline restricted to one body of knowledge or expertise. Quality management is for everyone in the company to know and to understand in detail.

We have shown that quality management has two levels: basic requirements of specification, time and cost, and higher level requirements covering service and customer focus issues. We accept quality has a price but the cost of not performing can be unknown and is probably unknowable.

We also discussed a hierarchy of quality methods ranging from inspection at the end of the process, to no inspection by supervisors and the reliance on suppliers and each worker in the process to get it right first time, every time. For such a bold approach to be viable – e.g. no supervisors, no inspectors – workers must be empowered. But more than that, they must want to be empowered, and managers must believe and trust. For most companies this is a desirable goal but probably not something to be attempted overnight!

We also commented on ISO accreditation. We say that ISO certification may be a step on the way to TQM but it is only that – a small and expensive step. We suggest that a true TQM company does not need the crutch of ISO certification.

With financial management we introduced key concepts and ratios. Unless the operations manager understands these ratios he or she will always be at the mercy of the accountants. Some time was spent on ROI and some time on cost cutting. Both these areas are of particular concern to the factory manager. ROI can be used to prevent the acquisition of much-needed equipment. Cost cutting, if applied 5% across the board, will inevitably hit the factory the hardest. Other sections probably do have some slack or spare capacity, but seldom the factory. It is important that factory managers understand ROI and can defend themselves against ill-judged cost cutting exercises.

For information technology we have taken a more general approach. This section is equally applicable to all functions of the organization. The key issue in any new IT system is knowing what you want, going with a system with local support, and initially making do with off-the-shelf software. We have not discussed uninterrupted power supply, disaster recovery, the need to back-up files and so on. All these issues are nuts and bolts and should be second nature to your IT manager. This text was not written for the professional IT manager; it aims rather to give the average manager an understanding of the strategy of IT implementation.

During the past five years we have experienced the growth of e-business applications and enabling infrastructures that have rapidly increased productivity by streamlining existing business processes. We have also seen over the past few years some dramatic failures of pure-play e-commerce companies.

The time has come to take a fresh look at Internet technology. We need to move away from the rhetoric of 'dot.com revolution' and see the Internet as a powerful enabling technology that can be used in almost any business and part of almost any strategy. The key question is now not whether to deploy Internet technology, but how to deploy it.

CASE EXAMPLE 5: FIT SIGMA at an SME, Sweden

Background

The Solectron factory in Ostersund, Sweden, where AXE switchboards are manufactured, employs approximately 1000 people. The site was formerly part of Ericsson Network Core Products AB. Solectron, as an independent company, was experiencing tough competition even at the crest of the 'telecom boom'. With the downturn of the market from 2000, the competition became increasingly fierce. The management were toying with the idea of launching a Six Sigma initiative, but their initial enquiry revealed that they would be set back by at least $1 million if they began a formal Black Belt training programme with the Six Sigma Academy at Scottsdale, Arizona.

Approach

Solectron applied the FIT SIGMA methodology – 'Fitness for the purpose' – albeit not consciously under the FIT SIGMA label (see Basu and Wright, 2003).

Ericsson, the parent company of previous years, had already embarked upon a Six Sigma initiative; the Black Belt training programme was in full swing. Solectron decided to send a promising manager to a Black Belt training course via the Ericsson deployment plan.

Implementation

The young manager duly returned to Ostersund with great enthusiasm and applied a preliminary 'base line analysis' rooted in a simple checklist. The results were then presented to the management and a customized programme was drafted. The training programme was extensive, but Solectron relied on the Black Belts from Ericsson and also retained the same consultants as and when required.

Ten members of the top management team attended a one-day course on Six Sigma, 14 people were trained as Black Belts on a 7 month part-time programme and 20 more attended a 2 day course.

Results and learning points

Six Sigma applications at this factory saved US$0.5 million during the first year of the project. This amounted to about $500 per employee, but was actually closer to a huge $36 000 per employee trained in Six Sigma methods. A modest start in terms of savings per Black Belt perhaps, but the investment was also a fraction of a 'pure-play' Six Sigma initiative. More significantly, this customized approach enabled Solectron to have a launch pad to gain a much-needed competitive advantage.

The key learning point of Solectron was that it was possible to gain significant benefits by adopting Six Sigma principles customized to the size and capability of the organization.

Chapter 9

Intellectual Capital

> *How beauteous mankind is! O brave new world,*
> *That has such people in't!*
>   William Shakespeare, *The Tempest*

The last, but definitely not the least, pillar of Total Operations Solutions is Intellectual Capital. There is a widespread recognition of the need to manage knowledge, intellectual property and intangible assets, but there is no consensus in the extant literature as to the best way to measure such items. The measurement of intellectual capital is an area of further research and beyond the scope of this book. We explore a better understanding of the elements of intellectual capital and provide a framework for its assessment in the context of the competitive values of the total organization.

It is now accepted that 'the most successful companies are the ones who use their intangible assets better and faster' (Bontis *et al.*, 1999). Kaplan and Norton (2004) argue that unlike financial and physical assets, intangible ones are more difficult for competitors to imitate. They go on to say that employees' skill, IT systems and organizational cultures are worth far more to many companies than their tangible assets.

An organization becomes a winner over its competitors by attaining high performance with best practices and by sustaining it through the efforts of its people. Certainly innovation is a competitive weapon, but new product designs and formulations can be copied, and usually sooner than later. Likewise new technology and materials are procurable by competitors on an open market. The success factor for attaining and sustaining a high performance which will distinguish one organization from another will be the quality of its people. People power includes quality of and consistency of performance. Many researchers (e.g. Fitz-Enz, 2000; Wright and Race, 2004), have established that in a knowledge economy it is undeniable that 'human capital' can be the ultimate driver of all value growth.

The study of human resources and industrial psychology is a fascinating field. Capital (balance sheet) assets depreciate with time while human resources can appreciate with experience and appropriate learning programmes. It may sound a cliché, but knowledge, skills and initiative of employees are a company's most valuable asset. The challenge with knowledge is that it is more difficult to manage than capital assets. Knowledge is stored in the heads of employees rather than stocked in a bank, warehouse or in a machine. Knowledge takes time and money to acquire and it should not be lightly disposed of with restructuring and the loss of skilled people. Properly encouraged, people can learn new skills.

Throughout human existence knowledge has been preserved and transferred through a variety of means, such as storytelling, letter writing, in books and stored in libraries (even Cleopatra had a library – famously burned by Mark Anthony). This was to continue for centuries until new technology brought about a fundamental change that was to reshape the future of information acquisition, preservation and dissemination. With the rapid application of desktop computers, information technology (IT) in the 1970s and 1980s was regarded as a necessary commodity, like telephone. Subsequently IT developed information communication technology (ICT) and e-business. Changes brought about by ICT include those that can be attributed to the development of the World Wide Web application and the subsequent widely available Internet technology (Theunissen and Theunissen, 2004). This has brought about increased global competition and globalization. The potency of ICT, including integrated systems such as ERP and CRM (customer relationship management), provides an organization with the readiness and competitiveness of information capital and knowledge management.

To harness and sustain the potential of both human capital and information capital invariably requires a customer-focused organization and leadership. It is also important to assess how well an organization can respond, mobilize and sustain the change agenda required to adapt to a dynamic business environment. All new strategies require leaders to identify and implement changes and the organization structure and culture of the business needs to be conducive to making these changes.

The three final foundation stones related to the management of intellectual capital, are:

18 Leadership and organization capital: This covers the structure of the organization, the culture of the organization (how we do things around here), calibre of the management team, leadership and flexibility, team working and empowerment.
19 Human resource policies and human capital: This includes a defined policy to attract highly skilled employees, the development of workers, flexibility in work systems and reward systems and also the skills and knowledge of employees.
20 Knowledge management and information capital: Nothing is static in today's world. Information capital comprising organization's database, information systems and technology infrastructure is changing daily. Training and educational programmes with appropriate resources and facilities and sharing of best practices are essential at all levels of the organization.

Foundation 18: Leadership and organization capital

Academics and practitioners agree that the major obstacle to the implementation of a change programme, such as total quality management, is the structure and culture of the organization. A bureaucratic, top-down structure will result in a culture where the management does the thinking, makes the plans and gives orders, and the people on the factory floor will be expected to wield the screwdrivers and to obey the orders. The culture will be such that the lower echelons will not be expected or encouraged to make suggestions.

If an organization is serious about harnessing the power of the people then the structure will have to be such that people at all levels are encouraged to make suggestions, and that communication will become multidirectional, that is up and down the 'chain of command' and across functional and departmental borders.

In a customer-focused business manufacturing managers and logistics managers in particular must be adaptable to the needs for organizational change. They are the people closest to the factory operatives on whom the quality of the product depends.

The organization's culture, missions and commitments begin at the top of the organization. It is essential that everyone should clearly know what is expected and what is acceptable. Top management should be seen and known at least by sight at all levels of the organization. Top management has to be visible and has to lead by example. It is expected that the management team will consist of high calibre professionals with people skills. Management however has to be continuously appraising their own performance and the management structure.

Too often the attitude is that total quality management can be achieved by issuing a new mission statement that says all the right things such as 'people are our greatest resource', and by introducing flexibility, team work and empowerment in the factory. The philosophy is that quality of product is a factory issue, and there is no need to change the structure of the rest of the organization.

Organizational structure

The traditional organization structure followed by many manufacturing companies is based on functions (see Figure 9.1). With this type of structure we are likely to find divisions such as financial, marketing, technical and personnel. Within each division we might

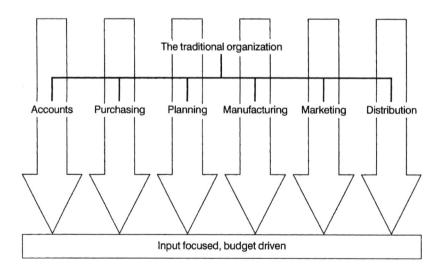

Figure 9.1   The traditional organization

find responsibilities by function, as an accounts department, a purchasing department, a planning department and so on. Typically each function or department is driven by a budget. Each manager, or functional head, guards their 'territories' from other functional barons. Their prime concern is often to keep expenses within budget. In addition to the waste of effort in internal 'in-fighting' and in 'empire building' the issue becomes serious when a customer seeking some information is passed from one department to another, with no department prepared to accept responsibility. We discussed some problems of traditional organizational structures in Chapters 3 and 4.

The leading-edge companies, realizing that the main objective of business is to create added value outputs and not inputs, are moving towards 'flat' organizations. There is, however, a danger of adopting the latest organizational 'fad' without thinking through what is appropriate for the business and the steps required to change the existing team. Another approach is the matrix approach, where people work for one department but have responsibility for a project in another department. This approach tries to superimpose a cross-functional team onto a rigid budget-driven departmental structure. The limitations of a 'matrix organization' are readily apparent, as depicted in Figure 9.2. (For example, the confusion that arises with two or more bosses during a project or a decision process and the conflicting requirements and priorities for individual members.)

One radical approach to organizational changes is the borderless organization, as shown in Figure 9.3. This is particularly effective in

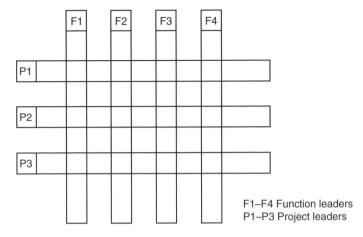

Figure 9.2   The matrix organization

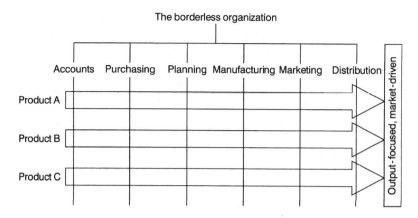

Figure 9.3   The borderless organization

supply chain management. In a borderless organization the focus is on the customer and therefore the organization is market-driven, rather than budget-driven, and responsibility for dealing with a customer's query is the responsibility of everyone.

It is easier to modify a piece of equipment from what is shown on an engineering drawing than it is to change an organizational structure from what is drawn on a piece of paper. Organizations tend to grow around the existing organizational chart rather than taking a clean slate approach. Ideally organizational changes should follow a holistic approach, including identifying resistance, conflict resolution, listening, feedback and communication planning. Kolodny (1993) suggests a 'step by step road map' for the implementation of significant organizational changes (see also Carnall, 1999).

Management profile

Management of people in an organization has always been important, but in the 1990s it has become even more so due to global competition, shorter product life cycles, rapid introduction of new technology and the impact of corporate programmes (such as total quality management and business process re-engineering). We have discussed the need for the whole of an organization to be involved in a culture change to total quality and not just the factory. None the less, the factory is central to the improvement process.

If one compares the companies that have excelled, either in performance or in a quality programme, with those that have not, the difference is in the strength of manufacturing management. All organizations have access to the same books, approaches, consultants and seminars. Similarly, the improvement possible through new manufacturing and information technologies is available to all. The failure of implementation lies with attempting to limit a change to one part of the organization, or in the calibre of existing managers. No matter how good the implementation programme is, unless the factory managers are of sufficient calibre, world class manufacturing will not be achieved.

The new generation manager will have a manufacturing background and, to gain the benefits of a borderless organization, will have a comfortable interface with every business function – marketing, finance, logistics and personnel. A survey by De Meyer and Ferdows (1990) confirmed that five out of the top ten manufacturing action plans relate to integration. A model for developing such a demanding management profile is to recruit high calibre technical graduates into a well-structured corporate management training scheme. For the first two years the trainee should be employed in a meaningful role in one of the core value added functions of purchasing, logistics or in a manufacturing unit. From our experience, little benefit will be gained by moving a trainee every two months or so from department to department. Trainees need to be able to feel that they are contributing; they will be keen, young, well-educated and adaptable, and in high demand. There is no sensible reason as to why they should not be able to provide a useful contribution right from the start.

After the initial two years the trainee can be appointed to an industrial engineer's position, or something similar. Industrial engineers, in this sense, are not traditional 'time and motion study people', but change agents in company-wide programmes such as TQM, BPR and MRP II implementation. After two or three years as an industrial engineer, the new generation manager can then move to other management roles in marketing, manufacturing, or supply chain management. To become a fully rounded manager, after between five to ten years, sponsorship through a part-time MBA programme such as offered by the Henley Management College should be considered.

In the past chief executives have had an accounting background, and in some cases marketing backgrounds. In the future, the chief executive is more likely to hold an engineering or science degree, supported by a postgraduate qualification such as an MBA from a specialist management studies institution.

Obstacles in organization

In spite of discussions about departments working together to satisfy internal customers and the end users (the real customers), in practice there are often strong personal reasons for resistance to change, including power, paradox, perplexity and paradigm (the four Ps of change).

Power

A survey by the Hay Group UK (1995) suggests that senior managers are consumed by power and that they only pay lip service to change. Usually it is more important for the next promotion of a senior manager to show how well he or she has run their empire, met the budget and satisfied their boss than it is to cooperate with other managers. Buzzwords are learnt, the right motions are gone through, good reasons are found as to why a change programme failed and the achievements of other objectives are highlighted in annual appraisal reviews. If the person who eventually gets to the top is the best at playing these internally focused games, such a person is unlikely to be able to lead an organization in global competition.

Paradox

It is an apparent paradox that two contradictory concepts can both be true in a company. For example, in a multi-product manufacturing business one product group is promoting employee empowerment, which is totally different from the business process re-engineering projects of another product group. One group is advocating asset utilization for its high-volume products while the other group is striving for flexibility for its large variety of products. The reality is that both camps are right but that they are not moving in the same direction, thus a sense of polarization is created within the company. To get people moving in the same direction, leadership from the top, a common goal and the means of self-assessment are necessary for lower level staff to feel some sense of belonging or ownership.

Perplexity

Another problem is the perplexity of the change of direction and nature of work that people encounter in business. Change is a dynamic process that requires continuous review, but if the change process is not properly handled people get confused: for example, if a company is trying to rebuild an organization, but before the change is halfway through senior management decide to launch another programme, the previous work is of little value.

It is said that people prefer not to change, that they are more comfortable with what they know. In reality, people of the twenty-first century are very used to change and very adaptable. Never have so many people travelled abroad for pleasure (or had the wherewithal to do so) as have this generation. How quickly most of us have adapted to cell phones, personal computers and concepts such as virtual reality. It is not change that perplexes people, it is the reason for change. If change has to occur then the reason has to be carefully explained, and the change process has to be carefully planned so as to involve all members of the organization. Unless the members of the organization understand the purpose of the change, then change will be difficult to effect.

Paradigm

Psychologically, a change process is too much to handle for many managers who like to follow the chartered routes of traditions. The paradigm is 'Why bother to change if it worked in the past?' It is difficult to break out of the mould, and many managers once they get to a senior position may pick up the styles, premises and approaches of their predecessors. Privileges of rank, such as the large corner office, the cocktail cabinet, the reserved parking space, will be clung to. Partly this will be the new executive's own vanity and partly it will be to satisfy the expectations of friends and family. We have visited one very successful world class organization where the chief executive does not have an office or a reserved parking space. He does not need a reserved parking space because he is always first to work in the morning. He has a desk, but he shares a large office with

executives responsible for finance, marketing, planning and manufacturing. Thus team work is not only espoused by senior management, it is openly practised.

In order to remove organizational obstacles we need effective
leadership, appraisal of managers beyond budget performance and
a continuous learning process. There is a fundamental need for a
paradigm shift in many organizations, for managers to move from
being managers to becoming leaders.

Leadership

The style and quality of leadership must come from the top and then
filter through to managers and subsequently down to empowered
employees. Alfred Sloan, chief executive of General Motors from
1923, did for management what Henry Ford did for the shop floor.
Sloan set three clear objectives for managers:

- To determine a company's strategy
- To design its structure
- To select its control systems.

Sloan's approach, particularly to the design of a rigid structure
and control systems relying on supervision, is now vulnerable in
global competition. None the less, the logic of designing a structure
and control system to meet the strategy, rather than first establishing
a structure and then trying to develop a strategy independent of the
structure, is difficult to refute.

The shift is now from a boss approach to a leadership approach.
For example, the boss controls staff while the leader inspires them
(e.g. Richard Branson of Virgin). The boss depends on authority and
the leader depends on goodwill. The boss shows who is wrong, the
leader shows what is wrong. However, even 'inspirational' leadership
requires perspiration too. Charisma alone does not bring about results
in a business. Academics and psychologists of 'human engineering'
believe that the leadership styles (e.g. autocratic, consultative, par-
ticipative and democratic) should be adaptive to the idiosyncrasies
of human behaviours. There is no one ideal leadership style.

Management gurus have suggested two essential qualities of leadership. One is industry foresight and vision, the other is innovation.
Hamel and Prahalad (1994) clearly established that 'top managers

must recognize that the real focus for their companies is the opportunity to compete for the future'. The other quality is related to the first and involves the innovative attitude to encourage and convert crude ideas into results. As expressed by Drucker (1969):

> *A top management that believes its job is to sit in judgment will inevitably veto new ideas ... Only a top management that sees its control function as trying to convert into purposeful action the half baked idea for something new will actually make its organization – whether company, university, laboratory or hospital – capable of genuine innovation and self-renewal.*

Christopher Bartlett of the Harvard Business School and Sumantra Ghosal of the London Business School (1994) focus on two other 'post Sloanist' processes of leadership. The first is 'competence building' by linking up the superior depth and breadth of all the employees' talents, and the second process is entrepreneurism through letting loose independent spirits through small business units. (Bartlett and Ghosal cite successful companies such as Kao, 3M, Canon and Intend.)

Organizational capital

In addition to an appropriate organization structure and the leadership provided by management, the competitive strength of an organization or the organization capital is underpinned by its core competence, intellectual property, customer assets, process capital and team work. Some practitioners (e.g. Sveiby, 1997) prefer the term 'structural capital', which includes policies, culture, distribution channels and other organizational capabilities developed to meet market requirements as well as intellectual property. There are overlaps between human capital, organizational capital and information/knowledge capital in various models of intellectual capital proposed by practitioners (Brooking, 1996; Edvinson and Mallone, 1997; Roos and Roos, 1997; Kaplan and Norton, 2004).

According to Hamel and Prahalad (1994), core competence is defined as an organization-based capability that integrates the skills of a set of practitioners from different business units and creates superior value for the client. It is an organizational version of unique individual know-how. Similar concepts of core competence are found in the works of Drucker (1992), Porter (1995) and Godbout (2000).

Intellectual property is guarded zealously with patent rights by research-based organizations such as pharmaceutical and ICT industries. Roos and Roos (1997) divide organization capital to manage current business process (process capital) and capabilities to develop new businesses (innovation capital).

Customer assets are all market-related intangibles, including brands, goodwill, client list, customer loyalty, distribution channels and so on. Kaplan and Norton (2004) have emphasized that no asset has greater potential for an organization than the collective knowledge possessed by all employees. A sustainable culture of motivating team work and knowledge-sharing is a crucial element of organization capital and a success factor of knowledge management.

Foundation 19: HR policies and human capital

In most companies the function once known as 'personnel' is now 'human resource management'. The change in name signalled a change in emphasis. Human resource managers of today deal with issues more far-reaching and complex than those previously handled by personnel managers. Apart from having to understand, and advise on, continuously changing employment and work place-related legislation (such as health and safety, employment contracts, and so on), organization structures have changed. The old hierarchical organization chart model where everyone knew their place has given way to 'borderless' organizations with flexible work practices and the need for continuous retraining and education. The implication of these challenges is being experienced by all levels of management in every function. Life may have seemed simpler in the 1960s and 1970s but one should not forget the disastrous effects of the poor industrial relations of those years.

Human resources become a competitive strength of human capital when HR policies lead to the recruitment, retention and development of a self-motivating workforce. Much has been written about motivation and many motivation theories have been developed, from Adam Smith (1776) to Maslow (1943) to Herzberg (1966) to Wright and Race (2004), but in reality few organizations have a workforce of highly skilled self-motivated employees. The turnover of staff in a knowledge-based industry is much higher than that in a traditional manufacturing or utility industry. There are an abundance of organizational theories and HR policies. In this foundation stone we address key HR policies related to:

- Skills flexibility structure
- Team structuring
- Industrial relations.

The need for continuous learning is discussed under the heading of knowledge management.

Skills flexibility structure

A company needs a clear policy regarding the structure of skills flexibility. The issues mostly revolve around the flexibility within engineering skills (e.g. between mechanical and electrical) and the flexibility between production and maintenance. The key principles of skills flexibility should include:

- Defining job categories to accommodate a common career development plan covering both engineering and production.
- Merging of maintenance and production for shift operations.
- Understanding the importance of specialist technical skills.

The titles and categories of factory jobs can vary depending on the location, language and available skills. However, the following model illustrates a representative skill path from which a specific structure can be developed.

Skill path model

- *Level 1*: Operators to be responsible for machine operations, machine setting adjustments, simple changeovers, cleaning, lubrication, simple inspections and preventative maintenance tasks on one or more machines under their control. Machine operations include knowing the standards of quality required and the ability and authority to take corrective action to achieve set standards.
- *Level 2*: (a) Craftspeople to be able to (as assigned) carry out corrective maintenance, major changeover, equipment settings, fault diagnostics, inspection and preventative maintenance tasks as well as normal machine

operations as described for Level 1. (b) Team leaders will have at least the same knowledge as the craftspeople but will have additional manufacturing responsibilities such as achievement of output targets to a desired quality standard. Other responsibilities will include organization of the team and the organizing of resources needed by the team to do their jobs (cleaning materials, oils and lubricants, tools, spares, etc.).

- *Level 3*: Technicians will be able to repair units, and will have specialist skills in mechanical, electrical and ICA (instrumentation, control and automation). They will be able to assist with Level 2 predictive maintenance analysis, and be involved in long-term trouble-shooting and the design of processes/systems for trouble-free machines.
- *Level 4*: Engineering or manufacturing supervisors/managers will have higher technical education and training to solve complex longer-term problems, develop maintenance strategies, advise production on optimum line speed and provide on-the-job training support to other levels.

The traditional electrician will no longer be required. In Level 2 craftspeople will be trained in basic electrical skills. The specific electrical and ICA know-how will be at Level 3.

Factories will apply a high degree of flexibility depending on the availability of skills at the different levels. The level of demarcation – should there be any at all – would be based on the capability and skills of employees, not on their job titles or union cards. The recruitment, training and development for each level will be covered in foundation stone 20, training and continuous learning.

It is important that before a task is assigned to a particular level, all the elements of the task are analysed to determine the skill overlap, as illustrated in Figure 9.4. Multi-skilling can be an exciting concept but it can present a potential risk in safety and quality if the details of the job and skills are not properly matched: 'a little knowledge is a dangerous thing'.

Skills flexibility in a manufacturing process can only be effective when the long-standing barriers between maintenance and production are broken down to form an integrated manufacturing operation. The first step is to implement a 'manufacturing-based' organization, as shown in Figure 9.5. In this model the maintenance engineer (area engineer) and his team are physically located in the production area. The area engineer reports to the manufacturing manager and also retains a functional link with the factory chief engineer regarding engineering policy. The next step is an integrated organization where the manufacturing manager is responsible for the reliability

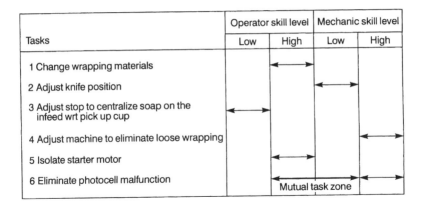

Tasks	Operator skill level		Mechanic skill level	
	Low	High	Low	High
1 Change wrapping materials		←→		
2 Adjust knife position			←→	
3 Adjust stop to centralize soap on the infeed wrt pick up cup	←→			
4 Adjust machine to eliminate loose wrapping				←→
5 Isolate starter motor		←→		
6 Eliminate photocell malfunction		←——— Mutual task zone ———→		

Figure 9.4   Task sharing in a packing machine

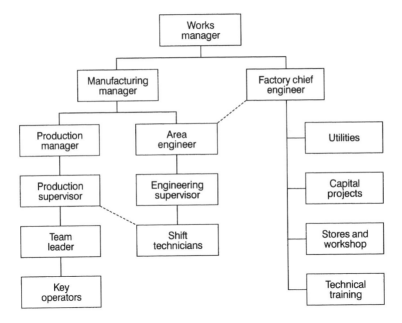

Figure 9.5   Manufacturing-based organization

of his assets and maintains an advisory link with the chief engineer. This is illustrated in Figure 9.6. There will continue to be a role for the chief engineer with factory services, projects, planned or expert maintenance, planning the installation of new systems, and technical training. Overall the number of levels will reduce, depending on the available skills, and the jobs of supervisors and technicians in both maintenance and production will merge.

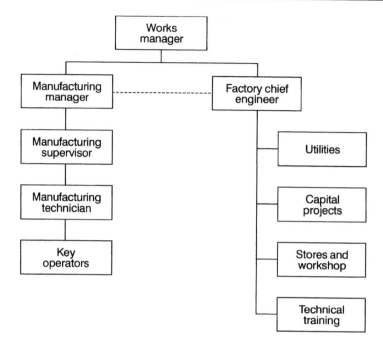

Figure 9.6 Integrated organization

Another important issue is the recognition of the need for high level skills, technical expertise and the special aptitude required in a high-tech operation or high-tech maintenance. The model in Figure 9.7 illustrates the skill levels in a high speed packaging machine. The depth of knowledge required at the expert level is so diverse for mechanical, electrical and control engineering that it may be prudent not to seek flexibility at these levels. An instrument technician may be an expert in programmable logic control (PLC), but will not necessarily be adept at diagnosing the faults in a 'Geneva' mechanism. Using the analogy that a multi-skilled craftsman is a general practitioner, then an expert technician in a particular field is a neurologist.

Team structuring

The traditional concepts of manual flow-line manufacturing and division of labour as detailed in Adam Smith's pin-making example (1766), the repetitive short-cycle progressive assembly line of Henry

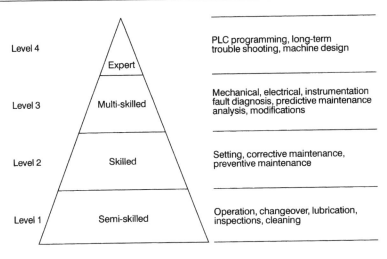

Figure 9.7   Skill profile in a high speed packaging machine

Ford and the standardization of work by time and motion studies of Taylor and the Gilbreths have been challenged, particularly in the past two decades. The tedium of assembly line work has been well documented and analysed by Wild (1975), and illustrated in the classic Charlie Chaplin movie *Modern Times*. The monotony of short-cycle work has been further aggravated by a number of factors, including the higher educational attainment of workers, the increased unemployment benefits of the labour force, the increased official concern over RSI or OOS (repetitive strain injury or occupational overuse syndrome) and the impact of the 'quality movement'. The experience of Japan's quality circles, and kaizen, where volunteers of workers form teams to improve safety, manufacturing or quality problems, have proved successful in increasing and sustaining productivity. With kaizen, companies involve workers in teams with designated team leaders by allowing them a good deal of autonomy in planning and managing daily activities. However, what is not often understood is that with the Japanese model empowerment only goes so far. Teams are encouraged to look for new systems and to suggest improvements, but they are not empowered to implement their suggestions until they have been tested to see how a change in one section will affect work in other sections. Once a new idea is adopted it is documented and becomes standard practice. No deviation is allowed from a standard practice until it has been fully tested, and then if found to be a better method it will become the new standard practice. In many ways this is not far removed from Taylorism, in so far as Taylor's aim was to involve workers in finding the best method and then implementing the best method as standard practice. Over the years Taylorism became corrupted to the stage where time and motion study people (work study) found the best method and imposed the best method on the worker. With the Japanese method the workers are involved in finding the better method and in imposing the better method on themselves.

In order to alleviate the tedium of repetitive assembly work and its detrimental effect on productivity during the 1960s and 1970s many companies, especially in Scandinavia, applied two facets of job restructuring. These were job enlargement through increased task length, and job enrichment involving a greater motivational content of the job. Some companies also applied organized or self-organized job satisfaction. The case examples reported by Wild (1975) showed improved results to a varying degree in productivity, employee turnover, absenteeism and quality. However, as the emphasis of job restructuring was upon the design, or redesign, of individual manual jobs, with increased automation and mechanization of assembly work, the impact of job restructuring became less significant. Manufacturing companies, which are primarily concerned with machine and process operations rather than assembly, have also sought the improvement of work organization. Thus all types of manufacturing companies are showing interest in group or team work structures. Despite the interest in team working, one cannot ignore the failure of the Volvo experiment at Uddevalla where a team of workers completely assembled cars at the one static workstation. The experimental factory at Uddevalla was opened in 1989 and closed in 1992. Also closed was the Kalmar factory, which had opened in 1974. Kalmar also used a team approach to car assembly, but limited to a team completing a full element of the production process in cycles of three to four minutes. Berggren (1994) believes that at Uddevalla, Volvo showed that there is a viable alternative to assembly line production. He lists external factors such as lack of dedicated suppliers, poor quality components, old-fashioned design and so on as the reasons for failure rather than the failure of the team work approach *per se*. None the less, despite Berggren's well-presented case, there can be little argument that the traditional assembly line model is still the most efficient method of car assembly.

In addition to the principles and case examples on group working as reported by Wild (2002), other methods of team structuring have developed more recently. One such example is Schumacher's work structuring approach (1993), which adapted tools based on industrial engineering principles, such as transformation analysis and TIED (technical, informational, error, direction) analysis.

Transformation analysis involves the breaking down of tasks into basic transformation (BT), supplementary transformation (ST), ancillary operations (AO), transportation (T) and storage (S). This is comparable to the flow process chart analysis of industrial engineering comprising operation (O), inspection (à), transport (é), delay (D) and storage (Ñ). Transformation analysis is used to streamline a task into value added (BT and ST) and cost added (AO, T and S) and also for work grouping ('whole task'). TIED analysis is designed to test the relationship between various activities by examining the links between them in each category of technical, information, error (or quality) and directional. Activities in each of these categories is scored between 0 and 4 and totals compared. The higher the score, the closer the link. TIED analysis is comparable to the critical examination of industrial engineering. Schumacher's approach of work structuring involves the following seven key principles:

1 Work should be organized around 'basic transformations' in the process of forming 'whole tasks'.
2 The basic organizational unit should be the primary work group (4–10 people).
3 Each work group should include a designated leader.
4 Each work group and their leader should plan and organize their own work.
5 Each work group should be able fully to evaluate its performance against agreed standards of excellence.
6 Jobs should be structured so that work group members can personally plan, do and evaluate at least one transformation in the process.
7 All work group members should have an opportunity to participate formally in the group's and the organization's common tasks.

However, as reported by Klein (1989), team structuring can also create problems. In Klein's example of 'the engine plant', team structuring included self-managed work teams with multi-skilled workers, an explicit commitment to 'factory culture', achievement of schedules set by the team and freedom to perform assembly tasks in the manner they thought best. Initially the performance of the team was highly satisfactory. But, when the company introduced a just-in-time inventory system, because the plant no longer had a buffer stock, the team came under severe delivery pressures. Just-in-time allowed no slack in the system and the team, without measured standards, could not meet the cost or delivery targets. In effect, the team lost its autonomy over methods and its flexibility through a lack of buffer stock. (Note the similarities to the Volvo experiment. The team was limited by the lack of support or by factors outside of its direct control.)

A solution to the above problem is demonstrated by two large automobile factories. One is a GM–Toyota joint venture, New United Motor Manufacturing Inc. (NUMMI, see Adler, 1993) and the other is Ford–Volkswagen's Autoeuropa (Santos, 1995). In both cases the *carte blanche* autonomy of the team was changed to a collaboration with industrial engineering. In this partnership team leaders were given comprehensive training in work study and operators (not industrial engineers) wrote methods specifications. The industrial engineer acted as a consultant or facilitator. Teams maintained their autonomy, work methods went through systematic improvement and self-planning was according to measured standards. The collaboration of industrial engineering with team structuring clearly provides a balance of empowerment motivation and efficiency.

Other important factors are related to job design and team structuring ergonomics and human factors. According to a recent study by Professional Physical Therapy Services (PPTS), USA, 'The cost of implementing ergonomic changes was relatively small when compared to the total costs of functional restoration of injured persons' (Arendt, 1995). The common work place injuries such as RSI or OOS and cumulative trauma disorder (CTD) can be prevented by appropriate work place design and work practices.

Safety and health

'Occupational safety, health and ergonomics might be considered a moral issue, but even the Romans realized that well-maintained slaves were more efficient and more valuable' (Wright and Race, 2004: 17). Given that the average adult in full-time employment can expect to spend about a quarter of his or her life at the work place, it can well be argued that employers have not just a legal but a moral obligation to provide a safe working environment, and that the worker, who 'sells' his or her time, has a right to a safe and healthy work place. History amply demonstrates that voluntary arrangements do not provide adequate safety standards and rigorous legislation has been necessary down the years, but the fault has not always been with employers. Employees are often found to take short cuts in spite of potential dangers, as is perhaps borne out by statistics that show that most accidents to most people still occur in the home.

Wright and Race point out that 'most health and safety requirements of workers are only common sense. It is common sense to have adequate light, correct temperatures, proper ventilation, noise controls and so on (2004: 117).

Ergonomics

Ergonomics is the science that seeks to improve the physical and mental well-being of workers by optimizing the function of human–machine environments. In today's office workers are surrounded by machines, most of them electronic, and long hours are spent hunched over keyboards and in front of VDU screens. In particular, ergonomics concentrates on:

- Fitting the work demands to the efficiency of people, to reduce physical and mental stress
- Providing information for the design of machines, keyboards, etc. so that they can be operated efficiently
- The development of adjustable workstations and chairs etc. so that individuals can self-adjust the workstation to meet their needs
- Providing information on correct body posture to reduce fatigue and to minimize OOS (occupational overuse syndrome – formerly known as RSI or repetitive stress injury)
- Giving guidelines for lighting, air conditioning, noise limits and so on.

The following website provided by the US Department of Labour Occupational Safety and Health Administration is recommended: www.osha.gov/SLTC/computerworkstation.

Industrial relations

The rapid changes in flexible working practices demand an examination and reassessment of key issues in organizations and these include industrial relations practices.

During the post-war growth period trade unions in the Western world assumed considerable power. The model of labour relations was basically confrontational. Relative power determined the winner of the face-to-face confrontation between management and unions. This was played out in contract negotiation and collective bargaining. Throughout the late 1960s and 1970s the recurring industrial disputes resulted in companies performing poorly. In many cases the impact was far reaching; for example, the miners' strike in the UK destabilized the economy and effectively brought down the government.

As we have indicated earlier, freer trade and deregulation along with improved logistics and communication technology now have exposed companies to global competition, particularly from lower-wage newly industrialized countries. The realization of this fact, particularly over the past decade, has changed the industrial relations scene. In addition to going through their internal restructuring, unions have merged and have accepted the need to work with management.

At the early stage of engineering flexibility in the UK unions were reluctant to accept changes and signed agreements primarily because of additional 'flexibility payments' (Cross, 1985). In recent years radical changes in the business environment have prompted unions to take the initiative of formalized flexibility agreements, which have helped to attract new businesses in the UK (e.g. Nissan, Siemens, Sony and Toyota).

Flexible work practices, such as the semi-autonomous or self-directed work teams, have potential problems from an industrial relations perspective. They come into conflict with job classifications and social security entitlements. Work structuring and empowerment initiatives have occurred, with people reduction and demands for concessions. Direct employee involvement, such as peer discipline within a team, can also undermine the role of the union. Therefore, if these anomalies are not addressed with a mutual trust between management and union lasting good industrial relations will remain fragile. The success of flexible working practices will be assured only if management works with the unions rather than around the unions or against them. A formal collaboration between management and unions would eliminate some of the mutual mistrust. If a company does not have a trade union then its role should be adopted by an *authoritative* work council, and not a token body whose contribution is to determine such matters as the colour of napkins in the canteen!

Nancy Day reports that there are many successful models of 'union–management collaboration' (1994). One such model, as promoted in Canada, is called 'strategic alliance' (see Wright, 1995). This initiative contains four elements of sustainable processes:

- *Element 1*: Principle-driven. Management and union must understand and accept the fundamental principle that management–union cooperation should benefit all.
- *Element 2*: Fostering commitment. Commitment to the partnership can be demonstrated by contractual agreement and investment of resources.
- *Element 3*: Internal and external support. Leaders of both management and unions must ensure that understanding and support are secured throughout the organization.
- *Element 4*: Adherence to procedures. Procedure (or 'process') refers to the jointly determined ground rules upon which alliance stands.

Although the necessity of joint initiatives or 'strategic alliances' has been recognized, their implementation has a long way to go. Mills (1994) found that only 20% of 224 large US companies had given serious consideration to participating alliance between management and unions.

Foundation 20: Knowledge management and information capital

Almost 400 years ago, Francis Bacon stated that 'Knowledge is power'. Drucker (1995) added that 'Knowledge has become the key economic resource and the dominant, if not the only, source of competitive advantage.'

Webster's Dictionary defines knowledge as 'familiarity or understanding gained through experience or study'. In a FIT SIGMA initiative an essential sustainable driver of performance management is the sharing of knowledge and best practice (Basu and Wright, 2003). Although not explicit in his 14-point philosophy, Deming (1986) advocated the principle 'to find the best practices and train the worker in that best way'.

The essential ingredient for benefiting from knowledge management is the establishment of a 'learning organization' culture. The development of a 'learning organization' culture does not happen overnight – it takes time, it requires the appropriate infrastructure to be in place. Our experience is that time and money spent in knowledge management is an investment in the most valuable resource of competitive advantage – people. The success of knowledge management is underpinned by three key processes essential in a learning organization:

- Sharing of best practice
- Information capital
- Learning programmes.

Sharing of best practice

Good practice for knowledge sharing is to:

- Systematically capture knowledge from proven 'good practices'
- Select examples of 'best practices' based upon added value to the business
- Do not differentiate between the sources, regardless of level of technology or economic power
- Inculcate knowledge sharing between all units.

Unless members at all levels of a company participating in sharing knowledge believe that their business can benefit from it, then the exercise has little value. If a company believes that they already know the best way or that the 'best practice' is not appropriate to their circumstances, then sustainable improvement simply will not happen. The support structure for such a knowledge-sharing process should include:

- A champion as a focal point to coordinate the process
- A regular best practice forum to learn from each other and to network
- Internal and external benchmarking to assess targets and gaps
- Continuous communication through websites, newsletters, videos and a 'visual organization'.

Information capital

The discipline of knowledge management is essentially holistic and complementary to many related disciplines, and in particular to organization development and information management. Malholtra (2003) identifies two main streams of knowledge management (KM), namely one that focuses on the 'hard' aspects of KM (i.e. the technology) and one that focuses on the 'soft' aspects of KM (i.e. the people). Information and communication technology (ICT) has driven the KM wave, particularly in Europe, the USA and Japan. It is important to recognize that although people and processes are crucial to effective KM, the competitive advantage of KM still remains in the domain skill of information management, and this advantage leads to the information capital of an organization.

According to Kaplan and Norton (2004), information capital is a measure of how well the company's strategic IT portfolio of infrastructure and applications supports the critical internal process of the business. The infrastructure relates to hardware (such as central servers and communication networks) and managerial expertise (such as standards, data security and disaster planning). The application comprises both processing applications (such as an ERP system or a CRM system) and analytical applications for sharing knowledge and best practice and applications for promoting the analysis of business advantages (such as customer profitability).

The advancement of knowledge management depends on the development of future technology. However, it is important to note that knowledge management is not information and communication technology. To echo the caution raised by O'Brien (2004), the practioners of KM should refrain from muddying the water by introducing aspects of artificial intelligence (AI) and intelligent systems (IS).

Learning programmes

Human resource management can create real strategic advantage by proper planning for people with the right skills and calibre to suit the corporate strategy. If it is recognized that 'people make things happen', then there will be a continuous need for recruitment, training and development of the workforce at all levels. Schonberger (1986) describes training as the catalyst for change programmes such as JIT, TQM and BPR. Implementation plans for change management programmes usually consist of boxes with words in them connected by arrows. Such a plan for world class manufacturing comprises half a dozen arrow-connected boxes, with the word training shown in each one: related to this, education and training are critical components of an empowered work environment and are essential for an effective alliance between management and unions.

In a terminology trap, there seems to be a status distinction with the terms training and education. For example, training is associated with imparting skills (how to do) and education with imparting knowledge (why it should be done). Training is thought of as being needed by people at a lower level than oneself, and education is for one's level and above (see also Tompkins, 1989). To overcome this implied snobbishness we use the term learning to cover both training and education. We see learning as including the development of people in their career progression.

The learning programmes of a leading-edge organization should comprise five elements:

- Continuous recruitment and development
- Learning programmes for implementing new technology
- Learning for company-wide change programmes
- Learning resources
- Learning performance

plus

- Annual appraisal.

Continuous recruitment and development

The quality of the final product depends on the materials used; therefore the development of people starts at the recruitment stage. Organizations of the future will require fewer people but the people will require a higher technical knowledge. The ability to attract high calibre people is an indication of the sustainable performance of a company. A 'blue chip' company can attract 'high fliers'. The recruitment policy of a leading manufacturing company, for example, should seek high qualifications at the entry level as follows:

- *Management trainees*: As a minimum requirement a management trainee should have a degree, with above average grades, from a reputable university.
- *Technicians*: All technicians should have a college or equivalent diploma in a suitable discipline. They will require a formal assessment after three years' training and experience before they are appointed as a technician.

- *Craftspeople*: A technical high school education is the minimum requirement for a craftsperson. One year of multi-skill training is required before their appointment as a craftsperson.
- *Operators*: Operators should have a technical high school education.

Learning for implementing new technology

The learning process for implementing new technology or processes usually starts at the design stage of the project. The strategy is to grow your own in-depth skills. The example of installing a PLC-controlled high speed laminated tube making machine for toothpaste in Chile (the first of its kind in the country) provides an example of such a training programme.

The chief engineer, manufacturing manager and project engineer visited the supplier in Switzerland to discuss the design specifications and then visited two users (in Germany and the UK) to assess the feasibility of the project. After the approval of the project proposal, which included a learning and service agreement with the supplier, an operation team comprising the supervisor, technician and key operator visited the supplier for a two-week hands-on learning programme. Additional visits to operating companies who had installed the machine further motivated the team.

The engineers from the Swiss supplier visited Chile during the commissioning of the machine. The visit plan included three days of classroom and hands-on learning. In spite of some language barriers, the engineers and key operators communicated well. The company was fortunate that they did not receive a 'sales representative' from the supplier but a genuine engineer with practical experience. The company formulated and installed its own internal on-the-job and off-the-job learning programme. The commissioning engineer (trainer) paid two more visits to Chile at six-month intervals.

Within 18 months the operational efficiency of the machine was sustained at over 80% and the in-house capability equalled that of the supplier.

Learning for a company-wide change programme

Change management and the need for learning in change management are covered in Foundation 15, Chapter 8. Learning is an essential component of a company-wide change programme whether it is TQM, Six Sigma, a strategic alliance between management and unions, or a change of structure to empowered teams. Employees require learning opportunities in work process and analysis skills (e.g. SPC) as well as so-called soft skills such as interrelating with team members. Line managers need to learn how to make the transition from an out-of-date autocratic management role to that of coach and mentor. The learning for all employees and managers must extend beyond skills and include learning about the need for 'cultural' change. It is essential to generate trust between all members by following the same learning process.

There are several models for company-wide learning programmes. We shall mention two: the first is from Oakland's 'total quality training cycle' (Oakland, 1992).

This model follows an eight-step continuous process and includes a series of integrated training programmes for everyone in the organization, as follows:

- Senior management: 8–20 hours of seminars per annum
- Middle management: 20–30 hours of seminars
- Supervisors and team leaders: 30–40 hours
- Seminars are followed up with workshops
- All other employees: a half day per week for six weeks.

The second model involves the five roles put forward by Hammer and Champy (1993). These are seen to be essential to make change happen for business process re-engineering. These roles are:

- The leader: a senior executive who authorizes and motivates the overall effort.
- The process owner: a manager with responsibility for a specific process.
- The re-engineering team: a group of individuals dedicated to the re-engineering of a particular process who diagnose the existing process and who oversee the redesign and the subsequent implementation.
- The re-engineering committee: a policy-making body of senior managers who develop the organization's overall re-engineering strategy and who monitor its progress.
- The re-engineering czar: an individual responsible for developing re-engineering tools and techniques within the company and for achieving synergy across separate projects.

All the above roles need to know three things about the change process: the *why*, which is the vision and rationale for change, the *what*, which is those aspects of the organization that will be changed, and the *how*, which is the processes, tools and techniques used to design and implement the change.

Whichever model of learning programmes is applied, it is essential that management is committed and follows through with the programme; otherwise, these concepts become no better than fads. With fads employees become cynical and believe that 'this too shall pass'.

Learning resources

The commitment of an organization to continuous learning is reflected in corporate support in the form of investment time, money, key personnel and facilities. 'A learning organization should plan its people power to allow for the time required for both on-the-job and off-the-job learning of each employee. The total time will be variable depending on the change programmes of a particular company. For example Bell Canada allocates 15 days per year for each employee's training' (see Wright, 1995). Significant research also shows that training and multi-skilling also improve a firm's ability to cope where technology is constantly evolving (Dwyer, 2000).

However, training for the sake of training will not be effective. 'Training and development that is linked to the needs of the business, of the job, and of employees provides the greatest payoff for the investment' (Knuckey *et al.*, 2002: 61).

There should be a budget for learning programmes and the measurable cost of training and education should be expressed as a percentage of annual sales. The amount allowed should be no less than 0.5% of sales and in some companies it is reported to be 2% of sales.

The use of a third party for specialist learning is usually successful. Each manager, supervisor and team leader should have responsibilities for the learning of their own personnel. In addition, a learning organization should provide a full-time and experienced facilitator or learning manager to coordinate the continuous learning programmes of the company. For multi-skilled crafts learning and TPM technical learning programmes, a competent engineering supervisor should be available to assist.

The company should provide dedicated learning facilities on site, including a learning centre (equipped with personal computers, appropriate training videos and presentation facilities) and a learning workshop (equipped with work benches, mechanical, electrical and control equipment, illustrated drawings and manuals, etc.). A multi-site or multinational company should benefit from a corporate learning centre for carrying out both internal and external seminars. An on-site library of books, periodicals and internal reports is a good resource for self-education and information.

Learning performance

The effectiveness of the education and training programmes of a company is usually assessed in terms of input as it is not easy to measure their output. The input measures are often expressed as:

- Number of learning hours per employee
- Learning expenditures as a percentage of annual sales (as discussed above, up to 2% of sales)
- Number of courses and seminars conducted.

Staff turnover is an indirect output measure of learning performance. A well-structured management development programme, and a reputation as a company that provides good learning opportunities, will attract high calibre candidates to an organization. A learning programme must be integrated with career development. If the management approach to human resources is well defined and considered, then most staff will repay their learning with longer service to the company. When a company loses people soon after they have been trained, then it may have got its training right but everything else is wrong.

Another assessment of learning performance involves the accreditation of learning programmes against national standards. One such scheme is 'Investor in People' in the UK. The scheme comprises four principles of employee development standards set by the Department of Education and Employment:

- A commitment from the top to develop all employees
- Regular reviews of learning and development needs
- Actions to train and develop individuals throughout their employment
- Evaluation of achievement in learning and development.

The assessment indicators stem directly from the standard. If a company measures up to the national standard as assessed by Training and Enterprise Councils (TECs), then it receives an accreditation certificate of 'Investor in People'.

The drive to continuously acquire new knowledge and transfer it to skilled people to achieve its business objective is the fundamental spirit of a learning organization. A learning organization is a leading organization. The self-analysis methodology as outlined in this book presents an opportunity to identify the gaps and learning needs.

Annual appraisal

The learning programmes for craftsmen, operators and office staff should include appraisal procedures and, where appropriate, a formal personal development plan. The effectiveness of a management appraisal programme is a key source of both the motivation and disgruntlement of managers. A poorly designed and implemented appraisal scheme can generate legions of demotivated 'underachievers'. On the other hand, when the scheme contains agreed objectives based on measurable parameters and the appraiser has no axe to grind then the scheme can be effective for identifying the development needs of the appraisee. The scheme loses its credibility when the agreed action points are not followed. A leading edge company can create a competitive edge with the aid of a properly administered appraisal scheme. The appraisal must be aimed at producing a personal development plan.

Any learning scheme should be well publicized, equitable and available to all.

Summary

In this chapter we have looked at intellectual capital comprising organization, people and knowledge. The key elements of intellectual capital are shown in a model in Figure 9.8.

We contend that people are the greatest resource of a company. People can be treated as servants, mere ciphers who are expected to do what they are told and to obey orders without question. Contrary to popular opinion such people do not make good soldiers. The military have long valued people with initiative and intelligence. Likewise, in the organization, people power, if properly harnessed, is a tremendous force to a company seeking a competitive edge.

INTELLECTUAL CAPITAL		
Organization capital	Human capital	Knowledge capital
Organization structure Leadership Customer focus Core competence Intellectual property Process capital Teamwork	Employees Flexible working practice Team structuring Industrial relations	Sharing best practices Information capital Learning programmes

© Ron Basu

Figure 9.8   A model for intellectual capital

We began the chapter by looking at organizational structures. We hope it is no surprise to our readers that we favour a flat structure with an empowered workforce. Such a structure requires two things: managers who are prepared to trust the workers and who are prepared to share information and decision-making, and workers who are prepared to accept responsibility. To move too quickly to such a structure would be dangerous. Such a structure needs the right culture. Cultural change takes time and has to be carefully planned.

People are not fools; hidden agendas are soon exposed. People will react honestly to honesty and fair play, but once trust has gone it is hard to regain. To an extent people do only work for money, but an empowered workforce with clear guidelines and who are encouraged to make suggestions and who are listened to, will provide a higher return for the wages they receive than those who are suspicious or even resentful of the bosses. Gaining the respect of the workers means involving them in decision-making, seeking their opinions and listening to them. Gone, thankfully, are the days of union and workers ranked against the bosses, of demarcation and of mutual mistrust. But we have to work hard to keep it that way.

Today we look for flexible working practices, and for unions or other representative bodies to work with management to safeguard and to grow employment opportunities. We see huge benefits accruing to a company that provides learning opportunities for all the people of the organization – opportunities that are not only on-the-job but off-the-job. We make the point that any learning plan should be open and well publicized. A set amount should be budgeted for learning each year.

Knowledge sharing is a strategic priority for a learning organization. A good idea is wasted when it is used only once. For knowledge sharing to matter, it must be underpinned by information management systems and continuous learning programmes. In this chapter we give several models of career path development and each involves a learning component.

CASE EXAMPLE 6: Sharing of best practice at GE Capital

Background

General Electric Inc., with its global business of over US$120 billion per annum, has been voted by Fortune as the 'most respected company'. GE is also known as the 'Cathedral of Six Sigma' and the high profile of the programme under the leadership of Jack Welch has been well publicized. GE licensed Six Sigma technology in 1994 from the Six Sigma Academy, rolled out the programme worldwide and achieved $2 billion savings in 1999.

GE Capital is the financial services arm of GE and accounted for approximately 40% of the group's turnover in 2001.

Approach

One heartening early success story at GE Capital relates to benchmarking and the sharing of good practice. GE Capital fielded about 300 000 calls a year from mortgage customers who had to use voicemail or call back 24% of the time because employees were unavailable. A Six Sigma team found that one of their 42 branches had a near perfect rate of answered calls.

Implementation

The team carried out a benchmarking exercise between all branches. They analysed the systems, process flows, equipment, physical layout and stopping of the 'best in class' branch and then cloned it to the other 41 branches.

Results and learning points

As a result, a customer has a 99.9% chance of obtaining a GE person on their first try. The success of this benchmarking exercise has contributed to knowledge-sharing between business units and subsidiaries of General Electric Inc. on a global scale.

Chapter 10

Alignment of Methodology

Vision without action is a day dream
Action without vision is a nightmare
Japanese Proverb

In this chapter we link Total Operations Solutions to TQM, Six Sigma, Lean Sigma and FIT SIGMA. Chapter 8 shows that if an organization is serious about effecting and maintaining improved performance then a total quality management culture is required. Achieving such a culture is not easy; sustaining it is even harder. The same applies to achieving and sustaining benefits of a quality initiative. This chapter considers the use of FIT SIGMA for achieving and sustaining the benefits of Total Operations Solutions.

The Malcolm Baldridge award, the Deming quality award, the European Foundation of Quality, have all served to give TQM a high profile. One count suggests that there are over 400 TQM tools and techniques (Pyzdec, 2000). However, this high profile has paradoxically contributed to a level of scepticism, especially by middle managers and staff. Promises have not been realized, high profile organizations that have claimed to be practising TQM have gone into decline. Staff have seen slogans and mission statements published which focus on customer service and 'our people' followed by redundancies and drastic cuts in training budgets. This chapter shows how to avoid this.

World class and best practice

The term world class is generally attributed to Hayes and Wheelwright (1984), who related best practice to German and

Japanese firms competing in export markets. Schonberger (1986) used the term 'best practice' to describe manufacturers making rapid and continuous improvement. World class in the 1990s was extended to include lean production (see Womack *et al.*, 1990), and also to service industries (see Basu and Wright, 2003).

Fry *et al.* (1994) and Harrison (1998) say best practice refers to any organization that performs as well or better than the competition in quality, timeliness, flexibility and innovation. Knuckey *et al.* (1999: 23) explain that 'the logic behind best practice is simple: because operational outcomes are a key contributor to competitiveness and business performance, and because best practice should improve operational outcomes, by implication good practice should lead to increased competitiveness. Best practice should lead to world class service'.

Knuckey *et al.* (1999: 137), on behalf of the New Zealand Ministry of Commerce, found from research of 1173 New Zealand manufacturing firms that the 'main sources of competitive advantage' and 'best practice' is;

- Goodwill and trust with suppliers and distributors
- Trust, goodwill and commitment from employees to the firm's goals
- Reputation with clients.

After a follow-up survey of 2756 manufacturing and service industries firms in New Zealand, Knuckey *et al.* (2002: 23) observe that 'best practice is a moving target – what was regarded as best practice in the 1990s is not necessarily regarded as best practice today'. Their 1999 list of 'best practice' for 'competitive advantage' is enlarged to include leadership, integrated management processes and coherence across activities and practices, and openness to new information and ideas (2002: 200).

Why best practice and world class is essential

There is no doubt that people today are more travelled, better educated and consequently more discerning than ever before. Customers know what is on offer elsewhere, they have experiences, and their expectations have been raised by advertising and marketing. Likewise shareholders, and other financial stakeholders, can be excused for wondering why the rapid technological advances of the past decade have not resulted in increased performance and higher returns on investment. At the same time, the well-publicized and promised benefits of technology have led customers to expect, even demand, improved products and service at less cost. Quality service, reliable products, value for money and, in the public sector, accountability are now taken for granted. Competitors are global, standards are world class and organizations that fail to meet world class performance will soon be found out.

In Chapter 8 we identified a hierarchy of four levels for quality management: inspection, control, assurance and TQM. To recap, quality inspection and quality control rely on supervision to make sure that no mistakes are made. This is the most basic approach to quality inspection and detection and correction of errors. The next level, quality control, is to inspect, correct, investigate and find the causes of problems and to take actions to prevent errors re-occurring. Both methods rely on supervision and inspection. The third level, quality assurance, includes the setting of standards with documentation and also includes the documentation of the *method* of checking against the specified standards. Quality assurance generally also includes a third party approval from a recognized authority, such as is found with the ISO 9000/2000 series. With quality assurance, inspection and control are still the basic approach, but in addition one would also expect to find a comprehensive quality manual, the recording of quality costs and, perhaps, use of statistical process control and the use of sampling techniques for random and the overall auditing of quality systems.

Quality inspection and control and quality assurance are aimed at achieving an agreed consistent level of quality first by testing and inspection, then by rigid conformance to standards and procedures, and finally by efforts to eliminate causes of errors so that the defined accepted level will be achieved.

As we said in Chapter 8, this cold and sterile approach implies that once a sufficient level of quality has been achieved, then, apart from maintaining that level which in itself might be hard work, little more need to be done with little input expected from staff members. It is a top-down approach to quality based on control and implies that the bosses know what is best, they set the standards, and they inspect and control to see that the standards are adhered to. This does not mean that management is ignoring what the customers want or what the competition is doing. It just means that the managers believe they know what is best and know how this can be achieved.

We also said in Chapter 8 that TQM is on a different plane. Total quality management includes all the previous levels of setting standards and the means of measuring conformance to standards. In doing this, statistical process control (SPC) may be used, systems will be documented and accurate and timely feedback of results will be given. With TQM, ISO accreditation might be sought, but an organization that truly has embraced TQM does not need the ISO stamp of approval. (ISO is discussed in some detail in Chapter 8.) Any organization seeking to reach world class status and wishing to maintain this status will need a vision of quality which goes far beyond mere conformance to a standard. The culture will be for every member of the organization to have a customer focus and a passion for quality and continuous improvement.

However, TQM is more than having a culture of quality; tools are required to achieve a level of quality. Six Sigma and Lean Sigma provide the necessary tools. Six Sigma is a rigorous process and when combined with the speed and agility of Lean Sigma has produced definitive solutions for better, faster and cheaper business processes. Total Operations Solutions enables the systematic identification and eradication of non-value added activities, an optimum value flow is achieved, cycle times are reduced and defects eliminated, resulting in an all-improved bottom line. While managers might understand the grey areas of distinction between different quality initiatives the crucial question is 'How do we sustain the results?'.

The biggest obstacle appears to be the packaged approach of various programmes causing a paucity of customized local solutions. Furthermore, due to the 'top-down' directive, middle managers are often not 'on board'. The initiative is not owned by employees. Additional and complementary areas of concern include:

- Some star performers of Six Sigma have shown poor business results (e.g. site closures by Motorola).
- Incomplete initiatives (e.g. Marconi abandoned Six Sigma during the economic downturn of 2001).
- Change of management and loss of sponsors (e.g. the decline of Six Sigma at Allied Signal after the departure of Larry Bossidy).
- External push by high powered consultants (e.g. the dominance of the Air Academy consortium in the GSK programme).
- Excellent early results not sustained (e.g. Ratheon relaunched Lean Sigma after a drop in performance).

- High start-up costs impede small and medium sized enterprises (the initial training start-up cost for Six Sigma is reported to be over $1 million).
- Still regarded as tools for manufacturing (in spite of the success of Six Sigma in GE Capital).

The dramatic bottom-line results and extensive training deployment of Six Sigma and Lean Sigma must be sustained with additional features for securing the long-term competitive advantage of a company. If Lean Sigma provides agility and efficiency, then measures must be in place to develop a sustainable fitness. The process to do just that is FIT SIGMA. In addition, the control of variation from the mean in the Six Sigma process (σ) is transformed to company-wide integration in the FIT SIGMA process. FIT SIGMA is therefore FIT Σ. Furthermore, the philosophy of FIT SIGMA should ensure that it is indeed fit for all organizations – whether large or small, manufacturing or service.

FIT SIGMA is a solution for *sustainable* excellence in *all operations*. It is a quality process beyond Six Sigma. The fundamentals underpinning FIT SIGMA are shown in Figure 10.1. Taken individually, the main components of these cornerstones are not new, but they do constitute proven processes. The combination of components forms the total FIT SIGMA process. The elements are:

- *Fitness for the purpose*
  - Initial assessment
  - All functions
  - Any size of organization

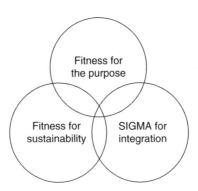

Figure 10.1   FIT SIGMA (Σ) fundamentals (© Performance Excellence Ltd)

- *Sigma (Σ) for improvement and integration*
  - Appropriate Six Sigma tools
  - Learning deployment
  - Project plan and delivery
- *Fitness for sustainability*
  - Performance management
  - Senior management review (S&OP)
  - Self-assessment and certification
  - Knowledge management.

Fitness for the purpose

Joseph Juran coined the phrase 'fitness for the purpose' relating to the basic requirements for quality. In the context of FIT SIGMA, 'fitness for the purpose' has wider implications. Here, 'fitness' means that the FIT SIGMA methodology is tailored to 'fit' all types of operations (whether manufacturing, service or transport) as well as all sizes of organizations (whether a multi-billion dollar global operation or a small local enterprise). The customization of the improvement programme to identify the right fit appropriate to the type and size of operation is determined by a formalized initial assessment process.

Initial assessment

With Total Operations Solutions the approach is to use 200 questions to establish a level of performance against world class standards. These questions are shown in the Appendix. This approach is a form of internal benchmarking. This initial assessment process enables continuing periodic self-assessment.

All functions

Although it is possible to consider each function independently, each function is interrelated. Our approach, with the 200 questions, enables the identification of weaknesses. The synergy that results from the benefits contributed by all elements as a whole far exceeds the aggregate of benefits from individual elements. The integrated approach is truly more than the sum of its elements.

Any size

The 200 questions can be customized to suit any type or size of industry. This is not a rigid approach in search of problems, but an adaptable solution fit for any organization, no matter what type of industry or size.

It is essential that the key players of the company believe in the approach. The initial assessment is similar to that of a Six Sigma 'base line analysis'. With Six Sigma (and Lean Sigma) 'base line analysis' is carried out to identify areas of improvement. However, unlike Six Sigma and Lean Sigma, with Total Operations Solutions (and also for FIT SIGMA) the benchmarking exercise is carried out before staff are taught the methodology. In Six Sigma parlance the education programme is known as learning deployment.

Sigma for improvement and integration

The FIT SIGMA 'improvement' aspect is essentially based upon proven tools and processes of Six Sigma and Lean Sigma.

Appropriate Six Sigma tools

Six Sigma/Lean Sigma tools are not original. The basic tools are:

- Pareto analysis
- Flow process charts
- Tolerance charts (UCL/LCL control charts)
- Cause and effect (Ishikawa) analysis
- Input–process–output (IPO) analysis
- Brainstorming
- Scatter diagram
- Histogram
- The seven wastes (muda)
- The five Ss.

More advanced tools include:

- Failure mode and effect analysis (FMEA)
- Design of experiments (DOE)
- Design for Six Sigma (DFSS).

Details of these tools can be found in *Implementing Quality* (Basu, 2004).

Knowledge of all these tools is not essential. The approach is to adapt what is the most suitable for the organization, making the best use of existing knowledge. Enquiring minds will, naturally, want to improve their knowledge and capabilities.

Learning deployment

In order to achieve long-term benefits it is essential that the organization provides the opportunity for employees at all levels to gain an understanding of analytical tools. To achieve this we recommend a learning deployment plan, to take place *after* the initial assessment using the 200 questions. The plan will vary according to existing quality knowledge and the size of the organization.

As a guide, the proven Six Sigma learning deployment programme allows:

- Leadership training for senior management – 2 days
- Expert training for approximately 1% of employees (at senior and middle management level) – 4–6 weeks
- Supervisor training for approximately 10% of employees – 1 week
- Appreciation training for all employees – 2 × half days.

The issue is not whom should be trained, but who should be the trainer. To gain the right level of training it could well be necessary to involve a consultant. The other approach is to send a dedicated staff member on a recognized quality management course, and for that member to act as the 'internal' consultant.

Project plan and delivery

A FIT SIGMA programme is in effect a project and the basic rules and approaches of project management apply. The essential requirements are a sponsor or 'torch bearer', trained team leaders, open two-way communication and RACI.

RACI means the definition of roles for:

- Responsibility
- Accountability
- Consulting
- Information.

Following the initial assessment a project brief is required, which will include:

- Project organization
- Time plan
- Learning deployment
- Project selection criteria (importance, payback etc.)
- Key deliverables and benefits.

Fitness for sustainability

In a Lean programme the reduction of overhead and cutting out of non-value added activities are all excellent accomplishments but they may be like a dieting plan to lose weight without incorporating appropriate fitness routines. With Total Operations Solution, as in a FIT SIGMA programme, the sustainability of performance is instilled right through the process and not just after the implementation of the education stage.

Performance management

There is little doubt, even in the present environment of advanced information technology, that a company's performance is governed by quarterly or annual financial reports. These reports create an immediate impact on the share value of the company and consequently the majority of performance measures are still rooted to the traditional accounting practice. Senior managers are usually driven to improve the share price, and often they have personal share options in the company which provides a further incentive to do so. Thus the traditional accounting model of balance sheets and profit and loss performance statements are still used to judge the success of management and of the organization. By their very nature these are backward-looking historical documents. Thus although we operate in an age where information is close to being real time, performance is still judged on past results.

In Chapter 8 basic financial measures were introduced. Such traditional measures can be extended to assess customer service (market effectiveness) and resource utilization (operations efficiency). Wild (2002) argues that the three aspects of customer service – specifications,

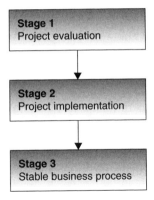

Figure 10.2 Key stages in performance measurement

cost and timing – can be measured against set points or targets. Given many resources as input to a process, resource utilization can be measured as 'the ratio of useful output to input'. Resource utilization is cost-driven while the objective of customer service is to add value.

The models of financial accounting, customer service and resource utilization may also be applicable to some areas of FIT SIGMA, but they are not the key aspects of FIT SIGMA. They are, however, most definitely covered in the 200 benchmarking questions of Total Operations Solutions.

Kaplan and Norton (1996c) argued that 'a valuation of intangible assets and company capabilities would be especially helpful since, for information age companies, these assets are more critical to success than traditional physical and tangible assets'. They have created the 'Balanced Scorecard', as was illustrated in Figure 7.8.

The Balanced Scorecard retains traditional financial measures, customer services and resource utilization (internal business process), and also includes additional measures for learning (people) and growth (innovation). This approach complements measures of past performance with drivers for future development. The Balanced Scorecard can be applied to a stable business process following the introduction of Total Operations Solutions.

Performance management in FIT SIGMA aims to be 'fit for the purpose', likewise with Total Operations Solutions.

With Total Operations Solutions once the benchmarking has been completed (the 200 questions have been answered and plotted) then actions will be planned to correct identified weaknesses and to build on strengths. These actions are best managed by a series of projects.

There are three key stages of a FIT SIGMA initiative in the context of performance measuring, as shown in Figure 10.2, and likewise these stages are incorporated into Total Operations Solutions.

Focus on strategic goals

As with FIT SIGMA, with Total Operations Solutions larger projects are selected based upon an organization's strategic goals and requirements. The viability of the project is then established based on certain quantifiable criteria including ROI (return on investment). Although attempts must be made to show an 'order of magnitude' of ROI data, the emphasis should be focused more on strategic goals and requirements.

With Total Operations Solutions, before any improvement project is commenced five factors are considered.

1 What is the project's value to the business in terms of overall financial performance? This factor can be applied by monitoring the savings on a monthly basis.
2 What resources will be required? How much will they cost? The time scale of the project is also included in this factor.
3 What metrics will be used to monitor the performance of specific large projects. Examples are DPMO (Defects Per Million Opportunities) and RTY (Rolled Throughput Yield).
4 What will the impact be on the external market? It will be important to monitor customer service and sales revenue to ensure that there is no erosion due to key people's commitment to the project.
5 That the project does not take on a life of its own, and that it continues to align with the overall mission and strategy of the business.

A recurring challenge for companies who have invested significant time and resources in implementing proven improvement plans such as Six Sigma is how to ensure their sustainable performance beyond the duration of a one-off corporate exercise. The annual review of the change programme during the budget planning is ineffective because 12 months is a long time in a competitive market place. In order to steer the benefits of the programme and the business objectives to a sustainable future, the senior managers who are in the driving seats must have a clear view of both the front screen and the rear view mirrors and they must look at them as frequently as possible to decide on their direction and optimum speed.

In recent years the pace of change in technology and the market place dynamics have been so rapid that the traditional methodology of monitoring actual performance against pre-determined budgets set at the beginning of the year may no longer be valid. It is fundamental that businesses are managed based on current conditions and up-to-date assumptions; there is also a vital need to establish an effective communication link, both horizontally across functional divisions and vertically across the management hierarchy, to share common data and decision processes. One such solution to these continuous review requirements is Sales and Operations Planning (S&OP).

Senior management review (S&OP)

Sales and Operations Planning (S&OP) has become an established company-wide business planning process in the Oliver Wight MRP II methodology. The diagram in Figure 10.3 shows the five steps in the process that will usually be present and the process can be adapted to specific organizational requirements.

1 *New product review*: Many companies follow parallel projects related to the new products in R&D, Marketing and Operations. The purpose of this review process in Step 1 is to review the different objectives of various departments at the beginning of the month and resolve new product-related assumptions and issues. The issues raised will impact upon the demand plan and the supply chain at a later stage of the process.

2 *Demand review*: Demand planning is more of a consensus art than a fore-casting science. Demand may change from month to month depending

Figure 10.3   Senior management review process (S&OP)

on market intelligence, customer confidence, exchange rates, promotions, product availability and many other internal and external factors. In Step 2, this review, at the end of the first week of the month, between Marketing, Sales, IT and Logistics, establishes agreement and accountability for the latest demand plan identifying changes and issues arising.

3 *Supply review*: In the current climate of increasing outsourcing and supply partnership, the capacity of supply is highly variable and there is a need to ensure the availability and optimization of supply every month. In Step 3, this review, usually on the second week of the month, between Logistics, Purchasing and Production, establishes the production and procurement plans and raises capacity, inventory and scheduling issues.

4 *Reconciliation review*: Issues would have been identified in previous reviews of new products, demand and supply. The reconciliation step goes beyond the balancing of numbers to assess the business advantage and risk for each area of conflict. In Step 4, this review looks at issues from the business point of view rather than departmental objectives. This is also known as the Pre-S&OP Review and its aim is to minimize issues for the final S&OP stage.

5 *Senior management review*: Senior managers or board members, with an MD or CEO in the chair, will approve the plan that will provide clear visibility for a single set of members driving the total business forward. The agenda includes the review of key performance indicators, business trends of operational and financial performance, issues arising from previous reviews and corporate initiatives. This is a powerful forum to adjust business direction and priorities. Step 5 is also known as the Sales and Operations Planning (S&OP) Review.

In each process step the reviews must address a planning horizon of 18–36 months in order to make a decision for both operational and strategic objectives. There may be a perceived view that S&OP is a process of aggregate/volume planning for supply chain. However, it is also a top level forum to provide a link between business plan and strategy. The continuous improvement and sustainability of company performance by a FIT SIGMA programme can only be ensured in the longer term by a well-structured S&OP or Senior Management Review Process. The results and issues related to FIT SIGMA should be a regular item in the S&OP agenda. Figure 10.4 illustrates how a hierarchy of key performance indicators (KPI) can be applied and cascaded across the review processes.

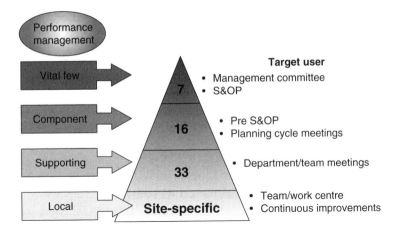

Figure 10.4 Balanced Scorecard: measures and hierarchy

Self-assessment and certification

In order to maintain a wave of interest in the quality programme and also to market the competitive advantage of quality, many companies dedicated the effort to the pursuit of an approved accreditation such as ISO or an award such as the Malcolm Baldridge Award (in the USA) and derivatives of the Baldridge Award in other countries. The certification and awards have had a chequered history. After a peak in the early 1990s, the Baldridge Awards gradually lost their impact in the USA and companies (e.g. GE, Johnson & Johnson) started developing their own customized quality assessment process. Encouraged by the customer demand for the ISO stamp of approval there was a rush for ISO 9000 certification in the 1990s, but companies became disillusioned by the auditors ensuring compliance with current procedures without necessarily improving standards. A number of consultancy companies attempted to introduce their own awards to progress an improvement programme (e.g. Class 'A' by Oliver Wight).

It is essential to incorporate a self-assessment process in order to sustain a performance and improvement culture. Total Operations Solutions provides a self-monitoring checklist of 200 questions which can be adapted to meet any type or size of organization.

There are several examples where a company achieved an external award based on a set of criteria but without improving business performance. There are also cases where, after the initial publicity, the performance level and pursuit for excellence were not maintained.

If the process is not underpinned by self-assessment then the award will gradually lose its lustre. We therefore recommend that a FIT SIGMA programme should adopt a self-assessment process developed from proven processes. Two such processes are described below: 'EFQM' and 'Total Solutions'.

EFQM (European Foundation of Quality Management)   The EFQM award is derived from America's Malcolm Baldridge National Quality Award. There are similar accolades available in other countries, such as the Canadian Excellence Awards and the Australian Quality Award.

The EFQM Award was established in 1991. It is supported by the European Union and the countries in the EU have their own support unit (e.g. British Quality Foundation in the UK). As shown in Figure 10.5, the EFQM model provides a set of checklist questionnaires under nine categories, each containing maximum points. They are:

Leadership	100 points
People management	90 points
Policy and strategy	80 points
Resources	90 points
Processes	140 points
People satisfaction	90 points
Customer satisfaction	200 points
Impact on society	60 points
Business results	150 points
Total	1000 points

The first five categories (Leadership to Processes) are 'enablers' and the remaining four categories are 'performance' related.

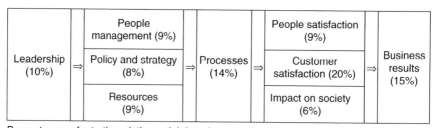

Percentages refer to the relative weighting given to criteria

Figure 10.5   The EFQM model

'Total Solutions' 'Total Solutions' enables self-assessment against 20 defined areas (called 'foundation stones') to identify areas of improvement for achieving the full potential of the business. The business is built from these foundation stones up, and consists of the 'six pillars' of Total Solutions (see Figure 2.1). These pillars are comprised as follows:

- Marketing and Innovation
- Supply Chain Management
- Environment and Safety
- Facilities
- Procedures
- People.

Self-assessment is done through 200 questions, ten for each foundation stone. Although the checklist is aimed at manufacturing operations, it can be adapted easily to service operations. A 'spider diagram' can be constructed from scores of each foundation stone to highlight the current performance profile and gaps (see Figure 10.6). In Total Manufacturing Solutions (Basu and Wright, 1997) the aim was to determine a Manufacturing Correctness Factor; in Total Operations Solutions the aim is to determine the Operational Excellence Factor. This is further discussed in Chapter 12.

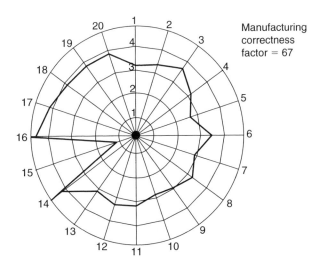

Figure 10.6 Example of a spider diagram giving a manufacturing correctness profile (Basu and Wright, 1997)

Our methodology of the self-assessment for a FIT SIGMA programme comprises the following features:

1 Establish the policy of external certification or customized self-assessment in line with the company culture and business characteristics.
2 Develop or confirm the checklist of assessment.
3 Train internal assessors in the common company assessment process (one assessor for every 500 employees as a rough guide). The assessors should also carry out normal line or functional duty.
4 Train experts (Black Belts) and department managers in the self-assessment checklist and process.
5 Carry out quarterly self-assessment by departmental managers.
6 Ensure six-monthly (at the initial stage) and annual (at the later stage) assessments by the internal assessors.
7 Analyse gaps and implement measures to minimize the gap.
8 Consider corporate awards, depending on the performance attained, by the CEO.
9 Review the checklist with the change of business every two years.
10 Consider external accreditation if it adds value to the business.

The above methodology is applicable to all types of business, both manufacturing and service, and all sizes of operations, whether large, medium or small. A larger organization is likely to have its own resources to develop and maintain the process; a smaller organization may require the assistance of external consultants to develop the process (Basu and Wright, 2003).

CASE EXAMPLE: Janssen–Cilag applies 'Signature of quality' for continuous self-improvement

Janssen–Cilag is the pharmaceutical arm of the Johnson & Johnson Group with their European Head Office based in High Wycombe, Buckinghamshire. The origins of the company lie as far back as the 1940s, with three companies initially in existence: Ortho Pharmaceutical in the UK, Cilag Chemie in Switzerland and Janssen Pharmaceutica in Belgium. The merger was completed in 1995 and Janssen–Cilag is now among the top ten pharmaceutical companies in the world. The company markets prescription medicines for a range of therapeutic areas of gastroenterology, fungal infections, women's health, mental health and neurology.

The commitment of the company to the values and standards laid out in 'Our Credo' drives management to strive continually for excellence in a number of overlapping areas. Based upon the principles of the Baldridge Award, the Quality Management team of Janssen–Cilag developed a self-assessment process known as 'Signature of Quality (SoQ)'. The process is supported by a checklist on a carefully constructed questionnaire in five interdependent areas:

- Customer focus
- Innovation
- Personnel and organizational leadership
- Exploitation of enabling technology
- Environment and safety.

SoQ is managed as a global process from the US office and each site is encouraged to prepare and submit a comprehensive quality report meeting the requirements. The assessment is carried out by specially trained Quality Auditors and a site may receive an SoQ Award based upon the results of the assessment.

SoQ has been reported to be successful in Janssen–Cilag as a tool for performing a regular 'health check' and as a foundation for improvement from internal benchmarking.

(From Basu and Wright (2003) *Quality Beyond Six Sigma*)

Knowledge management

Knowledge once gained is too important to lose. The key principles of knowledge management in FIT SIGMA methodology are:

1 Systematically capture knowledge from proven 'good practices'
2 Select examples of best practice which provide added value to the business
3 Inculcate knowledge between all functions.

It is essential to establish a learning organization culture. Unless staff at all levels are sharing in knowledge, and truly believe that the business can benefit from shared knowledge, the gathering of knowledge will have achieved little. If an organization believes that they already know what the best practice is and are satisfied with incremental improvement they will be left behind. History shows that knowledge progresses in leaps and bounds. The development of a learning culture does not just happen, words are not enough. The support structure required to develop a knowledge-sharing culture needs:

- A champion as a focal point to coordinate the process
- Regular 'best practice' forums, to promote learning, sharing and networking
- Internal and external benchmarking using the 200 questions
- Continuous communication through websites, newsletters, etc.

Summary

FIT SIGMA is a natural extension of the third wave of the Quality Movement offering a historically proven process to improve and sustain performance of all businesses, both manufacturing and services, whether big or small.

FIT SIGMA is not a statistic. It is both a management philosophy and an improvement process. The underlying philosophy is that of a total business-focused approach underpinned by continuous reviews and a knowledge-based culture to sustain a high level of performance. In order to implement the FIT SIGMA philosophy, a systematic approach is recommended. The process is not a set of new or unknown tools; in fact, these tools and cultures have been proven to yield excellent results in earlier waves.

The differentiation of FIT SIGMA is the process of combining and retaining the success factors. Its strength is that the process is not a rigid programme in search of problems, but an adaptable solution for a specific company or business.

Total Operations Solutions provides the necessary process for self-benchmarking to enable the level of fitness, to indicate where actions have to be taken to get fit, and to provide a method for regular self-monitoring of fitness. The objective is to know initially how unfit the organization is, to take action to correct and to improve fitness, and finally to maintain fitness.

Chapter 11

Strategy for
Improved Value

Probable impossibilities are to be preferred to improbable possibilities.
Aristotle

Once gaps in performance have been established (see Chapter 12), the natural reaction is to take immediate, almost urgent, action to correct the situation. However, we caution patience. Having come this far, it is important not to take precipitate action. Our philosophy is that there is no such thing as a quick fix. The best results are achieved by careful consideration of all factors.

A vital stage between gap analysis and the implementation phase is the selection of the appropriate improvement strategy. Following the results of the self-analysis and performance gap analysis the team should develop a recommendation for change. A lack of in-depth investigation of what is appropriate for a company has caused many sound change programmes such as TQM and even Six Sigma to fail. Recently business writers have been warning of the dangers of adopting 'management fads' or 'quick fixes' (Richards, 1995; Miller and Hartwick, 2002; Pettigrew, 2004). We liken what has often happened to the application of wonder drugs by a doctor without the diagnosis of the illness, and without taking into account the condition of the patient, with the 'cure' being more dangerous than the ailment.

Miller and Hartwick observe that 'Fads are simple, prescriptive, falsely encouraging, one size fits all, easy to cut and paste, in tune with the Zeitgeist', and so on. They conclude that enduring tools, what they describe as 'classics', 'arise not from the writings of academics or consultants but emerge out of practitioner responses to economic, social and competitive challenges'.

Determining what is a 'fad' and what is an enduring tool can be difficult, likewise dismissing a new tool as a 'fad' may well be an expensive lost opportunity. Miller and Hartwick urge managers when evaluating a business approach or technique to consider 'Does the approach have a track record for performance and measurable outcomes in similar companies facing similar challenges? Does it address problems or opportunities that are high priorities for our company? Are the changes it would require within our company's capabilities and resources? Yes answers to these questions suggest an approach likely to pay off and endure.'

In short, it is nothing less than a sound strategy to review fundamental criteria before adopting an improvement programme. We suggest that the three key criteria are improvement category (as described below), core strengths and the present position.

Improvement category

The approaches and characteristics of an improvement programme depend on both the degree of change (i.e. technical or strategic) and the pace of change (i.e. fast or longer term). Figure 11.1 illustrates the four broad categories of performance improvement. This type of conceptual mapping has been widely used by consultants. The categories are focused improvement (fast tactical change), continuous improvement (longer-term tactical change), focused restructuring (fast strategic change), process re-engineering (longer-term strategic change).

A tactical change usually involves small-scale incremental improvements. A strategic change represents improvements in much larger steps and has a deeper time horizon.

		Pace of change	
		Fast	Longer term
Degree of change	Tactical	Focused improvement	Continuous improvement
	Strategic	Focused restructuring	Process re-engineering

Figure 11.1   Improvement categories

- *Focused improvement*: This type of improvement may not appear to be radical but it is achieved within a short time scale and very often without any significant capital expenditure. Such changes are also relatively easy to implement and therefore form a big part of a company's cost-effectiveness programme.
- *Continuous improvement*: The application of total quality, flexible working practices and total productive maintenance are examples of the continuous improvement category. These types of programmes are invariably company-wide, requiring cultural change over a long period.
- *Focused restructuring*: Focused restructuring often aims at combining activities and departments. Such major organizational changes resulting from an acquisition or site closure may require an immediate downsizing or structural re-organization. Focused restructuring often aims at combining activities and departments.
- *Process re-engineering*: Business process re-engineering results in strategic changes with a deep time horizon and is achieved by redesigning the core processes of a business. The new operating model is often influenced by the success of processes adopted by benchmarking partners.

The choice of a particular improvement approach should depend on a company's specific requirements and commitments. It is also likely that a company may apply a carefully selected portfolio of all improvement approaches. However, the key message is that the selection should be based upon your own self-analysis and not be ruled by the pressure of fashion or fads.

The company's core strengths

As we discussed in Chapter 9, a company must identify its core values. Collins (1995) emphasizes that leading-edge companies have successfully adapted to a changing world without losing their core values. They have understood the difference between fundamental principles and daily practices. For example, according to Collins, Disney has diversified its product strategy from cartoons, to feature films, to theme parks (Disney Land), but has maintained its central ideology (vision), of bringing happiness to people.

It is important to identify a limited number of core principles (usually not more than five) and any improvement programme or change process must not deviate from these fundamental ideals. A core ideology does not arise from the pursuit of competitive advantage. Core values must be distinguished from, and not confused with, business practices or 'sacred cows'. Once core principles are clearly understood, and encapsulated in the mission statement, then, and only then, is it safe to consider changes.

Furthermore, a company's core strengths need to relate to its product and marketing strategy. A change programme must take into account the strategic measures in pursuit of exploiting a dominant position. For example, a ruthless cost-effectiveness programme is a sensible approach in mature markets. Similarly, knowledge gained in developing markets may significantly benefit mature markets. Improvement programmes related to quality logically should be applicable to products with a shorter life cycle, whilst those related to performance should be more appropriate for established products.

An aid to the selection of an improvement strategy (based on the criterion of a company's core strengths) should be derived from the understanding of its mission and objectives rather than from the self-analysis of the 200 questions. In short, when you understand your own mission and objectives you understand your core strengths. The 200 questions identify areas where corrective action is required. But your strategy for improvement must be based on your prevailing culture and ideals.

The company's present position

Following a self-analysis with the 200 questions, and a further review of the performance versus practice matrix, a company can locate its position within one of the five categories, namely leaders, behaviourists, structuralists, plodders and laggers (see Figure 12.7, p. 285). The choice of an improvement strategy can be significantly influenced by your identity with one of these five categories. Let us examine how this approach can be applied.

Leaders

This category of companies has achieved world class performance and global market leadership. They can sustain their advantages by continuing the application of best practices. For these companies there may not be any road map to follow, as they themselves are creating it. Nevertheless, they cannot afford any form of complacency, or any slippage, as the pressure to stay at the premier league is decidedly tough. In any event, our philosophy is that perfection is never attained, there is always room for improvement. Therefore, in addition to maintaining a continuous improvement culture and retaining their core strengths, their improvement strategy should contain:

- Further expansion and penetration capability with cost-effective products in the global market
- Continuous investment in improving relationships with stakeholders (e.g. investors, suppliers, customers and employees)
- A relentless pursuit to innovative new products and new business concepts.

Behaviourists

Companies in this category will have invested heavily in TQM initiatives and have a best practice culture. The systems (including IT), procedures and infrastructure for change programmes are in place. Employee involvement and team work are actively encouraged by management. These are continuous learning companies but are yet to reap the benefits of their efforts. There are two groups in this category. For the group with a small performance gap, because the infrastructure of best practice programmes and change culture is already in place, they should find the route to world class status reasonably straightforward.

On the other hand, the behaviourists, with a large performance gap, will have to face the reality that the rest of the journey is going to require discipline and a concerted company-wide effort. The momentum of TQM initiatives may have been lost and perhaps members of the company might be disillusioned.

To re-energize and to re-kindle enthusiasm for continuous improvement programmes the improvement strategy for behaviourists will need to include:

- A market-led strategy towards reducing operating costs and improving customer service
- Programmes focused on performance improvement and cost-effectiveness

- Abandonment of change programmes that are not delivering results and that are seen as fads by many employees.

Structuralists

The structuralist group of companies are profitable and usually have a dominant share of local and regional markets. They may be ahead of the game in their own patch but in fact may well be vulnerable to emerging global competition. Their business strategy has been to emphasize targets and results and to date this has been successful, but in general they have neglected to develop a change culture and a philosophy of best practice. It is likely that without adopting a best practice culture, and without the appropriate people and systems infrastructure, they may not go the distance to join the leaders' league.

This group first has to recognize that action and change are needed and then to adopt an improvement strategy. The strategy should include:

- Carefully designed continuous improvement programmes to enhance change culture and continuous learning
- Programmes for meeting product safety, and industrial safety environmental protection
- Additional emphasis on longer-term plans for improving human resources issues, including flexible working practices.

Plodders

The companies in this group may possess pockets of excellence in both performance and practices, but their overall strengths are not good enough to compete in a global market. A high proportion of companies fall into this category. Their local strategies have shown good results in specific areas but they lack a coherent and potent leadership to benefit from the best practices of each unit. We have found that it is not uncommon to observe world class manufacturing lines alongside less efficient lines in the same manufacturing site. Another example in our experience is a manufacturing organization that has its own high street retailers. This organization has an admirable policy of seven-day stock turn in the retail outlets but the balance sheet showed that they held eight months of finished goods in their distribution warehouses, and a further seven months of raw materials at the factories.

Plodders will require radical changes in both performance and practices to progress towards the leaders league.

In addition to retaining the pockets of excellence the improvement strategy for 'plodders' should include:

- The recognition and removal of inhibitors so that their own people skills and best practices can be developed to their full potential
- Retention of the core values of the company, and a selective but aggressive application of business process re-engineering in the critical areas of the business
- Encouragement of networking and promotion of best practices within the organization.

Laggers

This is the lowest scoring group in both performance and practices. It is unlikely that these companies can become world class in the foreseeable future. It is however possible for a company to operate in a protected market without long-term best practice or high performance. But as local protection is on the wane, these companies must make drastic changes for their survival. There is no merit in rushing into automation or TQM. Many companies in this group will be working with limited human and financial resources. Changing business procedures will have limited impact as these will only speed up poor processes.

In addition to holding onto the strengths, if any, in selected products, the improvement strategy for 'laggers' should be focused on short-term changes including:

- Aggressive restructuring, downsizing and asset utilization programmes
- Systematic simplification of business processes (namely, industrial engineering) toward high performance and quality with minimum investment
- Continuous learning and communication programmes to develop the company's human resources and also to sustain the morale of the workforce
- Practical longer-term plans for both continuing business and possible mergers with more profitable organizations.

Summary

Recently much attention has been focused on the danger of management fads reinforcing scepticism and resistance to change amongst management. There are also doubts about endangering the core values of a business by following fashionable, but inappropriate, business practices.

In this chapter we have identified the types of improvement processes and provided a systematic approach of adopting an improvement strategy that is most likely to be appropriate for the particular business. Naturally, the categorization of a manufacturing business and the selection of a strategy is not always clear-cut. In the real world a perfect model does not exist and there will always be a 'grey area' of overlap. None the less, our methodology provides a useful guideline for enhancing the proportion of objective analysis, thus helping the selection of improvement programmes.

Chapter 12

Data Collection and Gap Analysis

*I have spent a fortune travelling to distant shores and looked at lofty
mountains and boundless oceans, and yet I haven't found time to take
a few steps from my house to look at a single dew drop on a single
blade of grass.*
    Rabindranath Tagore

Travellers accept that even if they have a good road map with land-
marks and milestones they will get lost if they do not know where
they are. In the quest for operational excellence the first task is to
carry out a health check of your organization. A health check is not
an audit. Audits are usually formal, conducted by experts external to
the organization. A health check, on the other hand, is a less formal
self-assessment conducted by people from within the organization.

In previous chapters we have described the six pillars of an
organization and the 20 underpinning foundation stones. We have
developed 200 questions – 10 questions for each foundation – for
carrying out a self-assessment health check of an organization (see
the Appendix).

The traditional assessment processes, such as ISO, MBNQA or
EFQM, are usually carried out as audits by external consultants
while a health check by 200 questions is designed to be conducted by
an internal team of the organization. We believe that there are
substantial benefits to be gained from designing your own benchmarking or health check process rather than following a consulting
firm's standards. We are not suggesting that you should 'reinvent'
the wheel, rather we explain how – by using the results from the
200 questions – you can tailor-make your own benchmarking
process. After all, every business is to some extent unique and each

organization will have its own culture and way of doing things. This culture should not be unduly upset; any new process should consider a cultural fit.

The important success factors of conducting one's own assessment include:

- Employees know more about a company's business than any outside expert possibly can
- A customized own benchmarking process will promote either a detailed or a less structured approach to fit the existing culture of an organization
- Own benchmarking is likely to generate an ownership for a solution and dispel any distrust towards glib 'off-the-shelf' approaches.

Outside consultants can bring in experience, expertise and can be objective. They can often act as a catalyst to make things happen. They may also provide support to under-resourced organizations. None the less, our recommendation is that you will gain the most benefits by first carrying out your own self-assessment. The experience of Johnson & Johnson in the early 1900s, as reported by Biesadra (1992), was that by relying heavily on consultants the company initially achieved only 5% of what was finally achieved through internal benchmarking activities. Costs and cycle times of achieving results greatly reduced when the strategy changed from using external consultants to own employees. The quality of results was also greatly improved.

In this chapter we discuss the requirements and provide guidelines for conducting a health check as the starting point of an operational excellence programme. There are four parts in this health check process:

- Data preparation
- Self-assessment
- Gap analysis
- Improvement strategy.

Data preparation

Following your decision to embark upon a benchmarking project the next stage is to organize a multi-functional team. Team members should be senior and experienced people and all functions of the business should be represented. The first step for this team is to understand the company's organization and business activities. It is likely that the background and experience of team members will be varied and some may not have a clear understanding of the total business. People from engineering and technical backgrounds may understand detailed procedures of technical operations, while people from sales, marketing and service backgrounds may be more conversant with broader issues related to customers.

The synergy of the team should be greatly enhanced by comparing each member's understanding of the company with regard to the following basic questions:

- What is the core business of the company?
- Who are the main customers?
- Who are the top three competitors?
- Which sectors of the business are the most and least profitable?
- What is the size of the business in terms of sales, assets and people?

Although agreement on the answers to the above questions will promote a synergy for the team, the 200 questions cannot be considered until substantial amounts of data are collected and in some cases collated. The detailed preparation of data, and the understanding of the business process, can largely be derived from the following basic existing information:

- Annual operating plans for the past five years showing actual sales trends and profitability by product
- Long-term strategic plans, or study reports, giving market forecast by product and sectors
- Internal company reports and databases on competitors' market share and innovation programmes
- Current information on customers and distribution channels
- Expenditure programme (budget) for the next five years regarding innovation, marketing and capital projects
- Written policies and programmes on product safety, industrial safety and environmental protection
- Non-financial performance measures regarding:
  - customer service
  - plant efficiency

- plant utilization
- maintenance effectiveness
- Quality programmes and ISO certification if appropriate
- Information technology policy, and existing hardware and software application programs
- Organizational structures, management development and learning programmes
- Annual financial reports
- Marketing research reports and databases.

For the team to gain an in-depth understanding of the total process further analysis will be needed. One useful way to describe and analyse a business is by process mapping or process flow diagrams. This approach is illustrated in Figure 12.1. However, the description and analysis of the business may not need to be as complicated as this illustration. A simple value stream map can also indicate the total business process at a high level (see Basu, 2004: 118–121). Once the business process is mapped, the team possibly

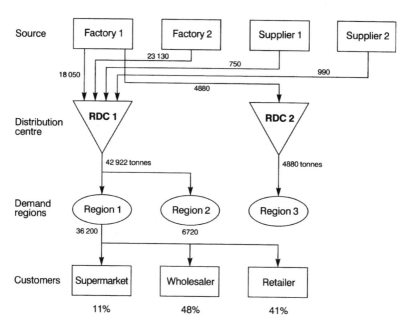

Figure 12.1 Flow diagram of sourcing and distribution of a product

might identify some areas of bottlenecks before carrying out a detailed self-assessment.

The next stage for the team is to study and understand the six pillars and the 20 foundation stones as described in Chapters 4–9. It is vital for the team to review all aspects of the 20 foundation stones so as to identify and understand which factors are critical to achieving excellence for your business. The well-known value chain model of Porter (1990) is a useful way of aligning your business with the six pillars in order to comprehend their characteristics. Figure 12.2 shows a model of our six pillars based upon Porter's value chain. We have three primary pillars of performance activities (Marketing and Innovation, Infrastructure Facilities and Supply Chain Management). They are supported by the three secondary pillars of practices (Environment and Safety, Systems and Procedures and Intellectual Capital). The combination of performance and practices gives excellence, as depicted in our model.

As in Porter's model, one can focus the business needs by analysing the relative value of each pillar and the reason for its existence with regard to the business. In our model the pillars of primary activities are profit-driven and the aim is the achievement of higher performance standards. The pillars of secondary activities are service-driven and the aim is for achieving best practices.

Although not essential, it is helpful to obtain published reports on outstanding or 'world class' performance achieved by other companies in your organization's area of interest. It is not necessary to search for a world class company to be a benchmarking partner. A wealth of information is available in published reports and this should be sufficient to provide an understanding of what is achievable. Several 'best practice' databases are now available in the USA and

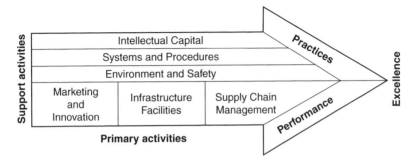

Figure 12.2   Value chain (after Porter, 1990)

Europe which will enable you to assess your organization against the reputed best.

Guide to assessment

A potential danger of performing a self-assessment by means of our 200 questions lies in its deceptive simplicity. Your own benchmarking may not be conceptually complicated but it will be extremely rich in detail. We have not applied any psychological expertise in the formulation of our questions, but it is evident that without adequate guidelines your teams could be at a disadvantage. It is often tempting to 'guess' a rating if the basis for the rating of a specific question is not properly qualified. In this chapter and the Appendix we have used a rating method for our questions. Guidelines for answering and rating each question can be found in ASK 2.0 interactive software.

Bogan and English (1994) give four categories of questions for this type of survey, as follows:

1 Multiple choice

   Example: What type of maintenance policy do your engineers follow?
   a) Breakdown
   b) Time-based preventive
   c) Predictive
   d) Inspection based?

2 Forced choice

   Example: Are you satisfied with forecasting methods and techniques?
   Yes   ☐
   No   ☐

3 Open-ended

   Example: What suggestions do you have to improve your customer service?

4 Scales

   Example: Rate the following on a scale of 1 to 5 with 1 being 'poor' and 5 being 'excellent'
   How good is the success ratio of new products?

The difficulty with multiple choice questions is that they provide a set of answers and sometimes the choice given does not adequately fit the situation. With forced choice (yes/no questions), not shading at all is provided. Seldom will answers be black or white.

With open-ended questions, however, too much leeway is given, a large amount of subjectivity is allowed and frequently answers stray from the question. In addition sometimes respondents find difficulty in replying to open-ended questions if they have to prepare a written answer.

We decided that the scaled method of questions would provide the best method for our purposes. The scale has a sufficient span to permit a reasonably accurate rating by an experienced team. Black and white type answers are avoided and subjectivity is confined within the limits of the five-point scale.

Some questions relate to areas where data is measurable (e.g. our question number 131: 'Do you have a dash board of key performance measurements and how well is it monitored?'). In this case it is relatively easy to apply a rating scale, provided a range of performance level can be defined for each scale. But it has to be clearly understood that it is essential to have a good understanding of what best practice is, that is to say, what exactly is the standard we are trying to measure against. A 'complacent' rating of 0.4 and 0.5 for every one of the 200 questions will render the exercise meaningless. The other danger is that once a rating is given it takes on an aura of accuracy which may be entirely misleading unless the rating has been given with full knowledge of all factors by an experienced team.

As many questions do not lend themselves to a quantifiable answer, the answers by necessity will rely on interpretation by team members. We recognize that interpretation may give scope for some inconsistency by teams. It is our intention to develop a piece of 'knowledge-based' software incorporating guidelines for all 200 questions. In the meantime, as a guideline, the following indicative sample is provided.

Question 1
How well do your managers in marketing and sales know the relative importance of main products (by volume, profit and trends)?

Poor (0.1)
No measurement of sales volume, value of profit by product. Total sales are usually reported by region or salesperson.

Fair (0.2)
Some measurement by product of sales volume, value and profit. No trend analysis. Marketing and sales managers do not receive regular reports by products.

Good (0.3)
Regular reporting of sales volume, value and profit by products. Trend analysis is carried out. Generally marketing and sales managers are reasonably competent in the interpretation of figures.

Very good (0.4)
Good measurement and reporting of sales volume value and profits by products. Regular trend analysis. A computerized information system facilities ABC analysis by various parameters. Marketing and sales managers are trained and able to take actions from regular trends and performance reports for each product.

Excellent (0.5)
Very reliable and prompt measurement and reporting of sales volume, value and profits by product. Trends are plotted on computer systems which are accessible by sales and marketing managers. Managers are capable of analysing data (e.g. ABC analysis) and take action on an interactive real time basis.

It would have been ideal to list detailed guidelines for all the 200 questions, but that would create an imbalance in the book with relatively low added value. This apparent deficiency can only be redressed by adequate training and exchanging assessment of 'non-quantifiable' questions between team members. We also propose to develop software containing guidelines (see Appendix).

Self-assessment

After achieving a good understanding of the foundation stones, data preparation and guide to assessment the internal team embarks on the actual health check of the organization in three steps, such as verification of data, agreement of scores and data analysis.

Verification of data

Following data preparation and preliminary data collection the team should verify key information through a series of carefully selected interviews. One simple rule the team must follow is open communication. People being interviewed, or providing information, have to be reassured that there is no ulterior motive. It has to be made clear that the objective is to carry out a 'health check' of the total business and not of any one person or department.

Agreement of scores

After following the hints given above (Guide to assessment), it is useful for each member of the team to carry out a 'dry run' in order to ensure that all questions can be adequately answered. The team can then have an open discussion to exchange views on doubtful areas. The next stage is relatively straightforward, with each member of the team, without collaborating with other members, ticking off their assessment of appropriate scores against each question. Finally, the team will meet together to review all answers and to agree a set of scores.

We emphasize that regardless of the type or priorities of a manufacturing business, the first assessment must include answers to all 200 questions. No question should be given a 'nil' score.

Data analysis

The objective of data analysis is to bring order out of the scores for the 200 questions. Data analysis can be done in a number of ways. We recommend four simple but effective means of data analysis:

- Rating profile
- Operational Excellence Factor (OEF)

1   Understanding the market place

1 How well do your managers in marketing and sales know the relative importance of main products?

1	0.1	0.2	(0.3)	0.4	0.5

2 How good (precise) are your analyses of trade needs and consumer habits?

2	0.1	(0.2)	0.3	0.4	0.5

3 How often do you conduct market research of trade needs and consumer habits?

3	0.1	(0.2)	0.3	0.4	0.5

4 How well are customer complaints handled/ recorded? Are there set procedures and do staff use the procedures?

4	(0.1)	0.2	0.3	0.4	0.5

5 How well do your sales and marketing team know the relative importance of factors that affect customer satisfaction?

5	0.1	0.2	(0.3)	0.4	0.5

6 How systematic, and scientific, are your advertising and promotion activities?

6	0.1	0.2	0.3	(0.4)	0.5

7 How close is the link between your sales, marketing, planning and operations functions?

7	0.1	(0.2)	0.3	0.4	0.5

8 How often do staff other than sales and marketing visit your major customers?

8	0.1	0.2	(0.3)	0.4	0.5

9 How well do you know international tariff, tax and trade regulations?

9	0.1	0.2	(0.3)	0.4	0.5

10 How aware are you of opportunities and constraints for emerging markets?

10	0.1	(0.2)	0.3	0.4	0.5

Figure 12.3   Example of a rating profile

- 'Spider' diagram
- Histogram.

Rating profile

As illustrated in Figure 12.3, a rating profile is drawn simply by joining scores of all 200 questions. It provides two useful pointers:

- It ensures that all questions have been assessed with scores in a scale 0.1 to 0.5.
- It easily offers a rough guide to the 'health' related to each question. Other diagrams show performance measures by a foundation stone and not by individual questions.

Table 12.1 Calculating the Operational Excellence Factor

Foundation stone	*Score*
1 Understanding the market place	5
2 Understanding the competition	4
3 Product and process innovation	4
4 Enterprise resource planning	4
5 Supply chain management	4
6 Distribution management and working with customers	5
7 Product safety	2
8 Occupational safety and health	3
9 Environment and resource management	3
10 Sourcing strategy	4
11 Appropriate technology	5
12 Flexibility and lean processes	3
13 Reliability and maintenance	4
14 Performance management and Balanced Scorecard	4
15 Quality management	3
16 Financial management	3
17 Information and communication technology	2
18 Leadership and organization capital	3
19 Human resource policies and human capital	2
20 Knowledge management and information capital	3
Operational Excellence Factor	70

Operational Excellence Factor (OEF)

OEF is the aggregate total of scores for each foundation stone expressed as a number, the maximum possible value being 100 (see Table 12.1).

'Spider' diagram

Operational Excellence Factor is a new concept. It provides a useful indicator of the overall performance of the business. But it does not highlight the strengths and weaknesses of individual foundation stones. The purpose of a spider diagram is to do just that. It has been used before in modified forms and under various names, such as 'arachnid' diagram, radar chart, measured matrix chart or M2. As illustrated in Figure 12.4, the chart consolidates various performance scores by arraying different foundation stones along the radius or spokes of a circular graph.

Greatest opportunities for improvement are highlighted by the size of gaps between the centre point and the radius. Different target goals, appropriate for each foundation stone, can be set on the

1 Understanding the market place
2 Understanding the competition
3 Product and process innovation
4 Enterprise resource planning
5 Supply chain and supplier partnership
6 Distribution management and working with customers
7 Product safety
8 Occupational safety and health
9 Environment and resource management
10 Sourcing strategy
11 Appropriate technology
12 Flexibility and lean processes
13 Reliability and maintenance
14 Performance management and Balanced Scorecard
15 Quality management
16 Financial management
17 Information and communication technology
18 Leadership and organization capital
19 Human resource policies and human capital
20 Knowledge management and information capital

Figure 12.4 Operations Excellence profile ('spider diagram')

diagram to identify the target gaps. The 'spider' diagram offers a number of positive features including:

- It complements the Operational Excellence Factor by highlighting how OEF is made up.
- It illustrates the total business performance levels with a single graph.
- It pinpoints the performance gaps for each foundation stone.
- It focuses the management attention on total manufacturing solutions rather than on isolated performance figures produced for a specific area or foundation stone.

Histogram

A histogram has the same objective as a spider diagram, i.e. to illustrate the performance levels of all foundation stones in a single graph. The difference is that a histogram shows linear rather than radial results.

Some users have found a histogram, as illustrated in Figure 12.5, visually easy to interpret and to measure gaps with respect to targets. The target or best practice figures can be presented alongside the actual performance for each foundation stone, as shown in Figure 12.6.

Computer-aided analysis

We all know that effective computer systems are good enabling tools for successful projects. Software should be able to assist teams, particularly at the data preparation stage of the project. Some

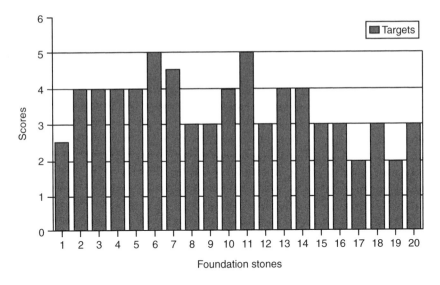

Figure 12.5 A histogram of scores of foundation stones

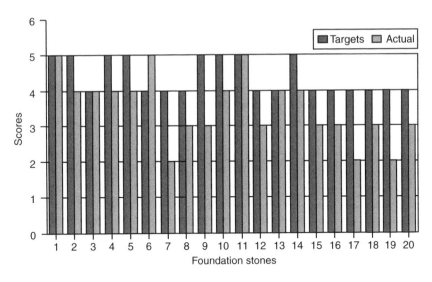

Figure 12.6 A histogram of scores for targets and actual

examples of available software applications are:

- Spreadsheet programs (e.g. Excel, Lotus 1-2-3) to help teams store data, calculate performance figures, and carry out trend analysis

- Process mapping programs to enable teams to prepare flow charts of various business processes
- Graphics programs (e.g. PowerPoint) to assist teams display data and results
- Word-processing programs to prepare questionnaires, interim reports, etc.
- CD-ROM libraries, Lotus Notes and databases to carry out literature searches and for best practice examples
- e-Mail systems to communicate between team members and key people.

It is not essential to hunt for all the software options. The use of existing technology with which the team members are familiar should be adequate for their preparation work. However, it would be extremely useful if the team had access to specially designed software to:

- Provide guidelines for assessing the answers of all 200 questions
- Compute the total score of each foundation stone and thus determine the manufacturing correctness factor
- Produce spider diagrams and histograms
- Include flexibility such as user-defined questions.

We have developed such a software on Microsoft Windows which meets the above user requirements and have named it ASK 2 (Advanced Self-Analysis Kit). It is designed to incorporate guidelines to 200 questions and to enable users to 'self-appraise' against world class standards.

Performance *vs.* practice analysis

The inclusion of performance *vs.* practice analysis was prompted by the success of a benchmark study carried out jointly by IBM and the London Business School and reported by Hanson *et al.* (1994).

Continuing the value chain approach, as shown in Figure 12.2, we can classify the six pillars and their associated foundation stones into two groups:

(a) Performance pillars (primary activities)
    1 Marketing and innovation (foundation stones 1–3)
    2 Supply chain management (foundation stones 4–6)
    3 Infrastructure facilities (foundation stones 10–14)
(b) Practice pillars (support activities)
    – Environment and safety (foundation stones 7–9)

 — Systems and procedures (foundation stones 15–17)
 — Intellectual capital (foundation stones 18–20)

There are 11 foundation stones for the performance pillars accounting for a maximum score of 55. Similarly the nine remaining foundation stones constituting practice pillars contain a maximum score of 45.

In order to achieve and sustain a leading competitive advantage, an organization must show 'very good' or 'excellent' results in both performance and practice indices. There are companies who score primarily in 'performance'-based primary activities. Other companies achieve excellent results in 'practice' parameters, perhaps through management approach, but fail to do well in 'performance' parameters. A number of organizations have the potential to quickly improve their status but a large group is lagging behind. As discussed in Chapter 11, we have divided companies into five groups based on their practice and performance scores, as illustrated in the 'practice performance map' (see Figure 12.7).

Leaders ('world class') These are the companies achieving high scores in practice (36–45) and performance (44–55). The Operational Excellence Factor for these companies will be over 70. These

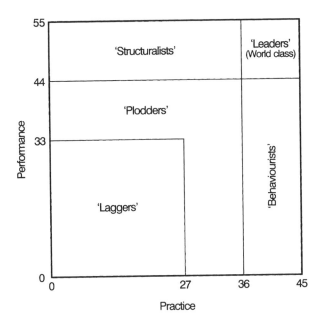

Figure 12.7   Practice performance map

companies are capable of competing with the best of the world's enterprises.

Behaviourists These companies have a high score in practice (36–45), but relatively low scores in performance (less than 44). Their total OEF will range between 47 and 84. These companies are promising because they have the supply infrastructure and the change culture. With a structured improvement programme towards higher performance levels they can reach the 'leaders' category.

Structuralists These are organizations with a high score in performance (44–55) but a lower score in practice (less than 36). Their OEF values will range from 53 as high as 90. These companies appear to be ahead in the game, but in the longer term they are not likely to sustain their performance advantages. In order to move towards the 'leaders' category they will need to invest in time and resources in best practices and training.

Plodders The fourth group of companies possess medium scores for both practice (27–35) and performance (33–43). Their OEF values could be between 42 and 78. These companies may have potential but they lack both performance and practices to compete in the world stage. They will require a long-term improvement programme with significant changes to their company policy, operation and practices.

Laggers The lowest scoring group in both practice (less than 27) and performance (less than 33) constitute the category of laggers, about whom no more can be said.

Gap analysis

The purpose of the gap analysis is to study the performance gaps and to identify the underlying factors that explain the causes of the gap. With accurate measurements and systematic analysis it will become easy to pin-point areas for attention. The improvement of results for the whole organization is the ultimate goal, and gap analysis is a powerful approach to achieve these results.

The key steps of the analysis include establishing the targets for performance or best practice, normalizing the measured performance levels achieved, analysing the performance gaps and their causes by using simple graphical tools and developing an improvement strategy. If the study does not lead to a practical improvement plan, it would be a waste of effort and all the charts would merely be decorative wallpaper.

Setting targets

For total operations solutions to have a real impact, in general a company should set its sights on the leaders position. If the outcome of your self-analysis indicates your organization is either a behaviourist or a structuralist then going for gold in all weak areas may be justifiable. But the 'search for the holy grail' in each foundation stone may take the laggers forever. Bogan and English (1994) advise, 'The holy grail-like search will make you an "industrial tourist" but not an effective bench-marker.'

Therefore, after positioning your business from the scores of self-analysis, the rational next step is to modify or confirm your targets in accordance with your mission statement and business objectives. You need to go beyond the rhetoric in your mission statement to understand what critical factors in your business must be altered to enhance your competitive edge. You may have a low score in a particular foundation stone (say, product safety), but if your business priority depends on this foundation stone then you should set a higher target.

We suggest that you should establish your targets at two levels. First, each foundation stone should have an average target score of 0.4 or 0.5. Only if a foundation stone is not relevant to your business, and this will be rare, may a target value lower than 0.4 be considered. By default the target score is 0.5. The second level of target involves the quantitative measures for selected questions. For example, you may set a target of distribution cost as 2% of sales for question number 49.

If your OEF is over 75 then you are a contender for 'world class' or 'leaders' league and your target scores for each foundation stone should be 0.5. Staying at the top is as challenging as trying to get there!

In our example shown in Figure 12.6, the target scores for eight foundation stones were set at the highest level (i.e. 0.5) whilst the targets for the remaining 12 foundation stones were set at 0.4.

Normalizing performance

It is an essential requirement to normalize all measures when the benchmarking is done by comparing performance across companies. This is achieved by expressing all indicators and indices with common denominators. Established procedures are available (see Karlof and Ostblom, 1993) for normalizing non-comparable factors in an intercompany benchmarking project. The non-comparable factors can be due to:

- Differences in operative content (e.g. order picking by cases or by full pallets)
- Differences in scope of operation (e.g. maintenance costs with materials and parts or labour only cost)
- Differences in cost structure (e.g. operating costs including depreciation or excluding depreciation)
- National differences (e.g. postal services in sparsely populated Canada or those in the densely populated Netherlands).

In the self-analysis exercise, the degree of non-comparability is likely to be less significant where the assessment is carried out for a company with a small range of product manufacturing in one country compared to a multi-product in a multinational company. For a multi-product multinational company the need for normalizing data should be critically reviewed. Very often the credibility of an exercise of this nature depends on how effectively performance measures can be expressed by a common base that is understood by both participants and stakeholders. Otherwise participants can be sceptical, saying, 'Our business is so special?'

It is important to ensure that appropriate units and methods of measurement have been applied to the quantitative parameters mentioned for the 200 questions.

Another issue related to 'normalization' is that we have given equal weighting to all 200 questions. Some team members of a company may believe that there should be different weighting for each pillar or foundation stone depending on the type or priority of a business. It is a logical consideration. However, as we have allocated a number of foundation stones – for example there are five foundation stones for the manufacturing facilities pillar – the sensitivity of differential weighting is not likely to be highly significant. Let us illustrate this point in Table 12.2.

Table 12.2 The effect of weighting scores

Pillars	Actual score	Normal weighting	Adjusted weighting	Correction factor	Adjusted score
1 Marketing and innovation	13	15	10	0.67	9
2 Supply chain management	13	15	15	1	13
3 Environment and safety	8	15	10	0.67	5
4 Infrastructure facilities	20	25	25	1	20
5 Systems and procedures	8	15	20	1.33	11
6 Intellectual capital	8	15	20	1.33	11
Totals	70	100	100	6.00	69

By applying higher weightings to procedures and people, and lower weightings to marketing/innovation and to environment and safety, the OEF changed from 70 to 69. The effect, however, is not significant. There is nevertheless some scope to adjust scores if the team applies extreme values of weighting (e.g. nil for Environment and Safety and 50 for Infrastructure Facilities). We believe that any manufacturing business must have all success factors or foundation stones, and thus extreme values of weighting should not occur.

Gap analysis tools

Gap analysis is a systematic process, but in general it is basically 'organized common sense'. Therefore the approach and tools for gap analysis in Total Operations Solutions should also be simple but effective. Very often by using well-publicized models, team members find that the models confuse the problem rather than clarify it. There is a danger of systematizing the problem rather than customizing the solution.

The practical tools are necessary both at the primary and secondary stages of analysis. The primary analysis involves a broad picture or 'a helicopter view' of the total business by identifying the overall performance gaps in each foundation stone.

The secondary analysis is concerned with the critical examination of the strengths and weaknesses identified by the primary analysis.

Both the computer-aided and graphical tools of the primary analysis can be applied at the secondary stage, particularly to audit results and to carry out sensitivity analysis. In addition, the team members can, depending on specific requirements, effectively apply:

- critical examination
- line graphs, bar charts, pie charts
- Pareto analysis
- 'total operations process map'
- 'Z charts'
- cause and effect diagram, and
- similar analysis tools such as SPC tools.

Perhaps only 'total operations process map' and 'Z charts' need some explanation, as other tools in the above list are well known. However, for the sake of completeness we shall comment on these tools in the context of secondary gap analysis. A comprehensive single source of reference of tools and techniques for all practitioners and students of operational excellence can be found in Basu's *Implementing Quality* (2004).

Critical examination is a powerful questioning tool of method study used by industrial engineers. It is not new. In fact, some managers and analysts have abandoned it because to them it is 'old hat' or 'déja vu'. None the less, critical examination can be eminently practical to understand the reasons for performance gap in a specific area. The technique is simple and comprises primary questions (to ensure that the current process is clearly understood) and secondary questions (to investigate suitable alternatives to the present process). The questions – primary and secondary – query purpose, place, sequence, person and means (what, where, when, who and how). Table 12.3 shows an example of typical questions used in critical examination. The principles of this tool can be gainfully applied to non-value added analysis and brain storming.

Line graphs are useful to describe a time series, such as comparing different companies' performances over time or for analysing the trends for relevant parameters of the same company. Figures 12.8(a) and 12.8(b) illustrate the trends of sales and profits for main products with reference to the secondary analysis of the results. (Refer to Question 1 of our 200 questions in the Appendix.)

Bar charts can be gainfully used in comparing a specific performance measure between companies or between different units of the

Table 12.3 Critical examination

	Primary questions		Secondary questions
	Stage 1	Stage 2	
Purpose	What is achieved?	Is it necessary? If yes, why?	What else could be done?
Place	Where is it done?	Why there?	Where else could it be done?
Sequence	When is it done?	Why then?	When else could it be done?
Person	Who does it?	Why that person?	Who else could do it?
Means	How is it done?	Why that way?	How else could it be done?

Source: Currie, 1964

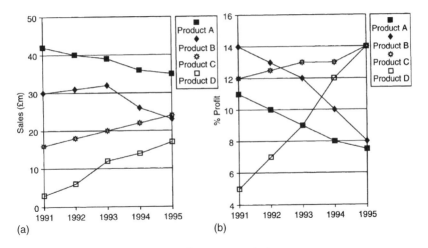

(a) (b)

Figure 12.8 Examples of line graphs in gap analysis

same company. Figure 12.9 shows an example of how return on capital employed is compared with reference to the results for Question 155 of the 200 questions.

Pie charts can vividly illustrate the share of a total task, cost profile, profit margin, etc., by its various elements. Figure 12.10 shows an analysis of a cost-effectiveness programme with regard to the secondary analysis of the results for Question 159.

Pareto analysis is a powerful tool for identifying A, B and C categories of products and activities so that appropriate priority and

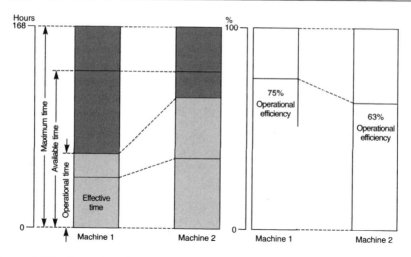

Figure 12.9 Examples of bar charts in gap analysis

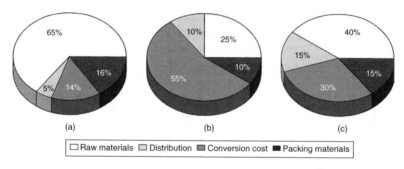

Figure 12.10 Examples of pie charts in gap analysis (a) Direct delivered cost. (b) Cost reduction efforts. (c) Savings achieved.

strategy can be applied. Figure 12.11 shows an example of Pareto analysis for stock holding with regard to Question 156.

There has been a considerable hype for promoting process mapping by the proponents of both TQM and BPR. In practice, however, process mapping has proved to be both harmful and helpful. For an analyst it has proved very useful to describe all details of a process and thus help to understand the interrelationship of various operations and factors. On the other hand, to an outsider this offers little value and tends, with a large number of boxes and arrows, to confuse. As we indicated earlier in this chapter (see data preparation) a simple flow diagram can be very useful to understand a business

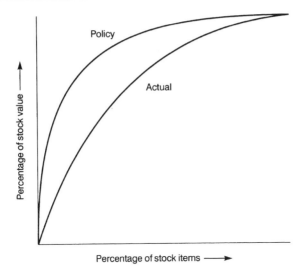

Figure 12.11 An example of Pareto analysis

process and further details can be left to a systems analyst if so desired. A 'total operations process map' is intended to be a simplified method of mapping to describe the various levels (from 'poor' to 'excellent') of each foundation stone.

During a gap analysis exercise this 'process map' can broadly locate where the business is at present and how far it has to go. It may also be expanded with a time scale as long as it does not complicate the purpose. Figure 12.12 gives an example of a 'total operations process map' which shows the present position of the business used in the example shown in Table 12.1.

The Z chart is one of the benchmark analyst's favourite tools for comparing the performance of a company against the benchmark of a competitor organization. This type of chart is fully described by Bogan and English (1994). Many companies have experienced failure of their strategic plans because they assessed a competitor's capability based on its current position. The Z chart quantifies the moving position. Thus a Z chart can be a powerful tool, particularly for strategic planning. Figure 12.13 shows an example of a Z chart.

One of the most widely used SPC tools in company-wide change programmes such as TQM and Six Sigma is the 'cause and effect diagram'. This is also popularly known as a 'fishbone diagram' because

You are here

Foundation stones	Level 1 POOR	Level 2 FAIR	Level 3 GOOD	Level 4 VERY GOOD	Level 5 EXCELLENT
1 Understanding the market place	Poor knowledge of products and market, isolated sales activities	Ad hoc market survey, isolated activities of marketing and manufacturing	Annual market survey, isolated activities of marketing and manufacturing	Annual market survey, direct communication, with marketing and manufacturing	First hand knowledge of market place, six-monthly market survey
2 Understanding the competition	Poor knowledge of true market size and competition	Knowledge of market size without the follow-up of competitors	Competitor intelligence in selected products	Analysis of published reports of key competitions, BCG matrix	Annual benchmark to assess the strengths of key competitors
3 Product and process innovation	Little focus on innovation, limited development activities	Restricted research and isolated innovation activities	Good research budget, but isolated innovation activities	Screening process of impractical ideas, reduction of innovation lead time	Generous research budget, over 80% new product success ratio, concurrent engineering
4 Enterprises resource planning	Ad hoc planning, high stock cover, no preferred supplier	Isolated planning, high stock cover, some agreement with suppliers	Isolated logistics planning, good stock management, some agreements with suppliers	Computerized MRP planning, effective stock management, cooperation with suppliers	Integrated planning system, JIT effective, EDI and partnership with suppliers
5 Supply chain and supplier partnership	Poor control over warehousing and transport, little interface with customers	Some control over warehousing and transport, some interface with customers	Good warehousing and transport by third party, sporadic control, work with customers	Effective warehouse and transport systems, some partnership with customers	Optimum distribution strategy, WMS and integration with key customers
6 Distribution management and working with customers	Low customer service, high stock and distribution cost	Medium customer service, high stock and distribution cost	High customer service, low supplier service, high stock and distribution cost	High customer service, high supplier service, high distribution cost. Low stock level	Low distribution cost, high customer and supplier services. Low stock level
7 Product safety	Lack of formal procedures of product safety needs	Ad hoc safety clearance, monitoring and training	Safety clearance for selected products, some monitoring and training	100% safety clearance, adequate monitoring at all stages, some training	100% safety clearance, excellent training and monitoring at all stages of supply chain
8 Occupational safety and health	Lack of formal procedures and facilities for industrial safety	Ad hoc application of safety standards and training	Safety standards and implements available, but partly implemented	Safety implements procedures, and training in place	ISRS certificate and HAZOP studies in place, excellent training
9 Environmental and resource management	Lack of effluent control and training	Adequate effluent control, lack of training	Compliance with legislation and some training	Effective effluent control and training	Full compliance of effluent control, effective non-waste technology
10 Sourcing strategy	Lack of clear sourcing strategy	Ad hoc studies on sourcing strategy	Credible internal manufacturing strategy	Credible support to sourcing policy	Full support to written sourcing strategy
11 Appropriate technology	Lack of a clear policy on technology	Ad hoc appraisal of technology and investment	Capital investment primarily based on ROI	Credible support to policy on technology and investment	Full support to written policy on technology and investment
12 Flexibility and lean processes	Lack of understanding of flexible manufacturing	Some applications of flexible manufacturing	Good understanding, partial application of flexible manufacturing	Credible support to flexible manufacturing	Full support to flexible manufacturing and quick change-over
13 Reliability and maintenance	Breakdown maintenance, low reliability, high cost	Time based maintenance, high maintenance cost	Condition based maintenance, some maintenance control system	Partial TPM, high reliability, high maintenance costs	Full implementation of TPM, high reliability, low maintenance cost
14 Performance management and Balanced Scorecard	Low level of manufacturing performance, poor reporting system	Medium level manufacturing performance for some plants	Medium level manufacturing performance, limited IE support	Sporadically high manufacturing performance with limited IE support	High manufacturing performance with integrated industrial engineering support
15 Quality management	Lack of defined procedures and standards for quality	Quality management in selected areas without top management support	Some use of SPC tools and quality procedures	Use of SPC tools and customer/supplier culture	Baldridge award or ISO9000 winner, change culture
16 Financial management	Lack of defined financial management, poor ROI	Medium ROI, and cash flow, no cost effectiveness	Sporadically good ROI and cash flow, some cost effectiveness	Good ROI and cash flow, but ad hoc cost effectiveness	Excellent ROI, cash flow and cost effectiveness programmes
17 Information and communication technology	Lack of IT strategy, support and application in manufacturing	Some good application of hardware and software in manufacturing	Customized application software in all areas of business	Open system IT, strategy not implemented, integrated network	Open system IT strategy in place, integrated client-server network
18 Leadership and organization capital	Lack of leadership, organization and management development	Traditional layers of management, some good managers	Good management team without development plans	Good management team and creditable management development plan	Visionary leadership, and policy to attract and develop high calibre managers
19 Human resource policies and human capital	Restricted working practices, poor industrial relations	Traditional working practices, good industrial relations	Limited flexible working practices and some consultation with unions	Multiskilled workforce, limited consultation with unions	Effective partnership with unions and sustainable working practices
20 Knowledge management and information capital	Lack of learning resources and training plans	Selective training plans by external resources	Limited learning resources and selective training plans	Good learning resources and selective training plans	Learning organization with written training plans for all employees

Figure 12.12   Total operations process map. For enlarged version, see the very back of this book

of its obvious shape, as shown in Figure 12.14. During a gap analysis exercise a 'cause and effect diagram' can be effectively used to map and analyse the root causes of a problem.

As we all know, the effectiveness of a tool or technique depends on the choice for application, the skill of the user and the interpretation of results derived from its application. One should not

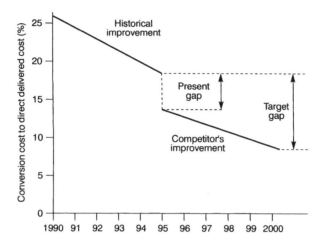

Figure 12.13   Example of a Z chart

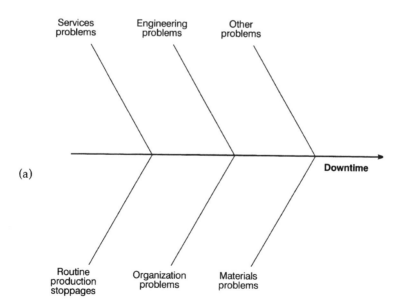

Figure 12.14   Cause and effect diagram

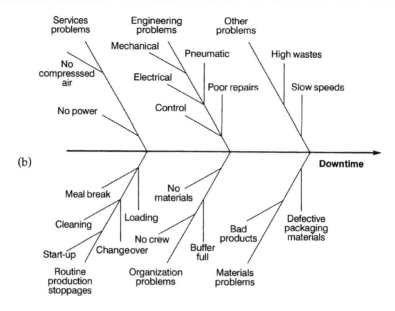

Figure 12.14 (*Continued*)

carry a tool kit in search of problems, it should be the other way round.

Lessons learnt

The quantitative analysis of the performance gap is only part of the gap analysis. An important by-product of the analysis is that it makes the team delve into the details of the business processes. This enables the team to identify and understand the underlying causes that explain why the performance gap exists. Although the main purpose of the gap analysis is the identification of opportunities for improvement, it also offers a number of other benefits, including:

- An understanding of the total business process and the success factors underpinning world class performance and best practices
- Bringing together the business perspectives of a multi-functional team, comprising marketing, technical, financial, logistics and human resources
- In-depth knowledge of foundation stones by specialists in the team, whether they are related to performance or practices
- A general improvement in performance and practices by focused attentions during the analysis even before the start of the implementation plan.

Improvement strategy

We emphasized in Chapter 11 that there is no such thing as a quick fix and the best results are achieved by careful consideration of all factors. Therefore, a vital stage between gap analysis and the implementation phase is the selection of the appropriate improvement strategy. The objective of the team is to search for the appropriate course of action by careful consideration of the results of the gap analysis and the alignment of the results with the company strategy. The danger of rushing into consultants' package solutions was underlined in Chapter 11. From the above it can be seen that Total Operations Solutions is by no means a quick fix.

As we suggested in Chapter 11 (see Figure 11.1), the approaches and characteristics of an improvement depend on both the degree of change (i.e. tactical or strategic) and the pace of change (i.e. fast or longer term). The four broad categories of improvement strategy are:

Focused improvement	fast and tactical
Continuous improvement	longer term and tactical
Focused re-structuring	fast and strategic
Process re-engineering/Six Sigma	longer term and strategic.

Summary

This chapter has discussed how initial data for analysis and rating can be drawn from information that already exists in the form of reports, plans and databases. A method of data analysis and our method of rating is detailed. Knowing where the data is, and how to rate it is one aspect. But perhaps the more important issue is the formation of a team to carry out the rating. The team will need to be drawn from senior people in each function.

The team will have to familiarize themselves with the complete structure and processes of the organization. Just by doing this the team members will become more valuable members of the organization! Team members will also have to read and understand Chapters 4–9 so as to understand what constitutes best practice, what is possible and what to look for. In their quest to understand the organization, team members will doubtless have to talk to and question people in each department as to what actually happens. Likewise when the rating process is being carried out team members will again have to refer back to the people who are doing the job to find out how things are actually done. It would be surprising if all this fact-gathering and questioning didn't cause speculation within the organization. It will therefore be absolutely essential for team members to be completely open in what they are trying to achieve. The aim is to improve the health of the organization and not to blame or to censure any one person or group of people.

The gathering of information, the familiarization of team members with the organization and processes of the organization and the gaining of understanding as to what is possible might seem to be a painstaking project. We would have to agree it is not easy, but the results will be far-reaching. In the long run we know our approach is a lot simpler and easier to implement than might at first be imagined.

We have shown how gap analysis is a powerful tool for identifying where action has to be taken for a company to achieve world class status. We demonstrate how systematic analysis and accuracy of measurement will show the way. Various techniques for analysis are considered. The very nature of this delving for information, by a team drawn from various key functions, will draw together functions and highlight commonality of purpose and the need for teamwork throughout the organization. This in itself will strengthen the company and bring forth untold advantages.

Chapter 13

Implementing the Strategy

Each morning sees some task begin,
Each evening sees it close;
Something attempted, something done,
Has earned a night's repose.
  H.W. Longfellow, 'The Village Blacksmith'

Many organizations start the improvement programme without going through the earlier stages of identifying the real requirements. This is usually the result of accepting the latest management fads without thinking through all the steps described in previous chapters. Change programmes that are not carefully planned and managed are doomed to failure, because not only is it likely that the improvement strategy will be wrong but also the necessary commitment and culture will not have been developed.

Many benchmarking projects have been well carried out and produced excellent reports and action plans, but due to poor implementation planning and a real will to make things happen little has been achieved. The knowledge gained through benchmarking of your own strengths and weakness can only lead to disillusionment of those involved, if no improvements are made or attempted. Disillusionment among a few key staff will be contagious and will result in a lowering of morale which will spread throughout the organization. Thus a benchmarking exercise, no matter how well carried out, if no follow up action is taken, will lead to negative results.

Therefore both benchmarking and implementation should be considered as one, and not as separate initiatives. Both are phases of a common continuous improvement process. As Bogan and English (1994) say, 'Segregating benchmarking planning and implementation planning is like separating Siamese twins who share vital organs.'

Making changes and improvements should be a continuous process, but to sustain continuous change is as difficult as initiating and implementing change. To keep the momentum going, it is necessary to evaluate if the change process has produced results and to keep developing ongoing improvement activities.

The success of any project is underpinned by management commitment, organization and resources. Building a commitment for all the stakeholders, inside and outside the company, involves the understanding of why improvement is needed and the nature of improvement. It is a common phenomenon for various factions to appreciate why a change is required but at the same time to believe that the need to change does not necessarily apply to them. As we have said in earlier chapters, the culture of the organization has to be such that everyone from the cleaner to the chief executive believes that they have a personal part to play in making changes. The prerequisite for change is the vision and the will to change based on a culture that will accept change. As top executives of Motorola are reported to have said, a thriving company constantly transforms itself while adhering to beliefs that are not subject to change.

It is vital that detailed discussion and agreement occur throughout the company as to what, how, when and where change should take place and who should be involved. There are many models for process maps and implementation steps for improvement programmes. The Strategic Planning Institutes' Council for Benchmarking has a five-step model (launch, organize, reach out, assimilate and act). We favour a four-stage process, as illustrated in Figure 13.1. This map covers the total improvement process. Our map is provided as a guide only.

Start-up

The key task for senior management is to decide what improvement opportunity areas have the greatest impact for the business. However, a significant number of companies that initiate a change programme do so because either they feel threatened for survival or they have become victims of a three-letter management fad. Our recommendation is that before any improvement is attempted, self-analysis to identify the weaknesses and the gaps in performance takes place. A self-analysis process does not start on its own. Any benchmarking programme, especially the one described in this book, requires full

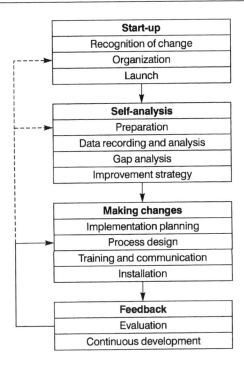

Figure 13.1 Total operations implementation process

commitment, preparation and organization. The start-up phase contains three major milestones:

- Recognition of change
- Organization
- Launch.

Recognition of need for change

It is vital that top management and the board wholeheartedly recognize the need for a change programme. This recognition may be prompted by a reaction to current company performance, threat from a new competitor, or a strategic change (e.g. merger or an internal report from any of the key stakeholders). The board and management must believe that serious action has to be taken.

The least risk approach is to conduct your own benchmarking in the systematic way we have detailed in the previous chapters. Take one step at a time and be patient; make big improvements through a series of small improvements, each being non-disruptive and 'right first time'. Major, panic-driven changes can destroy a company. Poorly planned change is worse than no change.

At this stage it may be helpful to conduct a limited number of consultation workshops with key stakeholders to acquire agreement and understanding about the need to change.

The objective of this will be to get the full commitment of top management and the support of the stakeholders.

The programme begins with the formation of a project team.

Organization

The organization phase involves a clear project brief, appointment of a project team and a project plan. The project brief must clearly state the purpose of the project and the deliverables expected from the project.

There is no rigid model for the structure of the project team. The basic elements of our recommended project structure are shown in Figure 13.2.

Steering committee

To ensure a high level of commitment and ownership to the project, the steering committee should be drawn from members of the board and include senior management. Their role is to provide support and resources, define the scope of the project consistent with corporate goals, set priorities and consider and approve the project team's recommendations.

Project leader

The project leader (manager has the wrong connotation), should be a person of high stature in the company, probably a senior manager, with broad experience in all aspects of the business and with good communication skills. He or she is the focal point of the project and also the main communication link between the steering committee and the project team members.

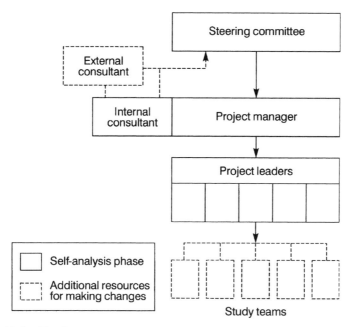

Figure 13.2 Total operations project organization

The project leader's role can be likened to that of a consultant. However if a line manager is given the task of project leadership as an additional responsibility to their normal job, then an experienced staff manager can be co-opted to support the leader. The role of the leader is to a great extent similar to Hammer and Champy's 'czar' (1993). The project leader's role is to:

- Provide necessary awareness and training for the project team, especially regarding multi-functional issues.
- Facilitate the work of various project groups and help them develop design changes.
- Interface with other departments and plants.

In addition to the careful selection of the project leader, two other factors are important in forming the team. First, the membership size should be kept within manageable limits. Second, the members should bring with them not only analytical skills but also in-depth knowledge of the total business covering marketing, financial, logistics, technical and human resources. The minimum number of team members should be three, and the maximum number should be six.

Any more than six can lead to difficulties in arranging meetings, communicating and in keeping to deadlines. The dynamics within a group of more than six people allows a pecking order to develop and for sub-groups to develop. The team should function as an action group, rather than as a committee that deliberates and makes decisions. Their role is to:

- Provide objective input in the areas of their expertise during the self-analysis phase, and
- To lead activities during the making changes phase.

For the project leader, the stages of the project include:

- Education of all the people of the company
- Gathering the data
- Analysis of the data
- Establishing study teams to recommend changes
- Regular reporting to the steering committee
- Regular reporting of progress company-wide to all the people of the company.

Obviously the project leaders cannot do all this work themselves, but they have to be the sort of people who know how to make things happen and who can motivate people to help make things happen. To assist in various phases study teams should be formed to work with the project leader.

Study teams

In general, study teams should be formed after the self-analysis phase, but in selected areas. However some members of study teams can assist in the original data collection phase and also in the analysis phase. The members of the study team represent all levels across the organization and are the key agents for making changes. Their role is to develop design changes and submit recommendations to the project leader.

External consultants

Use of an external consultant at various stages of the project might be useful to supplement your own resources. However a consultant cannot know your company as well as your own people do. It could be argued that a consultant will not only bring his or her expertise and experience but will also act as a catalyst during the total implementation process. Likewise, in the initial stages, consultants can be effectively used in training the people of your company in both analytical tools and in assisting with culture change. In our opinion the best time to employ a consultant is probably after your self-analysis has been completed and after the selection of a specific improvement strategy has been made. We recommend the employment of a consultant who is a specialist in a particular field. For example if the problem is with logistics then a consultant in that field could be employed. We do not favour using external consultants as project leaders.

Launch

It is critical that all stakeholders (e.g. managers, employees, unions, suppliers and key customers) who may be immediately impacted by the programme are clearly identified. Internal stakeholders must be consulted and kept fully informed at every stage of the programme. After the organization phase the next milestone is the formal launching of the programme. The nature of the launch can be either low key or a big bang. Our recommendation is that before the self-analysis a low-key, but definitely not a secretive, approach is more appropriate. Too much excitement and too high an expectation could be counterproductive if it leads to uncertainty. It will be only after self-analysis that an improvement strategy can be finalized. A high profile launch would therefore be more appropriate once the strategy has been approved by the steering committee.

The nature of the launch sets the tone for how future communication will take place and identifies the ownership of the project. It is absolutely essential that strong and visible support be given by senior management.

Self-analysis

After the start-up, the project team will be involved with the self-analysis stage of the project. This is basically do-it-yourself benchmarking. It is worth repeating that it is vital to assess your requirements before you start to implement any improvement programme.

We have described in detail in earlier chapters how team members can carry out a self-analysis and the basis on which they can recommend a suitable improvement strategy. The main steps and activities involved during this stage can be summarized as:

1 Preparation
    – Collect information about your own company
    – Analyse and understand your own business and processes
    – Study and understand the six pillars and 20 foundation stones as described in Chapters 4–9
    – Obtain published reports on the best practices of successful companies
    – Study and understand the 200 questions detailed in the Appendix
2 Data recording and analysis (see Chapter 12)
    – Carry out the assessment and scoring process for the 200 questions with regard to the best understanding of your own operations
    – Calculate your Operational Excellence Factor (OEF)
    – Conduct a primary analysis of the results with the aid of graphical presentations, including the 'spider diagram'
    – Conduct a performance *vs.* practices analysis and identify the category of your organization (leaders, behaviourists, structuralists, plodders or laggers)
3 Gap analysis
    – Identify the core values, priorities and mission of your company
    – Re-assess your target scores based upon your mission and core values
    – Re-examine the scores obtained during the primary analysis of the results given for the 200 questions
    – Identify your strengths/weaknesses and the gap between your target and actual performance as described in Chapter 12
4 Improvement strategy
    – Prepare a report of your key findings resulting from the self-analysis stage of the study. Include in the report recommendations for improvement programmes.

Making changes

In this phase the change process moves on to the action programme to make the changes happen. Having chosen the improvement strategy, the detailed work of implementing the changes will be influenced by the strategy. The strategy may be a confirmation of well-known improvement programmes (e.g. TPM for the factories and JIT for supply chain management). We have found it to be effective to name the total initiative (e.g. Project 'Utopia') so that everyone in the organization can identify it as a 'single issue improvement culture'.

There is an abundance of publications regarding change management and company-wide implementation programmes. In addition, how change is tackled will vary according to improvement strategy, as we have stated earlier. Therefore we shall outline key milestones of implementation planning, process design, learning and installation which are likely to be relevant for all programmes for making changes.

Your own benchmarking or self-analysis helps your company find its way through two aspects of change. First, it provides a road map describing areas that require more changes than others; second, the self-analysis phase of the programme provides insight and experience on how to establish a single culture that transcends divisional boundaries.

Implementation planning

It is possible that after spending several weeks with the self-analysis phase employees outside the core project group may demonstrate scepticism. If this shows signs of occurring it may be necessary for top management to relaunch the initiative, for example 'Utopia Stage Two'.

If this is done the project team will need reconfirmation. There is an obvious advantage of continuing with some of the same people involved in the self-analysis stage. Their experience, new-found company-wide knowledge, and their belief in the recommendations should not be undervalued. The number of those now directly involved will increase by the formation of study teams for the areas selected for study, and as discussed earlier specialist external consultants might now also be introduced.

The project leader will be responsible for writing implementation plans, indicating key tasks, responsibilities, deliverables, resource requirements and target dates. It is recommended that the project plan will include a critical path, and that periodic reviews and reports be made by the project leader to the steering committee.

Table 13.1 Process design

Improvement category	Programme design	Examples of process
Focused improvement	Labour productivity	Improved method and layout
Focused restructuring	Site development	Relocation of boiler house
Continuous improvement	Total productive maintenance	Lubrication and cleaning of machines by operators
Focused re-engineering	Supply chain re-engineering	Direct delivery to urban retailers

Process design

Process design relates to the actual transformation of an operation, procedure, organization or facilities from the current state to a desirable future state.

The nature of process design depends on the category of improvement, as illustrated in Table 13.1.

The design and redesign of a process by a study team must incorporate the ideas of the people who will actually be affected by the change. The tools of gap analysis can be systematically applied to develop and evaluate a process design. Innovation in process design will result from the readiness to abandon traditional thinking and to be able to imagine a 'green-field' approach to a process.

Some design processes (usually focused improvement) are accomplished at the project leader level and others (usually strategic changes and changes requiring capital expenditure) are approved through the steering committee. However, the steering committee should be kept informed of all changes and their progress. There is no advantage to be gained by being secretive. A world class organization does not have secrets or hidden agendas.

Training and communication

We have emphasized in Chapters 8 and 9, drawn from the experience of several companies, that training and communication are the life blood of a change process. The need to keep everyone in the company fully informed as to what is happening is so fundamental that we risk being pedantic. We will, however, list some of the key communication benefits and needs.

1 The objective is to share information and change processes among the stakeholders at all levels of the organization, e.g.:
   - Top management, and the board, must understand enough about the improvement programmes to know how the changes will affect the business. They must be able to know what is happening and to show leadership so that things will happen.
   - Study team education: The study team needs to have a detailed understanding of what is planned for their area and a good overall understanding of the big picture. They are the ones who will be responsible for working with and training people in process design changes in sections and units of the company.
   - Middle management and staff education: While not everyone can be on the study teams, everyone has a role to play in the improvement programme. Therefore everyone on the staff must be informed of how their work will be affected.
   - Employee training: No change process will work if the employees on the shop floor oppose it either directly or indirectly. Employee involvement and training are vital for an implementation plan. Many of the ideas for improvement in a programme such as TPM come from the operators.
   - Communication to unions: It is critical that the representatives of unions and other staff representative bodies are kept informed at critical stages of the implementation of how the change process will affect their members.
2 The communication among the stakeholders should be full and open. A change programme cannot be built upon any false pretence. Success depends on trust.
3 Although the study team may be responsible for making changes at the factory at floor level the employee learning programme should be properly structured:
   - There should be a learning manager with a focused role.
   - On-the-job learning should be accomplished through line supervisors.
   - An external human resources consultant may be valuable to guide the learning and to effect a culture change.

Installation

The installation phase involves the planning and physical actions necessary for putting the improved process into place. The project manager may co-opt industrial engineers to facilitate engineering changes. Separate capital proposals may be required, and these should be channelled through the steering committee. Other likely expenditure will include modification of equipment and for moving equipment. It is important that proper authorization is obtained for any expenditure before it is incurred. The project has to lead by example and cannot be seen to be taking short cuts.

The installation stage consists of a large number of concurrent and parallel activities including selection of equipment, revising layout, improvement of process capability, commissioning, training and so on. It is useful to prepare a project schedule showing the critical path and all the necessary resources. For very large projects, the expertise of external engineering consultants may be sought to carry out a front-end engineering study (e.g. feasibility study, conceptual engineering and preliminary engineering).

When a significant change in process design is involved, the installation should start with a pilot programme in a selected line or plant so that the process is proven and operations are understood by the employees. The project in the pilot area may run for several months as a learning centre. Some people understand a system conceptually but cannot accept it unless they can see it in action. Pilot projects can demonstrate results and validate the purpose of the change. It can be a great advantage to move along the learning curve by installing a pilot line ahead of a completely reorganized or new plant.

Another important issue of installation, unless the project is on a green-field site, is that it should be planned to create a minimum disruption to current operations. When a disruption is unavoidable, a stock build-up to cover a limited period of installation may be necessary to continue to meet the market demand. Factory house-keeping and safety standards should not be compromised during a change. Once again we repeat the project must lead by example, it cannot be seen to be condoning short-cuts or sloppy practices.

For some people (most of us) details are tedious and it may be difficult to maintain the momentum of earlier design efforts throughout the company. It is therefore important to include two actions in the installation programme:

Installation should be a logical extension of earlier activities for those people who were involved in the process design stage. They will believe and be committed to their recommendations. Installation activities should be continuously checked against target results and time frame.

Feedback

A change programme in total manufacturing solutions and the achievement of world class status is a never-ending journey toward continuous improvement. The phase of feedback involves the continuous need to sustain what has been achieved and to identify further opportunities for improvement.

It is at least as difficult to sustain changes as it is to design and install them. Keeping the change process going by regular feedback is a different process from that of making changes. It usually calls for different approaches and sometimes the responsibility of this phase may shift to a different team.

The feedback phase contains two interrelated milestones: evaluation and continuous development.

The progress of the changes should be monitored at regular intervals, usually by comparing the actual results with target performance levels. The audit team may decide to carry out a sample self-analysis by selecting from the 200 questions.

The frequency of sample analysis may be every year, in addition to the continuous monitoring of key performance indicators along the way.

Continuous development

The evaluation or audit may reveal that some changes are working well and some changes will need re-designing. There is a need to continuously align and adjust the performance level with specific needs.

A change programme can attain its full effect only by repetition. When you have been through the self-analysis for the first time you not only have a working model that can be used again, you also have a proven project organization experience to carry the changes through to their implementation.

You are likely to have a target moving progressively from internal, to external, to functional, to best practice. External targets refer to comparisons with competitors. Functional targets refer to comparisons with similar functions without regard to the type of industry in which they operate. Thus functional targets offer the greatest potential for funding major improvements. Our methodology should assist you, and external consultants if employed, to achieve both external and functional benchmarking.

Time scale

The time scale of total change process from start-up to feedback is expected to be several months and naturally the duration is variable. The time not only depends on the degree of the gaps in different foundation stones but also on risks involved and resources required. Four factors of the business can favourably affect the time scale:

- Full commitment of top management
- Good cash flow of the company
- Receptivity to change among the workforce
- Number of products retain a competitive niche in the market place.

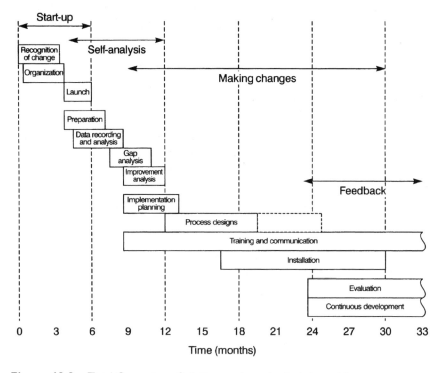

Figure 13.3   Total Operations Solutions: a hypothetical timetable

Given the existence of favourable factors, typical time scales for a change programme are likely to be as follows:

Start-up	2–6 months
Self-analysis	3–9 months
Making changes	15–24 months
Feedback	4–24 months (plus ongoing)
Total	24–63 months

Figure 13.3 shows a hypothetical summary schedule for implementing a Total Operations Solutions change process in a medium-sized company. The diagram depicts an order of magnitude only. In addition, the exact sequence of activity would vary according to the company undertaking the programme. The map is not linear as it may need frequent looping back to reflect the continuous learning with ongoing progress and development. However, there is no doubt that there is no short-cut route to a total improvement process.

Sustaining total operational excellence

Implementation of a major change programme is challenging, but it is even more challenging to sustain the benefits. In spite of the demonstrated benefits of many improvement techniques such as total quality management and Six Sigma, many attempts by companies to use them have ended in failure (Easton and Jarrell, 1998). Sterman *et al.* (1999) conclude that companies have found it extremely difficult to sustain even initially successful process improvement initiatives. Yet more puzzling is the fact that successful improvement programmes have sometimes led to declining business performance causing layoffs and low employee morale. In addition, business managers can be forgiven if they are often confused by the grey areas of distinction between quality initiatives such as TQM, Six Sigma, FIT SIGMA and Lean Sigma and techniques such as the Balanced Scorecard and EFQM. We discussed their distinctive features and alignment in Chapter 10 and explained the self-assessment process of an organization's business health by using the 200 questions of Total Operations Solutions in Chapter 12.

The key question is what is the process that could utilize these techniques and methodologies to the best advantage of an organization to sustain the benefits of a major change programme? A proven

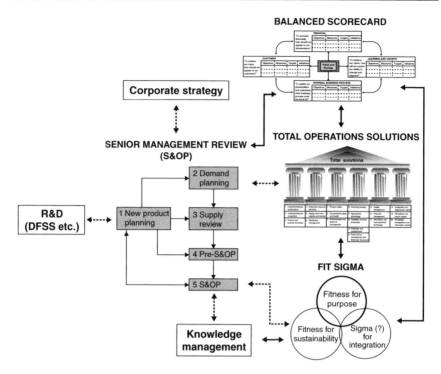

Figure 13.4   Total operations excellence

model based on the experience of GlaxoWellcome in the UK (now part of GlaxoSmithKline) is shown in Figure 13.4.

The monthly Senior Management Review meeting or the Sales and Operations Planning meeting is the central process to endorse the business plans and forecasts for at least up to 18 months. The Balanced Scorecard provides the performance of Key Performance Indicators and future pointers of the business. The periodic (say, every quarter) self-assessment by the 200 questions of TOpS (or a similar process such as EFQM) reflects the general health of the business, which are not detected by the Balanced Scorecard or other review meetings.

The results of Six Sigma/FIT SIGMA covering both the best practices and people development are captured and developed further as part of the management Knowledge Management process. The S&OP process is also the focal point to keep abreast with the Corporate Strategy and R&D pipeline and this process also influences the large projects of Six Sigma/FIT SIGMA programme.

The above process can be compared with a 'motor car' model. In the running and maintenance of a motor car the 'dash board' is the Balanced Scorecard and the self-assessment by TOpS questions (or EFQM) is like obtaining a MOT certificate in the UK. Similar regulatory processes of checking vehicle safety also exists in other countries (e.g. 'brake tag' in the USA and 'Shaaken' in Japan). The continuous TLC (tender loving care) of the motor car is equivalent to the S&OP process. Six sigma and FIT SIGMA are comparable to a major service or reconditioning of the motor car in a garage.

Summary

This chapter discusses how to make it all happen. Many a benchmarking exercise has produced excellent reports, many plans have been well researched and look good on paper. But until something actually happens, until some results are seen, all that has really occurred is expenditure in time and money. Our objective is not to waste your time and money, our objective is to get you a worthwhile pay back for your efforts.

Our methodology will enable you to determine your strengths and weaknesses and the gaps in your OEF. But our method calls for a systematic step-by-step approach. Short-cuts are always appealing, but believe us, our method *is* the short-cut – there are no further short cuts available.

Our implementation process begins with the start-up phase. This includes the board and the senior management first recognizing that change is essential and being committed to making changes happen. We then discuss the organization needed for implementing the change programme, including the establishment of a high-powered steering committee, appointment of a project leader and a project team drawn from all the key functions of the organization.

The project team will need to be kept small, it is an action group not a planning committee. The team will need careful briefing and will need to fully study this book. The team has the important role of carrying out the self-analysis and benchmarking of the company. To do so they will need to be able to understand each of the 200 questions, and also be able to dispassionately rate the company against each of the questions. Gathering of data for their use might at first sight seem to be an onerous task, but most of the information should already exist and on further examination should be found to be readily available. We discuss the help that the team will need to get the information they require, including assistance from people who will later form the nucleus of the study teams.

Once the gap analysis has been carried out, the next stage will be to develop an improvement strategy. At all stages the steering committee will need to be regularly advised by the project leader of the progress of the team. The strategy will come from recommendations of the project team, but will be determined by the steering committee.

At all stages of the project, it is essential that not only is the steering committee kept informed, but that all members of the organization right down to the lowest levels are kept appraised of the aims and activities of the project. Initially, while the data gathering and the analysis of the 200 questions are being carried out, many people might not be aware that much is happening. It may therefore be necessary to give the project a high profile relaunch once the strategy has been determined.

All the people of the organization have to understand the purpose of the project, believe in it and wholeheartedly support it. It goes without saying that the lead must come from the top of the organization. To get the full commitment of the whole organization, a major change in culture may be needed. Changing the culture is likely to be part of the improvement strategy.

In Figure 13.3 we give a hypothetical timetable for Total Operations Solutions to be implemented. This timetable shows that almost three years will be needed, but for some organizations the changes could take over five years to internalize. But even then you are not finished. The very essence of a quality programme designed for an organization to reach world class status is that there is no end to the progress. Change is continuous and inevitable.

Chapter 14

Case Studies

The bitterness of low quality is not forgotten
Nor can it be sweetened with low price
Marquis de Lavant (1734)

The following case examples provide insights for organizations that are achieving success in their business performance through the use of Six Sigma or related operational excellence programmes. The objective of including these case examples is to offer a set of proven practices through which an insight into the application of tools and techniques is given.

The case examples are taken from a large selection of real life experiences of many organizations around the world. We have not made any effort to make them tidy to suit any format or subject area. It is hoped that these cases provide a useful resource to stimulate discussions and training of self-assessment and help the implementation of an operational excellence programme. The cases may also be useful for analysis and discussion in learning programmes of an organization.

Case study 1: Six Sigma in Dow Chemical

Nature of the problem

The Dow Chemical Company, at just over 100 years old, is widely recognized as a technology-based manufacturing business. The company's ambition is to grow better and bigger by re-defining itself as a solutions-oriented science and technology company. Six Sigma is a key accelerator of that transformation.

With annual sales of US$28 billion, Dow serves customers in more than 170 countries and a wide range of markets that are vital to human progress, including food, transportation, health and medicine, personal and home care, and building and construction, among others. Dow is committed to the principles of sustainable development, focusing on delivering triple bottom line results – an approach that measures success by economic prosperity *and* environmental stewardship *and* corporate social responsibility. The company has approximately 50 000 employees around the world, 208 manufacturing sites in 38 countries and supplies more than 3200 products.

Effective from 6 February 2001 Union Carbide merged with a subsidiary of Dow Chemical Company and became a wholly owned subsidiary of the company. The December 1984 tragedy caused by a gas leak in Bhopal, India, continues to be a source of anguish for Union Carbide employees. Following the merger transaction there have been questions about Dow Chemical's position on the Bhopal tragedy and various demands from groups representing Bhopal victims that Dow Chemical assumes responsibility for the tragedy.

The modern era demands that businesses be more competitive, more productive and more customer-focused than ever before. The Internet, e-mail, fax machines, cell phones, pagers and other tools are accelerating the pace of commerce, requiring new levels of agility and flexibility. Remaining static and stagnant in this environment is not an option.

Dow's mission is 'To constantly improve what is essential to human progress by mastering science and technology.' Dow has set its aspirations purposefully high. These higher aspirations have fuelled the company's journey toward Six Sigma and business excellence. This mission is founded upon a long history of continuous improvement and corporate re-invention.

Throughout the early 1990s, Dow employed a number of measures to streamline and improve its competitive position. Value-based management tools were instituted. Quality performance mechanisms were put in place and re-engineering practices were implemented. In 1994, the company re-focused and re-shaped its strategy. The result of this effort was the Strategic Blueprint, the driving force behind all that Dow does.

Process and products

As a global leader in science and technology Dow provides innovative chemical, plastic and agricultural products and services to many essential consumer and industrial markets. There are over 3200 products in the company portfolio.

The chemical products include calcium chloride, caustic soda, sealants, emulsion polymers and fungicides. The main industrial users come from oil and gas, building and construction, paper, textiles and pharmaceutical industries.

The plastic products, such as resins, adhesive films, polymers, semi-conductors and polycarbonates, are extensively used in the automotive, electronic and engineering industries.

Agricultural products are aimed at crop protection, urban pest management, seeds and biotechnology solutions around the world.

In addition to physical products Dow is also engaged in specialist services, providing customized solutions to pharmaceutical, automotive and chemical industries. An example of such a service is the delivery of poorly soluble drug compounds based on advanced particle engineering technology.

Reasons for the application of Six Sigma

William Stavropoulos, the CEO of Dow Chemical, is reported to have once said, 'the most difficult thing to do is to change a successful company'. It is true that employees of companies enjoying a high profit margin with some dominance in the market are likely to be complacent and to feel comfortable with the status quo. Perhaps it is even more difficult to stay at the top or sustain success if the strategy and processes are not adaptable to change.

There are four critical and interrelated components that make up Dow's Strategic Blueprint: Competitive Standard, Value Growth, Culture and Productivity.

Competitive Standard

Dow's goal is to continue building world class leadership in all of our businesses and become best-in-class in customer loyalty. Competitive Standard objectives include:

- Actively manage Dow's business portfolio
- Hold businesses accountable for strategy and profit and loss results
- Align businesses to meet customer needs
- Focus externally to understand customers, competitors and market trends.

Value Growth

Dow's goal is to achieve earnings per share (EPS) growth of 10% per year, year-over-year, across the business cycle. Value Growth objectives include:

- Grow established businesses
- Leverage leading product and marketing positions
- Commercialize new products and services
- Expand geographically to capture emerging market opportunities
- Invest in Research and Development (R&D).

Culture

Dow's goal is to move to best-in-class in employee empowerment and environmental health and safety performance. Culture objectives include:

- Living our values people strategy
- Achieving our environmental health and safety goals.

Productivity

Dow seeks to sustain its position as the industry leader in productivity. Productivity objectives include:

- Leverage best practices around the world
- Optimize integration to enhance asset efficiency
- Re-engineer work processes
- Be the lowest cost supplier
- Be more efficient with asset utilization.

Following the development and implementation of the Strategic Blueprint, Dow continued its improvement journey. Global Workstations established a communications pipeline that allowed all employees around the world to share a common computer systems, thereby accelerating the pace and quality of communications. Through this period, Dow also implemented a People Success System for the development and growth of its human resources and established a Leadership Development Network to build on leadership skills and align the organization. The company also instituted Growth

Acceleration Initiatives to place increased focus on value growth and it launched strategic performance measures to track company performance against key metrics.

While the productivity measures implemented in the 1990s established strong competitive advantages for Dow, company leadership had higher aspirations. Dow leadership's vision extended beyond the role of leadership in the chemical industry and extended to business excellence. Dow set its corporate aspirations purposefully high. The company announced its intention to grow at rates that exceed the industry average without skipping a beat in terms of productivity. The drive toward business excellence was established to accelerate the implementation of business strategy by aligning all the company's businesses, functions, geographies and sites to corporate aspirations; enhancing focus on the market place, and ensuring the disciplined application of key processes to accelerate Value Growth.

In the late 1998, Dow leadership embarked on a search for an enabler that would drive the company to the next level of productivity, performance and value. Leadership teams visited a number of top tier global companies, holding discussions on the latest ideas and trends in productivity and improvement. The search led to Six Sigma.

Dow's implementation began by taking a four-month hiatus to formulate a breakthrough implementation strategy. Within the context of this planning, a number of key decisions were made that set apart Dow's implementation of Six Sigma from that of others. One decision was that Six Sigma at Dow would be integrated into the business strategies of the company rather than being relegated to a corporate role. Many quality programmes of the past that were relegated to corporate roles were plagued with responsibility but little authority. In effect, this decision added vigour to Dow's implementation of Six Sigma by placing accountability for results directly on the shoulders of the business leaders of the company.

Additionally, Dow wanted to distinguish its practice of Six Sigma beyond a focus on MAIC (Measure, Analyse, Improve, Control methodology of Six Sigma) by incorporating linkages to those strategic drivers that are at the centre of focus for the company. The first of those drivers is a concentrated emphasis on Six Sigma projects that drive customer loyalty. Secondly, Dow chose to create a Six Sigma linkage to the technology of leveraging. Throughout the 1990s, Dow instituted a global business model and a single information technology platform. With Dow's integrated business structure, single information systems platform and global technology centres, the company is uniquely qualified to leverage best practices from Six Sigma.

DMAIC methodology

DMAIC refers to a data-driven life cycle approach to Six Sigma projects for improving processes and is an essential part of a company's Six Sigma programme. DMAIC is an acronym for five interconnected phases: Define, Measure, Analyse, Improve and Control. The simplified definitions of each phase are:

- Define by identifying, prioritizing and selecting the right project
- Measure key process characteristics, the scope of parameters and their performances
- Analyse by identifying key causes and process determinants
- Improve by changing the process and optimizing performance
- Control by sustaining the gain.

Although DMAIC is a data-driven and quantitative technique, it is also a methodology that may not produce unique output from a given set of input data. We have therefore chosen an actual case from a subsidiary of Dow Chemical to illustrate a worked-out example (Basu, 2001).

Define

The Dow Chemical Company began using Six Sigma in 1998 to improve the operations of its subsidiary the FilmTec Corp. of Minneapolis, a manufacturer of membranes which was having difficulty in meeting customer demand.

Membrane quality is determined by two criteria: (a) flux or the amount of water the membrane lets through during a given period and (b) how much impurity is removed from the water.

Measure

Membrane elements were tested prior to shipping to ensure the prescribed quality standards. The specifications were assured but the speed with which customers were serviced suffered. The shortfall of customer service was costing FilmTec approximately $500 000 a year.

Analyse

Six Sigma tools and methodologies were used at FilmTec to reduce product and process variation. Statistical analysis was used to identify variables that affected membrane flux most significantly.

One of the variables identified for improvement was the concentration of a chemical component used in the manufacturing process. The problem stemmed from the inconsistencies in concentration caused by the interruptions in feeding the chemical in the manufacturing process. The feeding was done from a movable container that was replaced every day. When the empty container was replaced by a full one the chemical did not always reach the process area. Empty containers were often not noticed.

Improve

To reduce the variation, an inexpensive reservoir was added to feed the chemical while containers were exchanged. Additionally, a level transmitter with an alarm was installed to alert operators to containers that were nearly empty.

The improvements have been significant. For one of FilmTech's water membranes, the standard deviation of the product out of spec. was reduced from 14.5% to only 2.2%. This resulted in several benefits to FilmTec and its customers including the bonus that membranes were made available to customers faster than before.

Control

To sustain the gains from the project, the Six Sigma team made additional changes. Prior to DMAIC, numbers used to track trends were displayed in tabular form. However, the tables were difficult to read and had little impact on monitoring. Now measurements are displayed on Excel charts that illustrate graphically and with visual immediacy the trends in flux on the finished membrane. The results and learnings from this project were incorporated into a report and posted on the knowledge management website of Dow Chemical.

In order to emphasize the sustainability of gains during the Control phase some companies including Dow Chemical have added the process of Leverage (L) after control and thus extended DMAIC to become DMAICL.

Tools and techniques

At various stages of the DMAIC process Dow Chemical has made use of tools of techniques supported by an adequate training programme. These include:

Define stage	SIPOC diagram
	CTQ tree
	Project charter
Measure stage	Histogram
	UCL/LCL control chart
	Process capability measure (C_p/C_{pk})
	Pareto diagram
Analyse stage	Value stream
	Process map
	Cause and effect diagram
Improve stage	Brainstorming
	Mind map
Control stage	Gantt chart
	Activity network diagram

For specific Black Belt projects the company applied advanced techniques including FMEA (Failure Mode and Effect Analysis), DOE (Design of Experiments) and QFD (Quality Function Deployment). As indicated later, the managing implementation plan was based on the concept of Hoshin planning.

The descriptions and applications of all the above tools and techniques can be found in *Implementing Quality* (Basu, 2004). The terms 'tools' and 'techniques', which are frequently and interchangeably used in books and practices, are consciously differentiated here. As described in the book, 'tools' are related to improving quality, as are the tools used in constructing a building. A single 'tool' may be described as a device which has a clear role and defined application. A 'technique', on the other hand, may be viewed as a collection of tools. There is also a need for a greater intellectual thought process and more skill, knowledge, understanding and training in order to use them effectively. For example, control charts are a tool of statistics. The way this tool is used along with other tools (e.g. process capability measurement) is a 'technique' of statistical process control (SPC).

Key benefits achieved

While Dow does not release its aggregate Six Sigma results, it announced that at year-end 2001 the company was more than halfway toward its goal of achieving US$1.5 billion in cumulative earnings before interest and taxes (EBIT) from Six Sigma.

At the time of this writing, Dow has 1270 active Black Belts. This represents 2.4% of the company's current population. Although this is short of the 3% goal, the employee population has grown significantly in recent times due to major acquisitions. Twenty-three per cent of all Dow employees have been involved in a successful Six Sigma project. Currently, Dow has more than 2800 active Six Sigma (DMAIC) projects and more than 100 active Design for Six Sigma (DFSS) projects.

Despite challenging economic conditions, Dow fully expects to achieve its goal of US$1.5 billion in cumulative EBIT by 2003.

How benefits are calculated

As indicated above, Dow does not release details of how the financial benefits are worked out. However our internal communication revealed that Dow's approach is in sympathy with the approach adopted by Ericsson AB as a simplified 'Business Impact' model for larger projects. The approach is described in *Quality Beyond Six Sigma* (Basu and Wright, 2003).

The projects are categorized under three headings:

- Cost takeout
- Productivity
- Cost avoidance.

A variable weighting is allocated to each category as shown in Table 14.1. When sufficient data is not available to provide an accurate estimate of business impact an approach of 'derived importance' based upon scores for various categories is a practical alternative, as shown in Table 14.2.

Business impact = Cost takeout + 0.5 Productivity
+ 0.2 Cost avoidance − Implementation cost

Design packaging and Improve OEE were the chosen projects. This simple process, although it depends on experience-based subjective

Table 14.1 Project benefit categories

Level	Cost takeout	Productivity	Cost avoidance
Definition	'Hard' savings	'Soft' savings	Avoidance of anticipated cost is not in today's structure
	Recurring expense prior to Six Sigma	Increase of process capacity so you can 'do more with less', 'do the same with less', 'do more with the same'	
Example	Less people to perform activity	Less time required for an activity	Avoid purchase of additional equipment
	Less $ required for same item	Improved machine efficiency	Avoid hiring contractors
Impact	Whole unit	Partial unit	Not in today's cost
Weighting	100%	50%	20%

assessment of selected criteria, has proven to be a systematic way of prioritizing projects where the financial data are inadequate.

Key lessons learned

- *The value of constancy of purpose*: Dow began its focus on Six Sigma with top-down leadership endorsement. The power of that endorsement has been sustained and has grown since its implementation began. This 'constancy of purpose' sends a clear signal to the entire company about long-term expectations and true cultural change.
- *Financial rigor*: Dow instituted business rules and established a team of trained financial analysts to review and validate financial benefits from its Six Sigma projects. Applying financial rigour to project financials offers transparency and credibility to the company's implementation of Six Sigma.
- *Data capture and knowledge management*: Six Sigma drives a data-based decision-making process. In order to capture and leverage knowledge, a flexible and user-friendly database must be established. Dow has invested significantly in the construction and maintenance of its database system for Six Sigma. This investment is paying substantial dividends in terms of knowledge capture for leveraging and tracking of project metrics for ongoing improvement.

Table 14.2 Derived importance of projects

Projects	Cost takeout	Productivity	Cost avoidance	Employee satisfaction	Current performance	Feasibility	Derived importance
	High: 10 Low: 1	High: 5 Low: 1	High: 2 Low: 0	High: 3 Low: 1	Low: 10 High: 1	High: 10 Low: 1	Max. score 40
Design packaging	9	2	0	2	7	8	28
Improve OEE	5	4	2	2	10	10	33
Process control	1	2	2	1	5	9	20
Product development	7	1	2	3	2	2	17

- *A way to do work … not additive:* Many falsely believe that Six Sigma is additive or parallel. In other words, Six Sigma is often viewed as something else that the organization has to do rather than *the way in which work is done.* It is essential to clearly position Six Sigma as the way in which work is done. Most business roles involve solving problems and closing the gap between reality and a desired state. Six Sigma is a methodology, a tool set and a mindset that is ideally suited for solving problems. Used properly, Six Sigma accelerates business strategy.
- *Pipeline conundrum:* Reflecting back on its decision to implement via rapid transformation, Dow would consistently say that the approach it took was the right one at the right time. One challenge of implementation through rapid transformation is that it is possible to deplete the project pipeline. Keeping a robust pipeline is essential to maintaining and building momentum for Six Sigma implementation. Time spent up front in creating a project pipeline would be well spent.

Important factors for implementation

The Dow leadership team travelled to Scottsdale, Arizona to meet with the Six Sigma Academy in early 1999. Following a series of meetings, two businesses within the company implemented Six Sigma. In a matter of months, the first Six Sigma projects began to prove the promise of the methodology. Late in the summer of 1999, Dow leadership made a bold commitment, expanding the implementation to all its businesses and functions around the world. To lead the implementation of Six Sigma at Dow, Kathleen Bader was named to the post of Executive Vice President for Quality and Business Excellence.

Under the leadership of Kathleen Bader, the 'Staircase of Change Leadership' was employed to develop an implementation designed to drive change in a revolutionary, yet sustainable, manner (Bader, 2002). Each successive step in this staircase builds upon the previous step forming a solid foundation for change leadership. The steps in this staircase include:

- Vision
- Value
- Attitude
- Language
- Behaviours
- Best practices

- Leveraging
- Customer loyalty
- Articulate strategy
- Implementation
- Culture change
- Success.

The key features of each step are briefly described below.

Vision

Dow's stated vision for Six Sigma is: 'Dow will become recognized and lauded as one of the premier companies of the 21st century, driven by an insatiable desire to achieve a Six Sigma level of performance and excellence in all that we do.' Additionally, the Dow vision for Six Sigma was cast in the company's 1999 annual report to shareholders. In the letter to shareholders, the company declared: 'We expect Six Sigma to elevate our company to an entirely new level of operation performance, delivering $1.5 billion in EBIT cumulatively by 2003 from the combined impact of revenue growth, cost reductions, and asset utilization.'

Values

Dow widely communicates its corporate values – integrity, respect for people, unity, outside-in focus, agility and innovation – encouraging all employees to honour the relationships which make Dow successful and to see the world through the eyes of those whose lives are affected by the company. The implementation and methodology Six Sigma ties into and directly supports these values.

The premier performance values of Six Sigma are:

- Customers will be rewarded by higher productivity and quality of products and services; Dow will be rewarded by increased customer loyalty and business retention.
- Employees will be rewarded through more satisfying work, a greater sense of value to the company, more rewarding and competitive personal and professional growth; Dow will be rewarded because more satisfied employees means more satisfied customers.
- Shareholders will be rewarded by increased shareholder value; Dow will be rewarded by higher market capitalization.

- Society will be rewarded as Dow applies its Six Sigma mindset and technology to environmental, health and safety issues; Dow will be rewarded because EH&S is, quite simply, the sustainable thing to do.

Attitude

Early in the implementation, it was realized that Six Sigma was more than an extraordinary methodology and tool set for quality improvement. In its highest form, Six Sigma represents a mindset change that focuses on results, accountability and data-driven decision-making. In the environment of a large global corporation the unified, passionate attitude of leadership is essential to effective change. According to Kathleen Bader: 'Visionary leadership is rarely accidental. It is an attitude that imposes accountability, inaugurates change, inspires belief, invokes commitment, and induces results.'

Language

The soul of attitude is evidenced in language. The implementation of Six Sigma utilizes its own terminology. Utilizing the common language of Six Sigma was instituted as a leadership practice. Additionally, leadership was encouraged to utilize positive, solutions-oriented language to signal strong support for Six Sigma.

Behaviours

A listing of behaviours was communicated throughout the company in a variety of message forms including 34 road shows that took place at Dow sites around the world. These behaviours included: adopting intolerance for variation, measuring inputs not just outputs, demanding measurement and accountability, requiring sustainable gains, delivering on customer satisfaction to build loyalty, and leveraging for competitive advantage. The road shows, led by Kathleen Bader, sent a clear signal for expected change from Six Sigma at Dow.

Best practices

Dow undertook a diligent study of best practices in Six Sigma. The study looked at the implementations of best-in-class Six Sigma practitioners in order to identify key success factors and gaps. From this study came numerous best practices. Additionally, gaps were identified that were employed to differentiate Dow's implementation of Six Sigma. Specifically, these gaps were customer loyalty and leveraging.

Loyalty and leveraging processes and skills are embedded in Dow's Six Sigma Black Belt curriculum and are promoted widely throughout the company.

Customer loyalty

Dow's Values represent the cornerstone of how Dow works and behaves as a company. One of these values, outside-in focus, is critical to the company's future growth objectives. Dow believes its growth comes from looking for opportunities through the customer's eyes. Focusing on customer loyalty is a way to systematically gather customer input, ensuring that our business strategies are grounded by information from the market. By taking the outside-in approach, we are validating that our business efforts are focused on the things that matter most to our customers.

The application of customer loyalty to Dow's implementation of Six Sigma is much more than lip service and good intention. Up to 25% of all Six Sigma projects at Dow are focused on driving a Customer Loyalty differential. The Dow focus on customer loyalty is based on understanding what the customer states is important, and the fact that a business can objectively derive a measurable change in competitive advantage based on customer loyalty metrics. The customer loyalty pyramid provides the framework for the development of the customer loyalty process from qualifiers, through essential and defining characteristics and on to the drivers of customer loyalty. Moving a customer from being satisfied to being loyal can create powerful, sustainable business impact. Dow has implemented a process model that drives this critical transformation.

Leveraging

Leveraging is defined as the effective multiple implementation of demonstrated best practices. Breakthrough quality, coupled with Dow's unique ability to instantaneously transmit a Six Sigma solution from Texas to Terneuzen to Taiwan, turns ideas into impact on the bottom line. Breaking down silos and unleashing the power of leveraging across every Dow business, around the world, is having a multiplier effect on the company's implementation of Six Sigma.

There are three levels of leveraging Six Sigma best practices that exist within Dow. First, leveraging takes place within individual businesses and functions. The next level of leveraging is across businesses and functions. Big Company leveraging projects offer huge potential in terms of pay-off because Big Company projects span the entire global organization. To establish a leveraging mindset, Dow has developed tools and processes that enable the acceleration of leveraging. Leveraging is an integral component of Black Belt training at Dow. Additionally, Dow has established a database that captures a wide range of Six Sigma project information. Within this database, key word searches and flags that readily identify projects with leverageable components are commonly used. Furthermore, Dow has established Leveraging Champions within each of its businesses. The purpose of these Leveraging Champions is to data mine for leveraging opportunities and continually promote the idea of leveraging throughout the company.

Articulated strategy

The strength of the Six Sigma methodology will change corporations through an evolutionary process. However, the drivers for change facing Dow created an urgency that wouldn't wait for evolution. What was needed was transformation. As with any plan of attack, a detailed and rigorous strategy is required.

The Six Sigma breakthrough strategy implemented at Dow wove together three leading edge processes. The Stages of Change model, as proposed by Dave Ulrich from the University of Michigan, suggests that individuals go through four stages of change – from Awareness to Sustaining stages. Through this process, behaviours are first unfrozen. New behaviours are then defined then institutionalized. Finally, the new behaviours are reinforced in the Sustaining phase. The Management of Change bubble chart was also utilized. The components of this chart were synthesized from a number of organizational behaviour studies. This chart contains six cultural change elements that must be addressed during implementation of change. The Stages of Change model and the Management of Change model were overlaid against a Managing Implementation plan or MI. MI is based on the concepts of Hoshin Kanri (or Hoshin planning). The MI plan incorporates vision along with 3–5-year strategic objectives. Finally, annual objectives result from this plan. Objective metrics to evaluate progress against this plan and clearly identified areas of accountability are critical. The matrix of strategy formed by these three processes set the implementation of Six Sigma at Dow in motion in a focused and clear direction.

Implementation

Full-scale implementation of Six Sigma at Dow began early in 2000. Successive training waves, each containing approximately 200 Black Belts, were conducted following the full-scale launch. Each business and function within Dow has a Business Champion to drive the implementation. Furthermore, Local Champions are in place to make certain that Black Belts are supported at the local level with viable project charters and barrier-breaking support. Process Owners are also identified to make sure that control plans stay in place and gains are sustained for the long term.

Culture change

A Six Sigma resource commitment was established by the company. This commitment calls for 3% of all employees to be Six Sigma Black Belts. Black Belts are expected to fulfil a two-year, full-time commitment to Six Sigma. The two-year commitment begins when their first project goes into realization. In addition to culture change being facilitated by having 3% of all employees as Six Sigma Black Belts, Dow employs numerous other levers to effect cultural change. For example, employee compensation plans are tied to Six Sigma results. Top leadership has established an expectation that all employees have at least one personal goal tied to Six Sigma. Additionally, the company has established an expectation that all of its professional-level employees must be engaged in a successful Six Sigma project by year-end 2005.

Success

There is an old maxim that goes: 'Nothing succeeds like success'. In its implementation of Six Sigma, Dow has exceeded each one of its financial results targets. Dow's Six Sigma implementation is generating significant financial results and is effectively driving positive, powerful cultural change.

Conclusions

Although Dow Chemical Company may not have received the same level of publicity as Motorola and General Electric the contribution of the company to Six Sigma movement is none the less undiminished. In addition to the proven success factors Dow has offered at least three distinctive elements in its approach. These are 'attitude', 'leverage' and 'articulated strategy' (alignment with the concept of Hoshin Kanri). Six Sigma at Dow is quality with an attitude: an attitude that inspires commitment and makes things happen. The three levels of leveraging Six Sigma best practices enable the sharing and sustaining of the benefits across the organization. By aligning the strategic objectives of implementation with the concept of Hoshin planning over 3–5 years the project is steered in a focused and clear direction.

Six Sigma is now embedded in the corporate culture of Dow. In his address to shareholders in the Annual Report of 2003, Bill Stavropoulos said, 'Application of Six Sigma's proven approach to efficiency remains an essential part of the way we operate, helping to deliver productivity gain as well as other, sometimes surprising, contributions to our bottom line. Some of the tax benefits we gained in 2003, for example, were direct results of the work of a dedicated Six Sigma team'.

Acknowledgements

This case study is based upon the information provided by Kathleen Bader and Jeff Schatzer of Dow Chemical Company, USA, during the publication of *Quality Beyond Six Sigma* by R. Basu and J. N. Wright (Butterworth Heinemann, 2003).

Case study 2: The Dell Direct model

Background

Dell Computer today is a market leader in Personal Computers (PCs), with a world market share of around 20% and an operating profit greater than any of its competitors. Michael Dell, the founder, still not 40 years old, was the fourth wealthiest person in the USA in 2001.

As the story goes, Michael Dell started a part-time business from his dormitory when he was a student at the University of Texas in early 1980s. He was assembling and upgrading PCs. When these low-cost PCs generated a huge demand he dropped out of university and founded Dell Computer. Doubtless, his early success owed a lot to the booming PC market in the late 1980s and early 1990s. However, Dell should also be credited with two key aspects of his supply strategy. First, he bypassed the traditional retail channels by selling direct to customers. Second, his focused customers were medium and large corporate accounts, rather than individual consumers. (Individual customers were included only when on-line buying was introduced.)

The Direct model

The Dell Direct model, as it became known, proved to be a highly successful supply chain strategy with two key advantages:

- There was no margin for the retail channel and thus Dell could pass this on customers by undercutting its competitor's prices.
- The direct interaction with customers enabled Dell to receive more accurate and rapid information about market demand and requirements. This allowed Dell to adapt and respond more quickly.

'You actually get to have a relationship with the customer,' says Michael Dell, 'and that creates valuable information, which, in turn, allows us to leverage our relationship with both suppliers and customers.'

The emergence of Internet and on-line e-commerce further strengthened the power of the Dell Direct model. Dell also modified their supply chain strategy in two key areas. First, it opened the on-line channel to consumers for household applications. Even in the UK every household is getting used to receiving Dell leaflets encouraging them to order on-line. The consumer has the choice to buy a Compaq, HP, IBM or Toshiba model from the high street shops or wait for Dell computers, expecting better value for money. Second, the company moved to make-to-order manufacturing and supply process. The PC was only built after the customer ordered it, reducing Dell's costs further.

Outsourcing

In the IT world, outsourcing is almost always a way to get rid of a problem a company has not been able to solve itself. Dell appears to apply its outsourcing of its after-sales service with a difference. With their service providers, they are working to set quality measures and, more important, to build data linkages that makes it visible in real time how they are doing, for example, how long it takes to request a service.

Establishing how many partners Dell would need has been a process of trial and error. They accept that when you operate on the cutting edge of technology things do not always work as planned. Where the technology is fairly stable (e.g. monitors) they expect their partnerships to last a long time. Others will be more volatile. However, regardless of how long these relationships last, the suppliers share information with Dell in a real-time fashion. The technology available today really boosts the value and transparency of information sharing.

Inventory stock cover is one of a handful of key performance measures Dell watches very closely. It is not just the financing cost. Computer components are changing very fast. Since the millennium all computer chips carry a six digit date code. For example, '2005 – 21' means it was built in the twenty first week of 2005. Dell carries 11 days of inventory while a competitor has 80, and when Intel comes out with a new 450 megahertz chip, Dell is going to get to market 69 days sooner. In addition to inventory, the real-time performance measures in the P&L (profit and loss) account that Dell regards as the best indicators are margins, average selling price and the overhead associated with selling.

Dell sees forecasting as a critical marketing and sales skill. They teach their sales account managers to lead large account customers through a discussion of their future PC needs. With smaller and on-line customers they have real-time information about what they are buying which is aided by knowledge of the latest promotions directly targeted to individuals through newspapers and magazine adverts. They also analyse data from their direct telephone sales people.

The challenge

The industry leaders IBM, Compaq and Apple started to take notice, but found it very hard to copy. The main reason is that the competitors were not prepared to risk upsetting their traditional and established retail channels by selling directly. When Michael Dell first started out with his direct-selling model the competitors thought he had failed to understand the customers' need to touch and see the product before buying it. Even when they recognized that the model was a success, the competitors struggled to react, most probably because they were stuck in an existing set of relationships with retailers and suppliers.

It is likely that competitors will find a way to replicate or offset the Dell Direct model. The Dell model and its position of market leader will continue to give it some advantage. However, the computer industry as a whole is facing threats and challenges and looking for opportunities to grow. The PC sales are slowing down and prices are falling further. There is another scenario looming in the horizon. Just as the PC replaced mini computers, and the mini computers replaced the main frame, it is only matter of time before something comes along to replace the PC.

Over recent past years Dell had limited success by diversifying into servers and printers. The company strategy does not seem to encourage higher levels of R&D expenditure. Thus Dell has done well in the low-end models of servers and printers but has struggled at the high-end with Sun for servers and HP for printers.

The biggest challenge facing Dell is where to look for growth.

The final message from Michael Dell: 'The direct model really delivers value to the customer all the way from distribution back through manufacturing and design. If you tried to divide Dell up into a manufacturer and a channel, you'd destroy the company's unique value.'

Case study 3: Business Process Excellence project in GlaxoSmithKline Turkey

Background

GlaxoSmithKline Turkey (GSK Turkey, previously known as GlaxoWellcome Turkey) was awarded MRP II 'Class A' certification in 1999 by business education consultants Oliver Wight Europe.

As part of the MRP II Class A programme, GSK Turkey installed a sales and operations planning (S&OP) process which is underpinned by a set of business planning meetings at various levels. In spite of the GlaxoWellcome and Smith Kline Beecham merger and the corporate

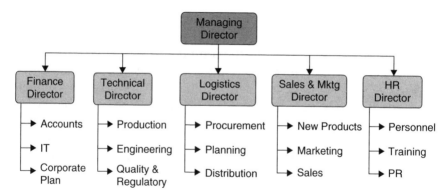

Figure 14.1   GSK Turkey organization chart

Lean Sigma initiative, the S&OP process has been continued by the company every month.

The rigour of the S&OP process, which is championed by the managing director, has helped the company to sustain and improve the business benefits and communication culture, especially when they were challenged by a number of initiatives in hand, including:

• Transfer of head office
• Rationalization of factory and warehouse
• Corporate Lean Sigma programme
• Merger of GlaxoWellcome and Smith Kline Beecham.

The organization structure of the company in general remained the same with some changes in personnel after the merger, as in Figure 14.1.

Project scenario

The situation was quite different, however, with GlaxoWellcome Turkey in the late 1990s. During the growth period of Zantac, Glaxo's blockbuster drug, a manufacturing plant was installed in 1984 at Gebze, an industrial town approximately 80 km from the head office in Istanbul. The Gebze factory gradually expanded to accommodate manufacturing and secondary packing facilities for antibiotics and tertiary packaging of imported Glaxo and Wellcome products for the local market. By the beginning of 1997 the Gebze factory was producing nearly 25% of the company turnover of over $100 million. A distribution warehouse was built in 1992 at the Gebze site and this was managed by the Logistics Department of the company. With the assistance of a local software consulting firm the IT Department implemented the financial module and limited planning modules of an enterprise resource planning (ERP) system called MFG-Pro. Although GlaxoWellcome Turkey was enjoying a period of growth both the internal communication and external customer service were not satisfactory. Some of the problems and challenges were:

- The customer order fill was only around 85% while the stock cover was over 6 months.
- The communication and interpersonal relationship between the head office (Istanbul) and the factory (Gebze) was poor.
- The distribution warehouse appeared to require additional storage capacity and modernization.
- Although an ERP system (MFG-Pro) was operational, it was not effective because of poor data accuracy and lack of understanding of the functionality.
- GW Turkey depended heavily on the supply from GlaxoWellcome Export (based in Ware, England) who could not assess the priority of GW Turkey.
- The corporate Global Supply Chain Programme (which required Y2K-enabled 'legacy' or new systems) demanded considerable resources from GW Turkey.

The challenges were compounded by an audit report by the US Food and Drug Administration (FDA). During an audit of the computer systems of a European factory supplying to the US market FDA issued a warning (Form 483) regarding the batch validation of the MRP (materials requirement) system of the factory. The corporate Quality Division of GlaxoWellcome mandated that all sites with links to the US market must conform to the validation policy for MRP systems while other sites (such as Gebze) were recommended to follow the policy.

Following a request from the Logistics Director of GW Turkey, the corporate Business Excellence Group from the UK visited Turkey, carried out a feasibility study and put forward the following recommendations in September 1997:

1 Changes:
   – Implement a company-wide sales and operations planning process (see Figure 10.3) supported by appropriate training

- Re-engineer the manufacturing resource planning (MRP II) process according to company requirements
- Update MFG-Pro planning modules to comply with re-engineered MRP II requirements and validation guidelines
- Install a performance management process to work towards MRP II Class A standards.

2 Time scale:
- MFG-Pro to be Y2K-enabled by the end of 1999
- The work on Business Process Excellence and MRP II processes would take 18 months leading to MRP II Class A.

3 Cost:
- $50 000 to be available from a corporate fund to ensure the validation on Y2K compliance of MFG-Pro
- The training, consulting and other costs for the Business Process Excellence project to be self-financing and supported by GW Turkey.

Project launch

GW Turkey launched a programme (known as EKIP) in January 1998 to improve company-wide communications and sustain a robust business planning process using MRP II 'best practice' principles.

The Logistics Director had been involved in a MRP II Class A project when he was previously working in Bristol Myer Squibs and was appointed as the Project Manager for EKIP. He invited two consultants from Oliver Wight (OW) Group, known to be specialists in MRP II processes, to run a two-day training workshop for managers. The OW consultants advised:

- To set up a project team with specific task groups for S&OP, demand management, production planning, MFG-Pro Update, quality and validation, performance management, and training and communication
- To achieve MRP II Class A the company should fulfil performance criteria (e.g. order fill 95%, BOM (bill of materials) accuracy 99%, MPS (master production schedule) performance 95%, supplier delivery performance 95%, inventory record accuracy 99%), MRP II process integrated with the software MFG-Pro and a sustainable S&OP process.

The Logistics Director decided that after the OW training workshop GW Turkey would do everything themselves except the software support from a local consulting firm to update MFG-Pro.

Corporate review

The supply chain problem escalated and the Logistics Director had to spend more time in the trouble shooting of day-to-day operations. In three months there was little progress with the EKIP except some Y2K-related systems specification for MFG-Pro and the formation of task groups. The relations between the Logistics Team at the head office and the Production Team at Gebze deteriorated further.

A key member of the Corporate Manufacturing and Supply Strategy Group of GlaxoWellcome Plc reviewed the status of Project EKIP and recommended a full-time Project Manager, a revised organization and a road map to Class A for GW Turkey. The Logistics Director continued to be part of the steering team and to be a key player in the success of the project.

Case Study 4: Cisco Systems

The company

Cisco is a leading new technology corporation that develops, manufactures, markets and supports Internet networking systems for both local and wide area networks. Founded in 1984, Cisco has over 26 000 employees worldwide and in February 2000 had a market capital of $490 billion, competing closely with Microsoft.

Cisco was among the very first in B2B communications history to leverage e-business across the entire value chain. Its customers include businesses of all sizes and government agencies, educational institutions and individual consumers.

Cisco occupies the number one or number two position in 18 of the 20 market segments it operates.

Because companies like Cisco move so rapidly, our information in this study cannot be viewed as completely up-to-date, but this does illustrate the success factors that they incorporate.

Drivers for e-business

The primary driver was Cisco's supply chain strategy. In the early 1990s the company began planning its global supply network strategy.

The management decided to outsource most of that work and use networking technology to link suppliers and distributors closely to in-house processes.

Cisco's supply chain network strategy comprised five initiatives:

- A *single enterprise system* for suppliers, manufacturers, distributors and customers
- *Real-time information-sharing* directly to contract manufacturers without delay
- *Direct fulfilment* of customer orders
- *Expediting new product introduction* to reduce the number of alterations during product development
- *Automated testing* to ensure quality on supplier lines.

The second driver was to excel customer service. Customers are now able to submit support requests, find answers to FAQs (frequently asked questions) on the Cisco website and obtain help in an electronic forum.

The e-business solution

Cisco Systems' solutions covered two interrelated areas. The back-end solution is a supply chain portal called MCO (Manufacturing Connection Online) and the front-end answer proved to be CICSO Connection Online, or CCO, a customer service portal.

The creation of MCO involved the consolidation of the access points of numerous manufacturing information systems into a single user interface via the company's intranet. MCO provides Cisco and its partners with access to real-time forecast data, inventory and purchase orders and customer orders.

The company automated customer service through CCO, comprising five key components:

- Market place
- Technical assistance
- Customer service of non-technical assistance
- An Internet Product Centre to enable users to submit orders
- Status agent to enable customers to ascertain the status of orders.

CCO is a comprehensive resource for customers, suppliers, sales force and business partners. This application also connects users directly to the Federal Express tracking service to determine in real time where their order is located.

Business benefits

The company has reduced the delivery time to users, on average from 23 down to ten days. This has been achieved by integrating suppliers earlier in the ordering process. Cisco has been saving over $100 million annually in its supply chain process and the costs are down by between 20 and 28%. Cisco's supply chain initiatives have eliminated inefficiencies for its suppliers and distributors.

The use of CCO has resulted in 98% accuracy for on-time shipments and a 25% increase in customer satisfaction since 1995. Product delivery lead times have been reduced by between two and five days. The company estimates that nearly 70% of product ordering is done through the Web, with CCO saving the company some £350 per year in operating expenses.

Cisco's skilled use of MCO and CCO portals and customer management reflect its commitment and leadership to the e-business culture.

The future

The dynamic growth of Cisco is linked to its forward-looking IT and e-business strategy. The company has built an open, standard-based, enterprise-wide information highway.

The Cisco strategy will assist its future suppliers to Web-enable their internal supply chain processes and so further integrate the value chain. The company is also working with its largest customers to place a Cisco server directly on those customers' premises as part of their own intranet. CICSO is clearly playing a leading role in the communications industry.

Chapter 15

The Reflective Practitioner

Open the second shutter so that more light can come in.
Johann Wolfgang Goethe

In Chapter 1 we said that the customer is the central focus for any organization, and that marketing was too important to be left to the marketing department; everyone in the organization should be vitally interested in marketing 'their' organization.

We are all now competing in a global market place. Make no mistake about it. There is nowhere to hide; national boundaries and governments no longer provide protection against overseas competitors.

As you have progressed through this book, you will have realized that it is not possible to separate service from manufacturing. We cannot think of any manufacturing organization that is not also competing in the level of service that it provides. In a global market place first-class service, in the sense of delivering the right product, in the right quantities, at the right time, and with good post-delivery follow up, is taken for granted.

The challenge is to eliminate non-value adding activities. Any activity and any input that does not add value for the customer merely adds to expenses and a lowering of profits. We have to be ruthless in the way we look at all costs. Obviously some non-value adding activities, such as completing regulatory returns, will by necessity occur. Your aim should be to establish what is adding value and what is not adding value, and what is necessary and what is not. If an activity is not adding value and is not deemed to be necessary, then, if you are to be competitive, it must be minimized.

This book shows how efficiency in manufacture and service can be achieved – and how eventually a company can become world class by attaining excellence in both performance and practices. Achieving world class status will not be easy and requires a total, not piecemeal, solution.

Total Operations Solutions (TOpS) is not a fad. We are not peddling a new panacea, a three-letter acronym which we try to fit to all situations. We recognize that all organizations are different and what will work for one organization will not necessarily be appropriate for another. We do not give specific answers, but we show how you can identify your own strengths and weaknesses and how, from an analysis of these strengths and weaknesses, you can determine what has to be done. It is not enough for a company to know that they are losing market share, or that they have a high turnover of good technical staff. Such facts are usually self-evident.

Our belief is that manifestations of obvious problems will only be symptoms of a deeper malady. In the search for a healthy company we stress that all six pillars have to be looked at. Even if one pillar is performing reasonably well, this might only be in comparison to the other pillars. It would be a mistake to take a short-cut and to try to get away with rating say only 50 of the 200 questions. If all the questions are honestly benchmarked it will be found, even in seemingly strong areas of performance, that weaknesses will be discovered. After all, in every area of human endeavour, be it sport, family, or business, there will always be room for improvement. The Japanese have a philosophy of continuous improvement in life and their word for this is *kaizen* (it is only in comparatively recent years that they have extended this word to include business endeavours).

We accept that this book originated with Total Manufacturing Solutions but our argument then was that if you are a manufacturing company then surely everything else that is done in the organization is to support the endeavours of the factory? Or do you take the view that you are a marketing company and the factory is only there to answer the needs of the marketing function? After all, it could be said that the marketing team is the interface with the customers, and therefore marketing knows what the customers want. Following this logic it would then be left to marketing to determine what shall be made (product), and because marketing 'know' what the market will pay (price) they would also determine the cost limits within which the factory must perform. Marketing would also have a fair say in how the product should be distributed (place) and, of course, how it should be advertised (promotion).

There are several dangers in this approach. At the opening of this chapter we used the words of David Packard (of Hewlett Packard), who said 'Marketing is too important to be left to the marketing department'. Kotler and Armstrong (1989) add that 'in a great marketing organization, you can't tell who's in the marketing department'. We don't disagree with these sentiments, but we would rephrase the statement to read 'in a world class manufacturing company you can't tell who's in manufacturing and who's in marketing'. Likewise, in a service organization it should not be possible to tell who is in operations and who is in marketing. There should be no back room! It is imperative that marketing, manufacturing and operations work as one. There is no room for functional divisions and jealousies.

Working together also means that, in the development of new products, marketing and operations must be closely associated.

In Chapter 4 we discussed new product/service development. It should go without saying that for a manufacturing organization new products are developed around the existing strengths and capabilities of the factory. But, hard to believe, for many organizations the factory is ignored when the specifications and design of a new product are being determined. The factory will then be given a difficult product to make that requires retooling and retraining, with delivery expected within an impossible time frame. Put like that it sounds ridiculous, but recently an impressive TV advertising campaign launched a new product that was not available to buy in the shops simply because the factory had been unable to perform on time! In this case the advertiser created a demand and made sales for the opposition.

But Total Operations Solutions goes beyond working together as a team within the organization. In our supply chain approach (see Chapter 5), we say that suppliers and customers should also be taken into our confidence and should become an integral part of the design process. While it is true that normally a customer only judges us on three occasions – that is, when placing an order, when the goods are received and when they get the account to pay – we believe that a world class organization would want to get closer to the customer than this. We see no reason why key customers should not be invited to give input to new product development, and we believe that customers should be encouraged to visit the factory at any time. Likewise with suppliers.

A surprisingly large number of companies have little loyalty for their suppliers. If the aim is to get the best price and to use buying power to squeeze suppliers, how can a company expect suppliers to be anything but a little suspicious of the company? But if suppliers are treated not as adversaries, but as part of the planning team, then there are real benefits to be gained for the company and for the supplier. Suppliers can be invaluable in making suggestions for new product design, new materials and methods. Through their market intelligence, from a different perspective from your market intelligence, they can add to your knowledge of what the competitors are up to.

Total Operations Solutions also considers health and safety issues and includes being a good citizen of the universe. Gone are the days when it was acceptable to pollute your own rivers and environment: now it is no longer acceptable to transfer production off shore and pollute someone else's environment or to exploit their labour force. Apart from the hypocrisy of such an approach it will only be a matter of time before you are caught out. In the long run, if not for ethical reasons but certainly for good commercial reasons, it pays to do it right first time, rather than be embarrassed into making expensive corrections later. Chapter 5 discusses product safety, industrial safety and environment protection. The ethics of producing good 'clean' products and providing safe working conditions do not need elaboration. The economic sense of doing so is also self-evident. Chapter 5 considers some of the actions that need to be taken to protect your products. It covers what to look for when receiving materials, how to store materials and how to prevent contamination during processing. Safety, accident prevention and emergency procedures are also covered.

Chapter 7 goes into the details of facilities. In this chapter we return to the theme of team work and the need for marketing, operations, customers and suppliers to work together and for all parties to understand the capabilities and strengths of the operation. The question of flexible manufacturing is considered. While we accept that there are considerable advantages from being flexible, we do make the point that forward planning and design can reduce the need to be flexible all of the time. We do not suggest that flexible manufacturing is a bad thing, or that in all circumstances it will benefit a company, but we do believe that many of the benefits of just-in-time can be achieved with large batches. It does not necessarily follow that making everything in batches of one just to achieve flexibility is always the best option. The aim is not flexibility, or just-in-time, or single-minute exchange of dies; the aim is efficiency. Economies of scale should still be considered as a viable option to flexible manufacturing and in some circumstances batch production will prove to be the more efficient option. The same principles apply to service industries. The real issue is efficient performance without losing customer benefits.

Operational performance is dependent on many things: the skills and ingenuity of the staff, the efficiency of the supply of the materials, the scheduling of work, the equipment we have and not least the reliability of the equipment. Quality includes the level of maintenance of the plant. We consider that maintenance is a competitive weapon.

To determine our manufacturing performance we are firm believers in measurement. The often maligned F.W. Taylor once said 'if it can't be measured it can't be managed'. We agree. And we say this applies to all aspects of a company, and thus we have 200 questions which enable you to obtain a benchmark measurement for the whole company and to extend them to include relations with suppliers and customers. With measurement of manufacturing performance we provide a series of quantifiable measurements which will give a precise measurement. Before any measurement should be attempted it is desirable that we know why we are measuring and what actions we can take as the result of the measurement. We say that the mere act of taking a measurement will mean time and effort, and that measurement in itself is not a value adding activity. If measurements are unreliable, or if the results are of interest only, there is no benefit in taking them. To justify the time and cost of taking a measurement it is important that the results are studied and that some concrete action is taken. The aim is to improve the quality of what we are providing, 'quality' being the reduction of non-value added activities and efficiency in our value adding activities.

Much of what we already measure is in the form of accounting information, and much time and effort go into recording this information. We are of the opinion that often data is gathered just for the sake of gathering it, and little effort is made to use constructively the information we already have. We actually don't need more information, but we must make sure that the information we are receiving is relevant and that we are using it to our advantage. In Chapter 8 we look at various standard accounting ratios and discuss the importance and relevance of each. This chapter also explains why we need a strategy for information technology. We live in an age where information has never before been so readily available. The danger is that we can get swamped with it. We also have to be aware of the pitfalls of computerization and of some of the basic safeguards that are required when considering a new system.

We have said earlier that quality is a cultural issue. Quality and the elimination of waste, the continuous search for better methods and processes should become so engrained into the psyche of the people of the organization that they are not even conscious that they are practising total quality management. Instinctively when things go wrong they will know what to do and will always react in the way that management would hope that they would react. Before this state can be achieved much learning has occurred.

Chapter 9 is our people chapter. The study of organizational cultures is not the study of organizations as such but is the study of the people who make up the organization. The hackneyed expression 'people are our greatest resource' is in fact more than a cliché. In the words of a New Zealand Maori proverb:

What is the important thing?
It is people
It is people
It is people.

In Chapter 9 we discuss our approach to learning and empowerment. We believe the key is through education and the provision of learning opportunities for everyone in the organization.

In the Appendix, with the 200 questions, we provide the basis for the answer of how Total Operations Solutions might be achieved. But, before the 200 questions can be asked, a philosophy and a method are needed.

Chapter 10 considers the philosophy of excellence and the magnitude of change needed to establish a culture of quality throughout a company. Cultural changes cannot be limited to just one section of an organization; any attempt to do so will be doomed to failure. The whole company, from the chief executive to the cleaner, must share the same vision and have the same goals. Likewise it is not possible for any one function to work in isolation or to remain aloof. Although it is important that direction and leadership come from the top of the company, unless everyone at all levels shares the same passion for manufacturing correctness and excellence, it won't happen. The culture has to be all-pervasive. Changing a culture does not happen overnight. But unless the decision to change is made and steps are taken to effect a change it will never happen. Changing a culture will not be an easy task.

Once the culture is right (the philosophy has been explained and accepted, i.e. everyone is living and breathing the philosophy), and the team (drawn from senior experienced people from each of the key functions) has been appointed and trained, and the data has been collected, then (and only then) can an attempt be made to seek answers to the 200 questions.

The method includes forming a team to ask the questions, and a system for the capture of data. These issues are covered in Chapter 12. Suffice it to say that as Total Operations Solutions embraces the whole organization, it follows as surely as night follows day that the team must be drawn from each major function of the organization. Much of the data on which to base the answers to the questions will already exist in the company. In Chapter 12 we discuss where data can be found.

Initially the 200 questions will not provide a solution. The 200 questions have been designed in such a way that the initial aim is to score or rate the organization against each question. There is no short-cut. Each question has to be considered and a rating agreed. In effect you will be using the questions as a means of benchmarking your organization. Having calculated a benchmark score the next stage is to analyse the results. The purpose of the analysis is to establish where the weaknesses are and to consider what actions are necessary to improve the situation. The gap between where your organization is and where it needs to be will be obvious once the rating has been completed. Each organization will have its own pattern of gaps. It is unlikely that any two organizations will have the same pattern. Improvement strategies are discussed in Chapter 11, and the management of the improvement process, plus the place of consultants in the improvement process, is considered.

From this examination we enable you to identify which of five categories of company yours currently falls into and what this means. An important issue in determining which category is the relationship and relative values of performance and practice issues. We explain how performance cannot be sustained if the supporting performance pillars are weak. For each category we highlight actions that might be taken so as to achieve (eventually) world class status. An indication of what various gaps mean is given in Chapter 12. Knowing your benchmark position and having determined what is required facilitates corrective action.

Chapter 13 explains the implementation process. We make the point that many organizations have gone through the agony of benchmarking, or have gone to lengths to determine strengths and weaknesses, but if nothing happens all the effort (time and money) will be for nothing. Implementation cannot be rushed into. Our approach is a structured approach centred on a project team. We stress the need for an 'open' programme well publicized throughout the company with no hidden agendas. Achieving Total Operations Solutions could well take in excess of five years and even then perfection will not be achieved. Ours is an ongoing programme.

Chapter 14 provides case examples. However, the overall emphasis is on self-examination to enable a company to benchmark against world class standards. The beauty of our approach is in its simplicity. You do not have to enter into a partnership with another organization and trade information to see how well you compare to their performance. With our approach, by gathering data for the 200 questions, and then by self-examination of your performance for each of the questions, you can establish your Operational Excellence Factor against our established world class standards. We give you the means to establish an external benchmark position without having to go outside the company!

In conclusion, we say that it is the achievement of operations performance and the application of best practices that give a company a sustainable leading edge. Further, we believe it important that it should not be forgotten that history proves that strong nations are those who are strong in manufacturing. The Industrial Revolution made Britain 'Great', mass production and innovation made the United States a world power, and manufacturing with a focus on quality made Japan economically strong. To sustain a strong healthy national economy a country needs efficient world class manufacturers. Today's issues are globalization and international competition. No longer are companies protected by national barriers and tariffs. For some this may be seen as a threat, but conversely, an efficient organization will see this as an opportunity. This book shows how to make the most of the emerging opportunities.

Appendix: 200 Questions

I keep six honest working men
(They taught me all I knew)
Their names are What and Why and When
and How and Where and Who.
      Rudyard Kipling, *The Elephant's Child*

The 200 questions are based upon our analysis and explanation of the 20 foundation stones of total operations as described in Chapters 4–9. Our emphasis is on a 'self-assessment' approach by an organization's own managers and staff. In Chapter 12 we discussed how a multi-functional team within an organization can carry out its own benchmarking to identify areas for progressive improvement. We also discussed the role of external consultants.

As explained in Chapter 1, we have 10 questions for each of the 20 foundation stones. We have listed and numbered the questions in the same order in which the foundation stones were introduced. The sequence of the questions does not imply a hierarchy of importance.

If there are any difficulties in interpreting the questions refer back to the relevant pillar/foundation stone chapter. The scale for scoring each question is: 0.1 (poor), 0.2 (fair), 0.3 (good), 0.4 (very good) and 0.5 (excellent). This allows a high degree of accuracy. Team member guidelines are given in Chapter 12.

When we use the word 'you' with questions, it can be taken to refer to you the reader, you as a member of a multi-functional benchmarking team, or you in the sense of your organization (and the management and planning team). Note that where the word 'product' is used it refers to deliverables, be they goods, transport or service.

'ASK 2.0': advanced self-analysis kit

The 'ASK 2.0' interactive software provides a truly practical way of assessing, monitoring and improving business performance. This invaluable and user-friendly tool can be used by managers, in both manufacturing and service sectors, for regular business assessment and also by individuals or class-based groups as part of regular training.

The software contains guidelines for scoring each of the 200 questions. Assessments are scored and a series of visual graphs are used to identify positioning in comparison to the ideal and previous assessments. The user can vary the setting of target scores and/or weighting for each of the 20 'foundation stones' as appropriate. An advanced version of the software enables the user to change or align questions to company requirements.

The 'ASK 2.0' software (CD + manual) for all versions of Windows™ is available from Performance Excellence Limited, Little Maltmans, Maltmans Lane, Gerrards Cross SL9 8RW, UK (order line tel.: +44(0)1753 886 701, fax: +44(0)1753 886 317).

Now for the questions!

---

1 Understanding the market place

Tick appropriate box

1　How well do your managers in marketing and sales know the relative importance of main products (by volume, profit and trends)?

☐　☐　☐　☐　☐
0.1　0.2　0.3　0.4　0.5

2　How good (precise) are your analyses of trade needs and consumer habits? (If you have your own consumer studies centre and it is effective a 0.5 rating is likely)

☐　☐　☐　☐　☐
0.1　0.2　0.3　0.4　0.5

3　How often do you conduct market research of trade needs and consumer habits? (Guesswork = 0.1, but if at least every year then a rating of 0.5 is warranted)

☐　☐　☐　☐　☐
0.1　0.2　0.3　0.4　0.5

4   How well are customer complaints
    handled/recorded? (Are there set
    procedures and do staff use the
    procedures?)

☐ ☐ ☐ ☐ ☐
0.1 0.2 0.3 0.4 0.5

5   How well do your sales and marketing
    team know the relative importance
    of factors that affect customer
    satisfaction? (Factors to consider are
    cost, quality, lead time, order fill,
    after-sales service)

☐ ☐ ☐ ☐ ☐
0.1 0.2 0.3 0.4 0.5

6   How systematic, and scientific, are your
    advertising and promotion activities?

☐ ☐ ☐ ☐ ☐
0.1 0.2 0.3 0.4 0.5

7   How close is the link between your sales,
    marketing, planning and operations
    functions?

☐ ☐ ☐ ☐ ☐
0.1 0.2 0.3 0.4 0.5

8   How often do staff other than sales
    and marketing visit your major
    customers?

☐ ☐ ☐ ☐ ☐
0.1 0.2 0.3 0.4 0.5

9   How well do you know international
    tariff, tax and trade regulations?

☐ ☐ ☐ ☐ ☐
0.1 0.2 0.3 0.4 0.5

10 How aware are you of opportunities
    and constraints for emerging markets
    (e.g. East Europe and China)?

☐ ☐ ☐ ☐ ☐
0.1 0.2 0.3 0.4 0.5

2   Understanding the competition

11 How well do you know the true market
    size and market share for your core
    products?

☐ ☐ ☐ ☐ ☐
0.1 0.2 0.3 0.4 0.5

12 How well do your managers in
    marketing, sales and operations know
    (and agree) who your top three
    competitors are in specific product
    categories?

☐ ☐ ☐ ☐ ☐
0.1 0.2 0.3 0.4 0.5

13 How well and how frequently is   ☐ ☐ ☐ ☐ ☐
    product analysed by growth, market   0.1 0.2 0.3 0.4 0.5
    share, profitability, etc. (for example
    BCG matrix)?

14 How good is your knowledge of the   ☐ ☐ ☐ ☐ ☐
    strengths and weaknesses of your top   0.1 0.2 0.3 0.4 0.5
    three competitors?

15 How well do you know and compare the   ☐ ☐ ☐ ☐ ☐
    service level which key competitors   0.1 0.2 0.3 0.4 0.5
    provide to your customers?

16 How well do you know your   ☐ ☐ ☐ ☐ ☐
    competitors' innovation programmes   0.1 0.2 0.3 0.4 0.5
    and success rates?

17 How well do you know your key   ☐ ☐ ☐ ☐ ☐
    competitors' acquisitions, expansion   0.1 0.2 0.3 0.4 0.5
    and divestment programmes?

18 How well do you know the capacities   ☐ ☐ ☐ ☐ ☐
    and utilization of competitors' or their 0.1 0.2 0.3 0.4 0.5
    suppliers' manufacturing units and
    distribution centres?

19 How effectively do you keep track of   ☐ ☐ ☐ ☐ ☐
    the emergence of new competitors?   0.1 0.2 0.3 0.4 0.5

20 How often do you take part in   ☐ ☐ ☐ ☐ ☐
    external benchmarking surveys related   0.1 0.2 0.3 0.4 0.5
    to your competition? (Seldom = 0.1,
    once a year = 0.5)

3   Product and process innovation

(Remember 'Product' refers to deliverables and can mean goods, transport or services, or any combination of these)

21 How generous is your budget for   ☐ ☐ ☐ ☐ ☐
    product and process innovation?   0.1 0.2 0.3 0.4 0.5
    (<0.25% of sales = 0.1, >2% of
    sales = 0.5)

22 How well has your product innovation lead time reduced over the past three years?

☐ ☐ ☐ ☐ ☐
0.1 0.2 0.3 0.4 0.5

23 How good is your success ratio for new products? (<10% = 0.1, >80% = 0.5)

☐ ☐ ☐ ☐ ☐
0.1 0.2 0.3 0.4 0.5

24 How well is product design carried out in parallel with process design?

☐ ☐ ☐ ☐ ☐
0.1 0.2 0.3 0.4 0.5

25 How well do you use an integrated multi-disciplined team for product development with full participation of manufacturing or suppliers?

☐ ☐ ☐ ☐ ☐
0.1 0.2 0.3 0.4 0.5

26 How well do you design a new product/ service with a focus on ease of production, process and delivery?

☐ ☐ ☐ ☐ ☐
0.1 0.2 0.3 0.4 0.5

27 How well do you apply project management for innovation?

☐ ☐ ☐ ☐ ☐
0.1 0.2 0.3 0.4 0.5

28 How effectively do you structure and apply a screening process so as to eliminate impractical ideas at each stage of development?

☐ ☐ ☐ ☐ ☐
0.1 0.2 0.3 0.4 0.5

29 How well do you carry out the analysis of product life cycles? (Not very well = 0.1, continuous = 0.5)

☐ ☐ ☐ ☐ ☐
0.1 0.2 0.3 0.4 0.5

30 How well do you involve major customers in new product/service development or improvement of existing product/services (including delivery of product/services)?

☐ ☐ ☐ ☐ ☐
0.1 0.2 0.3 0.4 0.5

4 Enterprise resource planning

31 How well is your vision/mission communicated and understood by staff?

☐ ☐ ☐ ☐ ☐
0.1 0.2 0.3 0.4 0.5

32 How well are all functions of the organization involved in annual planning?

☐ ☐ ☐ ☐ ☐
0.1 0.2 0.3 0.4 0.5

33 How well is performance against
goals monitored/measured:
(a) Internally   ☐ ☐ ☐ ☐ ☐
(b) Externally by consultants   ☐ ☐ ☐ ☐ ☐
(by accountants and other professionals)?   0.1 0.2 0.3 0.4 0.5

34 How effective is your master   ☐ ☐ ☐ ☐ ☐
scheduling process to ensure sufficient   0.1 0.2 0.3 0.4 0.5
resource (materials, stocks of finished
goods, people) to support the sales
plan and expected demand?

35 How good is your capacity planning?   ☐ ☐ ☐ ☐ ☐
(Do you use a rough-cut capacity plan   0.1 0.2 0.3 0.4 0.5
to develop a detailed capacity
requirement plan?)

36 How well is your purchase scheduling   ☐ ☐ ☐ ☐ ☐
managed? (What controls are there   0.1 0.2 0.3 0.4 0.5
in place?)

37 How well do you pursue a make-to-   ☐ ☐ ☐ ☐ ☐
order policy with an emphasis on   0.1 0.2 0.3 0.4 0.5
material velocity (stock turn)? (Large
stocks of raw materials, work in progress
and finished goods = 0.1, just-in-time
philosophy with little or no buffer
stock = 0.5)

38 How effectively are your business   ☐ ☐ ☐ ☐ ☐
processes supported by an ERP   0.1 0.2 0.3 0.4 0.5
system (e.g. SAP R/3)?

39 How good is your integrated point of   ☐ ☐ ☐ ☐ ☐
sale system?   0.1 0.2 0.3 0.4 0.5

40 How effective is the inclusion of key   ☐ ☐ ☐ ☐ ☐
suppliers in the planning process?   0.1 0.2 0.3 0.4 0.5

5   Supply chain and supplier partnership

41 How effective have you been in the   ☐ ☐ ☐ ☐ ☐
sharing of common coding and database   0.1 0.2 0.3 0.4 0.5
facilitated by Internet or electronic data

interchange (EDI) with suppliers and customers?

42 How effective have you been in the co-development of materials?

☐ ☐ ☐ ☐ ☐
0.1 0.2 0.3 0.4 0.5

43 How effective are you in sharing risks and cost savings with your suppliers?

☐ ☐ ☐ ☐ ☐
0.1 0.2 0.3 0.4 0.5

44 How good are you in meeting delivery as determined by customers?

☐ ☐ ☐ ☐ ☐
0.1 0.2 0.3 0.4 0.5

45 How well do you work with suppliers to improve each others processes?

☐ ☐ ☐ ☐ ☐
0.1 0.2 0.3 0.4 0.5

46 How satisfactory is your post-delivery performance in terms of invoice accuracy?

☐ ☐ ☐ ☐ ☐
0.1 0.2 0.3 0.4 0.5

47 How well do you record and seek causes for return of goods and/or customer complaints?

☐ ☐ ☐ ☐ ☐
0.1 0.2 0.3 0.4 0.5

48 How well is cost of non-conformance to quality standards communicated to staff (cost of rework, scrap, replacement, overtime, lost business)?

☐ ☐ ☐ ☐ ☐
0.1 0.2 0.3 0.4 0.5

49 How cost-efficient is your distribution operation when distribution cost is expressed as a percentage of sales? (Over 8% = 0.1, excellent, i.e. less than 1% = 0.5.)

☐ ☐ ☐ ☐ ☐
0.1 0.2 0.3 0.4 0.5

50 How easy is it for customers to contact the right person in your organization when they want to place an order or need knowledge of your product?

☐ ☐ ☐ ☐ ☐
0.1 0.2 0.3 0.4 0.5

6 Distribution management and working with customers

51 How well is your distribution/delivery strategy defined and is it regularly reviewed? (Does your strategy include third-party warehousing/transport?)

☐ ☐ ☐ ☐ ☐
0.1 0.2 0.3 0.4 0.5

52 How good is your design (type, size,   □ □ □ □ □
    location, etc.) and the operation of   0.1 0.2 0.3 0.4 0.5
    your warehouses (own and third
    party)?

53 If distribution/delivery problems occur   □ □ □ □ □
    are non-management staff authorized   0.1 0.2 0.3 0.4 0.5
    to contact contractors and suppliers to
    seek information?

54 How effective is your transport   □ □ □ □ □
    planning for both primary (trunking)   0.1 0.2 0.3 0.4 0.5
    and secondary (local delivery)
    operations?

55 How good is your formal distribution   □ □ □ □ □
    resource planning for each stock-keeping   0.1 0.2 0.3 0.4 0.5
    unit (SKU)?

56 How effectively does your organization   □ □ □ □ □
    span (across functions) the whole supply   0.1 0.2 0.3 0.4 0.5
    chain? (One executive responsible for
    planning, production and
    distribution = 0.5)

57 How closely is your operations   □ □ □ □ □
    manager involved with customers to   0.1 0.2 0.3 0.4 0.5
    achieve a precise specification of
    customers' needs?

58 How frequently and effectively do you   □ □ □ □ □
    analyse channels of distribution (e.g.   0.1 0.2 0.3 0.4 0.5
    supermarket, wholesaler, retailer)?

59 How well do you measure customer   □ □ □ □ □
    profitability by activity-based cost   0.1 0.2 0.3 0.4 0.5
    location?

60 Have you established a serious   □ □ □ □ □
    partnership with key customers to help   0.1 0.2 0.3 0.4 0.5
    them gain a competitive edge by
    providing an all-round package of
    customer service?

7 Product safety

(Some questions are purely for manufacturing operations thus extra questions have been included more applicable for service industries)

61 How effective is your safety clearance of new products and delivery of services?

☐ ☐ ☐ ☐ ☐
0.1 0.2 0.3 0.4 0.5

62 How well are your records of compliance regulatory bodies? (For example, for pharmaceutical products, records with FDA, MHRA etc.)

☐ ☐ ☐ ☐ ☐
0.1 0.2 0.3 0.4 0.5

OR

63 How well trained are your staff to understand and comply with legal issues such as copyright, disclosure and other regulatory requirements?

☐ ☐ ☐ ☐ ☐
0.1 0.2 0.3 0.4 0.5

64 How good is your installation and monitoring of water decontamination systems (chlorination, pasteurization)?

☐ ☐ ☐ ☐ ☐
0.1 0.2 0.3 0.4 0.5

65 How well have you incorporated hygiene design aspects especially for food products?

☐ ☐ ☐ ☐ ☐
0.1 0.2 0.3 0.4 0.5

66 How good are your quality assurance procedures and control at each stage of supply chain including sanitation, house keeping, storage and handling?

☐ ☐ ☐ ☐ ☐
0.1 0.2 0.3 0.4 0.5

67 How good are your selection and use of preservatives to prevent accidental contamination?

☐ ☐ ☐ ☐ ☐
0.1 0.2 0.3 0.4 0.5

68 How well is the receipt of raw and packaging materials controlled? Are tests desirable as part your receiving process?

☐ ☐ ☐ ☐ ☐
0.1 0.2 0.3 0.4 0.5

69 How good are your on-site laboratory facilities and resources? (Including staff qualified in microbiology where appropriate)

☐ ☐ ☐ ☐ ☐
0.1 0.2 0.3 0.4 0.5

70 How good and effective are your learning programmes for all employees regarding product/service/customer safety?

☐ ☐ ☐ ☐ ☐
0.1 0.2 0.3 0.4 0.5

8 Occupational safety and health

71 How frequently do staff have company-sponsored medical checks? (At all levels? Management only?)

☐ ☐ ☐ ☐ ☐
0.1 0.2 0.3 0.4 0.5

72 How effective is your accident prevention system and maintenance of equipment (e.g. low-voltage equipment, fire extinguishers, machine guards, sprinklers, smoke alarms, etc.)?

☐ ☐ ☐ ☐ ☐
0.1 0.2 0.3 0.4 0.5

73 How effective are your emergency procedures? Are there evacuation routes and procedures? Are drills carried out regularly?

☐ ☐ ☐ ☐ ☐
0.1 0.2 0.3 0.4 0.5

74 How safe is your work place? (In the office and the factory are working conditions suitable – consider noise, temperature, cleanliness, hygiene, space, and lighting; for hazardous material and equipment are permits current, is maintenance scheduled and up to date, are there regular inspections?)

☐ ☐ ☐ ☐ ☐
0.1 0.2 0.3 0.4 0.5

75 How well are staff made aware of measures to prevent stress and injury from prolonged repetitive work, such as long periods at computer workstations?

☐ ☐ ☐ ☐ ☐
0.1 0.2 0.3 0.4 0.5

76 How well have you implemented personal safety and protection measures, especially for employees in hazardous areas?

☐ ☐ ☐ ☐ ☐
0.1 0.2 0.3 0.4 0.5

77 How good is your organization of resources for first aid, health and safety, fire wardens, etc.?

☐ ☐ ☐ ☐ ☐
0.1 0.2 0.3 0.4 0.5

78 Do you have an accredited safety audit
(e.g. ISRS Certificate)?
☐ ☐ ☐ ☐ ☐
0.1 0.2 0.3 0.4 0.5

79 How effective are your learning
programmes for all employees regarding
work place safety?
☐ ☐ ☐ ☐ ☐
0.1 0.2 0.3 0.4 0.5

80 How well do you monitor the statistics
of absenteeism for health reasons and
accidents? (If work-related, what actions
are taken to overcome the causes?)
☐ ☐ ☐ ☐ ☐
0.1 0.2 0.3 0.4 0.5

9 Environment and resource management

81 Do you have an energy conservation
programme in place? (Is there a cross-
functional environmental committee in
place and how effective is it?)
☐ ☐ ☐ ☐ ☐
0.1 0.2 0.3 0.4 0.5

82 Are staff actively encouraged to make
energy waste/recycling suggestions and
are suggestions acted on?
☐ ☐ ☐ ☐ ☐
0.1 0.2 0.3 0.4 0.5

83 How well are you complying with
legislation and measuring up to public
concerns regarding environmental
issues?
☐ ☐ ☐ ☐ ☐
0.1 0.2 0.3 0.4 0.5

84 How well are you and your staff at all
levels aware of environmental issues
applying to your business and to your
customers businesses?
☐ ☐ ☐ ☐ ☐
0.1 0.2 0.3 0.4 0.5

85 How effective are you in avoiding/
detecting pollutant metals and materials
in plant and production or in the office
(such as asbestos, lead, cadmium,
mercury)?
☐ ☐ ☐ ☐ ☐
0.1 0.2 0.3 0.4 0.5

86 How good is your safety, health and
environmental reputation with
customers and the local community?
☐ ☐ ☐ ☐ ☐
0.1 0.2 0.3 0.4 0.5

87 Is your organization a member of an energy efficiency/sustainability environmental group of like-minded organizations?

☐ ☐ ☐ ☐ ☐
0.1 0.2 0.3 0.4 0.5

88 How effective are your environmental awareness learning sessions for all your personnel?

☐ ☐ ☐ ☐ ☐
0.1 0.2 0.3 0.4 0.5

89 How well do you monitor the safety and environmental standards of your business partners (e.g. raw material suppliers, co-packers, co-producers, contractors)?

☐ ☐ ☐ ☐ ☐
0.1 0.2 0.3 0.4 0.5

90 Do you present triple bottom-line reporting in your annual accounts?

☐ ☐ ☐ ☐ ☐
0.1 0.2 0.3 0.4 0.5

10 Sourcing strategy

91 How forward-looking is your written sourcing/sub-contracting/ manufacturing delivery/strategy?

☐ ☐ ☐ ☐ ☐
0.1 0.2 0.3 0.4 0.5

92 How relevant (effective) is your sourcing strategy to take advantage of global outsourcing opportunities?

☐ ☐ ☐ ☐ ☐
0.1 0.2 0.3 0.4 0.5

93 How well aligned are your operational objectives with the overall mission of the organization? (Are operational objectives quantified and performance monitored?)

☐ ☐ ☐ ☐ ☐
0.1 0.2 0.3 0.4 0.5

94 How well are internal operating costs benchmarked? (Do you know what best practice is for your industry?)

☐ ☐ ☐ ☐ ☐
0.1 0.2 0.3 0.4 0.5

95 How good and reliable is your long-term forecast of sales volume by main product/customer groups?

☐ ☐ ☐ ☐ ☐
0.1 0.2 0.3 0.4 0.5

96 How good and reliable are your analyses of your output capacity?

☐ ☐ ☐ ☐ ☐
0.1 0.2 0.3 0.4 0.5

97 How good is your evaluation of
strategic outsourced options
(Subjective = 0.1, SWOT
analysis = 0.5)

☐ ☐ ☐ ☐ ☐
0.1 0.2 0.3 0.4 0.5

98 How well have you analysed
your competitor's game plan and
strength regarding sourcing strategy?

☐ ☐ ☐ ☐ ☐
0.1 0.2 0.3 0.4 0.5

99 How forward-looking is your capital
expenditure plan?

☐ ☐ ☐ ☐ ☐
0.1 0.2 0.3 0.4 0.5

100 How well and how often do you review
your sourcing strategy with regard
to changing conditions?

☐ ☐ ☐ ☐ ☐
0.1 0.2 0.3 0.4 0.5

11 Appropriate technology

101 How well are volume and growth
considered when selecting
technology? (Is the product life
cycle analysed?)

☐ ☐ ☐ ☐ ☐
0.1 0.2 0.3 0.4 0.5

102 How well are product variety (and
trends) considered when selecting
technology?

☐ ☐ ☐ ☐ ☐
0.1 0.2 0.3 0.4 0.5

103 How well do you keep abreast of best
practice in use and changes in
technology?

☐ ☐ ☐ ☐ ☐
0.1 0.2 0.3 0.4 0.5

104 How well do you consider your staffs'
experience and skills when selecting
technology?

☐ ☐ ☐ ☐ ☐
0.1 0.2 0.3 0.4 0.5

105 How well is advantage taken of the
capacity, experience and local
representation of suppliers of new
technology?

☐ ☐ ☐ ☐ ☐
0.1 0.2 0.3 0.4 0.5

106 In the analysis of new technology
proposals, how effectively are
alternative solutions and value
engineering used/considered?

☐ ☐ ☐ ☐ ☐
0.1 0.2 0.3 0.4 0.5

107 How good is your evaluation of
investment proposals for new
technology in terms of return on
investment? (Conversely, is there a
danger that ROI analysis will leave
you with outdated equipment?)

☐ ☐ ☐ ☐ ☐
0.1 0.2 0.3 0.4 0.5

108 How good is your strategic approach to
new technology (e.g. are you aware
of new technology being introduced
by competitors)?

☐ ☐ ☐ ☐ ☐
0.1 0.2 0.3 0.4 0.5

109 When evaluating new technology how
well do you use the experience of
other users? How vulnerable is the
new technology?

☐ ☐ ☐ ☐ ☐
0.1 0.2 0.3 0.4 0.5

110 How good is your technology
development plan (both product and
process) with regard to your resources
and needs?

☐ ☐ ☐ ☐ ☐
0.1 0.2 0.3 0.4 0.5

12   Flexibility and lean process

111 How good is your understanding
of flexibility and lean processes?

☐ ☐ ☐ ☐ ☐
0.1 0.2 0.3 0.4 0.5

112 How well do your managers appreciate
the need for flexibility and lean
processes?

☐ ☐ ☐ ☐ ☐
0.1 0.2 0.3 0.4 0.5

113 How closely do marketing and
operations work together to standardize
common elements so as to minimize
the need for flexibility?

☐ ☐ ☐ ☐ ☐
0.1 0.2 0.3 0.4 0.5

114 How quickly can you respond to
changes in volume and variety
by flexible work systems?

☐ ☐ ☐ ☐ ☐
0.1 0.2 0.3 0.4 0.5

115 Without affecting the market, how
effective is your product and material
harmonization?

☐ ☐ ☐ ☐ ☐
0.1 0.2 0.3 0.4 0.5

116 How flexible and agile are your operational processes?

☐ ☐ ☐ ☐ ☐
0.1 0.2 0.3 0.4 0.5

117 How flexible/multi-skilled are your people? (In manufacturing an example is single minute exchange of dies, SMED)

☐ ☐ ☐ ☐ ☐
0.1 0.2 0.3 0.4 0.5

118 How well do you cope with changes to operation schedules (is planning data sufficiently reliable to permit rapid changes)?

☐ ☐ ☐ ☐ ☐
0.1 0.2 0.3 0.4 0.5

119 How effective have you been in implementing JIT and lean processes?

☐ ☐ ☐ ☐ ☐
0.1 0.2 0.3 0.4 0.5

120 Is your layout flexible and easily adapted?

☐ ☐ ☐ ☐ ☐
0.1 0.2 0.3 0.4 0.5

13   Reliability and maintenance

121 Do you have a maintenance plan/budget for:
   (a) plant and equipment,
   (b) IT Infrastructure
   (c) facilities (buildings, furniture, paint work, floor coverings, gardens, cleaning etc.)
   (d) maintenance and layout of the office environment

☐ ☐ ☐ ☐ ☐
☐ ☐ ☐ ☐ ☐
☐ ☐ ☐ ☐ ☐

☐ ☐ ☐ ☐ ☐
0.1 0.2 0.3 0.4 0.5

122 How good are your written maintenance policies for different types of assets?

☐ ☐ ☐ ☐ ☐
0.1 0.2 0.3 0.4 0.5

123 How well do you focus on right-first-time reliable equipment for new investments and continuously seek to improve/modify existing equipment?

☐ ☐ ☐ ☐ ☐
0.1 0.2 0.3 0.4 0.5

124 How well do you follow predictive and condition-based maintenance principles?

☐ ☐ ☐ ☐ ☐
0.1 0.2 0.3 0.4 0.5

125 How good are your maintenance staff in terms of specialist skills and experience?

☐ ☐ ☐ ☐ ☐
0.1 0.2 0.3 0.4 0.5

126 How good are your contracts/own maintenance infrastructure and third-party capability?

☐ ☐ ☐ ☐ ☐
0.1 0.2 0.3 0.4 0.5

127 How effective are your maintenance information and management systems for the control of assets and spares?

☐ ☐ ☐ ☐ ☐
0.1 0.2 0.3 0.4 0.5

128 How effectively have you achieved autonomous maintenance (empowered workforce) with TPM?

☐ ☐ ☐ ☐ ☐
0.1 0.2 0.3 0.4 0.5

129 How well is it understood throughout your organization that maintenance (no downtime) is a competitive weapon?

☐ ☐ ☐ ☐ ☐
0.1 0.2 0.3 0.4 0.5

130 How good are your maintenance contractors:
(a) prevention of problems
(b) speed of response when required
(c) effectiveness of response

☐ ☐ ☐ ☐ ☐
☐ ☐ ☐ ☐ ☐
☐ ☐ ☐ ☐ ☐
0.1 0.2 0.3 0.4 0.5

14 Performance management and Balanced Scorecard

131 Do you have a 'dash board' of key performance measurements and how well is it monitored?

☐ ☐ ☐ ☐ ☐
0.1 0.2 0.3 0.4 0.5

132 How good are your labour financial KPIs and trend?

☐ ☐ ☐ ☐ ☐
0.1 0.2 0.3 0.4 0.5

133 How good are your customer KPIs and trend?

☐ ☐ ☐ ☐ ☐
0.1 0.2 0.3 0.4 0.5

134 How good are your internal process KPIs and trend?

☐ ☐ ☐ ☐ ☐
0.1 0.2 0.3 0.4 0.5

135 How well do you compare when benchmarking your KPIs with:
(a) Competitors, local and overseas
(b) Other industries, local and overseas

☐ ☐ ☐ ☐ ☐
☐ ☐ ☐ ☐ ☐
0.1 0.2 0.3 0.4 0.5

136 How good are your regular performance audits and 'fitness' checks?

☐ ☐ ☐ ☐ ☐
0.1 0.2 0.3 0.4 0.5

137 How effectively is your performance management linked to regular senior management reviews (e.g. sales & operations planning)?

☐ ☐ ☐ ☐ ☐
0.1 0.2 0.3 0.4 0.5

138 How well is your performance linked to knowledge management (e.g. sharing of best practices)

☐ ☐ ☐ ☐ ☐
0.1 0.2 0.3 0.4 0.5

139 How effective and team-based are your performance improvement programmes (e.g. Six Sigma/FIT SIGMA)?

☐ ☐ ☐ ☐ ☐
0.1 0.2 0.3 0.4 0.5

140 How good are your resources for monitoring and improving performance (Black Belts etc.)?

☐ ☐ ☐ ☐ ☐
0.1 0.2 0.3 0.4 0.5

15   Quality management

141 How well practised is the TQM/Six Sigma concept in your organization (including customer supplier relationships internally and externally)?

☐ ☐ ☐ ☐ ☐
0.1 0.2 0.3 0.4 0.5

142 How effective are the commitments and support of top management in quality management?

☐ ☐ ☐ ☐ ☐
0.1 0.2 0.3 0.4 0.5

143 How well do you quantify quality targets and performance? (Are results displayed at the work place?)

☐ ☐ ☐ ☐ ☐
0.1 0.2 0.3 0.4 0.5

144 How effectively do you focus on preventing the cost of non-conformance?

☐ ☐ ☐ ☐ ☐
0.1 0.2 0.3 0.4 0.5

145 How well is the use of SPC tools understood at all levels?

☐ ☐ ☐ ☐ ☐
0.1 0.2 0.3 0.4 0.5

146 How well do you monitor the quality standards of approved suppliers?

☐ ☐ ☐ ☐ ☐
0.1 0.2 0.3 0.4 0.5

147 How clear is your written policy on quality? Is it readily available throughout your organization?

☐ ☐ ☐ ☐ ☐
0.1 0.2 0.3 0.4 0.5

148 How well documented is your
     standard procedure for all processes?
     Are your procedures reviewed and
     updated regularly?

☐ ☐ ☐ ☐ ☐
0.1 0.2 0.3 0.4 0.5

149 How successful have you been in
     achieving a quality award or
     accreditation to a quality standard
     (e.g. an EFQM award or ISO 9000
     accreditation)?

☐ ☐ ☐ ☐ ☐
0.1 0.2 0.3 0.4 0.5

150 How effective are your learning
     programmes for TQM/Six Sigma at
     all levels?

☐ ☐ ☐ ☐ ☐
0.1 0.2 0.3 0.4 0.5

16 Financial management

151 How well and clearly have key
     financial parameters been written into
     corporate strategic and annual operating
     plans?

☐ ☐ ☐ ☐ ☐
0.1 0.2 0.3 0.4 0.5

152 How well do your managers understand
     financial parameters and cost
     structures?

☐ ☐ ☐ ☐ ☐
0.1 0.2 0.3 0.4 0.5

153 What is your profit margin as a
     percentage of sales (return on sales?
     Is the trend upwards?)? (Less than
     5% = 0.1, over 15% = 0.5)

☐ ☐ ☐ ☐ ☐
0.1 0.2 0.3 0.4 0.5

154 How sound is your working capital
     position (e.g. have assets been sold
     to improve the position or was
     improvement from operating results)?

☐ ☐ ☐ ☐ ☐
0.1 0.2 0.3 0.4 0.5

155 How good is your return on capital
     employed (ROI)? (Less than 6% = 0.1,
     over 20% = 0.5)

☐ ☐ ☐ ☐ ☐
0.1 0.2 0.3 0.4 0.5

156 How good is your cash flow (consider
     debtors turn and stock turn ratios)?

☐ ☐ ☐ ☐ ☐
0.1 0.2 0.3 0.4 0.5

157 How rigorous and effective is your
     appraisal of capital proposals?

☐ ☐ ☐ ☐ ☐
0.1 0.2 0.3 0.4 0.5

158 How effective and up-to-date is your accounting system? (Is information relevant, clearly presented, timely and accurate?)
☐ ☐ ☐ ☐ ☐
0.1 0.2 0.3 0.4 0.5

159 How good are your cost-effectiveness programmes and achievements?
☐ ☐ ☐ ☐ ☐
0.1 0.2 0.3 0.4 0.5

160 How good is the trend of your share price?
☐ ☐ ☐ ☐ ☐
0.1 0.2 0.3 0.4 0.5

17   Information and communication technology

161 How user-friendly is your website compared to your competitors? (If no website score zero)
☐ ☐ ☐ ☐ ☐
0.1 0.2 0.3 0.4 0.5

162 How good are your hardware support agreements?
☐ ☐ ☐ ☐ ☐
0.1 0.2 0.3 0.4 0.5

163 How effective is your software strategy regarding selection of packages and knowing what to specify for own systems?
☐ ☐ ☐ ☐ ☐
0.1 0.2 0.3 0.4 0.5

164 Are your software packages integrated across all departments of the organization?
☐ ☐ ☐ ☐ ☐
0.1 0.2 0.3 0.4 0.5

165 How effective is the software for supply chain management including ERP and CRM?
☐ ☐ ☐ ☐ ☐
0.1 0.2 0.3 0.4 0.5

166 Can you order on-line from suppliers?
☐ ☐ ☐ ☐ ☐
0.1 0.2 0.3 0.4 0.5

167 Can your customers order on line?
☐ ☐ ☐ ☐ ☐
0.1 0.2 0.3 0.4 0.5

168 How effective is your e-business strategy to collaborate with both suppliers and customers?
☐ ☐ ☐ ☐ ☐
0.1 0.2 0.3 0.4 0.5

169 How good are your own IT resources
    and organization at developing and
    supporting IT applications? (Is there a
    disaster recovery plan? Has it been tested?)

☐ ☐ ☐ ☐ ☐
0.1 0.2 0.3 0.4 0.5

170 How effective is your strategy for
    selection, prototyping, training and
    implementing a company-wide IT
    application?

☐ ☐ ☐ ☐ ☐
0.1 0.2 0.3 0.4 0.5

18 Leadership and organization capital

171 How successful and effective have you
    been in implementing a 'flatter'
    organization with a reduced number of
    'layers' of managers?

☐ ☐ ☐ ☐ ☐
0.1 0.2 0.3 0.4 0.5

172 How effective is your organization
    in integrating supply chain-related
    activities under one senior manager?

☐ ☐ ☐ ☐ ☐
0.1 0.2 0.3 0.4 0.5

173 How good are your professional staff in
    their specialist function?
    (a) marketing
    (b) human resources
    (c) commercial
    (d) financial management

☐ ☐ ☐ ☐ ☐
☐ ☐ ☐ ☐ ☐
☐ ☐ ☐ ☐ ☐
☐ ☐ ☐ ☐ ☐
0.1 0.2 0.3 0.4 0.5

174 How good are your professional
    staff (see previous question) in
    understanding and cooperating with
    other functions.

☐ ☐ ☐ ☐ ☐
0.1 0.2 0.3 0.4 0.5

175 How good are your specialist managers
    with regard to their knowledge of
    technology in their area of expertise.

☐ ☐ ☐ ☐ ☐
0.1 0.2 0.3 0.4 0.5

176 How good are you in protecting and
    using customer data to business
    advantage?

☐ ☐ ☐ ☐ ☐
0.1 0.2 0.3 0.4 0.5

177 How effective is your organization in
    protecting patents and intellectual
    properties?

☐ ☐ ☐ ☐ ☐
0.1 0.2 0.3 0.4 0.5

178 Is there a formal system for storing and
retrieval of information?
(a) Customer ☐ ☐ ☐ ☐ ☐
(b) Supplier ☐ ☐ ☐ ☐ ☐
(c) Competitors ☐ ☐ ☐ ☐ ☐
(d) Product development ☐ ☐ ☐ ☐ ☐
0.1 0.2 0.3 0.4 0.5

179 How effective is your leadership as ☐ ☐ ☐ ☐ ☐
demonstrated by a vision of 0.1 0.2 0.3 0.4 0.5
competing for the future?

180 How effective is your leadership as ☐ ☐ ☐ ☐ ☐
demonstrated by encouraging 0.1 0.2 0.3 0.4 0.5
entrepreneurs in smaller units?

19 Human resource policies and human capital

181 How well are workers encouraged ☐ ☐ ☐ ☐ ☐
to become multi-skilled? (Do you 0.1 0.2 0.3 0.4 0.5
have learning programmes to
facilitate multi-skilling?)

182 How effective is your policy of ☐ ☐ ☐ ☐ ☐
recruitment to ensure high standards of 0.1 0.2 0.3 0.4 0.5
education and aptitude, as a foundation
for a flexible workforce?

183 How well have you removed the ☐ ☐ ☐ ☐ ☐
traditional barriers between functions 0.1 0.2 0.3 0.4 0.5
(e.g. operations and marketing)?

184 How good is your staff appraisal and ☐ ☐ ☐ ☐ ☐
staff development system? (Do staff 0.1 0.2 0.3 0.4 0.5
get regular feedbacks? Are goals
mutually agreed?)

185 How effective is continuous training ☐ ☐ ☐ ☐ ☐
and communication policy? 0.1 0.2 0.3 0.4 0.5

186 How good are your performance-based ☐ ☐ ☐ ☐ ☐
reward schemes? (Are they well 0.1 0.2 0.3 0.4 0.5
documented and freely available?)

187　How good is your team structuring with
　　　empowerment and designated team
　　　leaders?
　　　□　□　□　□　□
　　　0.1　0.2　0.3　0.4　0.5

188　How effectively are your team members
　　　trained in problem-solving techniques?
　　　(No training = 0.1, Black Belts working
　　　with teams = 0.5)
　　　□　□　□　□　□
　　　0.1　0.2　0.3　0.4　0.5

189　How good is your record for industrial
　　　relations in terms of hours lost due to
　　　industrial disputes?
　　　□　□　□　□　□
　　　0.1　0.2　0.3　0.4　0.5

190　How effective is your partnership with
　　　(a) unions
　　　(b) staff councils
　　　(c) social clubs etc.

□　□　□　□　□
□　□　□　□　□
□　□　□　□　□
0.1　0.2　0.3　0.4　0.5

20　Knowledge management and information capital

191　How effective is your on-the-job and
　　　off-the-job learning strategy? (Is
　　　your policy documented and freely
　　　available to all staff?)
　　　□　□　□　□　□
　　　0.1　0.2　0.3　0.4　0.5

192　How good are your learning programmes
　　　for implementing new technology?
　　　□　□　□　□　□
　　　0.1　0.2　0.3　0.4　0.5

193　How good is your database and
　　　information system in sharing best
　　　practices?
　　　□　□　□　□　□
　　　0.1　0.2　0.3　0.4　0.5

194　Are you an employer of choice?
　　　How does your staff turnover for the
　　　past three years compare to:
　　　(a) the competition
　　　(b) other local similar industries?

□　□　□　□　□
□　□　□　□　□
0.1　0.2　0.3　0.4　0.5

195　How well do you organize and
　　　implement learning programmes
　　　for a company-wide change process
　　　(e.g. TQM, Six Sigma)?
　　　□　□　□　□　□
　　　0.1　0.2　0.3　0.4　0.5

196 How good are your learning resources
in terms of full-time training staff,
facilities and learning materials?

☐ ☐ ☐ ☐ ☐
0.1 0.2 0.3 0.4 0.5

197 How well are employees encouraged
and supported to further their
general education at tertiary education
institutions? (Are general education
opportunities limited to certain levels
of employees?)

☐ ☐ ☐ ☐ ☐
0.1 0.2 0.3 0.4 0.5

198 How good is your learning performance
in terms of training hours/budget
for each level of employee?

☐ ☐ ☐ ☐ ☐
0.1 0.2 0.3 0.4 0.5

199 How good is your commitment to
learning in terms of total expenditure
as a percentage of sales?

☐ ☐ ☐ ☐ ☐
0.1 0.2 0.3 0.4 0.5

200 How successful are you as a learning
organization in terms of awards and
accredited programmes (e.g. 'Investor
in People')?

☐ ☐ ☐ ☐ ☐
0.1 0.2 0.3 0.4 0.5

Glossary

Best practice   Refers to any organization that performs as well or better than the competition in quality, timeliness, flexibility, and innovation. Best practice should lead to world-class performance.

Black Belts   Experts in Six Sigma methods and tools. Tools include statistical analysis. Black Belts are project leaders for Six Sigma initiatives; they also train other staff members in Six Sigma techniques.

BPR (Business Process Re-engineering)   This has been described as a manifesto for revolution. The approach is similar to taking a clean piece of paper and starting all over by identifying what is really needed to make the mission of the organization happen.

Brainstorming   A free-wheeling group session for generating ideas. Typically a group meeting of about seven people will be presented with a problem, and each member will be encouraged to make suggestions without fear of criticism. One suggestion will lead to another. All suggestions, no matter how seemingly fanciful, are recorded, and subsequently analysed. Brainstorming is useful for generating ideas for further detailed analysis.

Cause and effect diagram   The cause and effect, fishbone or Ishikawa diagram was developed by Kaoru Ishikawa. The premise is that generally when a problem occurs the effect is very obvious, and the temptation is to treat the effect. With the Ishikawa approach the causes of the effect are sought. Once these are known and eliminated, the effect will not be seen again. For example, working overtime is an effect; adding extra staff does not remove the cause. The question is, what caused the situation that led to overtime being worked?

COPQ (Cost of Poor Quality)   The cost of poor quality is made up of costs arising from internal failures, external failures, appraisal, prevention and lost opportunity costs – in other words, all the costs that arise from non-conformance to a standard. Chapter 3 discusses COPQ in some detail.

CTQ (Critical to Quality)   Six Sigma refers to CTQS. This simply means the identification of factors that are critical for the achievement of a level of quality.

DFFS (Design for FIT SIGMA™)   The steps are Define, Measure, Analyse, Design and Validate (see Chapter 3 for detailed discussion).

DMAIC   The cycle of Define, Measure, Analyse, Improve and Control.

DOE   The process of examining options in the design of a product or service. Controlled changes of input factors are made and the resulting changes to outputs noted. Losses from poor design include not only direct loss to the company from reworking and scrap, but also include those owing to user downtime due to equipment failure, poor performance and unreliability. Poor customer satisfaction will lead to further losses by the company as market share falls.

DPMO (Defects per million opportunities)   The basic measure of Six Sigma. It is the number of defects per unit divided by the number of opportunities for defects multiplied by 1 000 000. This number can be converted into a Sigma value – for example, Six Sigma = 3.4 per million opportunities.

E-business   Electronic-business is more than the transfer of information using information technology; it is the complex mix of processes, applications and organizational structures.

EFQM (European Foundation for Quality Management)   Derived from the American Malcolm Baldridge Quality Award, this is an award for organizations that achieve world-class performance as judged by independent auditors against a checklist. The checklist is detailed and extensive, and covers Leadership, People Management, Policy and Strategy, Partnerships and Resource, Processes, People Satisfaction, Customer Satisfaction, Impact on Society, and Business Results.

Fishbone diagram   The fishbone, Ishikawa, or cause and effect diagram was developed by Kaoru Ishikawa. The premise is that generally when a problem occurs the effect is very obvious, and the temptation is to treat the effect. With the Ishikawa approach the causes of the effect are sought. Once these are known and eliminated, the effect will not be seen again. For example, working overtime is an effect; adding extra staff does not remove the cause. The question is, what caused the situation that led to overtime being worked?

FIT SIGMA™   (see also **TQM**, **Six Sigma** and **Lean Sigma**) FIT SIGMA incorporates all the advantages and tools of TQM, Six Sigma and Lean Sigma. The aim is to get an organization healthy (fit) by using appropriate tools for the size and nature of the business (fitness for purpose) and to sustain a level of fitness. FIT SIGMA is a holistic approach.

Flow process chart   A flow process chart sets out the sequence of the flow of a product or a procedure by recording all the activities in a process. The chart can be used to identify steps in the process, value-adding activities and non-value-adding activities.

FMEA (Failure Mode and Effect Analysis)   This was developed in the aerospace and defence industries. It is a systematic and analytical quality planning tool for identifying, at the design stage of new products or services, what could go wrong during manufacture, or when in use by the customer. It is an iterative process, and the points examined are:

- What the function is
- Potential failure modes
- The effect of potential failure
- Review of current controls
- Determination of risk priority (occurrence, detection, and severity of failure)

- Identification of corrective actions to eliminate failures
- Monitoring of corrective actions and countermeasures.

FPY (First Pass Yield) Also known as RTY, this is the ratio of the number of completely defect-free units (without any kind of rework during the process) at the end of a process and the total number of units at the start of a process. The theoretical throughput rate is often regarded as the number of units at the start of the process. RTY/FPY is used as a key performance indicator to measure overall process effectiveness.

Green Belts Staff trained to be Six Sigma project leaders, Green Belts work under the guidance of Black Belts (see Black Belts).

Histogram A histogram is a descriptive and easy to understand chart of the frequency of occurrences. It is a vertical bar chart with the height of each bar representing the frequency of an occurrence.

Input–process–output diagram All operations or processes have inputs and outputs, and the process is the conversion of inputs into outputs. Analysis of inputs should be made to determine factors that influence the process – for example, input materials from suppliers meeting specification, delivery on time and so on. Examples of input–process–output diagrams for service and manufacturing industries are shown in Figures 3.5 and 3.6.

Ishikawa The Ishikawa, fishbone or cause and effect diagram was developed by Kaoru Ishikawa. The premise is that generally when a problem occurs the effect is very obvious, and the temptation is to treat the effect. With the Ishikawa approach the causes of the effect are sought. Once these are known and eliminated, the effect will not be seen again. For example, working overtime is an effect; adding extra staff does not remove the cause. The question is, what caused the situation that led to overtime being worked?

ISO 9000 To gain ISO 9000 accreditation, an organization has to demonstrate to an accredited auditor that they have a well-documented standard and consistent process in place that achieves a defined level of quality or performance. ISO accreditation will give a customer confidence that the product or service provided will meet certain specified standards of performance and that the product or service will always be consistent with the documented standards.

JIT (Just In Time) This was initially a manufacturing approach where materials are ordered to arrive just when required in the process, no output or buffer stocks are held, and the finished product is delivered direct to the customer. Lean Sigma incorporates the principles of JIT and relates to the supply chain from supplier and supplier's supplier, through the process to the customer and the customer's customer.

Kaizen *Kaizen* is a Japanese word derived from a philosophy of gradual day by day betterment of life and spiritual enlightenment. This approach has been adopted in industry and means gradual and unending improvement in efficiency and/or customer satisfaction. The philosophy is doing little things better so as to achieve a long-term objective.

Kanban *Kanban* is the Japanese word for card. The basic *kanban* system is to use cards to trigger movements of materials between operations in production so that a customer order flows through the system. Computer systems eliminate the need for cards, but the principle is the same. As a job flows through the factory, completion of one stage of production triggers the next so that there is no idle time, or queues, between operations. Any one job can be tracked to determine the stage of production. A *kanban* is raised for each customer order. The *kanban* system enables production to be in batches of one.

KPIs (Key Performance Indicators) Measurements of performance, such as asset utilization, customer satisfaction, cycle time from order to delivery, inventory turnover, operations costs, productivity, and financial results (return on assets and return on investment).

Lean Sigma (see also **JIT**) Lean was initially a manufacturing approach where materials are ordered to arrive just when required in the process, no output or buffer stocks are held, and the finished product is delivered direct to the customer. Lean Sigma incorporates the principles of Six Sigma, and is related to the supply chain from supplier and supplier's supplier, through the process to the customer and the customer's customer.

Mistake-proofing This refers to making each step of production mistake-free, and is also known as *Poka Yoke*. *Poka Yoke* was developed by Shingo (also see **SMED**), and has two main steps: (1) preventing the occurrence of a defect, and (2) detecting the defect. The system is applied at three points in a process:

1. In the event of an error, to prevent the start of a process
2. To prevent a non-conforming part from leaving a process
3. To prevent a non-conforming product from being passed to the next process.

MRP (II) (Manufacturing Resource Planning) Manufacturing resource planning is an integrated computer-based procedure for dealing with all of the planning and scheduling activities for manufacturing, and includes procedures for stock reorder, purchasing, inventory records, cost accounting, and plant maintenance.

Mudas *Muda* is the Japanese for waste or non-value-adding. The seven activities that are considered are:

1. Excess production
2. Waiting
3. Conveyance
4. Motion

5. Process
6. Inventory
7. Defects.
(For further detail, see Chapter 1.)

OEE (Overall Equipment Effectiveness)   This is used to calculate the effective performance of an equipment and identify losses. In total productive maintenance (TPM) it is defined by the following formula:

$$OEE = \text{Availability} \times \text{Performance rate} \times \text{Quality rate}$$

Pareto   Wilfredo Pareto was a nineteenth-century Italian economist who observed that 80 per cent of the wealth was held by 20 per cent of the population. The same phenomenon can often be found in quality problems. Juran (1988) refers to the vital few and the trivial many. The technique involves collecting data of defects, and identifying which occur the most and which result in the most cost or damage. Just because one defect occurs more often than others does not mean it is the costliest or that it should be corrected first.

PDCA (Plan–Do–Check–Act)   The PDCA cycle was developed by Dr W.E. Deming, and refers to: Planning the change and setting standards; Doing (making the change happen); Checking that what is happening is what was intended (i.e. that standards are being met): and Acting – taking action to correct back to the standard.

Performance Charts or UCL/LCL   Upper control and lower control limits are used to show variations from specification. Within the control limits, performance will be deemed to be acceptable. The aim should be to reduce the control limits over time, and thus control charts are used to monitor processes and the data gathered from the charts should be used to force never-ending improvements. These types of charts might also be known as Tolerance charts.

Poka Yoke   This refers to making each step of production mistake-free, and is also known as mistake-proofing. *Poka Yoke* was developed by Shingo (also see **SMED**), and has two main steps: (1) preventing the occurrence of a defect, and (2) detecting the defect. The system is applied at three points in a process:

1. In the event of an error, to prevent the start of a process
2. To prevent a non-conforming part from leaving a process
3. To prevent a non-conforming product from being passed to the next process.

QFD (Quality Function Deployment)   A systematic approach of determining customer needs and designing the product or service so that it meets the customer's needs first time and every time.

Qualitative Uses judgement and opinions to rate performance or quality. Qualitative assessment attempts to 'measure' intangibles such as taste, appearance, friendly service etc.

Quality Circles Quality circles are teams of staff who are volunteers. The team selects issues or areas to investigate for improvement. To work properly, teams have to be trained first in how to work as a team (group dynamics) and secondly in problem-solving techniques.

Quality Project Teams A top-down approach to solving a quality problem. Management determines a problem area and selects a team to solve the problem. The advantage over a Quality Circle is that this as a focused approach, but the disadvantage might be that members are conscripted rather than being volunteers.

Quantitative Means that which is tangible or can be measured – for example, the speedometer on a car measures and shows the speed.

RTY (Rolled Throughput Yield), *aka* **FPY (First Pass Yield)** This is the ratio of the number of completely defect-free units (without any kind of rework during the process) at the end of a process and the total number of units at the start of a process. The theoretical throughput rate is often regarded as the number of units at the start of the process. RTY/FPY is used as a key performance indicator to measure overall process effectiveness.

5 Ss These represent a set of Japanese words for excellent house keeping (*Sein*, sort; *Seiton*, set in place; *Seiso*, shine; *Seiketso*, standardize; and *Sitsuke*, sustain).

S & OP (Sales and Operations Planning) This is derived from MRP, and includes new product planning, demand planning, supply review to provide weekly and daily manufacturing schedules, and financial information (see also **MRP (II)**). S & OP is further explained in Chapter 6 (see Figure 6.10).

Scatter diagram Scatter diagrams are used to examine the relationship between two variables. Changes are made to each, and the results of changes are plotted on a graph to determine cause and effect.

Sigma The sign used for standard deviation from the arithmetic mean. If a normal distribution curve exists, one sigma represents one standard deviation either side of the mean and accounts for 68.27 per cent of the population. This is more fully explained in Chapter 3.

SIPOC (Supplier Input Process Output Customer) This represents a flow diagram and is used to define and examine an operation from the supplier to the customer.

Six Sigma Six Sigma is quality system that in effect aims for zero defects. Six Sigma in statistical terms means six deviations from the arithmetic mean, which equates to 99.99966 per cent of the total population, or 3.4 defects per million opportunities.

SMED (Single Minute Exchange of Dies) This was developed for the Japanese automobile industry by Shigeo Shingo in the 1980s, and involves the reduction of changeover of production by intensive work study to determine in-process and out-process activities and then systematic improve the planning, tooling, and operations of the changeover process. Shingo believed in looking for simple solutions rather relying on technology.

SoQ (Signature of Quality) A self-assessment process supported by a checklist covering customer focus, innovation, personnel and organizational leadership, use of technology, and environment and safety issues. It is useful in FIT SIGMA for establishing a company 'health' report.

SPC (Statistical Process Control) SPC uses statistical sampling to determine if the outputs of a stage or stages of a process are conforming to a standard. Upper and lower limits are set, and sampling is used to determine if the process is operating within the defined limits.

The Seven Wastes (see also *Muda*) *Muda* is the Japanese for waste or non-value-adding. The seven activities that are considered are:

1. Excess production
2. Waiting
3. Conveyance
4. Motion
5. Process
6. Inventory
7. Defects.

(See also Chapter 1.)

Tolerance charts or **UCL/LCL** Upper control and lower control limits are used to show variations from specification. Within the control limits performance will be deemed to be acceptable. The aim should be over time to reduce the control limits. Thus control charts are used to monitor processes and the data gathered from the charts should be used to force never ending improvements. These types of charts might also be known as Performance Charts.

TPM Total Productive Maintenance requires factory management to improve asset utilization by the systematic study and elimination of major obstacles – known as the 'six big losses' – to efficiency. The 'six big losses' in manufacturing are breakdown, set up and adjustment, minor stoppages, reduced speed, quality defects, and start up and shut down.

TQM Total Quality Management, is not a system, it is a philosophy embracing the total culture of an organization. TQM goes far beyond conformance to a standard, it requires a culture where every member of the organization believes that not a single day should go by without the organization in some way improving its efficiency and/or improving customer satisfaction.

UCL/LCL   Upper control and lower control limits are used to show variations from specification. Within the control limits, performance will be deemed to be acceptable. The aim should be to reduce the control limits over time, and thus control charts are used to monitor processes and the data gathered from the charts should be used to force never-ending improvements. These types of charts might also be known as Performance charts, or Tolerance charts.

World class   The term used to describe any organization that is making rapid and continuous improvement in performance and is considered to be using 'best practice' to achieve world-class standards.

Zero defects   Philip Crosby made this term popular in the late 1970s. The approach is right thing, right time, right place, and every time. The assumption is that it is cheaper to do things right the first time.

Bibliography

Adler, P.S. (1993) 'Time and motion regained', *Harvard Business Review*, 71 (1).

Ansoff, I. (1987) *Corporate Strategy*. Harmondsworth: Penguin Books.

Arendt, C.H., Landis, R.M. and Meister, A.B. (1995) 'The human side of change', IIE Solutions, *Industrial Engineering*, Atlanta, May.

Bader, Kathleen (2002) 'Six Sigma implementation – from start to finish', Six Sigma Summit, Café Royal, London, 22–23 January 2002.

Ballon, R.H. (1992) *Business Logistics Management*. New York: Prentice Hall.

Barsodi, R. (1929) *The Distribution Age*. New York: Appleton.

Bartlett, C. and Ghoshal, S. (1994) 'The changing role of top management', *INSEAD working papers*, London Business School Library.

Basu, R. (2001) 'Six Sigma to FIT SIGMA', IIE Solutions, *Industrial Emgineering*, Atlanta, July.

Basu, R. (2002) *Measuring eBusiness in the Pharmaceutical Sector*. London: Reuters Business Insight.

Basu, R. (2004) *Implementing Quality*. London: Thomson.

Basu, R. and Wright, J.N. (1997) *Total Manufacturing Solutions*. Oxford: Butterworth Heinemann.

Basu, R. and Wright, J.N. (2003) *Quality Beyond Six Sigma*. Oxford: Butterworth Heinemann.

Berggren, C. (1994) *The Volvo Experience: Alternatives to Lean Production in the Swedish Auto Industry*. Basingstoke: Macmillan.

Biesadra, A. (1992) 'Strategic benchmarking', *Financial Week*, September 29.

Bird, F.E. Jr and Germain, G.L. (1990) *Practical Loss Control Leadership*. International Loss Control Institute, USA.

Bogan, C.E. and English, M.J. (1994) *Benchmarking for Best Practices*. New York: McGraw-Hill.

Bontis, N., Dragonetti, N., Jacobsen, G. and Roos, G.(1999) 'The Knowledge Toolbox', *European Management Journal*, 17 (4).

Boyer, K.K. (1999) 'Evolutionary patterns of flexible automation and performance: a longitudinal study', *Management Science*, 45 (6): 824–842.

Bray, R. (2003) 'Procurement, under the lens', *Summit*, December 6 (6): 6.

Brooking, A. (1996) 'Intellectual capital – core asset for the Third Millennium enterprise', *International Thomson Business Press*, 8: 12–13.

Brown, R.M. and Blevins, T.F. (1989) 'Should America embrace Japanese management techniques?', *Advanced Management Journal*, Winter, 22–31.

Carnall, C. (1999) *Managing Change*. London: Prentice Hall.

Centre for Innovation in Corporate Responsibility (2004) www.circr.net (Canada).

Chesbrough, H.W. (2003) *Open Innovation*. Boston: HBS Publishing Corporation.

Christopher, M. (1992) *Logistics and Supply Chain Management*. London: Pitman Publishing.

Collins, J.C. (1995) 'Change is good – but first know what should never change', *Fortune*, 29 May.

Creech, B. (1994) *The Five Pillars of TQM*. New York: Truman Talley.

Currie, R.M. (1964) *Work Study*. BIM Publications.

Davidow, W. and Malone, M. (1992) *The Virtual Corporation*. New York: Harper Collins.

Day, N. (1994) 'Human resource futures', *Harvard Business School Bulletin*, December.

De Meyer, A. and Ferdows, K. (1990) *Removing the Barriers in Manufacturing*. INSEAD.

Dell, M. (2001) 'The power of virtual integration: an interview with Michael Dell', *Harvard Business Review*, 79 (5).

Deming, W.E. (1986) *Out of Crisis*. Cambridge, MA: MIT Centre of Advanced Engineering Study.

Department of Employment (1991) *Investor in People. The National Standard*. Sheffield: Department of Employment.

Dilworth, J.B. (1992) *Operations Management: Design, planning and Control for Manufacturing and Services*. New York: McGraw-Hill.

Drucker, P.F. (1969) *The Age of Discontinuity*. New York: Harper and Row.

Drucker, P. (1992) *Managing the Future – the 1990s and beyond*. New York: Tullman & Tattley.

Drucker, P. (1995) *Atlanta Monthly*, 11 September.

Dwyer, M. (2000) 'Options for improving information on job related education and training', *Report Prepared for the New Zealand Government*. Wellington, Department of Labour.

Easton, G.S. and Jarrell, S.L. (1998) 'The effects of total quality management on corporate performance', *Journal of Business*, 71 (2): 253.

Edvinson, L. and Malone, M. (1997) *Intellectual Capital*. New York: Harper Business.

Elkington, J. (1998) *Cannibals with Forks: The Triple Bottom Line of 21st Century Business*. Gabriola Island, BC: New Society Publishers.

Ettlie, J.E. (2000) *Managing Technology Innovation*. New York: J Wiley & Son.

Farrell, D. (2003) 'The real New Economy', *Harvard Business Review*, 81 (5).

Fitz-Enz, J. (2000) *The ROI of Human Capital: Measuring the Economic Value of Employee Performance*. American Management Association.

Forrester, J.W. (1961) *Industrial Dynamics*. New York: MIT Press (reprinted 1969).

Foster, B. (1996) 'Distribution reform cuts direct path to efficiency', *Best's Review*, 96 (5): 78–80.

Fry, T.D., Steele, D.C. and Sladdin, B.A. (1994) 'A service-oriented manufacturing strategy', *International Journal of Operations and Production Management*, 14 (10): 17–19.

Gartner G2 Report (2002) 'Consultants see hurdles for B2B', March, EyeforChem.com.

Garvin, D. (1984) 'What does product quality really mean?', *Sloan Management Review*, 25 (2).

General Electric (2000) Annual Report.

George, M.L. (2002) *Lean Six Sigma for Service*. New York, McGraw-Hill.

Gilmore, A. (2003) *Services, Marketing, and Management*. London: Sage.

Goldratt, E.M. (1992) *The Goal*. New York: North River Press.

Goodbout, A.J. (2000) 'Managing core competencies: the impact of knowledge management on human resources practices in leading edge organisations', *Knowledge and Process Management*, 7 (2).

Gronroos, C. (2000) *Service Management and Marketing*. New York: J Wiley & Son.

Hamel, G. and Prahalad, E.K. (1994) 'Competing for the future', *Harvard Business Review*, 72 (4).

Hammer, M. and Champy, J. (1993) *Reengineering the Corporation*. New York: Harper Business.

Hanson, P., Voss, C., Blackham, K. and Oak, B.J. (1994) *Made in Europe – A Four Nations Best Practice Study*. London Business School.

Harrison, A. (1998) 'Manufacturing strategy and the concept of world class manufacturing', *International Journal of Production and Operations Management*, 18 (4): 397–408.

Hartmann, E. (1991) 'How to install TPM in your plant', *8th International Maintenance Conference*, Dallas, 12–14 November.

Hay Group (1995) *People and Performance*. (Spring issue) Hay Group, London.

Hayes, P. and Wheelwright, S.C. (1984) *Restoring our Competitive Edge – Competing through Manufacturing*. New York: John Wiley and Sons.

Heller, Robert (n.d.) 'Business alliances: working with your business competitors instead of against them', *Thinking Managers*. www.thinkingmanagers.com/management/business-alliances.php. Accessed November 2004.

Henkoff, R. (1994) 'Delivering the goods', *Fortune*, 28 November, pp. 64–78.

Herzberg, F. (1966) *Work and the Nature of Man*. Cleveland, OH: World Publishing.

Hill, T. (1985) *Manufacturing Strategy*. New York: Macmillan.

Homlihan, J. (1987) *Exploiting the Industrial Supply Chain, Manufacturing Issues*. New York: Booz Allen & Hamilton.

Hopfenbeck, W. (1992) *The Green Manufacturing Revolution: Lessons in Environmental Excellence*. London: Prentice Hall.

Imai, M. (1986) *Kaizen: the Key to Japan's Competitive Success*. London: McGraw-Hill.

International Loss Control Institute (1991) Accredited Safety Auditors – Pre Course Reading. *International Loss Control Institute*, USA.

Jowitt, E.R. and Horwood, E. (1989) 'Hygiene Design and Operation of Food Plants', Unpublished paper. Chichester, UK.

Kaplan, R.S. (1996) *Implementing Balanced Scorecard*. Harvard Business School Publishing, Product No. 7342.

Kaplan, R.S. and Norton, D.P. (1996a) *The Balanced Scorecard*. Boston: Harvard Business School Press.

Kaplan, R.S. and Norton, D.P. (1996b) 'Linking the Balanced Scorecard to strategy', *California Management Review*, 39 (1): 53–77.

Kaplan, R.S. and Norton, D.P. (1996c) Using the Balanced Scorecard as a strategic management system. *Harvard Business Review*, 74 (1): 75–85.

Kaplan, R.S. and Norton, D.P. (2004) 'Measuring the strategic readiness of intangible assets', *Harvard Business Review*, 82 (1).

Karlof, B. and Ostblom, S. (1993) *Benchmarking. A Sign Post to Excellency and Productivity*. (trans J. Gilderson). New York: John Wiley and Sons.

Kesh, R. (2004) 'Impact of TPM, Hydrocarbon', *Business Management Asia*, March/April.

Klein, J.A. (1989) 'The human cost of manufacturing reform', *Harvard Business Review*, 67 (2).

Knuckey, S., Johnston, H. with Campbell-Hunt, C., Carlaw, K., Corbett, L. and Massey, C. (2002) *Firm Foundations*. Wellington, NZ: Ministry of Economic Development.

Knuckey, S., Leung-Wai, J. and Meskill, M. (1999) *Gearing Up*. Wellington, NZ: Ministry of Commerce.

Kolodny, H. (1993) *The Organization Change Process*. Toronto: University of Toronto Press.

Kotler, P. (2001) *Marketing Management*. Englewood Cliffs, NJ: Prentice Hall.

Kotler, P. and Armstrong, G. (1989) *Principles of Marketing*. Englewood Cliffs, NJ: Prentice Hall.

Koyak, P.R. (1993) *Releasing the Power of Technology*. Prism.

Levitt, T. (1980) 'Marketing success through differentiation – of anything', *Harvard Business Review*, 58 (1).

Lynch, R.L. and Cross, K.F. (1991) *Measure Up! Yardsticks for Continuous Improvement*. Oxford: Blackwell.

Lynn, M. (1995) 'Book sales rigging claim shakes industry', *Sunday Times*, 13 August.

Malhotra, Y. (2003) 'Is knowledge the ultimate competitive advantage?', *Business Management Asia*, Q2/3, September.

Maslow, A.H. (1943) 'A theory of human motivation', *Psychological Review*, 50: 370–96.

Massachusetts Institute of Technology (1976) *National Support for Science and Technology*. Cambridge, MA: MIT Press.

Mazur, L. (2002) 'Fad bandwagon is no cure for ailing business', *Marketing (UK)* p. 16.

MCA (2002) *Strategic Outsourcing*. London: Management Consultants Association.

Melnyk, S.A. and Swink, M. (2002) *Supply Chain Structure and Strategy*. New York: McGraw-Hill/Irwin.

MHRA (2004) *Safeguarding Public Health – Framework Document*. Department of Health, UK.

Miller, D. and Hartwick, J. (2002) 'Spotting management fads', *Harvard Business Review*, 80 (1): 26–28.

Miller, J.G., De Meyer, A. and Nakana, J. (1992) *Factories of the Future*. Boston, MA: Irwin.

Mills, Q. (1994) Harvard Business School Working Paper. www.hbs.edu/research/workingpapers.htm

Milne, R. (2004) 'Supply chain management', in J. Nevan Wright and P. Race (eds), *The Management of Service Operations*, 2nd edn. London: Thomson Learning.

Naylor, J. (1996) *Operations Management*. London: Pitman Publishing.

New, C.C. and Mayer, A. (1986) *Managing Manufacturing Operations in the UK*. London: British Institute of Management.

Norton, D.P. (1999) 'The Balanced Score Card: translating strategy into action', in Proceedings of an address to The Institute for International Resource, Auckland, May. See also www.bscol.com.

Novelli, B. (2004) 'The promise and the reality', *Modern Healthcare (Chicago)*, 16 August, 34 (33): 32.

O'Brien, J.A. (2004) *Management Information Systems: Managing Information Technology in the Business Enterprise*, 6th edn. New York: McGraw-Hill/Irwin.

Oakland, J.S. (1992) *Total Quality Management*. Oxford: Butterworth Heinemann.

Ohno, Taiichi (1988) *Toyota Production System*. Cambridge, MA: Productivity Press.

Parasuraman, A., Zeithamel, V. and Berry, L. (1985) 'A conceptual model of service quality', *Journal of Marketing*, 49 (Fall): 41–50.

Pettigrew, A.M. (2004) 'Business fads and quick fixes', *Report: Warwick University*. See also www.warwick.ac.uk/news/pr/business. Accessed November 2004.

Porter, M. (1985) *Competitive Strategy*. New York: Free Press.

Porter, M. (1990) *The Competitive Advantage of Nations*. New York: Free Press.

Porter, M. (1995) *Competitive Advantage*. New York: Free Press.

Professional Physical Therapy Services (1995) *Industrial Engineering*, April, p. 11.

Pyzdec, T. (2000) *The Complete Guide to Six Sigma*. www.qualityamerica.com.

Quinn, J.B. (1993) 'Leveraging intellect', *Executive Excellence*, 10 (10): 7–8.

Reid, R.D. and Sanders, N.R. (2004) *Operations Management: An Integrative Approach*. New York: Wiley and Sons.

Richards, L. (1995) 'Revive your company but avoid quick fixes', *Best's Review*, 95, September.

Roos, J. and Roos, G. (1997) *Intellectual Capital: Navigating in the Business Landscape*. London: Macmillan.

Royak, P.R. (1993) *Releasing the Power of Technology*. New York: Prism.

Royston, M.G. (1979) *Pollution Prevention Pays*. Oxford: Pergamon Press.

Santos, J.R.D. (1995) 'Re-Tayloring the shop floor', IIE Solutions, *Industrial Engineering*, Atlanta, May.

Sayle, A.J. (1991) *Meeting ISO 9000 in a TQM World*. AJSL, UK.

Schmenner, R.W. (1993) *Operations Management*. New York: Macmillan.

Schonberger, R. (1986) *World Class Manufacturing*. New York: Free Press.

Schroeder, R.G. (1993) *Operations Management's Decision Making in the Operations Function*. London: McGraw-Hill.

Schumacher, C. (1993) Seminar Notes on Workstructuring. *Workstructuring Ltd*, Godstone, Surrey.

Scott, C. and Westbrook, R. (1991) 'New strategic tools for supply chain management', *International Journal of Physical Distribution and Logistics Management*, 21 (1).

Shapiro, B.P. (1988) 'What the hell is "market oriented"?', *Harvard Business Review*, 66 (6).

Shingo, S. (1985) *A Revolution in Manufacturing*. The SMED System. Cambridge MA: Productivity Press.

Shirose, K. (1992) *TPM for Workshop Leaders* (trans. B. Talbot). Cambridge, MA: Productivity Press.

Simchi-Levi, D., Kaminsky, P. and Simchi-Levi, E. (2003) *Designing and Managing the Supply Chain*, 2nd edn. London: McGraw-Hill.

Skinner, W. (1969) 'Manufacturing – the missing link in corporate strategy', *Harvard Business Review*, 43 (3): 136–145.

Skinner, W. (1987) *Wanted: A New Breed of Manufacturing Manager*. Manufacturing Issues series. Booz Allen and Hamilton.

Slack, N., Chambers, S. and Johnston, R. (2004) *Operations Management*. London: Pearson Education.

Smith, A. (1776; 1950) *An Enquiry into The Nature and Causes of the Wealth of Nations. Book One*, 6th edn. London: Methuen.

Stalk, G. Jr (1988) 'Time – the next source of competitive advantage', *Harvard Business Review*, 66 (4).

Sterman, J.D., Keating, E.K., Olivia, R., Repenning, N.P. and Rockart, S. (1999) 'Overcoming the improvement paradox', *European Management Journal*, 17 (2): 120–134.

Sveiby, K.E. (1997) *The New Organisational Wealth: Managing & Measuring Knowledge Based Assets*, Berrett-Koehler Publication.

Swank, C.K. (2003) 'The lean service machine', *Harvard Business Review*, 81 (5): 123–129.

Taiichi, Ohno (1988) *Toyota Production System*. Cambridge, MA: Productivity Press.

Taylor, F.W. (1947) *The Principles of Scientific Management*. New York: Harper & Brothers.

The Economist (1995) 'The changing nature of leadership', June.

Theunissen, C.A. (1998) 'State Power and Intelligence in an Age of Knowledge', Unpublished doctoral thesis, Rand Afrikaans University, Johannesburg, South Africa.

Theunissen, C.A. and Theunissen, P.S. (2004) Unpublished paper. AUT and AIS: Auckland, New Zealand.

Theunissen, P.S. (1998) 'Informal Communication and Informal Communication Networks in Organisations: Development, Uses and Effects', Unpublished doctoral thesis, University of Pretoria, Pretoria, South Africa.

Tompkins, J.A. (1989) *Winning Manufacturing*. Norcross, GA: Engineering and Management Press. *USA Today*, 21 July 1998.

Wheelwright, S.C. and Hayes, R.H. (1985) 'Competing through manufacturing', *Harvard Business Review*, 63 (1).

Wild, R. (1975) *Work Organization*. London: John Wiley & Sons.

Wild, R. (1995) *Production and Operations Management*. London: Cassell.

Wild, R. (2002) *Operations Management*. London: Thomson Learning.

Wilson, D. (1984) *The Environmental Crisis*. London: Heinemann Educational.

Womack, J., Jones, D. and Roos, D. (1990) *The Machine that Changed the World*. New York: Rawson and Associates.

Wright, J., Nevan and Race, P. (2004) *The Management of Service Operations*, 2nd edn. London: Thomson Learning.

Wright, R. (1995) 'Managing labour relations in a new economy', *The Conference Branch of Canada*. Report 142-95, ISSN 0827-1070.

www.statistics.gov.uk. Accessed November 2004.

www.bbc.co.uk/science/hottopics. Accessed August 2004 'The Greenhouse Effect'.

www.canon.com/about/environment. Accessed November 2004.

www.census/gov/. Accessed November 2004.

www.dow.com

www.eiltd.net. August 2004.

www.triplebottomline.com.

Yip, G.S. (1992) *Total Global Strategy: Managing for Competitive Advantage*. London: Prentice Hall.

Zeichick, A., Scannell, E., Moore, C. and Krill, P. (2004) *InfoWorld* (San Mateo), 26 (33): 35–42.

Index

Foundation stones	Level 1 POOR	Level 2 FAIR	Level 3 GOOD	Level 4 VERY GOOD	Level 5 EXCELLENT
1 Understanding the market place	Poor knowledge of products and market, isolated sales activities	Ad hoc market survey, isolated activities of marketing and manufacturing	Annual market survey, isolated activities of marketing and manufacturing	Annual market survey, direct communication, with marketing and manufacturing	First hand knowledge of market place, six-monthly market survey
2 Understanding the competition	Poor knowledge of true market size and competition	Knowledge of market size without the follow-up of competitors	Competitor intelligence in selected products	Analysis of published reports of key competitions, BCG matrix	Annual benchmark to assess the strengths of key competitors
3 Product and process innovation	Little focus on innovation, limited development activities	Restricted research and isolated innovation activities	Good research budget, but isolated innovation activities	Screening process of impractical ideas, reduction of innovation lead time	Generous research budget, over 80% new product success ratio, concurrent engineering
4 Enterprises resource planning	Ad hoc planning, high stock cover, no preferred supplier	Isolated planning, high stock cover, some agreement with suppliers	Isolated logistics planning, good stock management, some agreements with suppliers	Computerized MRP planning, effective stock management, cooperation with suppliers	Integrated planning, JIT effective, EDI and partnership with suppliers
5 Supply chain and supplier partnership	Poor control over warehousing and transport, little interface with customers	Some control over warehousing and transport, some interface with customers	Good warehousing and transport by third party, sporadic control, work with customers	Effective warehouse and transport systems, some partnership with customers	Optimum distribution strategy, WMS and integration with key customers
6 Distribution management and working with customers	Low customer service, high stock and distribution cost	Medium customer service, high stock and distribution cost	High customer service, low supplier service, high stock and distribution cost	High customer service, high supplier service, high distribution cost. Low stock level	Low distribution cost, high customer and supplier services. Low stock level
7 Product safety	Lack of formal procedures of product safety needs	Ad hoc safety clearance, monitoring and training	Safety clearance for selected products, some monitoring and training	100% safety clearance, adequate monitoring at all stages, some training	100% safety clearance, excellent training and monitoring at all stages of supply chain
8 Occupational safety and health	Lack of formal procedures and facilities for industrial safety	Ad hoc application of safety standards and training	Safety standards and implements available, but partly implemented	Safety implements procedures, and training in place	ISRS certificate and HAZOP studies in place, excellent training
9 Environmental and resource management	Lack of effluent control and training	Adequate effluent control, lack of training	Compliance with legislation and some training	Effective effluent control and training	Full compliance of effluent control, effective non-waste technology
10 Sourcing strategy	Lack of clear sourcing strategy	Ad hoc studies on sourcing strategy	Credible internal manufacturing strategy	Credible support to sourcing policy	Full support to written sourcing strategy

Category	Level 1	Level 2	Level 3	Level 4	Level 5
11 Appropriate technology	Lack of a clear policy on technology	Ad hoc appraisal of technology and investment	Capital investment primarily based on ROI	Credible support to policy on technology and investment	Full support to written policy on technology and investment
12 Flexibility and lean processes	Lack of understanding of flexible manufacturing	Some applications of flexible manufacturing	Good understanding, partial application of flexible manufacturing	Credible support to flexible manufacturing	Full support to flexible manufacturing and quick change-over
13 Reliability and maintenance	Breakdown maintenance, low reliability, high cost	Time based maintenance, high maintenance cost	Condition based maintenance, some maintenance control system	Partial TPM, high reliability, high maintenance costs	Full implementation of TPM, high reliability, low maintenance cost
14 Performance management and Balanced Scorecard	Low level of manufacturing performance, poor reporting system	Medium level manufacturing performance for some plants	Medium level manufacturing performance, limited IE support	Sporadically high manufacturing performance with limited IE support	High manufacturing performance with integrated industrial engineering support
15 Quality management	Lack of defined procedures and standards for quality	Quality management in selected areas without top management support	Some use of SPC tools and quality procedures	Use of SPC tools and customer/supplier culture	Baldrige award or ISO9000 winner, change culture
16 Financial management	Lack of defined financial management, poor ROI	Medium ROI, and cash flow, no cost effectiveness	Sporadically good ROI and cash flow, some cost effectiveness	Good ROI and cash flow, but ad hoc cost effectiveness	Excellent ROI, cash flow and cost effectiveness programmes
17 Information and communication technology	Lack of IT strategy, support and application in manufacturing	Some good application of hardware and software in manufacturing	Customized application software in all areas of business	Open system IT, strategy not implemented, integrated network	Open system IT strategy in place, integrated client-server network
18 Leadership and organization capital	Lack of leadership, organization and management development	Traditional layers of management, some good managers	Good management team without development plans	Good management team and creditable management development plan	Visionary leadership, and policy to attract and develop high calibre managers
19 Human resource policies and human capital	Restricted working practices, poor industrial relations	Traditional working practices, good industrial relations	Limited flexible working practices and some consultation with unions	Multiskilled workforce, limited consultation with unions	Effective partnership with unions and sustainable working practices
20 Knowledge management and information capital	Lack of learning resources and training plans	Selective training plans by external resources	Limited learning resources and selective training plans	Good learning resources and selective training plans	Learning organization with written training plans for all employees